The Princeton Review®

ISEE®

PREP

The Staff of The Princeton Review

PrincetonReview.com

Penguin
Random
House

The Princeton Review
110 East 42nd St., 7th Floor
New York, NY 10017

Published in the United States by Penguin Random House LLC, New York.

Terms of Service: The Princeton Review Online Companion Tools ("Student Tools") for the retail books are available for only the two most recent editions of that book. Student Tools may be activated only twice per eligible book purchased for two consecutive 12-month periods, for a total of 24 months of access. Activation of Student Tools more than twice per book is in direct violation of these Terms of Service and may result in discontinuation of access to Student Tools Services.

ISBN: 978-0-593-51742-0
eBook ISBN: 978-0-593-51743-7
ISSN: 2994-760X

ISEE is a registered trademark of the Educational Records Bureau, which is not affiliated with The Princeton Review.

The Princeton Review is not affiliated with Princeton University.

The material in this book is up-to-date at the time of publication. However, changes may have been instituted by the testing body in the test after this book was published.

If there are any important late-breaking developments, changes, or corrections to the materials in this book, we will post that information online in the Student Tools. Register your book and check your Student Tools to see if there are any updates posted there.

Editor: Orion McBean
Production Editors: Kathy Carter and Sarah Litt
Production Artist: Deborah Weber

Printed in the United States of America.

10 9 8 7 6 5 4 3 2 1

The Princeton Review Publishing Team
Rob Franek, Editor-in-Chief
David Soto, Senior Director, Data Operations
Stephen Koch, Senior Manager, Data Operations
Deborah Weber, Director of Production
Jason Ullmeyer, Production Design Manager
Jennifer Chapman, Senior Production Artist
Selena Coppock, Director of Editorial
Orion McBean, Senior Editor
Aaron Riccio, Senior Editor
Meave Shelton, Senior Editor
Chris Chimera, Editor
Patricia Murphy, Editor
Laura Rose, Editor
Isabelle Appleton, Editorial Assistant

Penguin Random House Publishing Team
Tom Russell, VP, Publisher
Alison Stoltzfus, Senior Director, Publishing
Emily Hoffman, Assistant Managing Editor
Ellen Reed, Production Manager
Suzanne Lee, Designer
Eugenia Lo, Publishing Assistant

For customer service, please contact **editorialsupport@review.com**, and be sure to include:

- full title of the book
- ISBN
- page number

Acknowledgments

The Princeton Review would like to thank Shaina Walter Bowie for her hard work revising and developing test material for this book.

Contents

Get More (Free) Content
at **PrincetonReview.com/prep**

As easy as 1·2·3

1 Go to PrincetonReview.com/prep or scan the **QR code** and enter the following ISBN for your book: **9780593517420**

2 Answer a few simple questions to set up an exclusive Princeton Review account. (*If you already have one, you can just log in.*)

3 Enjoy access to your **FREE** content!

Once you've registered, you can...

- Read/print the Student and Caregiver Introductions with useful information on registering and taking the ISEE.

- Access additional online resources including: Primary and Lower Level test strategy, additional online drill questions, a student study guide, and more.

- Download a full-length ISEE Lower Level test and take online versions of the ISEE tests found in this book.

- Check for corrections or updates to this edition.

Need to report a potential **content** issue?

Contact **EditorialSupport@review.com** and include:
- full title of the book
- ISBN
- page number

Need to report a **technical** issue?

Contact **TPRStudentTech@review.com** and provide:
- your full name
- email address used to register the book
- full book title and ISBN
- Operating system (Mac/PC) and browser (Chrome, Firefox, Safari, etc.)

Look For These Icons Throughout The Book

 PROVEN TECHNIQUES

 APPLIED STRATEGIES

 ANOTHER APPROACH

 DON'T FORGET!

 WATCH OUT

 TIME-SAVING TIP

 TIME YOURSELF

 ONLINE PRACTICE TESTS

 ONLINE ARTICLES

The Princeton Review®

Full-service ISEE® Private Tutoring

Our Most Personalized Approach. Customized. Comprehensive. Reimagined.

ISEE Tutoring at a Glance

Top-Level Learning
- Expert tutors matched to your goals

Open Communication
- A custom dashboard with robust reporting

Practice Tools
- Exclusive Princeton Review printed materials

Convenience
- All tutoring options available for upper and middle levels

Comprehensive Tutoring
- 18 hours of customized instruction

Targeted Tutoring
- 10 hours of customized instruction

Scan to Learn More!

Interested in creating a custom Private Tutoring plan? Call 1-800-2-Review

Part I
The Basics

Chapter 1
Everything You Always Wanted to Know About the ISEE

WHAT IS THE ISEE?

The Independent School Entrance Examination (ISEE) is a standardized test made up of a series of multiple-choice questions and a writing sample. Lower, Middle, and Upper levels of the ISEE may be taken online or in a paper-based format, but the Primary levels are available only online. For all levels, the writing sample is not scored, but the other sections of the test are scored and your score report will show those scaled scores. You will also receive a percentile score for each section (between 1 percent and 99 percent) that compares your test scores with those of other test-takers from the previous three years. In addition, percentiles are then converted into stanines on a scale from 1–9.

Primary Level 2

Auditory Comprehension	6 questions	7 minutes
Reading	18 questions	20 minutes
Mathematics	24 questions	26 minutes
Writing Sample (unscored)	1 picture prompt	Untimed

Primary Level 3

Reading	24 questions	28 minutes
Mathematics	24 questions	26 minutes
Writing Sample (unscored)	1 picture prompt	Untimed

Primary Level 4

Reading	28 questions	30 minutes
Mathematics	28 questions	30 minutes
Writing Sample (unscored)	1 picture prompt	Untimed

Lower Level

Verbal Reasoning	34 questions	20 minutes
Quantitative Reasoning	38 questions	35 minutes
Break		5 minutes
Reading Comprehension	25 questions	25 minutes
Mathematics Achievement	30 questions	30 minutes
Break		5 minutes
Essay (unscored)	1 essay topic	30 minutes

Middle Level

Verbal Reasoning	40 questions	20 minutes
Quantitative Reasoning	37 questions	35 minutes
Break		5 minutes
Reading Comprehension	36 questions	35 minutes
Mathematics Achievement	47 questions	40 minutes
Break		5 minutes
Essay (unscored)	1 essay topic	30 minutes

Upper Level

Verbal Reasoning	40 questions	20 minutes
Quantitative Reasoning	37 questions	35 minutes
Break		5 minutes
Reading Comprehension	36 questions	35 minutes
Mathematics Achievement	47 questions	40 minutes
Break		5 minutes
Essay (unscored)	1 essay topic	30 minutes

> **Prepare Wisely**
> Print "What to Expect on the ISEE" from the ERB at isee.erblearn. org.

What's on the ISEE?

The Auditory Comprehension section (Primary Level 2 only) consists of an audio recording of a short passage followed by multiple-choice questions that can be listened to and seen on the screen. The Reading Comprehension section (all levels) tests your ability to read and understand short passages. These reading passages include both fiction and nonfiction. The Verbal Reasoning section of the ISEE (Lower, Middle, and Upper only) tests your knowledge of vocabulary using two different question types: synonyms and sentence completions. The Quantitative Reasoning and Mathematics Achievement sections test your knowledge of general mathematical concepts. All levels of the exam have problem-solving questions. The Middle and Upper Level exams also include quantitative comparison questions, which ask you to compare two columns of data. Remember, there is no guessing penalty on the ISEE. You should select an answer for every question.

Upper versus Middle versus Lower versus Primary Levels

There are, in effect, six different versions of the ISEE. The Primary 2 test is taken by students who are, at the time of testing, in the first grade. The Primary 3 test is taken by students who are in the second grade. The Primary 4 test is taken by students who are in the third grade. The Lower Level test is taken by students who are in the fourth and fifth grades. Students who are in the sixth and seventh grades take the Middle Level test. Students who are in the eighth, ninth, tenth, and eleventh grades take the Upper Level test.

Primary Level 2 has scaled scores ranging from 200 to 299 each for Reading (includes Auditory Comprehension) and Math. Primary Level 3 has scaled scores ranging from 300 to 399 each for Reading and Math. Primary Level 4 has scaled scores ranging from 400 to 499 each for Reading and Math. The Lower, Middle, and Upper levels all use the same scale: students receive four scaled scores ranging from 760 on the low end to 940 at the top.

There are few major differences between the structure of Lower, Middle, and Upper Level tests. There are some differences in content, however; for instance, vocabulary on the Middle Level test is less challenging than it is on the Upper Level test. The Middle and Upper Level tests cover the same general math concepts (arithmetic, algebra, geometry, charts, and graphs), but naturally, the Middle Level test will ask slightly easier questions than the Upper Level test. There are no quantitative comparison questions on the Lower Level test. The Lower Level test is 20 minutes shorter than the others.

Because the Lower Level ISEE tests both fourth and fifth graders, the Middle Level tests both sixth and seventh graders, and the Upper Level tests eighth, ninth, tenth, and eleventh graders, there are questions on the tests that students testing at the lower end of each of those groups might have difficulty answering. Younger students' scaled scores and percentiles will not be harmed by this fact. Both sets of scores take into consideration a student's age. However, younger students may feel intimidated by this. If you are at the lower end of your test's age group, there will be questions you are not supposed to be able to answer and that's perfectly all right.

The material in this book follows the content of the tests without breaking it down further into age groups or grades. Content that will appear only on the Upper Level test has been labeled as "Upper Level only." Students taking the Primary, Lower, and Middle Level tests do not need to work on the Upper Level content. Nevertheless, younger students may not have yet seen some of the material included in the Primary, Lower, and Middle Level review. Caregivers are advised to help younger students with their work in this book and seek teachers' advice or instruction if necessary.

HOW TO USE THIS BOOK

Before you dive into this book, go to your online Student Tools and download the Student and Caregiver Introductions. These resources are packed with a wealth of information to help prepare you for what to expect on the ISEE. Then download the Student Study Guide. We've broken down the contents of this book into 12 study sessions and suggested a timeline for you to follow.

Some of these sessions will take longer than others, depending on your strengths and weaknesses. If any of them takes more than two hours, take a break and try to finish the session the following day. You may want to do one, two, or three sessions a week, but we suggest you give yourself at least a day or two in between to absorb the information you've just learned. The one thing you should be doing every day is quizzing yourself on vocabulary and making new flashcards.

We also caution against thinking that you can work through this book during summer vacation, put it aside in September, and be ready to take the test in December. If you want to start that early, work primarily on vocabulary until about 10 weeks before the test. Then you can start on techniques, and they'll be fresh in your mind on the day of the test. If you've finished your preparation too soon and have nothing to practice on in the weeks before the test, you're going to get rusty. If you know you are significantly weaker in one of the subjects covered by the test, you should begin with that subject so you can practice it throughout your preparation.

Chapter 2
Learning
Vocabulary

THE IMPORTANCE OF VOCABULARY

Half of the ISEE Verbal section is synonyms, and you need to know the tested words to get those questions right. While Sentence Completions allow for a more strategic approach, the fact remains that knowing words is important to scoring points on these questions.

Having a strong vocabulary will also help you throughout your life: on other standardized tests (of course), in college, in your job, and when you read.

Flashcards
Making *effective* flash-cards is important. We'll address how to do so shortly!

BUILDING A VOCABULARY

The best way to build a great vocabulary is to keep a dictionary and flashcards on hand and look up any new words you encounter. For each word you find, make a flashcard, and review your flashcards frequently. We'll discuss effective ways of making flashcards shortly.

Reading a lot helps ensure that you will encounter new words. Read newspapers, magazines, and books. If you think you don't like reading, you just haven't found the right material to read. Identify your interests—science, sports, current events, fantasy, you name it—and there will be plenty of material out there that you will look forward to reading.

Not sure what you should read? Ask a favorite teacher or adult whose vocabulary you admire. Below are just a few suggestions based on your test level, but there are many other great things to read.

Test Level	Title
Middle	*The Hobbit* by J.R.R. Tolkien
	A Tree Grows in Brooklyn by Betty Smith
	To Kill a Mockingbird by Harper Lee
	The Outsiders by S.E. Hinton
Upper	Editorial and op-ed pages of *The Washington Post*, *The New York Times*, and *The Wall Street Journal*
	Time magazine
	The Economist
	The New Yorker
	Scientific American
	I Know Why the Caged Bird Sings by Maya Angelou
	The Glass Menagerie by Tennessee Williams
	The Kite Runner by Khaled Hosseini
	Invisible Man by Ralph Ellison
	The Lord of the Rings by J.R.R. Tolkien
	Narrative of the Life of Frederick Douglass by Frederick Douglass

You can also learn words through vocab-building websites, such as <u>vocabulary.com</u> or <u>quizlet.com</u>, which present drills in the form of rewarding games.

Finally, in the coming pages, you will find lists of words that you may see on the ISEE.

Making Effective Flashcards

Most people make flashcards by writing the word on one side and the definition on the other. That's fine as far as it goes, but you can do much better. An effective flashcard will provide information that will help you remember the word. Different people learn words in different ways, and you should do what works best for you. Here are some ideas, along with a couple of examples.

Relating Words to Personal Experience

If the definition of a word reminds you of someone or something, write a sentence on the back of your flashcard using the word and that person or thing. Suppose, for example, you have a friend named Scott who is very clumsy. Here's a flashcard for a word you may not know:

> *Maladroit*

> *Clumsy*
>
> *Tripping over his own feet yet again, Scott is quite maladroit.*

Relating Words to Roots

Many words are derived from Latin or Greek words. These words often have roots—parts of words—that have specific meanings. If you recognize the roots, you can figure out what the word probably means. Consider the word *benevolent*. It may not surprise you that "bene" means *good* (think *beneficial*). "Vol" comes from a word that means *wish* and also gives us the word *voluntary*. Thus, *benevolent* describes someone who is good-hearted (good wish). Your flashcard can mention the roots as well as the words *beneficial* and *voluntary* to help you remember how the roots relate to *benevolent*.

Often if you don't know the exact meaning of a word, you can make a good guess as to what the tone of the word is. For example, you may not know what "terse" means, but if a teacher said "My, you're being very terse today," you'd probably assume it meant something bad. Knowing the tone of words can be very helpful even if you can't remember the exact definition. As you go through your flashcards, you can separate them into three piles: positive, negative, and neutral. This will help you more rapidly recognize the tone of advanced vocabulary.

The table below provides some examples of common roots, along with their meanings and examples of vocabulary words that include them.

Root	Meaning	Example
ambi	both	ambidextrous
a/an/anti	not/against	amoral, antibiotics
anim	life	animated
auto	self	autograph
ben	good	beneficial
chron	time	chronology
cis/cise	cut/shorten	scissors, concise
cred	belief	credibility
de/dis	away from/not	deficient, dissent
equ	equal	equality, equate
fort	strength	fortress
gress	movement	progress
il/im/in	not	illegal, imperfect
laud	praise	applaud
loc/loq	speech	eloquent
mag/magna	great	magnify, magnificent
mal	bad	malicious
mis	wrong	mistake
ob	against	obstruct
pac	peace	pact, pacifier
path	feeling	sympathy, apathetic
phil/phile	love	philanthropy, bibliophile
ver	truth	verify
vit/viv	life	vital, revive

PEMDAS is a clever way of remembering the order of operations in math. You'll read more about that later in this book.

Other Methods

There are many other ways to remember words. If you are visually inclined, you might draw pictures to help you remember words. Others use mnemonics (a word that comes from a Greek word for memory), such as sound associations or acronyms (such as PEMDAS: Please Excuse My Dear Aunt Sally). Some people remember words if they speak the words and definitions out loud, in addition to writing flashcards. A great way to remember a word is to start using it in conversation. Ultimately, whatever works for you is the right approach!

Here are some words that could show up on test day. How many can you define? On a separate sheet of paper, write down the definitions of the words you know and have a parent or an adult check them. Then use your favorite dictionary to look up the rest and make flashcards.

ISEE MIDDLE LEVEL VOCABULARY LIST

abrupt	lure
adapt	meager
anxious	mimic
barren	noncommittal
braggart	notorious
capricious	obstinate
concise	omit
controversial	peak
drastic	predicament
duration	presume
economize	quest
endeavor	revere
falter	robust
flourish	soothe
gratified	steadfast
gullible	subtle
haphazard	tangible
homely	thrive
incident	unruly
inundate	urgent
irate	vibrant
jovial	vigorous
keen	willful
knack	wrath
lofty	yearn

You can find Lower Level vocabulary words when you register your book online following the instructions on the "Get More (Free) Content!" page.

ISEE UPPER LEVEL VOCABULARY LIST

acclaim	disuse	inquisitive	remorse
affluent	docile	jeopardy	renounce
allege	endorse	lavish	renown
aloof	epoch	lull	repel
ambition	equilibrium	memoir	resilience
appease	evade	muse	restraint
appraise	exemplify	mythic	revenue
arrogant	expenditure	neglect	rogue
asset	extravagant	novice	rue
audacious	facilitate	nuance	sage
augment	fastidious	obedient	sentimental
banter	fortify	obscure	shackle
belligerent	foster	obstruction	skeptical
cache	genuine	peeve	slander
chronic	hinder	persist	stamina
clarify	hoard	plausible	stronghold
console	ignorant	plunder	succumb
contrite	immune	profound	synopsis
crude	impeccable	prophet	timid
deception	impostor	provoke	transgression
demolition	impromptu	rebuke	tycoon
descendant	incessant	reckless	undermine
devious	incite	refine	verify
devout	incumbent	reluctant	vigilant
discern	indifferent	remedy	voracious

Chapter 3
Fundamental
Math Skills

INTRODUCTION

There are some basic math skills that are at the heart of many of the questions on your test. This chapter will go through the fundamental math content that you'll see on the ISEE, but you won't see any ISEE-style questions. Those are in Chapter 5. Much of the content in this chapter will likely be review, especially if you're preparing for the Upper Level test, but even the most difficult-seeming questions on the Upper Level exams are built on testing your knowledge of these fundamental skills. Make sure you read the explanations and do all of the drills before going on to the ISEE math chapter. Answers to these drills are provided in Chapter 4.

A Note to Middle Level Students

This chapter has been designed to give all students a review of the math found on the tests. There are four sections: "The Building Blocks," "Algebra," "Geometry," and "Word Problems." At the beginnings and ends of some of these sections, you will notice information about what material you should review and what material is only for Upper Level (UL) students. Be aware that you may not be familiar with all the topics on which you will be working. If you are having difficulty understanding a topic, take this book to adults and ask that person for additional help.

A Note to Primary and Lower Level Students

While you will find some of the early content in this chapter useful, this book is designed for students who are in 6th grade or older. For content that is specific to your test level, register your book and check out the online resources.

Lose Your Calculator!

You will *not* be allowed to use a calculator on the ISEE. If you have developed a habit of reaching for your calculator whenever you need to add or multiply a couple of numbers, follow our advice: put your calculator away now and take it out again after the test is behind you. Do your math homework assignments without it, and complete the practice sections of this book without it. Trust us, you'll be glad you did.

Write It Down; Get It Right!
You don't get points for doing the math in your head, so don't do it!

Write It Down

Do not try to do math in your head. You are allowed to write in your test booklet if you are taking a paper-based test. You *should* write in your test booklet. If you are taking a computer-based test, use scratch paper. Even when you are adding just a few numbers together, write them down and do the work on paper. Writing things down not only helps to eliminate careless errors but also gives you something to refer back to if you need to double-check your work.

NUMBERS & OPERATIONS

Math Vocabulary

Term	Definition	Examples	Test Level
Integer	Any number that does not contain either a fraction or a decimal. Can be positive, negative, or zero.	14, 3, 0, –3	ML, UL
Whole number	Positive integers and zero	0, 1, 17	All
Positive number	Any number greater than zero	$\frac{1}{2}$, 1, 104.7	ML, UL
Negative number	Any number less than zero	$-\frac{1}{2}$, –1, –104.7	ML, UL
Even number	Any number that is evenly divisible by two. **Note:** Zero is an even number!	–104, –2, 0, 2, 16, 104	All
Odd number	Any number that is not evenly divisible by two	–115, –11, –1, 1, 11, 115	All
Prime number	A number that has exactly two positive factors: 1 and itself. **Note:** One is **not** a prime number, but two **is**.	2, 3, 5, 7, 13, 131	LL, ML, UL
Digit	The numbers from 0 through 9	0, 2, 3, 7. The number 237 has digits 2, 3, and 7.	P3, P4, LL, ML, UL
Units (ones) digit	The digit in the ones place	For 281, 1 is in the units place.	P3, P4, LL, ML, UL
Consecutive numbers	Any series of numbers listed in the order they appear on the number line	3, 4, 5 or –1, 0, 1, 2	All
Distinct numbers	Numbers that are different from one another	2, 7, and 19 are three distinct numbers; 4 and 4 are not distinct because they are the same number.	All
Divisible by	A number that can be evenly divided by another	12 is divisible by 1, 2, 3, 4, 6, 12.	P4, LL, ML, UL
Sum	The result of addition	The sum of 6 and 2 is 8 because 6 + 2 = 8.	All
Difference	The result of subtraction	The difference between 6 and 2 is 4 because 6 – 2 = 4.	All
Product	The result of multiplication	The product of 6 and 2 is 12 because 6 × 2 = 12.	P4, LL, ML, UL
Quotient	The result of division	The quotient when 6 is divided by 2 is 3 because 6 ÷ 2 = 3.	P4, LL, ML, UL
Remainder	The amount left over when dividing	17 ÷ 5 leaves a remainder of 2.	LL, ML, UL
Rational number	A number that can be written as a fraction	$0.\overline{66}$ is rational because it can be written as $\frac{2}{3}$	LL, ML, UL

Term	Definition	Examples	Test Level
Irrational number	A number that cannot be written as a fraction	π or $\sqrt{2}$	UL
Multiple	The result of multiplying a number by an integer (not a fraction)	40 is a multiple of 8 ($8 \times 5 = 40$) and of 5 ($5 \times 8 = 40$).	ML, UL
Factor	Any numbers or symbols that can be multiplied together to form a product	8 and 5 are factors of 40 because $8 \times 5 = 40$.	ML, UL
Mean (or Average)	The result when you divide the sum of the values by the number of values	The mean of 5 and 7 is 6 because $(5 + 7) \div 2 = 6$.	ML, UL

The Rules of Zero

Zero has some funny rules. Make sure you understand and remember these rules.

- Zero is neither positive nor negative.
- Zero is even.
- Zero is an integer.
- Zero multiplied by any number is zero.
- Zero divided by any number is zero.
- You cannot divide by zero ($9 \div 0 = $ *undefined*).

Common Multiples

Make sure you are comfortable with multiplying integers up to 12. If you are having trouble with these, break out the flashcards. On one side of the card write down the multiplication problem, and on the other write down the answer. Now quiz yourself. You may also want to copy the table shown below so you can practice. For handy tips on using flashcards effectively, turn to Chapter 2 and read the section on flashcards.

	1	2	3	4	5	6	7	8	9	10	11	12
1	1	2	3	4	5	6	7	8	9	10	11	12
2	2	4	6	8	10	12	14	16	18	20	22	24
3	3	6	9	12	15	18	21	24	27	30	33	36
4	4	8	12	16	20	24	28	32	36	40	44	48
5	5	10	15	20	25	30	35	40	45	50	55	60
6	6	12	18	24	30	36	42	48	54	60	66	72
7	7	14	21	28	35	42	49	56	63	70	77	84
8	8	16	24	32	40	48	56	64	72	80	88	96
9	9	18	27	36	45	54	63	72	81	90	99	108
10	10	20	30	40	50	60	70	80	90	100	110	120
11	11	22	33	44	55	66	77	88	99	110	121	132
12	12	24	36	48	60	72	84	96	108	120	132	144

Practice Drill 1—Math Vocabulary (LL, ML, UL)

The following questions are for Lower, Middle, and Upper Levels only.

1. How many integers are there between −1 and 6? _____

2. List three consecutive odd integers. _____

3. How many odd integers are there between 1 and 9? _____

4. What is the tens digit in the number 182.09? _____

5. The product of any number and the smallest positive integer is _____

6. What is the product of 5, 6, and 3? _____

7. What is the sum of 3, 11, and 16? _____

8. What is the difference between your answer to question 6 and your answer to question 7?
   _____

9. List three consecutive negative even integers: _____

10. Is 11 a prime number? _____

11. What is the sum of the digits in the number 5,647? _____

12. What is the remainder when 58 is divided by 13? _____

13. 55 is divisible by what numbers? _____

14. The sum of the digits in 589 is how much greater than the sum of the digits in 1,207?
    _____

15. Is 21 divisible by the remainder of 19 ÷ 5? _____

16. What are the prime factors of 156? _____

17. What is the sum of the odd prime factors of 156? _____

18. 12 multiplied by 3 is the same as 4 multiplied by what number? _____

19. What are the factors of 72? _____

20. How many factors of 72 are even? _____

    How many are odd? _____

21. What is the mean of 6, 8, 11, and 15? _____

When You Are Done
Check your answers in
Chapter 4, page 96.

Working with Negative Numbers—Middle & Upper Levels

It is helpful to think of numbers as having two component parts: the number itself and the sign in front of it (to the left of the number). Numbers that don't have signs immediately to the left of them are positive. So +7 can be, and usually is, written as 7.

Adding

If the signs to the left of the numbers are the same, you add the two numbers and keep the same sign. For example:

$$2 + 5 = (+2) + (+5) = +7 \text{ or just plain } 7$$
$$(-2) + (-5) = -7$$

If the signs to the left of the numbers are different, you subtract the numbers and the answer takes the sign of the larger number. For example:

$$5 + (-2) = 5 - 2 = 3, \text{ and because 5 is greater than 2, the answer is } +3 \text{ or just plain } 3.$$
$$(-2) + 5 = 5 - 2 = 3, \text{ and because 5 is greater than 2, the answer is } +3 \text{ or just plain } 3.$$
$$(-5) + 2 = 5 - 2 = 3, \text{ and because 5 is greater than 2, you use its sign and the answer is } -3.$$

Subtracting

All subtraction problems can be converted to addition problems. This is because subtracting is the same as adding the opposite. "Huh?" you say—well, let's test this out on something simple that you already know. We know that $7 - 3 = 4$, so let's turn it into an addition problem and see if we get the same answer.

$$7 - 3 = (+7) - (+3)$$

Okay, so now we reverse only the operation sign and the sign of the number we are subtracting (the second number). The first number stays the same because that's our starting point.

$$(+7) + (-3)$$

Now use the rules for addition to solve this problem. Because the signs to the left are different, we subtract the two numbers $7 - 3 = 4$, and the sign is positive because 7 is greater than 3.

We have just proven that subtraction problems are really just the opposite of addition problems. Now let's see how this works in a variety of examples.

$3 - 7 = (+3) - (+7) = (+3) + (-7) = 7 - 3 = 4$ and, because 7 is greater than 3, the answer is -4.

$-9 - 3 = (-9) - (+3) = (-9) + (-3) = -12$

$13 - (-5) = (+13) - (-5) = (+13) + (+5) = +18$

$(-5) - (-8) = (-5) + (+8) = +3$

This is just one way to look at subtraction problems. If you have a way that works better for you, use that!

Practice Drill 2—Adding and Subtracting Negative Numbers (Middle & Upper Levels)

1. $6 + (-14) =$

2. $13 - 27 =$

3. $(-17) + 13 =$

4. $12 - (-15) =$

5. $16 + 5 =$

6. $34 - (+30) =$

7. $(-7) + (-15) =$

8. $(-42) + 13 =$

9. $-13 - (-7) =$

10. $151 + (-61) =$

11. $(-42) - (-42) =$

12. $5 - (-24) =$

13. $14 + 10 =$

14. $(-5) + (-25) =$

15. $11 - 25 =$

When You Are Done
Check your answers in Chapter 4, page 97.

Multiplying and Dividing

The rules for multiplying and dividing positive and negative integers are so much easier to learn and use than the rules for adding and subtracting them. You simply multiply or divide as normal, and then determine the sign using the rules below.

Positive ($\div$ or $\times$) Positive $=$ Positive

Negative ($\div$ or $\times$) Negative $=$ Positive

Positive ($\div$ or $\times$) Negative $=$ Negative

Negative ($\div$ or $\times$) Positive $=$ Negative

Here are some examples.

Helpful Trick
When multiplying numbers, simply count the number of negative signs. An even number of negative signs (-6×-3) means that the product must be a positive number. An odd number of negative signs (2×-5) means that the product must be negative.

$$6 \div 2 = 3 \qquad\qquad 2 \times 6 = 12$$

$$(-6) \div (-2) = 3 \qquad\qquad (-2) \times (-6) = 12$$

$$6 \div (-2) = -3 \qquad\qquad 2 \times (-6) = -12$$

$$(-6) \div 2 = -3 \qquad\qquad (-2) \times 6 = -12$$

If you are multiplying more than two numbers, simply work from left to right and deal with the numbers two at a time.

Simplify $2 \times (-5) \times (-10)$.

Step 1: multiply the first two numbers: $2 \times (-5) = -10$

Step 2: multiply the result with the third number: $(-10) \times (-10) = 100$

Practice Drill 3—Multiplying and Dividing Negative Numbers (Middle & Upper Levels)

1. $20 \div (-5) =$

2. $(-12) \times 3 =$

3. $(-13) \times (-5) =$

4. $(-44) \div (-4) =$

5. $7 \times 9 =$

6. $(-65) \div 5 =$

7. $(-7) \times (-12) =$

8. $(-10) \div 2 =$

9. $81 \div 9 =$

10. $32 \div (-4) =$

11. $25 \times (-3) =$

12. $(-24) \times (-3) =$

13. $64 \div (-16) =$

14. $(-17) \times (-2) =$

15. $(-55) \div 5 =$

When You Are Done
Check your answers in
Chapter 4, page 97.

Order of Operations—Lower, Middle, & Upper Levels

How would you attack this problem?

$$16 - 45 \div (2 + 1)^2 \times 4 + 5 =$$

To solve a problem like this, you need to know which mathematical operation to do first. The way to remember the order of operations is to use PEMDAS.

	Parentheses
	Exponents
Done at the same time from left to right $\Big\{$	**Multiplication**
	Division
	Addition $\Big\}$ **Done at the same time**
	Subtraction **from left to right**

You can remember the order of operations by using the phrase below:

"Please Excuse My Dear Aunt Sally"

Now, let's give it a try.

$16 - 45 \div (2 + 1)^2 \times 4 + 5 =$

1. **Parentheses:**

    $16 - 45 \div \underline{(2 + 1)}^2 \times 4 + 5 =$

    $16 - 45 \div (3)^2 \times 4 + 5 =$

2. **Exponents:**

$$16 - 45 \div (3)^2 \times 4 + 5 =$$

$$16 - 45 \div 9 \times 4 + 5 =$$

3. **Multiplication and division (from left to right):**

$$16 - 45 \div 9 \times 4 + 5 =$$

$$16 - 5 \times 4 + 5 =$$

$$16 - 20 + 5 =$$

First Things First
Make sure you remember PEMDAS whenever you see a question with more than one operation.

4. **Addition and subtraction (from left to right):**

$$16 - 20 + 5 =$$

$$-4 + 5 = \boxed{1}$$

Just take it one step at a time and you'll be able to do it in no time at all!

Practice Drill 4—Order of Operations (Lower, Middle, & Upper Levels)

1. $10 - 3 + 2 =$

2. $15 + (7 - 3) - 3 =$

3. $3 \times 2 + 3 \div 3 =$

4. $2 \times (4 + 6)^2 \div 4 =$

5. $420 \div (10 + 5 \times 12) =$

6. $20 \times 5 \div 10 + 20 =$

7. $3 + 5 \times 10 \times (7 - 6) \div 2 - 4 =$

8. $10 \times (8 + 1) \times (3 + 1) \div (8 - 2) =$

9. $12 + (5 \times 2)^2 - 33 \div 3 =$

10. $200 - (150 \div 3) \times 2^3 =$

When You Are Done
Check your answers in Chapter 4, page 97.

Factors (Middle & Upper Levels)

Factors are all the numbers that divide evenly into your original number. For example, 2 is a factor of 10; it goes in 5 times. However, 3 is not a factor of 10 because 10 divided by 3 does not produce an integer quotient (and therefore does not "go in evenly"). When asked to find the factors of a number, just make a list.

> The factors of 16 are
> 1 and 16 (always start with 1 and the original number)
> 2 and 8
> 4 and 4
> The factors of 18 are
> 1 and 18
> 2 and 9
> 3 and 6

Knowing some of the rules of divisibility can save you some time.

A number is divisible by	If...
2	it ends in 0, 2, 4, 6, or 8
3	the sum of the digits is divisible by 3
4	the number formed by the last two digits is divisible by 4
5	it ends in 0 or 5
8	the number formed by the last three digits is divisible by 8
9	the sum of the digits is divisible by 9
10	it ends in 0

Larger Factors
There's a quick way to figure out if a number is divisible by larger numbers. Simply take the two smaller factors and check both. If a number is divisible by both 2 and 3, then it's divisible by 6. If a number is divisible by both 3 and 4, then it's divisible by 12.

Factor Trees (Middle & Upper Levels)

To find the prime factors of a number, draw a factor tree.

Start by writing down the number and then drawing two branches from the number. Write down any pair of factors of that number. Now if one (or both) of the factors is not prime, draw another set of branches from that factor and write down a pair of factors for that number. Continue until you have only prime numbers at the end of your branches. Each branch end is a prime factor. Remember, 1 is NOT prime!

What are the distinct prime factors of 56? Well, let's start with the factor tree.

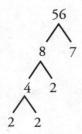

The prime factors of 56 are 2, 2, 2, and 7. Because the question asked for only the distinct prime factors, we have to eliminate the numbers that repeat, so we cross out two of the twos. The distinct prime factors of 56 are 2 and 7.

Multiples (Middle & Upper Levels)

Multiples are the results when you multiply a number by any integer. The number 15 is a multiple of 5 because 5 times 3 equals 15. On the other hand, 18 is a multiple of 3, but not a multiple of 5. Another way to think about multiples is to consider them "counting by a number."

The first seven positive multiples of 7 are:

$$
\begin{array}{ll}
7 & (7 \times 1) \\
14 & (7 \times 2) \\
21 & (7 \times 3) \\
28 & (7 \times 4) \\
35 & (7 \times 5) \\
42 & (7 \times 6) \\
49 & (7 \times 7)
\end{array}
$$

Practice Drill 5—Factors and Multiples (Middle & Upper Levels)

1. List the first five multiples of:

   2

   4

   5

   11

2. Is 15 divisible by 3 ?

3. Is 81 divisible by 3 ?

4. Is 77 divisible by 3 ?

5. Is 23 prime?

6. Is 123 divisible by 3 ?

7. Is 123 divisible by 9 ?

8. Is 250 divisible by 2 ?

9. Is 250 divisible by 5 ?

10. Is 250 divisible by 10 ?

11. Is 10 a multiple of 2 ?

12.   Is 11 a multiple of 3 ?

13.   Is 2 a multiple of 8 ?

14.   Is 24 a multiple of 4 ?

15.   Is 27 a multiple of 6 ?

16.   Is 27 a multiple of 9 ?

17.   How many numbers between 1 and 50 are multiples of 6 ?

18.   How many even multiples of 3 are there between 1 and 50 ?

19.   How many numbers between 1 and 100 are multiples of both 3 and 4 ?

20.   What is the greatest multiple of 3 that is less than 50 ?

When You Are Done
Check your answers in
Chapter 4, page 98.

Fractions—Primary 3 & 4, Lower, Middle, & Upper Levels

A fraction really just tells you to divide. For instance, $\frac{5}{8}$ actually means five divided by eight (which equals 0.625 as a decimal).

Another way to think of this is to imagine a pie cut into eight pieces. $\frac{5}{8}$ represents five of those eight pieces of pie.

The parts of a fraction are called the numerator and the denominator. The numerator is the number on top of the fraction. It refers to the portion of the pie, while the denominator is on the bottom of the fraction and tells you how many pieces there are in the entire pie.

$$\frac{\text{numerator}}{\text{denominator}} = \frac{\text{part}}{\text{whole}}$$

Reducing Fractions—Primary 4, Lower, Middle, & Upper Levels

Imagine a pie cut into two big pieces. You eat one of the pieces. That means that you have eaten $\frac{1}{2}$ of the pie. Now imagine the same pie cut into four pieces and you eat two. That's $\frac{2}{4}$ this time. But look, the two fractions are equivalent!

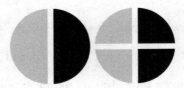

To reduce fractions, simply divide the top number and the bottom number by the same amount. Start out with small numbers like 2, 3, 5, or 10 and reduce again if you need to.

$$\frac{12}{24} \; \frac{\div 2}{\div 2} = \frac{6}{12} \; \frac{\div 2}{\div 2} = \frac{3}{6} \; \frac{\div 3}{\div 3} = \frac{1}{2}$$

In this example, if you happened to see that both 12 and 24 are divisible by 12, then you could have saved two steps. However, don't spend very much time looking for the largest number possible by which to reduce a fraction. Start out with a small number; doing one extra reduction doesn't take very much time and will definitely help prevent careless errors.

Practice Drill 6—Reducing Fractions (Primary 4, Lower, Middle, & Upper levels)

1. $\frac{6}{8} =$

2. $\frac{12}{60} =$

3. $\frac{20}{30} =$

4. $\frac{36}{96} =$

5. $\frac{24}{32} =$

6. $\frac{16}{56} =$

7. $\dfrac{1,056}{1,056} =$

8. $\dfrac{154}{126} =$

9. What does it mean when the number on top is larger than the one on the bottom?

When You Are Done
Check your answers in Chapter 4, page 98.

Improper Fractions and Mixed Numbers—Lower, Middle, & Upper Levels

Changing from Improper Fractions to Mixed Numbers

If you knew the answer to number 9 in the last drill or if you looked it up, you now know that when the number on top is greater than the number on the bottom, the fraction is greater than 1. That makes sense, because you also know that a fraction bar is really just another way of telling you to divide. So, $\dfrac{10}{2}$ is the same as $10 \div 2$, which equals 5, which is much greater than 1!

A fraction that has a greater numerator than denominator is called an *improper fraction*. You may be asked to change an improper fraction to a mixed number. A *mixed number* is an improper fraction that has been converted into a whole number and a proper fraction. To do this, let's use $\dfrac{10}{8}$ as the improper fraction that you are going to convert to a mixed number.

First, divide 10 by 8. This gives the whole number. 8 goes into 10 once.

Now, take the remainder, 2, and put it over the original fraction's denominator: $\dfrac{2}{8}$.

So the mixed number is $1\dfrac{2}{8}$, or $1\dfrac{1}{4}$.

Put Away That Calculator!
Remember that a remainder is just the integer left over after you've gotten the largest integer quotient possible from the division; it is not the decimal that a calculator gives you.

Practice Drill 7—Changing Improper Fractions to Mixed Numbers (Lower, Middle, & Upper Levels)

1. $\dfrac{45}{9} =$

2. $\dfrac{72}{42} =$

3. $\dfrac{16}{3} =$

4. $\dfrac{5}{2} =$

5. $\dfrac{8}{3} =$

6. $\dfrac{62}{9} =$

7. $\dfrac{15}{10} =$

8. $\dfrac{22}{11} =$

9. $\dfrac{83}{7} =$

10. $\dfrac{63}{6} =$

When You Are Done
Check your answers in
Chapter 4, page 99.

Changing Mixed Numbers to Improper Fractions

It's important to know how to change a mixed number into an improper fraction because it may be easier to add, subtract, multiply, or divide a fraction if there is no whole number in the way. To do this, multiply the denominator by the whole number and then add the result to the numerator. Then put this sum on top of the original denominator. For example:

$$1\frac{1}{2}$$

Multiply the denominator by the whole number: $2 \times 1 = 2$

Add this to the numerator: $2 + 1 = 3$

Put this result over the original denominator: $\dfrac{3}{2}$

$$1\frac{1}{2} = \frac{3}{2}$$

Practice Drill 8—Changing Mixed Numbers to Improper Fractions (Lower, Middle, & Upper Levels)

1. $6\dfrac{3}{7} =$

2. $2\dfrac{5}{9} =$

3. $23\dfrac{2}{3} =$

4. $6\dfrac{2}{3} =$

5. $7\dfrac{3}{8} =$

6. $7\dfrac{2}{5} =$

7. $10\dfrac{1}{16} =$

8. $5\dfrac{12}{13} =$

9. $4\dfrac{5}{9} =$

10. $33\dfrac{21}{22} =$

When You Are Done
Check your answers in Chapter 4, page 99.

Adding and Subtracting Fractions with a Common Denominator—Lower, Middle, & Upper Levels

To add or subtract fractions with a common denominator, just add or subtract the top numbers and leave the bottom numbers alone.

$$\frac{5}{7} + \frac{1}{7} = \frac{6}{7}$$

$$\frac{5}{7} - \frac{1}{7} = \frac{4}{7}$$

Adding and Subtracting Fractions When the Denominators Are Different—Lower, Middle, & Upper Levels

In the past, you have probably tried to find common denominators so that you could just add or subtract straight across. There is a different way; it is called the *Bowtie*.

No More "Least Common Denominators"
Using the Bowtie to add and subtract fractions eliminates the need for the least common denominator, but you may need to reduce the result.

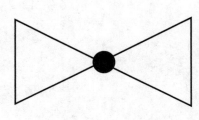

This diagram may make the Bowtie look complicated. It's not. There are three steps to adding and subtracting fractions.

Step 1: Multiply diagonally going up.
First **B** × **C**. Write the product next to **C**.
Then **D** × **A**. Write the product next to **A**.

Step 2: Multiply straight across the bottom, **B** × **D**.
Write the product as the denominator in your answer.

Step 3: To add, add the numbers written next to **A** and **C**.
Write the sum as the numerator in your answer.
To subtract, subtract the numbers written next to A and C. Write the difference as the numerator in your answer.

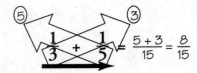

Practice Drill 9—Adding and Subtracting Fractions (Lower, Middle, & Upper Levels)

1. $\dfrac{3}{8} + \dfrac{2}{3} =$

2. $\dfrac{1}{3} + \dfrac{3}{8} =$

3. $\dfrac{4}{7} + \dfrac{2}{7} =$

4. $\dfrac{3}{4} - \dfrac{2}{3} =$

5. $\dfrac{7}{9} + \dfrac{5}{4} =$

6. $\dfrac{2}{5} - \dfrac{3}{4} =$

7. $\dfrac{10}{12} + \dfrac{7}{2} =$

8. $\dfrac{17}{27} - \dfrac{11}{27} =$

9. $\dfrac{3}{20} + \dfrac{2}{3} =$

Upper Level Only

10. $\dfrac{x}{3} + \dfrac{4x}{6} =$

11. $\dfrac{2x}{10} + \dfrac{x}{5} =$

12. $\dfrac{3y}{6} - \dfrac{y}{12} =$

When You Are Done
Check your answers in Chapter 4, page 100.

Multiplying Fractions—Middle & Upper Levels

Multiplying can be a pretty simple thing to do with fractions. All you need to do is multiply straight across the tops and bottoms.

$$\frac{3}{7} \times \frac{4}{5} = \frac{3 \times 4}{7 \times 5} = \frac{12}{35}$$

Dividing Fractions—Middle & Upper Levels

Dividing fractions is almost as simple as multiplying. You just have to flip the second fraction and then multiply.

$$\frac{3}{8} \div \frac{2}{5} = \frac{3}{8} \times \frac{5}{2} = \frac{15}{16}$$

Dividing fractions can be easy as pie; just flip the second fraction and multiply.

> **Remember Reciprocals?**
>
> A reciprocal results when you flip a fraction—that is, exchange the numerator and the denominator. So the reciprocal of $\frac{2}{3}$ is what? Yep, that's right: $\frac{3}{2}$.

Practice Drill 10—Multiplying and Dividing Fractions (Middle & Upper Levels)

1. $\dfrac{2}{3} \times \dfrac{1}{2} =$

2. $\dfrac{5}{8} \div \dfrac{1}{2} =$

3. $\dfrac{4}{5} \times \dfrac{3}{10} =$

4. $\dfrac{24}{15} \times \dfrac{10}{16} =$

5. $\dfrac{16}{25} \div \dfrac{4}{5} =$

When You Are Done
Check your answers in Chapter 4, page 101.

Decimals—Lower, Middle, & Upper Levels

Remember, decimals and fractions are just two different ways of writing the same thing.

Be sure you know the names of all the decimal places. Here's a quick reminder.

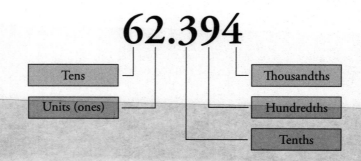

Adding Decimals

To add decimals, just line up the decimal places and add.

$$
\begin{array}{r}
48.02 \\
+\ 19.12 \\
\hline
67.14
\end{array}
$$

Subtracting Decimals

To subtract, do the same thing. Line up the decimal places and subtract.

$$
\begin{array}{r}
67.14 \\
-\ 48.02 \\
\hline
19.12
\end{array}
$$

Multiplying Decimals—Middle & Upper Levels

To multiply decimals, first count the number of digits to the right of the decimal point in the numbers you are multiplying. Then, multiply and, on the product, count that same number of spaces from right to left—this is where you put the decimal point.

$$
\begin{array}{r}
0.5 \\
\times\ 4.2 \\
\hline
2.10
\end{array}
$$
(two digits to the right of the decimal point)

Dividing Decimals—Middle & Upper Levels

To divide, move the decimal points in both numbers the same number of spaces to the right until you are working with an integer in the divisor.

$$12.5 \div 0.25 = 0.25\overline{)12.5}$$

Now move both decimals over two places and solve the problem.

$$25\overline{)1250}^{50}$$

And you're done! Remember: you do not put the decimals back into the problem.

Practice Drill 11—Decimals

Lower, Middle, & Upper Levels

1. $1.43 + 17.27 =$

2. $2.49 + 1.7 =$

3. $7 - 2.038 =$

Middle & Upper Levels

4. $4.25 \times 2.5 =$

5. $0.02 \times 0.90 =$

6. $180 \div 0.03 =$

7. $0.10 \div 0.02 =$

When You Are Done
Check your answers in Chapter 4, page 101.

Converting Fractions to Decimals and Back Again

From Fractions to Decimals

As we learned when we introduced fractions a little earlier, a fraction bar is really just a division sign.

$$\frac{10}{2} \text{ is the same as } 10 \div 2, \text{ or } 5$$

In the same sense:

$$\frac{1}{2} = 1 \div 2, \text{ or } 0.5$$

In fact, we can convert any fraction to its decimal equivalent by dividing the top number by the bottom number:

$$\frac{11}{2} = 11 \div 2 = 5.5$$

From Decimals to Fractions

To change a decimal to a fraction, look at the digit furthest to the right. Determine what place that digit is in (e.g., tenths, hundredths, and so on) and then put the decimal (without the decimal point) over that number (e.g., 10, 100, and so on). Let's change 0.5 into a fraction.

5 is in the tenths place, so we put it over 10.

$$\frac{5}{10} \text{ reduces to } \frac{1}{2}$$

Practice Drill 12—Converting Fractions to Decimals and Back Again (Lower, Middle, & Upper Levels)

Fill in the table below by converting the fractions to decimals, and vice versa. The fractions and decimals in this table are those most often tested on the ISEE, so memorize them now and save yourself time later.

Fraction	Decimal
$\dfrac{1}{2}$	0.5
$\dfrac{1}{3}$	
$\dfrac{2}{3}$	
	0.25
	0.75
$\dfrac{1}{5}$	
	0.4
	0.6
$\dfrac{4}{5}$	
	0.125

When You Are Done
Check your answers in Chapter 4, page 102.

Percents—Middle & Upper Levels

Percentages are really just an extension of fractions. Let's go back to that pie we were talking about in the section on fractions. Let's say we had a pie that was cut into four equal pieces. If you ate one piece of the pie, then we could say that the *fractional part* of the pie that you have eaten is:

$$\frac{1}{4} = \frac{\text{(the number of pieces you ate)}}{\text{(the total number of pieces in the pie)}} = \frac{\text{part}}{\text{whole}}$$

Now let's find out what percentage of the pie you have eaten. Percent literally means "out of 100." When we find a percent, we are really trying to see how many times out of 100 something happens. To determine the percent, you simply take the fractional part and multiply it by 100.

$$\frac{1}{4} \times 100 = \frac{100}{4} = 25\%$$

You've probably seen percents as grades on your tests in school. What does it mean to get 100% on a test? It means you got every question correct. Let's say you got 25 questions right out of a total of 25. So we put the number of questions you got right over the total number of questions and multiply by 100.

$$\frac{25}{25} = 1 \times 100 = 100\%$$

Let's says that your friend didn't do as well on this same test. He answered 20 questions correctly. Let's figure out the percentage of questions he got right.

$$\frac{20}{25} = \frac{4}{5} \times 100 = 80\%$$

What percentage did he get wrong?

$$\frac{5}{25} = \frac{1}{5} = 20\%$$

Notice that the percentage of questions he got right (80%) plus the percentage of questions he got wrong (20%) equals 100%.

Practice Drill 13—Percents (Middle & Upper Levels)

1. A bag of candies contains 15 butterscotches, 20 caramels, 5 peppermints, and 10 toffees.

   a) The butterscotches make up what percentage of the candies?_____

   b) The caramels?_____

   c) The peppermints?_____

   d) The toffees?_____

2. A student answered 75% of the questions on a test correctly and left 7% of the questions blank. What percentage of the questions did the student answer incorrectly?_____

3. Salma's closet contains 40 pairs of shoes. She has 8 pairs of sneakers, 12 sets of sandals, 16 pairs of boots, and the rest are slippers.

   a) What percentage of the shoes are sneakers? _____

   b) Sandals?_____

   c) Boots?_____

   d) Slippers?_____

   e) How many pairs of slippers does Salma own? _____

4. A recipe for fruit punch calls for 4 cups of apple juice, 2 cups of cranberry juice, 3 cups of grape juice, and 1 cup of seltzer. What percentage of the punch is juice?_____

5. Five friends are chipping in for a birthday gift for their teacher. David and Jakob each contribute $13. Stephanie, Kai, and Janice each contribute $8.

   a) What percentage of the total did Stephanie, Kai, and Janice contribute?
      _____

   b) What about David and Jakob?_____

When You Are Done
Check your answers in Chapter 4, pages 102–103.

More Percents—Middle & Upper Levels

Another place you may have encountered percents is at the shopping mall. Stores offer special discounts on their merchandise to entice shoppers to buy more stuff. Most of these stores discount their merchandise by a certain percentage. For example, you may see a $16 shirt that is marked 25% off the regular price. What does that mean?

Percents are not "real" numbers. In the above scenario, the shirt was not $25 less than the regular price (then the store would have to pay you money!), but 25% less. So how do you figure out how much that shirt really costs and how much money you are saving?

To find how much a percent is in "real" numbers, you need to *first take the percent and change it to a fraction*.

Because percent means "out of 100," to change a percent to a fraction, simply put the percent over 100.

$$25\% = \frac{25}{100} = \frac{1}{4}$$

Now let's get back to that shirt. Multiply the regular price of the shirt, $16, by the fraction.

$$\$16 \times \frac{1}{4} = \$4$$

Tip:
Changing a decimal to a percent is the same as changing a fraction to a percent. Multiply the decimal by 100 (move the decimal two spaces to the right). So 0.25 as a percent is $0.25 \times 100 = 25\%$.

This means 25% of 16 is $4. You get $4 off the original price of the shirt. If you subtract that from the original price, you find that the new sale price is $12.

Guess what percentage the sale price is of the regular price? If you said 75 percent, you'd be right!

Practice Drill 14—More Percents (Middle & Upper Levels)

Fill in the missing information in the table below.

Fraction	Decimal	Percent
$\frac{1}{2}$	0.5	50%
$\frac{1}{3}$		
	$0.6\overline{6}$	
		25%
	0.75	
$\frac{1}{5}$		
		40%
	0.6	
$\frac{4}{5}$		
		12.5%

1. 25% of 84 =

2. $33\frac{1}{3}$ % of 27 =

3. 20% of 75 =

Tip:
The word *of* in word problems means multiply!

4. 17% of 300 =

5. 16% of 10% of 500 =

6. A dress is marked down 15% from its regular price. If the regular price is $120, what is the sale price of the dress? The sale price is what percentage of the regular price of the dress?

7. Wei goes to school 80% of the 365 days of the year. How many days does Wei go to school?

8. Atlas answered all 36 questions on her history test. If she got 25% of the questions wrong, how many questions did she get right?

When You Are Done
Check your answers in Chapter 4, pages 103–104.

9. During a special one-day sale, the price of a television was marked down 20% from its original price of $100. Later that day, the television was marked down an additional 10%. What was the final sale price?

Percent Change—Upper Level Only

There is one special kind of percent question that shows up on the ISEE: percent change. This type of question asks you to find by what percent something has increased or decreased. Instead of taking the part and dividing it by the whole, you will take the difference between the two numbers and divide it by the original number. Then, to turn the fraction to a percent, divide the numerator by the denominator and multiply by 100.

For example:

The number of people who streamed *Umbrella Academy* in its second season was 3,600,000. During the first season, only 3,000,000 streamed the show. By approximately what percent did the audience increase?

$$\frac{\text{The difference}}{\text{The original}} = \frac{600,000}{3,000,000} \quad \text{(The difference is } 3,600,000 - 3,000,000.\text{)}$$

$\% \text{ change} = \frac{\text{difference}}{\text{original}} \times 100$

The fraction reduces to $\frac{1}{5}$, and $\frac{1}{5}$ as a percent is 20%.

Practice Drill 15—Percent Change (Upper Level Only)

1.   During a severe winter in Conway, the temperature dropped suddenly to
      10 degrees below zero. If the temperature in Conway before this cold spell
      occurred was 10 degrees above zero, by what percent did the temperature drop?

2.   Primo Burger wants to attract more customers by increasing the size of its patties. From now
      on, Primo's patties are going to be 4 ounces larger than before. If the size of its new patty is
      16 ounces, by approximately what percent has the patty increased?

When You Are Done
Check your answers in
Chapter 4, page 104.

Basic Exponents—Middle & Upper Levels

Exponents are just another way to indicate multiplication. For instance, 3^2 simply means to multiply three
by itself two times, so $3^2 = 3 \times 3 = 9$. If you remember that rule, even higher exponents won't seem very
complicated. For example:

$$2^5 = 2 \times 2 \times 2 \times 2 \times 2 = 32$$

The questions on the ISEE don't generally use exponents higher than four or five, so this is likely
to be as complicated as it gets.

The rule for exponents is simple: when in doubt, write it out! Don't try to figure out two times
two times two times two times two in your head (just look at how silly it looks written down
using words!). Instead, write it as a math problem and just work through it one step at a time.

What would you do if you were asked to solve this problem?

$$Q^3 \times Q^2 =$$

Let's look at this one carefully. Q^3 means $Q \times Q \times Q$ and Q^2 means $Q \times Q$. Put them together and you've
got:

$$(Q \times Q \times Q) \times (Q \times Q) =$$

How many Qs is that? Count them. Five! The answer is Q^5. Be careful when multiplying exponents like this
so that you don't get confused and multiply the actual exponents, which would give you Q^6. If you are ever
unsure, don't spend a second worrying; just write out the exponent and count the number of things you are
multiplying.

> **When in Doubt,
> Write It Out!**
> Don't try to compute
> exponents in your head.
> Write them out and
> multiply!

Basic Roots—(Middle & Upper Levels)

A square root (also called a "radical expression") is just the "undoing" of squaring a number.
$2^2 = 2 \times 2$ or 4, so the square root of 4 is 2.

You will see square roots written this way on tests: $\sqrt{4}$.

Use the Common Multiples table on page 16 to make flashcards of the first 12 perfect squares and their
square roots.

For example, since $4 \times 4 = 16$, that means $\sqrt{16} = 4$. Write $\sqrt{16}$ on one side of your flashcard and 4 on the other side.

Cube roots and other larger roots work the same way as square roots—they "undo" exponents. So since $2^3 = 2 \times 2 \times 2 = 8$, that means $\sqrt[3]{8} = 2$.

Practice Drill 16—Basic Exponents and Square Roots (Middle & Upper Levels)

1. $2^3 =$

2. $2^4 =$

3. $3^3 =$

4. $4^3 =$

5. $\sqrt{81} =$

6. $\sqrt{100} =$

7. $\sqrt{49} =$

8. $\sqrt{64} =$

9. $\sqrt{9} =$

10. $\sqrt[3]{125} =$

11. $\sqrt[3]{64} =$

12. $\sqrt[4]{16} =$

When You Are Done
Check your answers in Chapter 4, page 105.

Advanced Exponents—Upper Level Only

Adding and Subtracting with Exponents

When adding or subtracting expressions with exponents, the bases and exponents have to match. $3^2 + 3^2 = 2(3^2)$ When a variable is involved, the bases and exponents have to match, and you'll just add or subtract the coefficients (the number to the left of the variable): $9x^2 - 4x^2 = 5x^2$

Multiplying and Dividing Exponents with the Same Base

You can multiply and divide exponents *with the same base* without having to expand out and calculate the value of each exponent. The bottom number, the one you are multiplying, is called the base. (However, note that to multiply $2^3 \times 5^2$ you must calculate the value of each exponent separately and then multiply the results. That's because the bases are different.)

To multiply, add the exponents.

$$2^3 \times 2^4 = 2^{3+4} = 2^7$$

To divide, subtract the exponents.

$$2^8 \div 2^5 = 2^{8-5} = 2^3$$

To take an exponent to another power, multiply the exponents.

$$(2^3)^3 = 2^{3 \times 3} = 2^9$$

Anything raised to the first power is itself:

$$3^1 = 3 \qquad x^1 = x$$

Anything raised to the 0 power is 1:

$$3^0 = 1 \qquad x^0 = 1$$

> **For exponents with the same base, remember MADSPM:** When you *Multiply* with exponents, *Add* them. When you *Divide* with exponents, *Subtract*. When you see *Powers* with exponents, *Multiply*.
>
> Exponents can be combined ONLY when the expression involves multiplication or division. Pay attention to the operation that is used in the problem when dealing with exponents!

Negative exponents mean reciprocal: flip it over and get rid of the negative sign in the exponent.

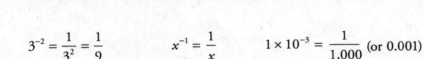

$$3^{-2} = \frac{1}{3^2} = \frac{1}{9} \qquad\qquad x^{-1} = \frac{1}{x} \qquad\qquad 1 \times 10^{-3} = \frac{1}{1,000} \text{ (or 0.001)}$$

Advanced Square Roots—Upper Level Only

Sometimes you'll be given square roots in which the number under the root sign is not a perfect square. When that's the case, factor the number under the square root sign and separate into two separate square roots. To simplify $\sqrt{8}$, first factor 8 into 4 and 2. $\sqrt{8} = \sqrt{4 \times 2}$. When there's multiplication or division under the square root sign, the operation can be broken apart into separate roots: $\sqrt{8} = \sqrt{4 \times 2} = \sqrt{4} \times \sqrt{2}$. Now simplify the square root of the perfect square. $\sqrt{4} = 2$, so $\sqrt{4} \times \sqrt{2} = 2 \times \sqrt{2}$, which is written as $2\sqrt{2}$.

This also works in the opposite direction. When multiplying or dividing, the numbers under two (or more) radical signs can be combined.

$$\sqrt{32} \times \sqrt{2} = \sqrt{32 \times 2} = \sqrt{64} = 8$$

Always be on the lookout for perfect squares as "hidden" factors or multiples of the numbers you're given! In order to add or subtract radical expressions, the number under the radical sign must be the same and you'll add or subtract the coefficients.

$$7\sqrt{3} - 4\sqrt{3} = 3\sqrt{3}$$

You may need to simplify the radical expression before adding or subtracting:

$$\sqrt{32} - \sqrt{8}$$

$$\sqrt{32} = \sqrt{16 \times 2} = \sqrt{16} \times \sqrt{2} = 4 \times \sqrt{2} = 4\sqrt{2}$$

$$\sqrt{8} = \sqrt{4 \times 2} = \sqrt{4} \times \sqrt{2} = 2 \times \sqrt{2} = 2\sqrt{2}$$

Now that the numbers under the radical sign match, subtract the coefficients:

$$4\sqrt{2} - 2\sqrt{2} = 2\sqrt{2}$$

Practice Drill 17—Advanced Exponents & Roots (Upper Level Only)

Simplify each expression.

1. $3^5 \times 3^3 =$

2. $7^2 \times 7^7 =$

3. $5^3 \times 5^4 =$

4. $15^{23} \div 15^{20} =$

5. $4^{13} \div 4^4 =$

6. $10^{10} \div 10^6 =$

7. $(5^3)^6 =$

8. $(8^{12})^3 =$

9. $(9^5)^5 =$

10. $(2^2)^{14} =$

11. $3^4 + 3^4 =$

12. $7x^6 - 3x^6 =$

13. $\sqrt{24} =$

14. $\sqrt{500} =$

15. $\sqrt{3} \times \sqrt{48} =$

16. $\sqrt{150} \div \sqrt{6} =$

17. $\sqrt{18} + \sqrt{72} =$

18. $\sqrt{200} - \sqrt{50} =$

When You Are Done
Check your answers in
Chapter 4, page 105.

Matrices

Occasionally you may see questions in the Mathematics Achievement section that test matrices—a way of organizing numbers into rows and columns. A matrix is indicated by the large brackets around the numbers. On the ISEE, you're most likely to see a question that asks you to either add or subtract matrices. Let's take a look at an example:

$$\begin{bmatrix} 5 & 6 \\ 7 & 8 \end{bmatrix} + \begin{bmatrix} 1 & 3 \\ 4 & 9 \end{bmatrix} = ?$$

In order to add or subtract matrices, the dimensions of each matrix need to match. Here, both matrices are two rows by two columns (2×2), so the resulting matrix will also be 2×2. All you need to do is match up the numbers in the same position and add or subtract them!

$$\begin{bmatrix} a & b \\ c & d \end{bmatrix} + \begin{bmatrix} e & f \\ g & h \end{bmatrix} = \begin{bmatrix} a+e & b+f \\ c+g & d+h \end{bmatrix}$$

So in the example expression,

$$\begin{bmatrix} 5 & 6 \\ 7 & 8 \end{bmatrix} + \begin{bmatrix} 1 & 3 \\ 4 & 9 \end{bmatrix} = \begin{bmatrix} 5+1 & 6+3 \\ 7+4 & 8+9 \end{bmatrix} = \begin{bmatrix} 6 & 9 \\ 11 & 17 \end{bmatrix}$$

Review Drill 1—Numbers & Operations

1. Is 1 a prime number?

2. How many factors does 100 have?

3. $-10 + (-20) =$

4. $100 + 50 \div 5 \times 4 =$

5. $\dfrac{3}{7} - \dfrac{1}{3} =$

6. $\dfrac{4}{5} \div \dfrac{5}{3} =$

7. $1.2 \times 3.4 =$

8. $\dfrac{x}{100} \times 30 = 6.$ Find the value of x.

9. $1^5 =$

10. $\sqrt{16} =$

11. What are the first 10 perfect squares?

When You Are Done
Check your answers in
Chapter 4, page 106.

12. $\begin{bmatrix} 17 & 21 \\ 31 & 9 \end{bmatrix} - \begin{bmatrix} 4 & 12 \\ 19 & 6 \end{bmatrix} =$

ALGEBRAIC CONCEPTS—LOWER, MIDDLE, & UPPER LEVELS

An Introduction

If you're a Lower or Middle Level student, you may not yet have begun learning about algebra in school, but don't let that throw you. If you know how to add, subtract, multiply, and divide, you can solve an algebraic equation. Lower Level students need to understand only the section below titled "Solving Simple Equations." Middle Level students should complete all of the "Solving Simple Equations" drills and as much of the Upper Level material as possible. Upper Level students need to go through the entire Algebra section carefully to make sure they can solve each of the question types.

> **The Case of the Mysteriously Missing Sign**
> If there is no operation sign between a number and a variable (letter), the operation is multiplication.

Solving Simple Equations

Algebraic equations involve the same basic operations that you've dealt with throughout this chapter, but instead of using only numbers, these equations use a combination of numbers and letters. These letters are called *variables*. Here are some basic rules about working with variables that you need to understand.

- A variable (usually x, y, or z) replaces an unknown number in an algebraic equation.
- It is usually your job to figure out what that unknown number is.
- If a variable appears more than once in an equation, that variable is always replacing the same number.
- When a variable is directly to the right of a number, with no sign in between them, the operation that is holding them together is multiplication (e.g., $3y = 3 \times y$).
- You can add and subtract like variables (e.g., $2z + 5z = 7z$).
- You cannot add or subtract unlike variables (e.g., $2z$ and $3y$ cannot be combined).

To solve simple algebraic equations, you need to think abstractly about the equation. Let's try one.

$$2 + x = 7$$

What does x equal?

Well, what number plus 2 gives you 7? If you said 5, you were right and $x = 5$.

$$2y = 16$$

> In the first equation, we subtracted 2 from both sides. In the second equation, we divided both sides by 2.

What does y equal?

Now you need to ask yourself what multiplied by 2 gives you 16. If you said 8, you were right! $y = 8$.

Tip: You can check to see if you found the right number for the variable by replacing the variable in the equation with the number you found. So in the last problem, if we replace y with 8 and rewrite the problem, we get $2 \times 8 = 16$. And that's true, so we got it right!

Practice Drill 18—Solving Simple Equations (Lower, Middle, & Upper Levels)

1. If $35 - x = 23$, then $x =$

2. If $y + 12 = 27$, then $y =$

3. If $z - 7 = 21$, then $z =$

4. If $5x = 25$, then $x =$

5. If $18 \div x = 6$, then $x =$

6. If $3x = 33$, then $x =$

7. If $65 \div y = 13$, then $y =$

8. If $14 = 17 - z$, then $z =$

9. If $\frac{1}{2}y = 24$, then $y =$

10. If $136 + z = 207$, then $z =$

11. If $7x = 84$, then $x =$

12. If $y \div 2 = 6$, then $y =$

13. If $z \div 3 = 15$, then $z =$

14. If $14 + x = 32$, then $x =$

15. If $53 - y = 24$, then $y =$

When You Are Done
Check your answers in
Chapter 4,
pages 106–107.

Manipulating an Equation—Middle & Upper Levels

To solve an equation, your goal is to isolate the variable, meaning that you want to get the variable on one side of the equation and everything else on the other side.

$$3x + 5 = 17$$

To solve this equation, follow these two steps.

Step 1: Move elements around using addition and subtraction. Get variables on one side and numbers on the other. Simplify.

Step 2: Divide both sides of the equation by the *coefficient*, the number in front of the variable. If that number is a fraction, multiply everything by the denominator.

For example:

$$3x + 5 = 17$$

$$\underline{-5 \quad -5}$$

Subtract 5 from both sides to get rid of the 5 on the left side.

$$3x \quad = 12$$

$$\underline{\div 3 \qquad \div 3}$$

Divide both sides by 3 to get rid of the 3 on the left side.

$$x \quad = 4$$

Remember: Whatever you do to one side, you must also do to the other.

Practice Drill 19—Manipulating an Equation (Middle & Upper Levels)

1. If $8 = 11 - x$, then $x =$

2. If $4x = 20$, then $x =$

3. If $5x - 20 = 10$, then $x =$

4. If $4x + 3 = 31$, then $x =$

5. If $m + 5 = 3m - 3$, then $m =$

6.   If $2.5x = 20$, then $x =$

7.   If $0.2x + 2 = 3.6$, then $x =$

8.   If $6 = 8x + 4$, then $x =$

9.   If $3(x + y) = 21$, then $x + y =$

10.   If $3x + 3y = 21$, then $x + y =$

11.   If $100 - 5y = 65$, then $y =$

When You Are Done
Check your answers in
Chapter 4, page 107.

Manipulating Inequalities—Middle & Upper Levels

Manipulating an inequality is just like manipulating an equation that has an equals sign, except for one rule: if you multiply or divide by a negative number, flip the inequality sign.

Let's try an example.

Helpful Trick
Think of the inequality
sign as an alligator, and
the alligator always
eats the bigger meal.

$$-3x < 6$$

Divide both sides by –3, and then flip the inequality sign.

$$x > -2$$

Practice Drill 20—Manipulating an Inequality (Middle & Upper Levels)

Solve for x.

1. $4x > 16$

2. $13 - x > 15$

3. $15x - 20x < 25$

4. $12 + 2x > 24 - x$

5. $7 < -14 - 3x$

When You Are Done
Check your answers
in Chapter 4,
pages 107–108.

Functions—Middle & Upper Levels

In a function problem, an arithmetic operation is defined and then you are asked to perform it on a number. A function is just a set of instructions written in a strange way.

The function # is defined as $x = 3x(x + 1)$

On the left there is usually a variable with a strange symbol next to or around it.
In the middle is an equals sign.

On the right are the instructions. These tell you what to do with the variable.

What follows will be a question that asks you the value of the expression when the variable is a particular number.

What does #5 equal?

#5 = $(3 \times 5)(5 + 1)$ *Just replace each x with a 5!*

Here, the function (indicated by the # sign) simply tells you to substitute a 5 wherever there was an x in the original set of instructions. Functions look confusing because of the strange symbols, but once you know what to do with them, they are just like manipulating an equation.

Sometimes more than one question will refer to the same function. The following drill, for example, contains multiple questions about one function. In cases such as this, the first question tends to be easier than the second.

Another way functions may be tested is by naming a function with a variable instead of a strange symbol.

The function f is defined by $f(x) = 3x(x+1)$. What is the value of $f(5)$?

This is the exact same question as the previous one, just formatted a little differently. You're still going to replace each *x* with a 5.

$$f(5) = (3 \times 5)(5 + 1)$$

$$f(5) = 15 \times 6 = 90$$

Practice Drill 21—Functions (Middle & Upper Levels)

1. If ❧*p* = 5*p* − 4, then what is the value of ❧6 ?)

2. If *f*(*x*) = 7*x*, then what is the value of *f*(5)?

3. If *p* and *q* are positive integers and *p* ◀ *q* is defined as $\frac{p}{q} + 3$, what is the value of 10 ◀ 2 ?

4. The function *s* is defined by $s(r) = r^2 - 4$. What is the value of *s*(3)?

When You Are Done
Check your answers in
Chapter 4, page 108.

MULTIPLYING EXPRESSIONS WITH FOIL (UPPER LEVEL ONLY)

First, Outside, Inside, Last

$$(x + 2)(x + 3)$$

FOIL stands for First, Outside, Inside, Last, an easy way to remember how to properly distribute all the terms of two binomials (expressions with two terms in them). Multiply the two First terms of each binomial, in this case $x \times x = x^2$. Then, multiply the Outside terms: $x \times 3 = 3x$. Next, multiply the Inside terms: $2 \times x = 2x$. Finally, multiply the Last terms by each other: $2 \times 3 = 6$. Add all these terms together to find that $(x + 2)(x + 3) = x^2 + 3x + 2x + 6$. Combine like terms to fully simplify: $x^2 + 5x + 6$.

Factoring with Binomials

To work in the opposite direction and factor a polynomial expression, create two sets of parentheses for the binomials and place a variable in each: $(x\quad)(x\quad)$. If the last term is positive, this means there must be either two plus signs or two minus signs. If both the middle and last terms are positive, there must be two plus signs, and if the middle term is negative when the last term is positive, there must be two minus signs. If the last term is negative, that means there must be one of each sign. Now, look at the last term. The two numbers in the parentheses must multiply to equal the last term and add to equal the middle term. Let's try an example:

$$x^2 + 6x + 9$$

Both terms are positive, so start with $(x + \quad)(x + \quad)$. Now, list the factors of 9: 1 and 9, 3 and 3. $1 + 9 \neq 6$, but $3 + 3 = 6$. Therefore, the expression should read $(x + 3)(x + 3)$. Let's try another:

$$x^2 - 3x - 10$$

This one has a negative sign before the last term, so start with $(x + \quad)(x - \quad)$ since a negative times a positive will equal a negative number. Now, list the factors of 10: 1 and 10, 2 and 5. Since the signs are opposite, there are more options of how to add the numbers, since $1 + -10$ and $-1 + 10$ are both options. However, neither equals -3. Try 2 and 5: $-2 + 5 = 3$, and $2 + -5 = -3$. Since the middle term must be negative, place the 2 with the plus sign and 5 with the minus sign: $(x + 2)(x + -5)$.

Practice Drill 22—Foiling & Factoring (Upper Level Only)

Multiply the following expressions.

1. $(x + 4)(x + 3)$

2. $(x - 4)(x - 3)$

3. $(x + 4)(x - 3)$

4. $(a + b)(a - b)$

5. $(a + b)(a + b)$

6. $(a - b)(a - b)$

7. If $x^2 + y^2 = 53$, and $xy = 14$, what is the value of $(x - y)^2$?

Factor the following expressions:

8. $x^2 + 13x + 42$

9. $y^2 - 3y - 10$

10. $x^2 - 12x + 35$

11. $y^2 + 11x + 24$

12. $a^2 - 5a - 14$

13. $b^2 - 11b + 30$

14. $k^2 + 16k + 63$

When You Are Done
Check your answers in Chapter 4, pages 108–109.

Solving Percent Questions with Algebra—Middle & Upper Levels

Percentages

Solving percent problems can be easy when you know how to translate them from "percent language" into "math language." Once you've done the translation, you guessed it—just manipulate the equation!

Whenever you see words from the following table, just translate them into math terms and go to work on the equation!

Percent Language	Math Language
% or "percent"	out of 100 $\left(\dfrac{x}{100}\right)$
of	times (as in multiplication) ($\times$)
what	your favorite variable (p)
is, are, were, was, did	equals (=)

For example:

24 is 60 percent of what?

$$24 = \frac{60}{100} \times m$$

Practice Drill 23—Translating and Solving Percent Questions (Middle & Upper Levels)

1. 30 is what percent of 250 ?

2. What is 12% of 200 ?

3. What is 25% of 10% of 200 ?

4. 75% of 20% of what number is 12 ?

5. 16% of what number is 25% of 80 ?

6. What percent is equal to $\frac{3}{5}$?

7. 30 is what percent of 75 ?

8. What is 11% of 24 ?

9. What percent of 24 is equal to 48 ?

10. 60% of what percent of 500 is equal to 6 ?

When You Are Done
Check your answers
in Chapter 4,
pages 109–110.

GEOMETRY & MEASUREMENT—PRIMARY 4, LOWER, MIDDLE, & UPPER LEVELS

An Introduction

Just as in the previous Algebraic Concepts section, this Geometry & Measurement section contains some material that is above the level tested on the Lower and Middle Level Exams. These students should not work on sections that are indicated for higher levels. While the ISEE separates Measurement from Geometry, many of the questions considered "Measurement" questions are about the attributes of geometric figures, so they are grouped together in this book.

Perimeter—Primary 4, Lower, Middle, & Upper Levels

The perimeter is the distance around the outside of any figure. To find the perimeter of a figure, just add up the lengths of all the sides.

What are the perimeters of these figures?

> **Perimeter**
> P = side + side + side...
> until you run out of sides.

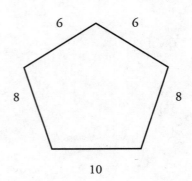

Perimeter = 6 + 6 + 8 + 8 + 10 = 38

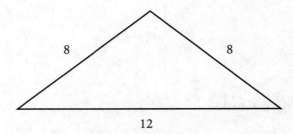

Perimeter = 8 + 8 + 12 = 28

Angles—Middle & Upper Levels

Straight Lines

Angles that form a straight line always total 180°.

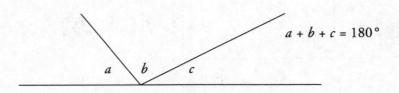

$$a + b + c = 180°$$

Triangles

All of the angles in a triangle add up to 180°.

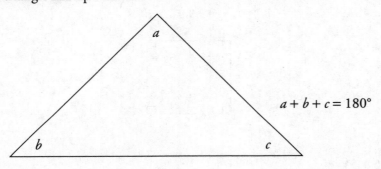

$$a + b + c = 180°$$

Four-Sided Figures

The angles in a square, rectangle, or any other four-sided figure always add up to 360°.

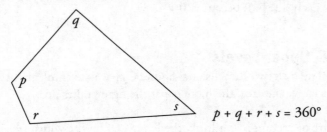

$$p + q + r + s = 360°$$

Angle Vocabulary

Supplementary Angles are angles that add up to 180°.

Complementary Angles are angles that add up to 90°.

Opposite Angles are the angles that are across from one another when two lines cross. They are always equal!

Vertex is the point at which two lines (or sides of a polygon) cross or meet.

Squares and Rectangles—Lower, Middle, & Upper Levels

A *rectangle* is a four-sided figure with four right (90°) angles. Opposite sides are equal in a rectangle. The perimeter is equal to the sum of the sides.

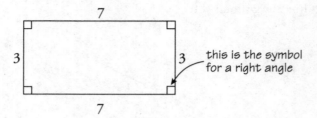

Perimeter = 3 + 3 + 7 + 7 = 20

A *square* is a special type of rectangle in which all the sides are equal.

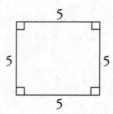

Perimeter = 5 + 5 + 5 + 5 = 20

Because all sides of a square are equal, you can find the length of a side by dividing its perimeter by four. If the perimeter of a square is 20, then each side is 5, because 20 ÷ 4 = 5.

Area—Lower, Middle, & Upper Levels

Area is the amount of space taken up by a two-dimensional figure. One way to think about area is as the amount of paper that a figure covers. The larger the area, the more paper the figure takes up.

To determine the area of a square or rectangle, multiply the length (*l*) by the width (*w*).

Area of a Rectangle
$A = lw$

Remember the formula:

$$\textbf{Area} = \textbf{length} \times \textbf{width}$$

What is the area of a rectangle with length 9 and width 4 ?

In this case, the length is 9 and the width is 4, so 9 × 4 = 36. Now look at another example.

Area of rectangle *ABCD* = 6 × 8 = 48

The area of squares and rectangles is given in *square feet, square inches,* and so on.

To find the area of a square, you multiply two sides, and because the sides are equal, you're really finding the square of the sides. You can find the length of a side of a square by taking the square root of the area. So if a square has an area of 25, one side of the square is 5.

> **Area of a Square**
> $A = s^2$

Volume—Lower, Middle, & Upper Levels

Volume is very similar to area, except it takes into account a third dimension. To compute the volume of a figure, you simply find the area and multiply by a third dimension.

For instance, to find the volume of a rectangular object, you would multiply the length by the width (a.k.a. the area of the base) by the height (the third dimension). Since a rectangular solid (like a box) is the only kind of figure you are likely to see in a volume question, simply use the formula below.

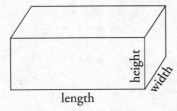

length × width × height = volume

> **Volume of a Rectangular Solid**
> $V = lwh$

For example:

>   What is the volume of a rectangular fish tank with the
>   following specifications?
>   length: 6 inches
>   height: 6 inches
>   width: 10 inches

There isn't much to it. Just plug the numbers into the formula.

>   length × width × height = volume
>   6 × 10 × 6 = 360

Practice Drill 24—Squares, Rectangles, & Angles—Lower, Middle, & Upper Levels

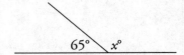

1. What is the value of *x* ?

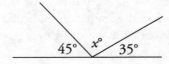

2. What is the value of *x* ?

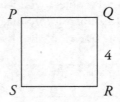

3. *PQRS* is a square. What is its perimeter? Area?

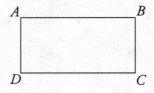

4. *ABCD* is a rectangle with length 7 and width 3. What is its perimeter? Area?

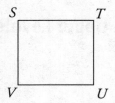

5.   *STUV* is a square. Its perimeter is 12. What is its area?

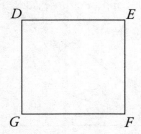

6.   *DEFG* is a square. Its area is 81. What is its perimeter?

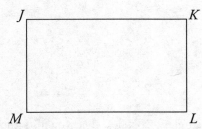

7.   *JKLM* is a rectangle. If its width is 4, and its perimeter is 20, what is its area?

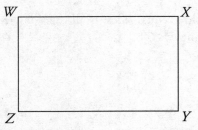

8.   *WXYZ* is a rectangle. If its length is 6 and its area is 30, what is its perimeter?

9.   What is the volume of a rectangular solid with height 3, width 4, and length 2 ?

When You Are Done
Check your answers in Chapter 4, page 110.

Triangles—Lower, Middle, & Upper Levels

A triangle is a geometric figure with three sides.

Isosceles Triangles

Any triangle with two equal sides is an isosceles triangle.

If two sides of a triangle are equal, the angles opposite those sides are always equal. Said another way, the sides opposite the equal angles are also equal.

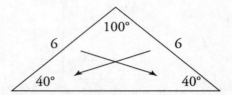

This particular isosceles triangle has two equal sides (of length 6) and therefore two equal angles (40° in this case).

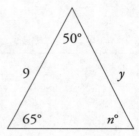

If you already know that the above triangle is isosceles, then you also know that y must equal one of the other sides and n must equal one of the other angles. Since $n = 65$ (65° + 50° + n° = 180°), then y must equal 9, because it is opposite the other 65° angle.

Equilateral Triangles

An equilateral triangle is a triangle with three equal sides. If all the sides are equal, then all the angles must be equal. Each angle in an equilateral triangle is 60°.

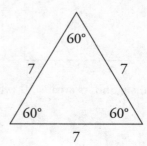

Right Triangles

A right triangle is a triangle with one 90° angle.

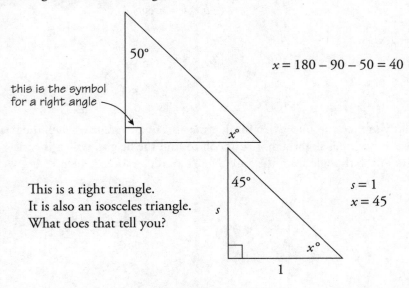

50°

this is the symbol
for a right angle

$x°$

$x = 180 - 90 - 50 = 40$

This is a right triangle.
It is also an isosceles triangle.
What does that tell you?

45°

s

$x°$

1

$s = 1$
$x = 45$

Area

To find the area of a triangle, multiply $\frac{1}{2}$ by the length of the base by the length of the triangle's

height, or $\frac{1}{2}b \times h$.

Lower Levels
The test-writers may give you the formula for the area of a triangle, but memorizing it will still save you time!

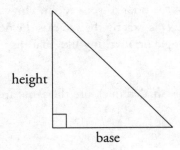

height

base

What is the area of a triangle with base 6 and height 3 ?

Just put the values you are given into the formula and do the math. That's all there is to it!

$$\frac{1}{2} b \times h = \textbf{area}$$

$$(\frac{1}{2})(6) \times 3 = \textbf{area}$$

$$3 \times 3 = 9$$

The only tricky point you may run into when finding the area of a triangle is when the triangle is not a right triangle. In this case, it becomes slightly more difficult to find the height, which is easiest to think of as the distance to the point of the triangle from the base. Here's an illustration to help.

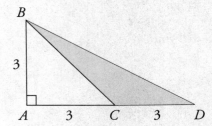

First look at triangle *BAC*, the unshaded right triangle on the left side. Finding its base and height is simple—they are both 3. So using our formula for the area of a triangle, we can figure out that the area of triangle *BAC* is $4\frac{1}{2}$.

Now let's think about triangle *BCD*, the shaded triangle on the right. It isn't a right triangle, so finding the height will involve a little more thought. Remember the question, though: how far up from the base is the point of triangle *BCD*? Think of the shaded triangle sitting on the floor of your room. How far up would its point stick up from the floor? Yes, 3! The height of triangle *BCD* is exactly the same as the height of triangle *BAC*. Don't worry about drawing lines inside the shaded triangle or anything like that, just figure out how high its point is from the ground.

Okay, so just to finish up, to find the area of triangle *BCD* (the shaded one), use the same area formula, and just plug in 3 for the base and 3 for the height.

$$\frac{1}{2} b \times h = \textbf{area}$$

$$(\frac{1}{2})(3) \times 3 = \textbf{area}$$

And once you do the math, you'll see that the area of triangle *BCD* is $4\frac{1}{2}$.

Not quite convinced? Let's look at the question a little differently. The base of the entire figure (triangle *DAB*) is 6, and the height is 3. Using your trusty area formula, you can determine that the area of triangle *DAB* is 9. You know the area of the unshaded triangle is $4\frac{1}{2}$, so what's left for the shaded part? You guessed it, $4\frac{1}{2}$.

Similar Triangles—Middle & Upper Levels

Similar triangles are triangles that have the same angles but sides of different lengths. The ratio of any two corresponding sides will be the same as the ratio of any other two corresponding sides. For example, a triangle with sides 3, 4, and 5 is similar to a triangle with sides of 6, 8, and 10, because the ratio of each of the corresponding sides (3:6, 4:8, and 5:10) can be reduced to 1:2.

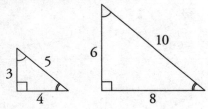

One way to approach similar triangles questions that ask you for a missing side is to set up a ratio or proportion. For example, look at the question below:

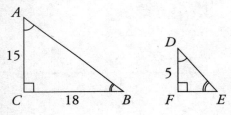

What is the value of *EF*?

These triangles are similar because they have the same angles. To find side *EF*, you just need to set up a ratio or proportion.

$$\frac{15}{18} = \frac{5}{EF}$$

Cross-multiply to get $15(EF) = 18(5)$.

Divide both sides by 15 to get $EF = 6$.

The Pythagorean Theorem—Upper Level Only

For all right triangles, $a^2 + b^2 = c^2$, where a, b, and c are the lengths of the triangle's sides.

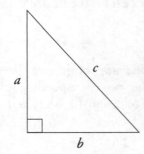

Always remember that c represents the *hypotenuse*, the longest side of the triangle, which is always opposite the right angle.

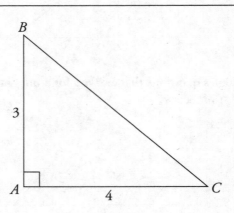

1.   What is the length of side BC?

Just put the values you are given into the formula and do the math, remembering that line BC is the hypotenuse:

$a^2 + b^2 = c^2$
$3^2 + 4^2 = c^2$
$9 + 16 = c^2$
$25 = c^2$
$5 = c$

So, BC is 5.

Practice Drill 25—Triangles (Lower, Middle, & Upper Levels)

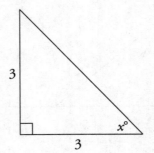

1.   What is the value of x ?

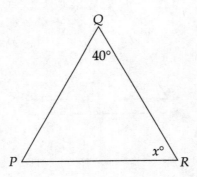

2.   Triangle PQR is an isosceles triangle. $PQ = QR$. What is the value of x ?

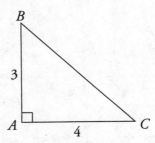

3.   What is the area of right triangle ABC ?

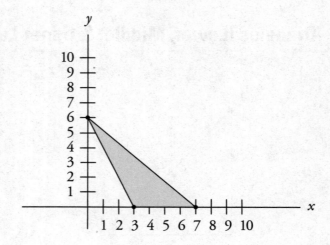

4. What is the area of the shaded region?

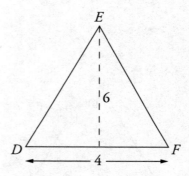

5. What is the area of triangle *DEF*?

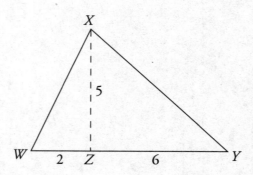

6. What is the area of triangle *WXZ*? Triangle *ZXY*? Triangle *WXY*?

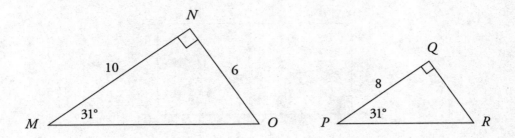

7. What is the length of line *QR*?

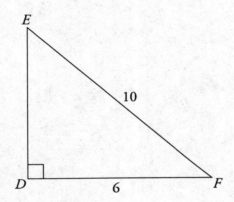

8. What is the length of side *DE*?

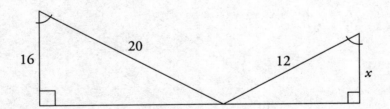

9. What is the value of *x*?

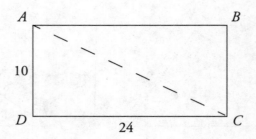

10. What is the length of the diagonal of rectangle *ABCD* ?

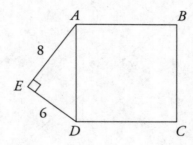

11. What is the perimeter of square *ABCD* ?

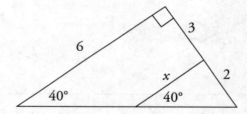

12. What is the value of *x* ?

When You Are Done
Check your answers
in Chapter 4, page 111.

Circles—Middle & Upper Levels

You are probably already familiar with the parts of a circle, but let's review them anyway.

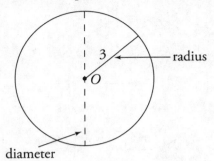

Diameter
$d = 2r$
Circumference
$C = \pi d$
Area
$A = \pi r^2$

Any line drawn from the origin (the center of the circle) to its edge is called a **radius** (*r*).

Any line that goes from one side of the circle to the other side and passes through the center of the circle is called the **diameter** (*d*). The diameter is two times the length of the radius.

Area and Circumference

Circumference (which is written as *C*) is really just the perimeter of a circle. To find the circumference of a circle, use the formula $2\pi r$ or πd. We can find the circumference of the circle above by taking its radius, 3, and multiplying it by 2π.

$C = 2\pi r$
$C = 2\pi 3$
$C = 6\pi$

The area of a circle is found by using the formula πr^2.

$A = \pi r^2$
$A = \pi 3^2$
$A = 9\pi$

You can find a circle's radius from its circumference by getting rid of π and dividing the number by 2. Or you can find the radius from a circle's area by getting rid of π and taking the square root of the number.

So if a circle has an area of 81π, its radius is 9. If a circle has a circumference of 16π, its radius is 8.

What's Up with π?

The Greek letter π is spelled "pi" and pronounced "pie." It is a symbol used with circles. Written as a number, π is a nonrepeating, nonending decimal (3.1415927…). We use π to determine the true length of circles. However, on the ISEE, we simply leave π as the Greek letter. So when figuring out area or circumference, make sure that you include π in your equation at the beginning and include it in every step of your work as you solve. Remember, π represents a number and it must always be included in either the area or circumference formula.

Practice Drill 26—Circles (Middle & Upper Levels)

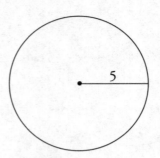

1. What is the circumference of the above circle? What is the area?

2. What is the area of a circle with radius 4 ?

3. What is the area of a circle with diameter 8 ?

4. What is the radius of a circle with area 9π ?

5. What is the diameter of a circle with area 9π ?

6. What is the circumference of a circle with area 25π ?

When You Are Done
Check your answers in Chapter 4, page 112.

3-D Shapes—Upper Level Only

While these question types tend to be few and far between, it is important you are prepared for them, just in case they do come up.

Boxes

A three-dimensional box has three important lines: length, width, and height.

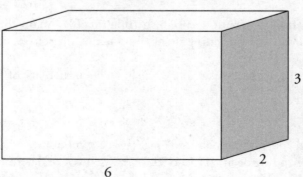

This rectangular box has a length of 6, a width of 2, and a height of 3.

The volume formula of a rectangular box is $V = lwh$.

$V = lwh$
$V = 6(2)(3)$
$V = 36$

Cubes

Cubes are just like rectangular boxes, except that all the sides are equal.

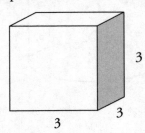

The volume formula for the cube is still just $V = lwh$, but since the length, width, and height are all equal it can also be written as $V = s^3$, where s = side.

$V = s^3$
$V = 3^3$
$V = 27$

Cylinders

Cylinders are like circles with height added. For a cylinder with a radius of r and a height of h, the volume formula is $V = \pi r^2 h$.

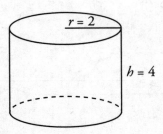

$V = \pi r^2 h$
$V = \pi 2^2 4$
$V = \pi 4(4)$
$V = 16\pi$

Practice Drill 27—3-D Shapes (Upper Level Only)

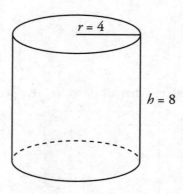

1.   What is the volume of this cylinder?

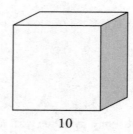

2.   What is the volume of this cube?

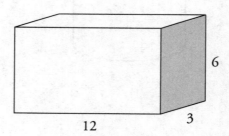

3.   What is the volume of this rectangular box?

6

4. A cube with a side length of 6 inches has 54 cubic inches of liquid poured into it. How many more cubic inches of liquid must be poured into the cube for it to be completely filled?

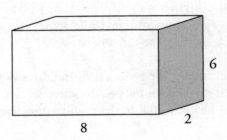

6

8   2

5. The rectangular box pictured is filled by identical cubes with side lengths of 2. How many cubes does it take to fill the rectangular box?

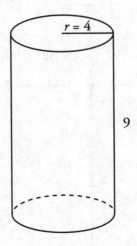

r = 4

9

6. The cylinder pictured is $\frac{1}{3}$ full of grain. What is the volume of the grain in the cylinder?

When You Are Done
Check your answers
in Chapter 4, page 112.

COORDINATE GEOMETRY—LOWER, MIDDLE, & UPPER LEVELS

The *xy*-Coordinate Plane

Coordinate geometry tests the same material as plane geometry, just on an *xy*-coordinate plane. Think of the *xy*-coordinate plane as a map of sorts: the *x*-axis runs left to right, similar to how east and west work on a map, and the *y*-axis runs up and down, or north and south. Both axes work like number lines in positive and negative directions, stretching infinitely in both directions. Ordered pairs (*x*, *y*) indicate where on the map to plot points, the first number always referring to the *x*-axis and the second always referring to the *y*-axis. The *x*- and *y*-axes cross one another at the *origin*, point (0, 0), and all other points are in reference to the origin. Everything to the right of the origin has a positive *x*-value while everything to the left has a negative *x*-value. Points above the *x*-axis have a positive *y*-value, while points below the *x*-axis have a negative *y*-value. Think of this concept as the equator splitting the earth in two.

Look at the following figure, for example. The point (4, 5) indicates to travel from the origin four in the positive direction on the *x*-axis, and then five in the positive direction on the *y*-axis. Similarly, point (–4, 5) travels in the negative direction on the *x*-axis, but in the positive direction on the *y*-axis.

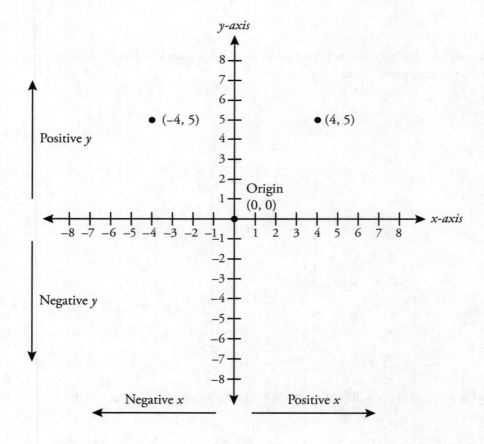

Try some on your own! Plot the following points: (1, 7), (–1, 7), (1, –7)

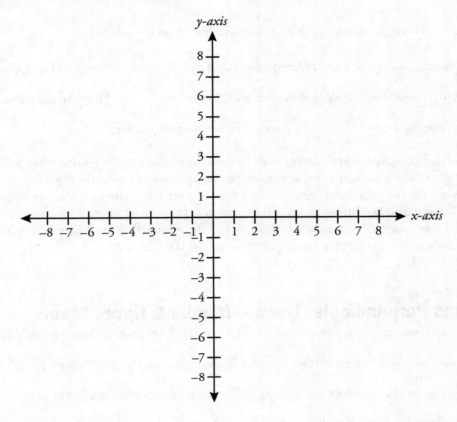

What kind of shape do these points create if you connect them? If you answered triangle, you are correct. Connecting points to create shapes can very easily turn a coordinate geometry question into a plane geometry question.

Formula of a Line

Coordinate planes are also useful for plotting lines, shapes, and curves. For these tests, it is especially useful to understand how the formula of a line works. The most common form of the line formula is called *slope-intercept form* because it shows the *slope* and the *y-intercept*:

$$y = mx + b$$

The *x* and *y* in the formula represent the two parts of an ordered pair. *m* represents the *slope* and shows how steep or shallow the line's incline or decline is. A positive slope means that the line will rise from left to right and a negative slope will descend from left to right. To find *m*, you will need two points along the line to find the rise over run. Any two points define a line by connecting them together, so it does not matter which you use. The "rise" refers to the change in the *y*-axis, and the "run" to the change in the *x*-axis. Use the following formula to calculate the slope and be sure to remain consistent as to which point you call the first point and which you call the second so the order matches in the numerator and denominator.

$$m = \frac{\left(y_2 - y_1\right)}{\left(x_2 - x_1\right)}$$

Let's try an example:

Points (2, 6) and (–1, 0) lie on a certain line. What is its slope?

Use the slope formula using the (x, y) ordered pairs. Let's call (2, 6) the first point, (x_1, y_1), and (–1, 0) the second, or (x_2, y_2). Therefore, the slope equation will read $m = \dfrac{(0-6)}{(-1-2)}$. Simplify the numerator and the denominator to find that $m = \dfrac{-6}{-3} = 2$. This slope will be an upward slope.

The other important component to slope intercept form is the *y-intercept*, the y-value when x is zero. You can find this point if you know the slope and any point. In the previous example, the slope is 2, and you already know two points. The formula should read $y = 2x + b$, so to solve for b, choose a point to plug in for x and y. Try using (2, 6), for example. The equation will become $6 = 2(2) + b$. Multiply 2 by 2 to find that $6 = 4 + b$. Then, subtract 4 from both sides to isolate b. Since $b = 2$, the point (0, 2) must also be a point on the same line. The final equation to the line containing all these points is $y = 2x + 2$.

Parallel and Perpendicular Lines—Middle & Upper Levels

Lines *parallel* to each other will have the same slope and different y-intercepts, meaning that they will travel in the same direction and never intersect; thus the two equations are said to have "no solutions." Lines that are *perpendicular* to one another intersect at a 90° angle. Therefore, their slopes will be the negative reciprocals of one another. For example, if the slope of one of the lines is 2, the slope of the line perpendicular would be $-\dfrac{1}{2}$. If the slope were $\dfrac{5}{8}$, the slope of the line perpendicular would be $-\dfrac{8}{5}$. Sometimes two equations will actually be equations for the same line, in which case they would have "infinitely many solutions." For example, $y = 2x + 3$ and $4x - 2y = -6$ are both equations for the same line. The second equation can be rearranged into $2y = 4x + 6$ and then reduced to $y = 2x + 3$ if you divide both sides by 2.

Does each of the following equations describe a line that is parallel to, perpendicular to, or the same as the line $y = 3x + 2$?

i. $y = -\dfrac{1}{3}x + 2$

_____

ii. $x + 3y = 6$

_____

iii. $y = 3x + 3$

_____

iv. $3x - y = 3$

_____

v. $9x - 3y = -6$

_____

The original equation is in slope-intercept form, so you can easily tell that it has a slope of 3. Parallel lines will also have a slope of 3, but a different y-intercept. Perpendicular lines will have a slope of $-\frac{1}{3}$. Lines that are the same will have a slope of 3 and a y-intercept of 2. The first equation is perpendicular since it has a slope of $-\frac{1}{3}$. The second equation is in standard form, but rearranges into $y = -\frac{1}{3}x + 2$, so it is perpendicular. When an equation is in standard form ($ax + by = c$), the slope will always be $-\frac{a}{b}$. The third equation is parallel since the slope is 3, but the y-intercept is different. The fourth equation is parallel since it has a slope of 3 $\left(-\frac{a}{b} = \frac{-3}{-1} = 3\right)$ and a y-intercept of –3. The fifth equation is the same line. If you divide both sides by 3, you get $3x - y = -2$, which rearranges into $y = 3x + 2$.

Practice Drill 28—Coordinate Geometry (Middle & Upper Levels)

1. What is the slope of a line perpendicular to $y = -\frac{1}{4}x + 12$?

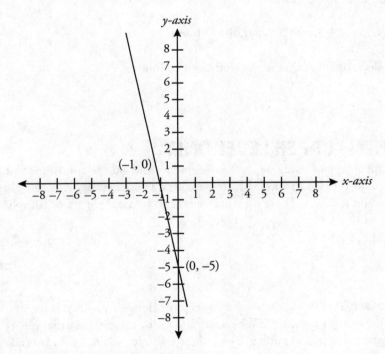

2. What is the equation of the line shown above?

3. What could be the fourth coordinate of a parallelogram with the points (3, –4), (3, 8), and (–4, –4)?

4. What is the slope of the line containing points (–2, 12) and (3, 5)?

5.

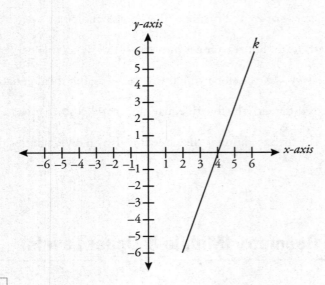

When You Are Done
Check your answers
in Chapter 4, page 113.

Which value would be greater?

a) the slope of a line that is parallel to line *k*

b) the slope of a line that is perpendicular to line *k*

TRIGONOMETRY—UPPER LEVEL ONLY

Trigonometry is a helpful way of using angle measurements and side relationships to find missing information about triangles of all types. On the ISEE, test-makers will generally stick to right triangles, either isolated or in real-world applications. These measurements can be used for more complicated shapes, though these will not appear on this test.

SOHCAHTOA

SOHCAH… what? SOHCAHTOA is a helpful mnemonic device to help you remember the basic relationships of trigonometry. S stands for *sine*, C for *cosine*, and T for *tangent* for an angle, θ. Each of these represents ratios between the sides and hypotenuse of a right triangle. O, A, and H stand for *opposite, adjacent,* and *hypotenuse* sides of the triangle. The hypotenuse is always the longest side of a right triangle, opposite the right angle. The opposite and adjacent sides are the legs of a right triangle. The mnemonic spells out the following expressions:

$$\sin\theta = \frac{opposite}{hypotenuse} \qquad \cos\theta = \frac{adjacent}{hypotenuse} \qquad \tan\theta = \frac{opposite}{adjacent}$$

SOH stands for $\sin\theta = \dfrac{opposite}{hypotenuse}$, CAH stands for $\cos\theta = \dfrac{adjacent}{hypotenuse}$, and TOA stands for $\tan\theta = \dfrac{opposite}{adjacent}$.

Which side is adjacent and which is opposite? It all depends on which angle you are relating the sides to. Take a look at the following triangle:

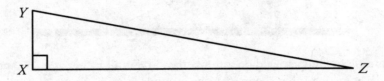

In the figure above, YZ is the hypotenuse because it is opposite the right angle. Angle Z is opposite side XY and adjacent to side XZ (since it's touching the angle). Likewise, Angle Y is opposite side XZ and adjacent to XY.

Let's try an example.

What is the length of side BC?

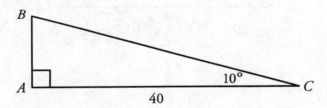

Identify BC. In this case, it is the hypotenuse of the triangle. The other pieces of information will determine which measurement to use of SOHCAHTOA. Since side AC and angle C are given, it seems most convenient to use cosine, as AC is adjacent to angle C. Cosine is the CAH of SOHCAHTOA, which stands for Cosine = Adjacent/Hypotenuse. Therefore, $\cos 10° = \dfrac{40}{BC}$. Multiply both sides of the equation by BC to find that $BC \cos 10° = 40$. Finally, divide both sides by $\cos 10°$ to find that $BC = \dfrac{40}{\cos 10°}$.

Practice Drill 29—Trigonometry (Upper Level Only)

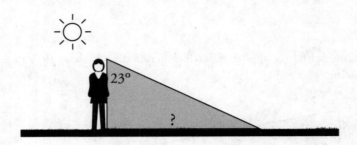

1. Samin is standing in an open field on a sunny day. The sun hits her at a 23° angle. If Samin is 1.5 meters tall, how long is her shadow on the ground?

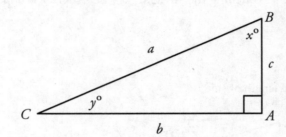

2. What is cos x?

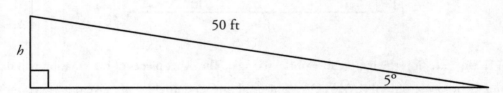

3. A 50-foot ramp contains a 5° incline. How high is h shown above?

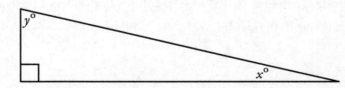

4. $\cos x° = \dfrac{24}{25}$. What is sin $y°$?

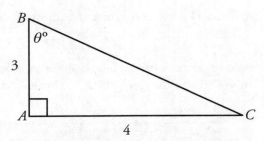

5.   Triangle *ABC* contains sides with lengths 3 and 4 as shown above. What is sin θ?

NON-GEOMETRIC MEASUREMENT

Proportions—Lower, Middle, & Upper Levels

Proportions show relationships between two sets of information. For example, if you wanted to make cookies and you had a recipe for a dozen cookies but wanted to make two dozen cookies, you would have to double all of the ingredients. That's a proportion. Here's how we'd look at it in equation form.

$$\overset{\times 2}{\overbrace{\frac{4 \text{ cups of flour}}{1 \text{ dozen cookies}} = \frac{8 \text{ cups of flour}}{2 \text{ dozen cookies}}}}_{\times 2}$$

Whenever a question gives you one set of data and part of another set, it will ask you for the missing part of the second set of data. To find the missing information, set up the information in fractions like the one above. Be careful to put the same information in the same place. In our example, we have flour on top and cookies on the bottom. Make sure both fractions have the flour over the cookies. Once we have our fractions set up, we can see what the relationship is between the two elements (in this case, flour and cookies). Whatever that relationship is, it's the same as the relationship between the other two things.

Ratios—Lower, Middle, & Upper Levels

A ratio is like a recipe. It tells you how much of each ingredient goes into a mixture.

For example:

To make punch, mix two parts grape juice with three parts orange juice.

This ratio tells you that for every two units of grape juice, you will need to add three units of orange juice. It doesn't matter what the units are; if you were working with ounces, you would mix two ounces of grape juice with three ounces of orange juice to get five ounces of punch. If you were working with gallons, you would mix two gallons of grape juice with three gallons of orange juice. How much punch would you have? Five gallons.

To work through a ratio question, first you need to organize the information you are given. Do this using the Ratio Box.

In a club with 35 members, the ratio of people wearing purple shirts to people wearing yellow shirts is 3:2. To complete your Ratio Box, fill in the ratio at the top and the "real value" at the bottom.

	PURPLE	YELLOW	TOTAL
Ratio	3	2	5
Multiplier			
Real Value			35

Then look for a "magic number" that you can multiply by the ratio total to get to the real value total. In this case, the magic number is 7. That's all there is to it!

	PURPLE	YELLOW	TOTAL
Ratio	3 +	2 =	5
Multiplier	7	7	7
Real Value	21	14	35

Averages

There are three parts to every average problem: total, number, and average. You may recall from the Math Vocabulary chart in Chapter 3 that the average is sometimes referred to as the mean. Most ISEE problems will give you two of the three pieces and ask you to find the third. To help organize the information you are given, use $T = AN$.

Total = **A**verage × **N**umber of Things

For example, if your friend went bowling and bowled three games, scoring 71, 90, and 100, here's how you would compute her average score using $T = AN$.

To find the total, you would simply add up the three scores, in this case 261.

The math becomes simple. $261 = A \times 3$. Divide both sides by 3 to get that your friend bowled an average of 87.

Get used to working with $T = AN$ by using it to solve the following problems.

Practice Drill 30— Proportions, Ratios, & Averages (Lower, Middle, & Upper Levels)

1. The average of 3 numbers is 18. What is two times the sum of the 3 numbers?

2. A group of friends decided to compare comic book collections. Nathan has 11 comic books, Serena has 16, Jose has 14, and Amira has 19. What is the average number of comic books per person?

3. Sofia scores 84, 85, and 88 on her first three exams. What must she score on her fourth exam to raise her average to an 89 ?

4. If a class of 6 students has an average grade of 72 before a seventh student joins the class, what must the seventh student's grade be to raise the class average to 76 ?

5. At Anna's Ice Cream Shop, ice cream cones are sold as single, double, or triple scoops. The ratio of single to double to triple scoops sold on a particular Saturday was 3:5:1. If the total number of cones sold was 45, how many double scoops were sold?

More Practice: Middle & Upper Levels

6. Rumi scored an average of 24 points over his first 5 basketball games. How many points must he score in his 6th game to average 25 points over all 6 games?

7. Dwan measured a total of 245 inches of rainfall in his hometown over one week. During the same week the previous year, his hometown had a total of 196 inches. How many more inches was the average daily amount of rainfall for the week this year than the week last year?

8. Brady's favorite recipe for bolognese sauce calls for 2 pounds of meat, 1 carrot, 1 onion, 1 stalk of celery, 1 cup of tomatoes, and 2 cups of chicken stock to feed 8 people. If Brady decides to serve bolognese at a dinner party for 24 people, how many cups of chicken stock will he need?

9. Emerson wants to find the mean number of pages in the books he has read this month. The books were 200, 220, and 260 pages long. He read the 200-page book twice, so it will be counted twice in the mean. If he reads one more book, what is the fewest number of pages it can have to make the mean no less than 230?

When You Are Done
Check your answers in Chapter 4, pages 114–116.

DATA ANALYSIS & PROBABILITY—LOWER, MIDDLE, & UPPER LEVELS

Probability describes how likely it is that something is going to happen. You might not have quantified it before, but it's something you do every day, whether you're flipping a coin or wondering if you'll need to take an umbrella. To make probability less vague, many people express the odds of something happening in terms of percents. For instance, a standard coin has two equal results: heads (50%) and tails (50%). If the weather report says that there's a 90% chance of rain, you probably want to take that umbrella. You might also see probability expressed as a number between 0 and 1—the chance of seeing a flying elephant being 0 and the chance of the sun rising tomorrow being 1.

Don't be distracted by the objects in the question or the method with which they're being assessed. Whether it's 20% or 0.2, whether dealing with marbles, cards, coins, food, or anything else, a probability question essentially boils down to finding a specific number of possibilities out of the total number of possibilities.

Independent Probability

The basic formula for probability is

$$probability = \frac{the\ number\ of\ what\ you\ want}{the\ total\ number}$$

For example, if a bag with 11 total gumballs has 6 red gumballs, the probability of randomly selecting a red gumball is $\frac{6}{11}$, or 0.54, or 54%.

A gumball is randomly selected from a jar that contains 5 blue gumballs, 15 red gumballs, and 30 yellow gumballs. What is the probability that the randomly selected gumball is red?

The question asks for probability, so use the formula $probability = \dfrac{the\ number\ of\ what\ you\ want}{the\ total\ number}$.

The question asks for the probability that a randomly selected gumball is red, so *the number you want* is the number of red gumballs, which is 15, and *the total number* is the number of gumballs, which is $5 + 15 + 30 = 50$. Therefore, the probability is $\dfrac{15}{50}$. Both the numerator and denominator are multiples of 5, so divide both by 5 to reduce to $\dfrac{3}{10}$.

"Not" Probability—Middle & Upper Levels

So-called "not" probability is just the probability that something will not happen. To find this, determine the probability that the event *will* happen and subtract that number from 1. It's often easier than calculating the probability of all other possible outcomes and adding all of those together to get the answer. Remember, the bag with 11 total gumballs has 6 red gumballs. The probability of randomly selecting a red gumball is $\dfrac{6}{11}$, so the probability of not selecting a red gumball is $1 - \dfrac{6}{11} = \dfrac{5}{11}$.

"Or" Probability—Middle & Upper Levels

Sometimes a question will ask for the probability of one event *or* another event taking place. To find this, add the individual probabilities. For example, take that same bag with 11 gumballs, 6 of which are red. Of the remaining 5, 3 are blue gumballs and 2 are yellow gumballs. The probability of getting a red gumball or a blue gumball is $\dfrac{6}{11} + \dfrac{3}{11} = \dfrac{9}{11}$. The probability of getting a blue gumball or a yellow gumball is $\dfrac{3}{11} + \dfrac{2}{11} = \dfrac{5}{11}$. Notice that this is the same as the probability of not getting a red gumball. The probability of getting a red gumball, a blue gumball, or a yellow gumball is $\dfrac{6}{11} + \dfrac{3}{11} + \dfrac{2}{11} = \dfrac{11}{11} = 1$. The probability is 1, because red, blue, and yellow are the only colors of gumballs in the bag, so one of these colors must be drawn.

COLORS OF THE RAINBOW SURVEY	
Color	Number of Students
Red	13
Orange	15
Yellow	17
Green	31
Blue	24
Indigo	6
Violet	29

The students at a school were surveyed and asked for their favorite color of the rainbow. What is the probability that a randomly selected student chose either red or yellow as her favorite color?

The question asks for the probability that a randomly selected student chooses either red or yellow, so add the probability that the student selects red to the probability that the student selects yellow. To find each of these, determine the total number of students in the poll. The total number is $13 + 15 + 17 + 31 + 24 + 6 + 29 = 135$. There are 13 students who select red, so the probability of selecting red is $\frac{13}{135}$. There are 17 students who select yellow, so the probability of selecting yellow is $\frac{17}{135}$. Therefore, the probability of selecting red or yellow is $\frac{13}{135} + \frac{17}{135} = \frac{30}{135} = \frac{10}{45} = \frac{2}{9}$.

"And" Probability—Middle & Upper Levels

On ISEE probability questions, it is important to decide if there are any events that happen independently from each other, or if one event affects another. For instance, if a question asks about flipping a coin four times, does one coin flip influence the next? The answer is no. A coin flip will come out to either heads or tails every time, so the probability of getting tails on each trial is $\frac{1}{2}$. However, in some cases, one event does affect the next, which is when you'll want to know about "and" probability. This concept still uses basic probability. Take the probability that each individual event happens and multiply them.

Once again, consider the bag with 11 gumballs, including 6 red gumballs. If two gumballs are selected at random, what is the probability that they will both be red? The probability that the first gumball will be red is $\frac{6}{11}$. However, the probability that the second gumball will be red is different. Once one red gumball is removed, only 5 red gumballs and 10 total gumballs remain, so the probability is $\frac{5}{10}$. To find the probability that both are red, multiply the two individual probabilities to get $\frac{6}{11} \times \frac{5}{10} = \frac{6}{11} \times \frac{1}{2} = \frac{3}{11} \times \frac{1}{1} = \frac{3}{11}$.

Adrian has 3 T-shirts, 4 long-sleeved shirts, and 7 tank tops. If he selects two shirts at random, what is the probability that both shirts will be tank tops?

To find the probability that both shirts will be tank tops, find the probability that each individual shirt will be a tank top. There are 7 tank tops and $3 + 4 + 7 = 14$ total shirts, so the probability that the first shirt will be a tank top is $\frac{7}{14}$. Once one tank top is removed, there are 6 tank tops and 13 total shirts remaining, so the probability that the second shirt will be a tank top is $\frac{6}{13}$. Therefore, the probability that both will be tank tops is $\frac{7}{14} \times \frac{6}{13} = \frac{1}{2} \times \frac{6}{13} = \frac{1}{1} \times \frac{3}{13} = \frac{3}{13}$.

Practice Drill 31—Probability

Lower, Middle, & Upper Levels

1. A basket of marbles contains 15 blue marbles. If the probability of not selecting a blue marble is $\frac{4}{9}$, how many marbles are in the basket?

2. A bowl of fruit contains 4 apples, 6 kiwis, and 5 cherimoyas. If one fruit is selected from the bowl at random, what is the probability that it will be an apple or a kiwi?

Middle & Upper Levels

3. A box of cookies has 2 chocolate chip, 4 pecan, 7 oatmeal raisin, and 3 peanut butter cookies. If two cookies are selected at random, what is the probability that both cookies will be pecan?

4. A jar of cookies contains 5 chocolate chip, 4 oatmeal raisin, 4 snicker doodles, and 2 red velvet. Sandy chooses two cookies from the jar without replacement. What is the probability that she will choose a chocolate chip cookie first and a red velvet cookie second?

When You Are Done
Check your answers in Chapter 4, pages 116–117.

CHARTS AND GRAPHS—ALL LEVELS

Charts

Chart questions usually do not involve much computation, but you must be careful. Follow these three steps and you'll be well on the way to mastering any chart question.

1. Read any text that accompanies the chart. It is important to know what the chart is showing and what scale the numbers are on.
2. Read the question.
3. Refer to the chart and find the specific information you need.

If there is more than one question about a single chart, the later questions will tend to be more difficult than the earlier ones. Be careful!

Here is a sample chart.

Don't Be in Too Big a Hurry
When working with charts and graphs, make sure you take a moment to look at the chart or graph, figure out what it tells you, and then go to the questions.

Club Membership by State, 2021 and 2023

State	2021	2023
California	300	500
Florida	225	250
Illinois	200	180
Massachusetts	150	300
Michigan	150	200
New Jersey	200	250
New York	400	600
Texas	50	100

There are many different questions that you can answer based on the information in this chart. For instance:

What is the difference between the number of members who came from New York in 2021 and the number of members who came from Illinois in 2023 ?

This question asks you to look up two simple pieces of information and then do a tiny bit of math.

First, the number of members who came from New York in 2021 was 400.

Second, the number of members who came from Illinois in 2023 was 180.

Finally, look back at the question. It asks you to find the difference between these numbers. 400 − 180 = 220. Done.

The increase in the number of members from New Jersey from 2021 to 2023 was what percent of the total number of members in New Jersey in 2021 ?

Do you remember how to translate percentage questions? If not, go back to the percentage discussion earlier in the chapter.

In 2021, there were 200 club members from New Jersey. In 2023, there were 250 members from New Jersey. That represents an increase of 50 members. To determine what percent that is of the total amount in 2021, you need to ask yourself, "50 (the increase) is what percent of 200 (the number of members in 2021)?"

Translated, this becomes:

$$50 = \frac{g}{100} \times 200$$

With a little bit of simple manipulation, this equation becomes:

$$50 = 2g$$

and

$$25 = g$$

So from 2021 to 2023, there was a 25% increase in the number of members from New Jersey. Good work!

> Which state had as many club members in 2023 as a combination of Illinois, Massachusetts, and Michigan had in 2021 ?

First, take a second to look up the number of members who came from Illinois, Massachusetts, and Michigan in 2021 and add them together.

$$200 + 150 + 150 = 500$$

Which state had 500 members in 2023? California. That's all there is to it!

Graphs

Some questions will ask you to interpret a graph. You should be familiar with both pie and bar graphs. These graphs are generally drawn to scale (meaning that the graphs give an accurate visual impression of the information), so you can always guess based on the figure if you need to.

The way to approach a graph question is exactly the same as the way to approach a chart question. Follow the same three steps.

1. Read any text that accompanies the graph. It is important to know what the graph is showing and what scale the numbers are on.
2. Read the question.
3. Refer back to the graph and find the specific information you need.

This is how it works.

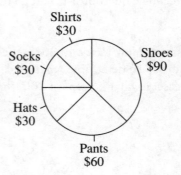

The graph in Figure 1 shows Emily's clothing expenditures for the month of October. On which type of clothing did she spend the most money?

This one is easy. You can look at the pieces of the pie and identify the largest, or you can look at the amounts shown in the graph and choose the largest one. Either way, the answer is shoes because Emily spent more money on shoes than on any other clothing items in October.

Emily spent half of her clothing money on which two items?

Again, you can find the answer to this question two different ways. You can look for which two items together make up half the chart, or you can add up the total amount of money Emily spent ($240) and then figure out which two items made up half (or $120) of that amount. Either way is just fine, and either way, the right answer is shoes and shirts.

Practice Drill 32—Charts and Graphs

Questions 1–3 refer to the following summary of energy costs by district.

District	2019	2023
A	400	600
B	500	700
C	200	350
D	100	150
E	600	800

(All numbers are in thousands of dollars.)

1. In 2023, which district spent twice as much on energy as District A spent in 2019?

2. Which district spent the most on electricity in 2019 and 2023 combined?

3. The total increase in energy expenditure in these districts, from 2019 to 2023, is how many dollars?

Questions 4 and 5 refer to the bar graph, which shows the number of games owned by five students.

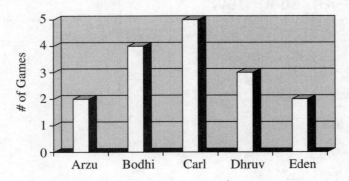

4. Carl owns as many games as which two other students combined?

5. Which one student owns one-fourth of the games accounted for in the bar graph?

Middle & Upper Levels

Questions 6–8 refer to Matt's weekly time card, shown below.

Day	In	Out	Hours Worked
Monday	2:00 P.M.	5:30 P.M.	3.5
Tuesday			
Wednesday	2:00 P.M.	6:00 P.M.	4
Thursday	2:00 P.M.	5:30 P.M.	3.5
Friday	2:00 P.M.	5:00 P.M.	3
Saturday			
Sunday			

6. If Matt's hourly salary is $16, what were his earnings for the week?

7. What is the average number of hours Matt worked on the days he worked during this particular week?

8. The hours that Matt worked on Monday accounted for what percent of the total number of hours he worked during this week?

When You Are Done
Check your answers in Chapter 4,
pages 117–118.
You can make a chart to
see how you've
been doing!

Review Drill 2—Mixed Review

1. If one-third of *b* is 15, then what is *b* ?

2. If $7x - 7 = 49$, then what is *x* ?

3. If $4(y - 5) = 20$, then what is *y* ?

4. $8x + 1 < 65$. Solve for *x*.

5. 16 is what percent of 10 ?

6. What percent of 32 is 24 ?

7. What is the area of a triangle with base 7 and height 6 ?

8. What is the diameter of a circle with an area of 49π ?

9. What is the radius of a circle with a circumference of 12π ?

10. What is the area of a circle with a diameter of 10 ?

When You Are Done
Check your answers in
Chapter 4, page 118.

Chapter 4
Fundamental
Math Skills Drills:
Answers and
Explanations

NUMBERS & OPERATIONS

Practice Drill 1—Math Vocabulary

1.	6	0, 1, 2, 3, 4, 5
2.	1, 3, 5	Many sets of integers would answer this question correctly.
3.	3	3, 5, and 7
4.	8	The tens digit is two places to the left of the decimal.
5.	That number	The smallest positive integer is 1, and any number times 1 is equal to itself.
6.	90	$5 \times 6 \times 3 = 90$
7.	30	$3 + 11 + 16 = 30$
8.	60	$90 - 30 = 60$
9.	$-6, -4, -2$	2, 4, and 6 are consecutive positive even integers and the question wants negative. Other sets of consecutive negative even integers would also answer the question correctly.
10.	Yes	11 is divisible only by 1 and itself.
11.	22	$5 + 6 + 4 + 7 = 22$
12.	6	13 goes into 58, 4 times. $4 \times 13 = 52$ and $58 - 52 = 6$.
13.	1, 5, 11, 55	1, 5, 11, and 55 will all divide into 55 evenly.
14.	12	$5 + 8 + 9 = 22$ and $1 + 2 + 0 + 7 = 10$. $22 - 10 = 12$
15.	No	The remainder of $19 \div 5$ is 4. And 21 is not divisible by 4.
16.	2, 2, 3, 13	Draw a factor tree.
17.	16	$3 + 13 = 16$
18.	9	$12 \times 3 = 36$ and $9 \times 4 = 36$.
19.	1, 2, 3, 4, 6, 8, 9, 12, 18, 24, 36, 72	Remember that factors are the numbers that can be multiplied together to get 72.
20.	There are 9 even factors and 3 odd factors.	The even factors are 2, 4, 6, 8, 12, 18, 24, 36, and 72. The odd factors are 1, 3, and 9.
21.	10	Add the values. $6 + 8 + 11 + 15 = 40$. Then divide by the number of values. $40 \div 4 = 10$.

Practice Drill 2—Adding and Subtracting Negative Numbers

1. −8
2. −14
3. −4
4. 27
5. 21
6. 4
7. −22
8. −29
9. −6
10. 90
11. 0
12. 29
13. 24
14. −30
15. −14

Practice Drill 3—Multiplying and Dividing Negative Numbers

1. −4
2. −36
3. 65
4. 11
5. 63
6. −13
7. 84
8. −5
9. 9
10. −8
11. −75
12. 72
13. −4
14. 34
15. −11

Practice Drill 4—Order of Operations

1. 9 Do addition and subtraction from left to right. $10 - 3 = 7$, then $7 + 2 = 9$.

2. 16 Parentheses first! $7 - 3 = 4$, then do addition and subtraction from left to right. $15 + 4 = 19$, then $19 - 3 = 16$.

3. 7 Multiplication and division happen before addition and subtraction. $3 \times 2 = 6$ and $3 \div 3 = 1$, then $6 + 1 = 7$.

4. 50 Parentheses, then exponents, then multiplication and division (from left to right). $4 + 6 = 10$, then 10 squared is 100, then $2 \times 100 = 200$, and $200 \div 4 = 50$.

5. 6 Work inside the parentheses first, doing the multiplication before the addition. $5 \times 12 = 60$, then $10 + 60 = 70$. $420 \div 70 = 6$.

6. 30 Multiplication and division first, from left to right, then addition. $20 \times 5 = 100$, then $100 \div 10 = 10$, then $10 + 20 = 30$.

7. 24 Parentheses first, then multiplication and division (from left to right). $7 - 6 = 1$, then $5 \times 10 = 50$, then $50 \times 1 = 50$, then $50 \div 2 = 25$. Next do the addition and subtraction (from left to right). $3 + 25 = 28$, and $28 - 4 = 24$.

8. 60 Parentheses first, then multiplication and division (from left to right). $8 + 1 = 9$, $3 + 1 = 4$, and $8 - 2 = 6$. Then $10 \times 9 = 90$, $90 \times 4 = 360$, and $360 \div 6 = 60$.

9. 101 Parentheses, then exponents, then division, then addition and subtraction (from left to right). $5 \times 2 = 10$, 10 squared $= 100$. $33 \div 3 = 11$. Then $12 + 100 = 112$, and $112 - 11 = 101$.

10. −200 Parentheses first, then exponents, then multiplication and division (from left to right), then subtraction. $150 \div 3 = 50$. $2^3 = 8$, and $50 \times 8 = 400$. Then $200 - 400 = -200$.

Practice Drill 5—Factors and Multiples

1. 2, 4, 6, 8, 10
   4, 8, 12, 16, 20
   5, 10, 15, 20, 25
   11, 22, 33, 44, 55
2. Yes   3 goes into 15 evenly 5 times.
3. Yes   Use the divisibility rule for 3. The sum of the digits is 9, which is divisible by 3.
4. No   The sum of the digits is 14, which is not divisible by 3.
5. Yes   The only factors of 23 are 1 and 23.
6. Yes   The sum of the digits is 6, which is divisible by 3.
7. No   The sum of the digits is 6, which is not divisible by 9.
8. Yes   250 ends in a 0, which is an even number and is divisible by 2.
9. Yes   250 ends in a 0, which is divisible by 5.
10. Yes   250 ends in a 0, which is divisible by 10.
11. Yes $2 \times 5 = 10$
12. No   There is no integer that can be multiplied by 3 to equal 11.
13. No   2 is a factor of 8.
14. Yes $4 \times 6 = 24$
15. No   There is no integer that can be multiplied by 6 to equal 27.
16. Yes $3 \times 9 = 27$
17. 8   6, 12, 18, 24, 30, 36, 42, 48
18. 8   Even multiples of 3 are really just multiples of 6.
19. 8   Multiples of both 3 and 4 are also multiples of 12.
   12, 24, 36, 48, 60, 72, 84, 96
20. 48 $3 \times 16 = 48$

Practice Drill 6—Reducing Fractions

1. $\dfrac{3}{4}$

2. $\dfrac{1}{5}$

3. $\dfrac{2}{3}$

4. $\dfrac{3}{8}$

5. $\dfrac{3}{4}$

6. $\dfrac{2}{7}$

7. 1

8. $\dfrac{11}{9}$

9. If the number on top is larger than the number on the bottom, the fraction is greater than 1.

Practice Drill 7—Changing Improper Fractions to Mixed Numbers

1. 5

2. $1\frac{5}{7}$

3. $5\frac{1}{3}$

4. $2\frac{1}{2}$

5. $2\frac{2}{3}$

6. $6\frac{8}{9}$

7. $1\frac{1}{2}$

8. 2

9. $11\frac{6}{7}$

10. $10\frac{1}{2}$

Practice Drill 8—Changing Mixed Numbers to Improper Fractions

1. $\frac{45}{7}$ $\frac{7 \times 6 + 3}{7} = \frac{45}{7}$

2. $\frac{23}{9}$ $\frac{9 \times 2 + 5}{9} = \frac{23}{9}$

3. $\frac{71}{3}$ $\frac{3 \times 23 + 2}{3} = \frac{71}{3}$

4. $\frac{20}{3}$ $\frac{3 \times 6 + 2}{3} = \frac{20}{3}$

5. $\frac{59}{8}$ $\frac{8 \times 7 + 3}{8} = \frac{59}{8}$

6. $\frac{37}{5}$ $\frac{5 \times 7 + 2}{5} = \frac{37}{5}$

7. $\frac{161}{16}$ $\frac{16 \times 10 + 1}{16} = \frac{161}{16}$

8. $\frac{77}{13}$ $\frac{13 \times 5 + 12}{13} = \frac{77}{13}$

9. $\frac{41}{9}$ $\frac{9 \times 4 + 5}{9} = \frac{41}{9}$

10. $\frac{747}{22}$ $\frac{22 \times 33 + 21}{22} = \frac{747}{22}$

Practice Drill 9—Adding and Subtracting Fractions

1. $1\dfrac{1}{24}$ or $\dfrac{25}{24}$ Multiply using Bowtie to get $\dfrac{9}{24}+\dfrac{16}{24}=\dfrac{25}{24}=1\dfrac{1}{24}$.

2. $\dfrac{17}{24}$ Multiply using Bowtie to get $\dfrac{8}{24}+\dfrac{9}{24}=\dfrac{17}{24}$.

3. $\dfrac{6}{7}$ Did you use the Bowtie? You didn't need to because there was already a common denominator there!

4. $\dfrac{1}{12}$ Multiply using Bowtie to get $\dfrac{9}{12}-\dfrac{8}{12}=\dfrac{1}{12}$.

5. $2\dfrac{1}{36}$ or $\dfrac{73}{36}$ Multiply using Bowtie to get $\dfrac{28}{36}+\dfrac{45}{36}=\dfrac{73}{36}=2\dfrac{1}{36}$.

6. $-\dfrac{7}{20}$ Multiply using Bowtie to get $\dfrac{8}{20}-\dfrac{15}{20}=-\dfrac{7}{20}$.

7. $4\dfrac{1}{3}$ or $\dfrac{13}{3}$ Multiply using Bowtie to get $\dfrac{20}{24}+\dfrac{84}{24}=\dfrac{104}{24}=\dfrac{13}{3}=4\dfrac{1}{3}$.

8. $\dfrac{2}{9}$ Did you use the Bowtie? You didn't need to because there was already a common denominator there! Subtract to get $\dfrac{6}{27}=\dfrac{2}{9}$.

9. $\dfrac{49}{60}$ Multiply using Bowtie to get $\dfrac{9}{60}+\dfrac{40}{60}=\dfrac{49}{60}$.

10. x Multiply using Bowtie to get $\dfrac{6x}{18}+\dfrac{12x}{18}=\dfrac{18x}{18}=x$.

11. $\dfrac{2x}{5}$ Multiply using Bowtie to get $\dfrac{10x}{50}+\dfrac{10x}{50}=\dfrac{20x}{50}=\dfrac{2x}{5}$.

12. $\dfrac{5y}{12}$ Multiply using Bowtie to get $\dfrac{36y}{72}-\dfrac{6y}{72}=\dfrac{30y}{72}=\dfrac{5y}{12}$.

Practice Drill 10—Multiplying and Dividing Fractions

1. $\dfrac{1}{3}$ $\dfrac{2 \times 1}{3 \times 2} = \dfrac{2}{6} = \dfrac{1}{3}$

2. $1\dfrac{1}{4}$ or $\dfrac{5}{4}$ $\dfrac{5}{8} \times \dfrac{2}{1} = \dfrac{5 \times 2}{8 \times 1} = \dfrac{10}{8} = \dfrac{5}{4}$

3. $\dfrac{6}{25}$ $\dfrac{4 \times 3}{5 \times 10} = \dfrac{12}{50} = \dfrac{6}{25}$

4. 1 $\dfrac{24 \times 10}{15 \times 16} = \dfrac{240}{240} = 1$

5. $\dfrac{4}{5}$ $\dfrac{16}{25} \times \dfrac{5}{4} = \dfrac{16 \times 5}{25 \times 4} = \dfrac{80}{100} = \dfrac{4}{5}$

Practice Drill 11—Decimals

1. 18.7   Don't forget to line up the decimals. Then add.

2. 4.19   After lining up the decimals, remember to add a 0 at the end of 1.7. Then add the two numbers.

3. 4.962   Change 7 to 7.000, line up the decimals, and then subtract.

4. 10.625   Don't forget there are a total of 3 digits to the right of the decimals.

5. 0.018   There are a total of 4 digits to the right of the decimals, but you do not have to write the final 0 in 0.0180.

6. 6,000   Remember to move both decimals right 2 places: $3\overline{)18000}$ with quotient 6000 and don't put the decimals back after dividing!

7. 5   Remember to move both decimals right 2 places: $2\overline{)10}$ with quotient 5 and don't put the decimals back after dividing!

Practice Drill 12—Converting Fractions to Decimals and Back Again

Fraction	Decimal	Fraction	Decimal
$\dfrac{1}{2}$	0.5	$\dfrac{1}{5}$	0.2
$\dfrac{1}{3}$	$0.3\overline{3}$	$\dfrac{2}{5}$	0.4
$\dfrac{2}{3}$	$0.6\overline{6}$	$\dfrac{3}{5}$	0.6
$\dfrac{1}{4}$	0.25	$\dfrac{4}{5}$	0.8
$\dfrac{3}{4}$	0.75	$\dfrac{1}{8}$	0.125

Practice Drill 13—Percents

1. a) 30% $\dfrac{\text{butterscotches}}{\text{total}} = \dfrac{15}{50} = \dfrac{3}{10}$ $\dfrac{3}{10} \times 100 = \dfrac{300}{10} = 30\%$

    b) 40% $\dfrac{\text{caramels}}{\text{total}} = \dfrac{20}{50} = \dfrac{2}{5}$ $\dfrac{2}{5} \times 100 = \dfrac{200}{5} = 40\%$

    c) 10% $\dfrac{\text{peppermints}}{\text{total}} = \dfrac{5}{50} = \dfrac{1}{10}$ $\dfrac{1}{10} \times 100 = \dfrac{100}{10} = 10\%$

    d) 20% $\dfrac{\text{toffees}}{\text{total}} = \dfrac{10}{50} = \dfrac{1}{5}$ $\dfrac{1}{5} \times 100 = \dfrac{100}{5} = 20\%$

2. 18%   100% = 75% + 7% + percentage of questions answered incorrectly

3. a) 20% $\dfrac{\text{sneakers}}{\text{total}} = \dfrac{8}{40} = \dfrac{1}{5}$ $\dfrac{1}{5} \times 100 = \dfrac{100}{5} = 20\%$

    b) 30% $\dfrac{\text{sandals}}{\text{total}} = \dfrac{12}{40} = \dfrac{3}{10}$ $\dfrac{3}{10} \times 100 = \dfrac{300}{10} = 30\%$

    c) 40% $\dfrac{\text{boots}}{\text{total}} = \dfrac{16}{40} = \dfrac{2}{5}$ $\dfrac{2}{5} \times 100 = \dfrac{200}{5} = 40\%$

    d) 10%   sneakers + sandals + boots + slippers = 100%
                 20% + 30% + 40% + slippers = 100%
                 slippers = 10%

e) 4   sneakers + sandals + boots + slippers = 40
        8 + 12 + 16 + slippers = 40
        slippers = 4

4. 90% $\dfrac{\text{juice}}{\text{total}} = \dfrac{4+2+3}{4+2+3+1} = \dfrac{9}{10}$ $\dfrac{9}{10} \times 100 = \dfrac{900}{10} = 90\%$

5. a) 48% $\dfrac{\text{Stephanie} + \text{Kai} + \text{Janice}}{\text{total}} = \dfrac{\$8 + \$8 + \$8}{2(\$13) + 3(\$8)} = \dfrac{24}{50}$ $\dfrac{24}{50} \times 100 = \dfrac{2400}{50} = 48\%$

    b) 52%   100% = Stephanie + Kai + Janice + David + Jakob
              100 = 48 + David + Jakob
              David + Jakob = 52

Practice Drill 14—More Percents

Fraction	Decimal	Percent	Fraction	Decimal	Percent
$\dfrac{1}{2}$	0.5	50%	$\dfrac{1}{5}$	0.2	20%
$\dfrac{1}{3}$	$0.3\overline{3}$	$33\dfrac{1}{3}\%$	$\dfrac{2}{5}$	0.4	40%
$\dfrac{2}{3}$	$0.6\overline{6}$	$66\dfrac{2}{3}\%$	$\dfrac{3}{5}$	0.6	60%
$\dfrac{1}{4}$	0.25	25%	$\dfrac{4}{5}$	0.8	80%
$\dfrac{3}{4}$	0.75	75%	$\dfrac{1}{8}$	0.125	12.5%

1. 21 $25\% = \dfrac{1}{4}$

          $\dfrac{1}{4} \times 84 = \dfrac{84}{4} = 21$

2. 9 $33\dfrac{1}{3}\% = \dfrac{1}{3}$

          $\dfrac{1}{3} \times 27 = \dfrac{27}{3} = 9$

3. 15 $20\% = \dfrac{1}{5}$

          $\dfrac{1}{5} \times 75 = \dfrac{75}{5} = 15$

4. 51 $17\% = \dfrac{17}{100}$ $\dfrac{17}{100} \times 300 = \dfrac{5100}{100} = 51$

5.   8 $16\% = \dfrac{16}{100}$

$10\% = \dfrac{1}{10}$

$\dfrac{16}{100} \times \dfrac{1}{10} \times 500 = \dfrac{8000}{1000} = 8$

6.   85%   The sale price is $102. 15% of $\$120 = \dfrac{15}{100} \times 120 = \dfrac{1800}{100} = 18$, and $\$120 - \$18 = \$102$. The sale price is 85% of the regular price: $100\% - 15\% = 85\%$.

7.   292 $80\% = \dfrac{4}{5}$

$\dfrac{4}{5} \times 365 = \dfrac{1460}{5} = 292$

8.   27   If she got 25% wrong, then she got 75% correct. 75% of $36 = \dfrac{3}{4} \times 36 = \dfrac{108}{4} = 27$.

9. $72   If $20\% = \dfrac{1}{5}$, then $\dfrac{1}{5} \times 100 = \dfrac{100}{5} = 20$. The original price ($\$100$) is reduced by $\$20$, so the new price is $\$80$. After an additional 10% markdown $\left(\dfrac{1}{10} \times 80 = \dfrac{80}{10} = 8 \right)$, the discounted price is reduced by $\$8$, so the final sale price is $80 - 8 = 72$.

Practice Drill 15—Percent Change

1.   200%   The question is testing percent change since it asks by what percent did the temperature drop? To find percent change, use this formula: $\%\ \text{change} = \dfrac{\text{difference}}{\text{original}} \times 100$. The change in temperature was $20°$: $10° - (-10°) = 20°$. Since the question asks for the percent the temperature dropped, the larger number will be the original number. Thus, the equation should read $\dfrac{20}{10} \times 100$, which reduces to $2 \times 100 = 200$.

2.   33%   The question is testing percent change since it asks by what percent did the patty increase? To find percent change, use this formula: $\%\ \text{change} = \dfrac{\text{difference}}{\text{original}} \times 100$. The change in patty size is 4, which is given in the question. The new patty size is 16 oz, so the original patty size must have been 12 oz since $16 - 4 = 12$. The equation will read $\dfrac{4}{12} \times 100$, which reduces to $\dfrac{1}{3} \times 100 = \dfrac{100}{3} = 33\dfrac{1}{3}$.

Practice Drill 16— Basic Exponents and Square Roots

1. 8 $2 \times 2 \times 2 = 8$
2. 16 $2 \times 2 \times 2 \times 2 = 16$
3. 27 $3 \times 3 \times 3 = 27$
4. 64 $4 \times 4 \times 4 = 64$
5. 9 $9^2 = 9 \times 9$ or 81, so $\sqrt{81} = 9$.
6. 10 $10^2 = 10 \times 10$ or 100, so $\sqrt{100} = 10$.

7. 7 $7^2 = 7 \times 7$ or 49, so $\sqrt{49} = 7$.
8. 8 $8^2 = 8 \times 8$ or 64, so $\sqrt{64} = 8$.
9. 3 $3^2 = 3 \times 3$ or 9, so $\sqrt{9} = 3$.
10. 5 $5^3 = 5 \times 5 \times 5 = 125$, so $\sqrt[3]{125} = 5$.
11. 4 $4^3 = 4 \times 4 \times 4 = 64$, so $\sqrt[3]{64} = 4$.
12. 2 $2^4 = 2 \times 2 \times 2 \times 2 = 16$, so $\sqrt[4]{16} = 2$.

Practice Drill 17—Advanced Exponents & Roots

1. 3^8 $3^5 \times 3^3 = 3^{5+3} = 3^8$

2. 7^9 $7^2 \times 7^7 = 7^{2+7} = 7^9$

3. 5^7 $5^3 \times 5^4 = 5^{3+4} = 5^7$

4. 15^3 $15^{23} \div 15^{20} = 15^{23-20} = 15^3$

5. 4^9 $4^{13} \div 4^4 = 4^{13-4} = 4^9$

6. 10^4 $10^{10} \div 10^6 = 10^{10-6} = 10^4$

7. 5^{18} $(5^3)^6 = 5^{3 \times 6} = 5^{18}$

8. 8^{36} $(8^{12})^3 = 8^{12 \times 3} = 8^{36}$

9. 9^{25} $(9^5)^5 = 9^{5 \times 5} = 9^{25}$

10. 2^{28} $(2^2)^{14} = 2^{2 \times 14} = 2^{28}$

11. $2(3)^4$ Adding two of the same term together is more simply written as multiplying that term by 2. The expression cannot be simplified further since there are now two different bases.

12. $4x^6$ $7 - 3 = 4$ and the bases and exponents stay the same.

13. $2\sqrt{6}$ $\sqrt{24} = \sqrt{4 \times 6} = \sqrt{4} \times \sqrt{6} = 2\sqrt{6}$

14. $10\sqrt{5}$ $\sqrt{500} = \sqrt{100 \times 5} = \sqrt{100} \times \sqrt{5} = 10\sqrt{5}$

15. 12 $\sqrt{3} \times \sqrt{48} = \sqrt{3 \times 48} = \sqrt{144} = 12$

16. 5 $\sqrt{150} \div \sqrt{6} = \sqrt{150 \div 6} = \sqrt{25} = 5$

17. $9\sqrt{2}$ $\sqrt{18} = \sqrt{9 \times 2} = 3\sqrt{2}$ and $\sqrt{72} = \sqrt{36 \times 2} = 6\sqrt{2}$. $3\sqrt{2} + 6\sqrt{2} = 9\sqrt{2}$

18. $5\sqrt{2}$ $\sqrt{200} = \sqrt{100 \times 2} = 10\sqrt{2}$ and $\sqrt{50} = \sqrt{25 \times 2} = 5\sqrt{2}$. $10\sqrt{2} - 5\sqrt{2} = 5\sqrt{2}$

Review Drill 1—Numbers & Operations

1. No — Remember, 2 is the smallest (and only even) prime number. 1 is NOT prime.
2. 9 — 1, 2, 4, 5, 10, 20, 25, 50, 100
3. −30
4. 140
5. $\dfrac{2}{21}$ — Multiply using Bowtie to get $\dfrac{9}{21} - \dfrac{7}{21} = \dfrac{2}{21}$.
6. $\dfrac{12}{25}$ — $\dfrac{4}{5} \times \dfrac{3}{5} = \dfrac{4 \times 3}{5 \times 5} = \dfrac{12}{25}$
7. 4.08 — Don't forget there are a total of 2 digits to the right of the decimals.
8. 20 — Multiply to get $\dfrac{30x}{100} = 6$. Multiply both sides by 100 to get $30x = 600$, and then divide both sides by 30 to get $x = 20$.
9. 1 — $1^5 = 1 \times 1 \times 1 \times 1 \times 1$. Note: 1 to any power will always equal 1.
10. 4 — $4^2 = 4 \times 4$ or 16, so $\sqrt{16} = 4$.
11. 1, 4, 9, 16, 25, 36, 49, 64, 81, 100
12. $\begin{bmatrix} 13 & 9 \\ 12 & 3 \end{bmatrix}$ Subtract the numbers in matching positions. $17 - 4 = 13$. $21 - 12 = 9$. $31 - 19 = 12$. $9 - 6 = 3$.

ALGEBRAIC CONCEPTS

Practice Drill 18—Solving Simple Equations

1. $x = 12$ — $35 - 12 = 23$
2. $y = 15$ — $15 + 12 = 27$
3. $z = 28$ — $28 - 7 = 21$
4. $x = 5$ — $5 \times 5 = 25$
5. $x = 3$ — $18 \div 3 = 6$
6. $x = 11$ — $3 \times 11 = 33$
7. $y = 5$ — $65 \div 5 = 13$
8. $z = 3$ — $14 = 17 - 3$
9. $y = 48$ — $\dfrac{1}{2} \times 48 = 24$
10. $z = 71$ — $136 + 71 = 207$

11. $x = 12$ $7 \times 12 = 84$

12. $y = 12$ $12 \div 2 = 6$

13. $z = 45$ $45 \div 3 = 15$

14. $x = 18$ $14 + 18 = 32$

15. $y = 29$ $53 - 29 = 24$

Practice Drill 19—Manipulating an Equation

1. 3   To isolate x, add x to both sides. Then subtract 8 from both sides. Check your work by plugging in 3 for x: $8 = 11 - 3$.

2. 5   To isolate x, divide both sides by 4. Check your work by plugging in 5 for x: $4 \times 5 = 20$.

3. 6   To isolate x, add 20 to both sides. Then divide both sides by 5. Check your work by plugging in 6 for x: $5(6) - 20 = 10$.

4. 7   To isolate x, subtract 3 from both sides. Then divide both sides by 4. Check your work by plugging in 7 for x: $4 \times 7 + 3 = 31$.

5. 4   To isolate m, add 3 to both sides. Subtract m from both sides. Then divide both sides by 2. Check your work by plugging in 4 for m: $4 + 5 = 3(4) - 3$.

6. 8   To isolate x, divide both sides by 2.5. Check your work by plugging in 8 for x: $2.5 \times 8 = 20$.

7. 8   To isolate x, subtract 2 from both sides. Then divide both sides by 0.2. Check your work by plugging in 8 for x: $0.2 \times 8 + 2 = 3.6$.

8. $\frac{1}{4}$ To isolate x, subtract 4 from both sides. Then divide both sides by 8. Check your work by plugging in $\frac{1}{4}$ for x: $6 = 8 \times \frac{1}{4} + 4$.

9. 7   To isolate $x + y$, divide both sides by 3. Check your work by plugging in 7 for $x + y$: $3(7) = 21$.

10. 7   To isolate $x + y$, factor out a 3 from both terms on the left side: $3(x + y) = 21$. Then divide both sides by 3. Check your work by plugging in 7 for $x + y$: $3(7) = 21$. Note that this question and the previous question are really the same equation. Did you see it?

11. 7   To isolate y, subtract 100 from both sides. Then divide both sides by -5. Check your work by plugging in 7 for x: $100 - 5 \times 7 = 65$.

Practice Drill 20—Manipulating an Inequality

1. $x > 4$ To isolate x, divide both sides by 4. The sign doesn't change!

2. $x < -2$ To isolate x, subtract 13 from both sides. Then divide both sides by -1. Since you divided by a negative number, flip the sign.

3. $x > -5$ First, combine like terms to get $-5x < 25$. Then divide both sides by -5. Since you divided by a negative number, flip the sign.

4. $x > 4$ To isolate x, add x to both sides. Subtract 12 from both sides. Then divide both sides by 3. The sign doesn't change!

5. $x < -7$ To isolate x, add $3x$ to both sides. Subtract 7 from both sides. Then divide both sides by 3. The sign doesn't change!

Practice Drill 21—Functions

1. 26 Follow the directions and substitute 6 in for p. Since $\clubsuit p = 5p - 4$, $\clubsuit 6 = 5(6) - 4$.
2. 35 Follow the directions and substitute 5 in for x. Since $f(x) = 7x$, $f(5) = 7(5)$.
3. 8 Follow the directions and substitute 10 in for p and 2 in for q. Since $p \blacktriangleleft q = \dfrac{p}{q} + 3$, $10 \blacktriangleleft 2 = \dfrac{10}{2} + 3$.
4. 5 Follow the directions and substitute 3 in for r. Since $s(r) = r^2 - 4$, $s(3) = 3^2 - 4$.

Practice Drill 22—Foiling & Factoring

1. $x^2 + 7x + 12$ FOIL: $x \times x = x^2$, $x \times 3 = 3x$, $4 \times x = 4x$, and $3 \times 4 = 12$. Add all these together to find that $x^2 + 3x + 4x + 12 = x^2 + 7x + 12$.

2. $x^2 - 7x + 12$ FOIL: $x \times x = x^2$, $x \times -3 = -3x$, $-4 \times x = -4x$, and $-3 \times -4 = 12$. Add all these together to find that $x^2 - 3x - 4x + 12 = x^2 - 7x + 12$.

3. $x^2 + x - 12$ FOIL: $x \times x = x^2$, $x \times -3 = -3x$, $4 \times x = 4x$, and $-3 \times 4 = -12$. Add all these together to find that $x^2 - 3x + 4x - 12 = x^2 + x - 12$.

4. $a^2 - b^2$ FOIL: $a \times a = a^2$, $a \times -b = -ab$, $a \times b = ab$, and $-b \times b = -b^2$. Add all these together to find that $a^2 + ab - ab - b^2 = a^2 - b^2$.

5. $a^2 + 2ab + b^2$ FOIL: $a \times a = a^2$, $a \times b = ab$, $a \times b = ab$, and $b \times b = b^2$. Add all these together to find that $a^2 + ab + ab + b^2 = a^2 + 2ab + b^2$.

6. $a^2 - 2ab + b^2$ FOIL: $a \times a = a^2$, $a \times -b = -ab$, $-a \times b = -ab$, and $-b \times -b = b^2$. Add all these together to find that $a^2 - ab - ab + b^2 = a^2 - 2ab + b^2$.

7. 25 FOIL out $(x - y)^2$ to find $x^2 - 2xy + y^2$. Since $x^2 + y^2 = 53$, substitute 53 to find $53 - 2xy$. Substitute 14 in for xy: $53 - 2(14) = 53 - 28 = 25$.

8. $(x + 6)(x + 7)$ Factor into two binomials. Since x^2 is the first term and both signs are positive, place an x and an addition sign in each of the binomial parentheses to find $(x + \quad)(x + \quad)$. Now, find two factors of 42 that also add up to 13. The factors 6 and 7 work, and since both binomials contain addition signs, the order does not matter.

9. $(y + 2)(y - 5)$ Factor into two binomials. Since y^2 is the first term and the second sign is negative, place a y and opposite signs in each of the binomial parentheses to make $(y + \quad)(y - \quad)$. Now, find two factors of 10 that also add up to -3. The factors 2 and -5 work, so place 2 in the binomial with the addition sign and 5 next to the subtraction sign.

10. $(x - 5)(x - 7)$ Factor into two binomials. Since x^2 is the first term, the last term is positive and the middle term is negative, place an x and a subtraction sign in each of the binomial parentheses to make $(x - \quad)(x - \quad)$. Now, find two factors of 35 that also add up to 12. The factors 5 and 7 work, and since both binomials contain subtraction signs, the order does not matter.

11. $(y + 8)(y + 3)$ Factor into two binomials. Since y^2 is the first term and both signs are positive, place a y and an addition sign in each of the binomial parentheses to find $(y + \quad)(y + \quad)$. Now, find two factors of 24 that also add up to 11. The factors 3 and 8 work, and since both binomials contain addition signs, the order does not matter.

12. $(a + 2)(a - 7)$ Factor into two binomials. Since a^2 is the first and both signs are negative, place an a and opposite signs in each of the binomial parentheses to make $(a + \quad)(a - \quad)$. Now, find two factors of 14 that also add up to –5. The factors 2 and –7 work, so place 2 in the binomial with the addition sign and 7 next to the subtraction sign.

13. $(b - 5)(b - 6)$ Factor into two binomials. Since b^2 is the first term, the middle term is negative and the last term is positive, place a b and a subtraction sign in each of the binomial parentheses to make $(b - \quad)(b - \quad)$. Now, find two factors of 30 that also add up to 11. The factors 5 and 6 work, and since both binomials contain subtraction signs, the order does not matter.

14. $(k + 9)(k + 7)$ Factor into two binomials. Since k^2 is the first term and both signs are positive, place a k and an addition sign in each of the binomial parentheses to find $(k + \quad)(k + \quad)$. Now, find two factors of 63 that also add up to 16. The factors 9 and 7 work, and since both binomials contain addition signs, the order does not matter.

Practice Drill 23—Translating and Solving Percent Questions

1. 12 Translation: $30 = \dfrac{x}{100} \times 250$. To solve, simplify the right side: $\dfrac{x \times 250}{100} = \dfrac{250x}{100}$, which reduces to $\dfrac{25x}{10}$. Multiply both sides by 10, and then divide both sides by 25. Check your work by plugging in 12 for x.

2. 24 Translation: $x = \dfrac{12}{100} \times 200$. To solve: $\dfrac{12 \times 200}{100} = \dfrac{2400}{100} = 24$.

3. 5 Translation: $x = \dfrac{25}{100} \times \dfrac{10}{100} \times 200$. To solve, reduce the right side: $\dfrac{1}{4} \times \dfrac{1}{10} \times 200$. Then simplify: $\dfrac{1 \times 1 \times 200}{4 \times 10} = \dfrac{200}{40} = 5$.

4. 80 Translation: $\dfrac{75}{100} \times \dfrac{20}{100} \times n = 12$. To solve, reduce the left side: $\dfrac{3}{4} \times \dfrac{1}{5} \times n$. Then simplify: $\dfrac{3 \times 1 \times n}{4 \times 5} = \dfrac{3n}{20}$. Multiply both sides by 20, and divide both sides by 3. Check your work by plugging in 80 in for n.

5. 125 Translation: $\dfrac{16}{100} \times n = \dfrac{25}{100} \times 80$. To solve, reduce both sides to get $\dfrac{4}{25} \times n = \dfrac{1}{4} \times 80$. Then, multiply to get $\dfrac{4n}{25} = \dfrac{80}{4}$. Next, cross-multiply to get $16n = 2,000$. Finally, divide both sides by 16. Check your work by plugging in 125 for n.

6. 60 Translation: $\dfrac{x}{100} = \dfrac{3}{5}$. To solve, cross-multiply to get $5x = 300$, and then divide both sides by 5. Check your work by plugging in 60 for x.

7. 40   Translation: $30 = \dfrac{x}{100} \times 75$. To solve, simplify the right side: $\dfrac{x(75)}{100} = \dfrac{75x}{100}$, which reduces to $\dfrac{3x}{4}$. Multiply both sides by 4, and divide both sides by 3. Check your work by plugging in 40 for x.

8. 2.64   or $2\dfrac{16}{25}$ or $\dfrac{66}{25}$

        Translation: $x = \dfrac{11}{100} \times 24$. To solve, $\dfrac{11}{100} \times 24 = \dfrac{11 \times 24}{100} = \dfrac{264}{100} = 2.64$.

9. 200   Translation: $\dfrac{x}{100} \times 24 = 48$. To solve, simplify the left side: $\dfrac{24x}{100}$, which reduces to $\dfrac{6x}{25}$. Then multiply both sides by 25, and divide both sides by 6. Check your work by plugging in 200 for x.

10. 2   Translation: $\dfrac{60}{100} \times \dfrac{n}{100} \times 500 = 6$. To solve, reduce the fraction to $\dfrac{3}{5}$ and simply the left side: $\dfrac{3 \times n \times 500}{5 \times 100} = \dfrac{1500n}{500} = 3n$. Then divide both sides by 3. Check your work by plugging in 2 for n.

GEOMETRY & MEASUREMENT

Practice Drill 24—Squares, Rectangles, and Angles

1. 115° $65° + x° = 180°$

2. 100° $45° + x° + 35° = 180°$

3. 16, 16   The perimeter of $PQRS$ is 16. $4 + 4 + 4 + 4 = 16$. Its area is also 16, since $4^2 = 16$.

4. 20, 21 $7 + 3 + 7 + 3 = 20$. The perimeter of $ABCD$ is 20. $7 \times 3 = 21$. The area of $ABCD$ is 21.

5. 9 $(12 \div 4 = 3)$. Therefore, the area is $3^2 = 9$. The area of $STUV$ is 9. If the perimeter is 12, then one side of the square is 3.

6. 36   The perimeter of $DEFG$ is 36. If the area is 81, then one side of the square is 9 ($\sqrt{81} = 9$). Therefore, the perimeter is $9 + 9 + 9 + 9 = 36$.

7. 24   The area of $JKLM$ is 24. If the perimeter is 20, then $4 + l + 4 + l = 20$. So the length (the other side) of the rectangle is 6. Therefore, the area is $6 \times 4 = 24$.

8. 22   The perimeter of $WXYZ$ is 22. If the area is 30, then $6 \times w = 30$. So the width (the other side) of the rectangle is 5. Therefore, the perimeter is $6 + 5 + 6 + 5 = 22$.

9. 24 $V = lwh = 2 \times 4 \times 3 = 24$.

Practice Drill 25—Triangles

1. 45°   Since two sides (legs) of the triangle are both 3, the angles that correspond to those sides are also equal to each other. 180° − 90° = 90°. Therefore, each angle is 45°, so $x = 45°$.

2. 70°   Since sides PQ and QR are equal, then $\angle QPR$ and $x°$ are also equal to each other. 180° − 40° = 140°. Thus, divide 140° by 2 to find that each remaining angle is 70°. So $x = 70°$.

3. 6   Plug the base and height into the area formula for a triangle: $A = \frac{1}{2}bh = \frac{1}{2}(4)(3) = 6$.

4. 12   In this case, count the height and base of the triangle by counting off the ticks on the coordinate plane. The height is 6 and the base is 4, which means that $A = \frac{1}{2}bh = \frac{1}{2}(4)(6) = 12$.

5. 12   Plug the base and height into the area formula for a triangle: $A = \frac{1}{2}bh = \frac{1}{2}(4)(6) = 12$.

6. $WXZ = 5$ $A = \frac{1}{2}bh = \frac{1}{2}(2)(5) = 5$

   $ZXY = 15$ $A = \frac{1}{2}(6)(5) = 15$

   $WXY = 20$ $A = \frac{1}{2}(2+6)(5) = 20$

7. 4.8   These are similar triangles since all the angles are the same. Set up a proportion to solve: $\frac{MN}{NO} = \frac{PQ}{QR}$, so $\frac{10}{6} = \frac{8}{QR}$. Cross-multiply to get 10(QR) = 6(8). Divide both sides by 10, and $QR = 4.8$.

8. $DE = 8$ Since this is a right triangle, use the Pythagorean Theorem to find the missing side length: $a^2 + b^2 = c^2$, so $a^2 + 6^2 = 10^2$. Subtract 36 from both sides and $a^2 = 64$. Take the square root of both sides, and a (or DE) = 8.

9. 9.6   These are similar triangles since all the angles are the same. Set up a proportion to solve: $\frac{16}{20} = \frac{x}{12}$. Cross-multiply to get 16(12) = 20(x). Divide both sides by 20, and $x = 9.6$.

10. 26   Remember that all angles in a rectangle are right angles. This diagonal (AC) cuts the rectangle into two right triangles, so use the Pythagorean Theorem to find the missing side length: $a^2 + b^2 = c^2$, so $10^2 + 24^2 = c^2$, and c (or AC) = 26.

11. 40   First, use the right triangle to find AD, which is one side of the square $ABCD$. $8^2 + 6^2 = c^2$, so $c = 10$. Since all sides of a square are equal, the perimeter is 10 + 10 + 10 + 10 = 40 (or 10(4) = 40).

12. 2.4   These are similar triangles since all the angles are the same. Set up a proportion to solve: $\frac{6}{3+2} = \frac{x}{2}$. Cross-multiply to get $5x = 6(2)$. Divide both sides by 5, and $x = 2.4$.

Practice Drill 26—Circles

1. Circumference = 10π. Area = 25π.

   Plug the radius into the circumference formula for a circle: $C = 2\pi r = 2\pi(5) = 10\pi$. Plug the radius into the area formula for a circle: $A = \pi r^2 = \pi(5)^2 = 25\pi$.

2. 16π Plug the radius into the area formula for a circle: $A = \pi r^2 = \pi(4)^2 = 16\pi$.

3. 16π Since $d = 2r$, the radius is 4 $(8 = 2r)$. Plug the radius into the area formula for a circle: $A = \pi r^2 = \pi(4)^2 = 16\pi$. Note: this is really the same circle as the previous question.

4. 3   Remember, you can find the radius from a circle's area by getting rid of π and taking the square root of the number, in this case 9.

5. 6   Find the radius from the circle's area by getting rid of π and taking the square root of 9. Then multiply the radius by 2 to find the diameter.

6. 10π Find the radius from the circle's area by getting rid of π and taking the square root of 25. Then, plug the radius into the circumference formula for a circle: $C = 2\pi r = 2\pi(5) = 10\pi$.

Practice Drill 27—3-D Shapes

1. 128π Plug the radius and height into the volume formula for a cylinder: $V = \pi r^2 h = \pi(4)^2(8) = 128\pi$.

2. 1,000   Plug the side length into the volume formula for a cube: $V = s^3 = 10^3 = 1,000$.

3. 216   Plug the length, width, and height into the volume formula for a rectangular box: $V = lwh = 12 \times 3 \times 6 = 216$.

4. 162   First, find the volume of the cube: $V = s^3 = 6^3 = 216$. Next, to find the remaining liquid needed to completely fill the cube, subtract the volume of liquid already poured into it: $216 - 54 = 162$.

5. 12   One way to solve this problem is to divide the length, width, and height into segments of 2. The length is 8, so 4 cubes could fit along the length of the rectangular box since each cube has a side length of 2. The width of the box is 2, so only 1 cube could fit along the width of the box. That means the bottom layer of the box could hold 4 cubes (4 cubes across by 1 cube deep). The height of the box is 6, so you could stack 3 cubes on top of each other to fill the box. If each layer has 4 boxes and 3 layers of cubes can be stacked, then a total of 12 cubes can fit into the box (4 boxes per layer times 3 layers equals 12 boxes).

6. 48π First, find the volume of the cylinder: $V = \pi r^2 h = \pi(4)^2(9) = 144\pi$. Since the grain fills only a third of the cylinder, then find $\frac{1}{3}$ of the volume, or $\frac{1}{3}(144\pi) = 48\pi$. Just treat the π like a variable in questions like these.

COORDINATE GEOMETRY

Practice Drill 28—Coordinate Geometry

1. 4   The slope of a perpendicular line is its negative reciprocal. The reciprocal of $\frac{1}{4}$ is 4, and since the original slope was negative, its reciprocal must be positive.

2. $y = -5x - 5$

    The formula of a line is $y = mx + b$, where m is the slope and b is the y-intercept. The y-intercept is −5, since this is where it crosses the y-axis. Therefore, the formula will read $y = mx - 5$. Now, either use the slope formula to find the slope, or simply plug in a point to x and y to find m. Try the point (−1, 0): $0 = m(-1) - 5$. Multiply m by −1 to find that $0 = -m - 5$. Add 5 to both sides to isolate m, so $5 = -m$. Multiply by −1 on both sides to get m alone, so $-5 = m$. Plug that into the formula to get $y = -5x - 5$.

3. (−4, 8)   Plot the points to see what these points look like on the xy-coordinate plane:

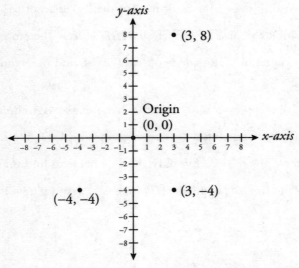

    The points start to outline a rectangle, which is a type of parallelogram. Since rectangles create right angles, the missing point should be in the top left corner, in line with the y-value of (3, 8). The point will also be in line with the x-value of (−4, −4). Therefore, the point will be (−4, 8).

4. $-\frac{7}{5}$ Use the slope formula and plug in the points given. To distinguish the points, arbitrarily call one of them point 1 and point 2. For instance, $(-2, 12) = (x_1, y_1)$, and $(3, 5) = (x_2, y_2)$. Now, use the slope formula $m = \dfrac{(y_2 - y_1)}{(x_2 - x_1)}$. The result is $(5 - 12) \div (3 - (-2)) = -\dfrac{7}{5}$.

5. a   The slope of line k is positive because it slopes upward from left to right. The slope of a line that is parallel will be the same as that of k, so it will be positive as well. The slope of a line perpendicular will be the negative reciprocal. Even though the slope of the line is not given in the question, the slope of the perpendicular line will have to be negative. Therefore, the slope of the parallel line will always be greater.

Practice Drill 29—Trigonometry

1. $1.5 \tan 23°$

    To find the length of the shadow on the ground, label the figure. Samin is 1.5 meters, and let the shadow length on the ground (the other leg of the triangle) equal x meters. Since the sides are the opposite and adjacent sides to the angle, 23°, use tangent: $\tan 23° = \dfrac{x}{1.5}$. Multiply by 1.5 on either side to isolate x to find that $1.5 \tan 23° = x$.

2. $\dfrac{c}{a}$

    The cosine is the adjacent side over the hypotenuse. The side adjacent to $x°$ is side c. Therefore, the cosine is c divided by the hypotenuse, a.

3. $50 \sin 5°$

    Since the hypotenuse is given and h is opposite of the 5°, use sine for a measurement: $\sin 5° = \dfrac{h}{50}$. Multiply by 50 on each side to find that $50 \sin 5° = h$.

4. $\dfrac{24}{25}$

    Label the figure using the cosine information: the leg adjacent to $x°$ is 24 and the hypotenuse is 25. To find sine of $y°$, use SOH of SOHCAHTOA. Therefore, $\sin y°$ equals the opposite divided by the hypotenuse. The side opposite $y°$ is 24, and the hypotenuse is 25, so $\sin y° = \dfrac{24}{25}$.

5. $\dfrac{4}{5}$

    $\sin\theta = \dfrac{opp}{hyp}$, so the opposite is 4, but the hypotenuse is unknown. Use the Pythagorean Theorem to find the hypotenuse: $a^2 + b^2 = c^2$, in which c is the hypotenuse and a and b are the legs. Therefore, $3^2 + 4^2 = c^2$. Simplify the exponents to find that $9 + 16 = c^2 = 25$. Take the square root of 25 to find the hypotenuse, which is 5. Now, plug 5 into the sine equation to find that $\theta = \dfrac{4}{5}$.

Non-Geometric Measurement

Practice Drill 30— Proportions, Ratios, & Averages

1. 108

    Use $T = AN$ to solve this question. Place 3 in for the *Number of items* and 18 in for the *Average*. Multiply these numbers to find the *Total*, which is 54. The question asks for twice the sum, which is the same as twice the *Total*, so $2 \times 54 = 108$.

2. 15

    When you see the word average, set up $T = AN$. To find the average number of comic books, start by finding the *Total* number: $11 + 14 + 16 + 19 = 60$. Put 60 in the *total* spot in $T = AN$. Then put 4, the number of friends, into the *Number of things* spot. Next, divide to find the average: $\dfrac{60}{4} = 15$.

3.   99   First, add the three scores to find Catherine's current point total. $84 + 85 + 88 = 257$. Next, set up a $T = AN$ with 4 in the *Number of items* place since there will be a fourth test, and 89 as the desired *Average* to find what the new *Total* will be with all four scores. Multiply 4×89 to find a total of 356. Subtract the totals to find that $356 - 257 = 99$. This means that she must score a 99 on the fourth test to raise her average to an 89.

4.   100   Use two $T = AN$ equations to organize the information in this question—every time you see the word *average,* set up a $T = AN$. There are 6 students with an average test score of 72. Place 6 in the *Number of items* place and 72 in the *Average* place. Find the *Total* number of points by multiplying $6 \times 72 = 432$. Make a separate $T = AN$ for the next portion of the question. If a seventh student joins the class, the *Number of items* place now contains 7, and the desired *Average* is 76. Multiply these together to find that $7 \times 76 = 532$. The difference between 532 and 432 is 100, so the seventh student must score 100 to change the average to 76.

5.   25   When the question asks about ratios, make a Ratio Box. Place the given information into the Ratio Box:

	SINGLES	DOUBLES	TRIPLES	TOTAL
Ratio	3	5	1	
Multiplier				
Actual				45

Add the three ratios to find the ratio total, which is 9. Next determine what times 9 equals 45, which is 5. Finally, multiply 5 by 5 to find the actual number of double scoops, which is 25. The correct answer is 25.

More Practice: Middle & Upper Levels

6.   30   Use two $T = AN$ equations to organize the information in this question—every time you see the word *average,* set up a $T = AN$ equation. The question states that *Rumi scored an average of 24 points over his first 5 basketball games.* Therefore, place 24 in the *Average* place in the equation, and 5 in the *Number of items* place. Multiply these numbers together to find that Rumi scored a *Total* of 120 points over the five games. To find how many points he must score on his sixth game to bring his average up to 25, use the second $T = AN$ to plug in the given information. Write 6 in the *Number of items* place to account for all six games, and 25 in the *Average* place since that's the desired average. Multiply these numbers to find he must score a total of 150 points over the entire 6 games. The difference between 150 and 120 is 30, so Rumi must score 30 points in the sixth game to raise his average to 25.

7.   7   The problem gives information about the weekly amount of rain, but the question asks about the *daily amount* instead. The daily amount will be the average (i.e., the amount of rain per day). Place 245 in the *Total* spot of the first $T = AN$ and 7 in the *Number of items* place. That gives you an *Average* of $\frac{245}{7} = 35$, which is the average daily amount for the current year. Do the same for the previous year in a second $T = AN$. This time, 196 goes in the *Total* spot and 7 goes in the *Number of items* place. That equals an average of $\frac{196}{7} = 28$. The question asks for *how many more inches,* so you will need to subtract the two daily amounts of rain: $35 - 28 = 7$.

8. 6   The recipe gives the amounts of ingredients needed to feed 8 people, but Brady wants to feed 24, so set up a proportion. $\dfrac{2 \text{ cups of stock}}{8 \text{ people}} = \dfrac{c \text{ cups of stock}}{24 \text{ people}}$ You cross-multiply to solve: $2 \times 24 = 8c$, so $48 = 8c$, so $c = 6$. You may also notice that Brady is serving 3 times the number of people as the recipe feeds, so you could get the same result by multiplying 2 cups by 3.

9. 270   Since the question mentions the mean, create a $T = AN$ equation. Emerson wants to have an average of 230 or more, so place 230 in the *Average* spot of the pie. In the *Number of items* place, write in 5 because he has already read 4 books that were 200, 200, 220, and 260 pages long, and he is going to read one more. Multiply to find the *Total* number of pages he must read: $5 \times 230 = 1{,}150$. He has already read $200 + 200 + 220 + 260 = 880$ pages, so find the difference between these two totals to see how many pages long the fifth book must at least be: $1{,}150 - 880 = 270$.

DATA ANALYSIS & PROBABILITY

Practice Drill 31—Probability

1. 27   The question asks for the number of marbles in the basket. The probability of not selecting a blue marble is $\dfrac{4}{9}$, so the probability of selecting a blue marble is $1 - \dfrac{4}{9} = \dfrac{9}{9} - \dfrac{4}{9} = \dfrac{5}{9}$. Use the probability formula: $probability = \dfrac{the \ number \ of \ what \ you \ want}{the \ total \ number}$. The probability is $\dfrac{5}{9}$, and the number of what you want is the number of blue marbles, which is 15. The question asks for the total number, so set this equal to x to get $\dfrac{5}{9} = \dfrac{15}{x}$. Cross-multiply to get $5x = 135$. Divide both sides by 5 to get $x = 27$.

2. $\dfrac{2}{3}$ The question asks for the probability that the fruit selected will be an apple or a kiwi, so get the sum of the probabilities that the fruit will be an apple and that the fruit will be a kiwi. There is a total of $4 + 6 + 5 = 15$ pieces of fruit. There are 4 apples, so the probability that the fruit is an apple is $\dfrac{4}{15}$. There are 6 kiwis, so the probability that the fruit is a kiwi is $\dfrac{6}{15}$. Therefore, the probability that the fruit is an apple or a kiwi is $\dfrac{4}{15} + \dfrac{6}{15} = \dfrac{10}{15} = \dfrac{2}{3}$.

3. $\dfrac{1}{20}$ The question asks for the probability that both cookies are pecan, so multiply the probabilities that each individual cookie will be pecan. There are 4 pecan cookies and $2 + 4 + 7 + 3 = 16$ total cookies, so the probability that the first cookie will be pecan is $\dfrac{4}{16}$. Once one pecan cookie is removed, there

are 3 remaining pecan cookies and 15 total cookies remaining, so the probability that the second

cookie will be pecan is $\frac{3}{15}$. Multiply the two to get $\frac{4}{16} \times \frac{3}{15} = \frac{1}{4} \times \frac{1}{5} = \frac{1}{20}$.

4. $\frac{1}{21}$ On the first trial, Sandy chooses a chocolate chip cookie, which has a probability of $\frac{5}{15}$. On the second trial, she chooses a red velvet cookie. There are 2 red velvet cookies, but now there are only 14 cookies remaining in the jar to choose from. The probability for the second trial is $\frac{2}{14}$. Multiply these together since these are independent of each other: $\frac{5}{15} \times \frac{2}{14} = \frac{1}{3} \times \frac{1}{7} = \frac{1}{21}$.

Practice Drill 32—Charts and Graphs

1.   E   First, find what District A spent in 2019: $400,000 (pay attention to the note below the table: the numbers are in thousands of dollars). Look for double this amount. $800,000 is listed in the table for the value in 2023 for District E.

2.   E   Add across to find which district spent the most, keeping in mind that these are all in the thousands (though this doesn't really matter to find the largest sum). District E has the largest sum: $600,000 + $800,000 = $1,400,000.

3. $800,000

     Remember that these numbers are in the thousands. Add down to find the sum of the values in 2017: $1,800,000. Do the same with the values in 2023 to find a sum of $2,600,000. Find the difference of these values: $2,600,000 − $1,800,000 = $800,000.

4.   Arzu and Dhruv

     Check the graph. Carl owns 5 games, so the other two people together must own a total of 5 games.

5.   Bodhi

     To find which student owns one-fourth of all the games, first add all the games to find a total. Your work from the previous question will help! Arzu = 2, Bodhi = 4, Carl = 5, Dhruv = 3, and Eden = 2, which yields a total of 16 games. $\frac{1}{4}$ of 16 is $\frac{1}{4} \times 16 = \frac{16}{4} = 4$, so Bodhi is the student who has 4 games.

6. $224   To find Matt's earnings for the week, first add up all his hours and then multiply by his hourly salary ($16/hour). He works 3.5 + 4 + 3.5 + 3 = 14 hours over the week, so 14 × 16 = 224.

7.   3.5   Remember, if you see the word *average*, you can use $T = AN$. The previous question helped you find the total number of hours Matt worked: 14. Put that number in the *Total* place. He worked 4 days—note the question says *on the days he worked,* not the number of days in a week. Put 4 in the *Number of items* place. Divide both sides by 4 to find the *Average*: $\frac{14}{4} = 3.5$.

8.   25   One way to solve this problem is to translate the words into math: *The hours he worked on Monday* is 3.5, *accounted for* is equals, *what percent* is $\frac{x}{100}$, and the *total hours he worked* is 14. The equation is $3.5 = \frac{x}{100} \times 14$. Simplify the right side: $\frac{x}{100} \times 14 = \frac{x(14)}{100} = \frac{14x}{100}$. Multiply both sides by 100 to get $350 = 14x$. Divide both sides by 14, and $x = 25$. You can also find a percent by dividing the desired amount by the total amount: Matt worked 3.5 hours on Monday and a total of 14 hours, so $\frac{3.5}{14} = \frac{35}{140} = \frac{1}{4}$, or 25%.

Review Drill 2—Mixed Review

1.   45   Translate the problem: $\frac{1}{3}(b) = 15$. Multiply both sides by 3, and $b = 45$. Check your work by plugging in 45 for b: $\frac{1}{3}(45) = 15$.

2.   8   To isolate x, add 7 to both sides. Then divide both sides by 7. Check your work by plugging in 8 for x: $7(8) - 7 = 49$.

3.   10   To isolate y, divide both sides by 4. Then add 5 to both sides. Check your work by plugging in 10 for y: $4(10 - 5) = 20$.

4. $x < 8$ To isolate x, subtract 1 from both sides. Then divide both sides by 8. The sign doesn't change!

5.   160   Translation: $16 = \frac{x}{100}(10)$. To solve, simplify the right side: $\frac{x}{100}(10) = \frac{x(10)}{100} = \frac{10x}{100}$, which reduces to $\frac{x}{10}$. Then, multiply both sides by 10. Check your work by plugging in 160 for x.

6.   75   Translation: $\frac{x}{100}(32) = 24$. To solve, simplify the left side of the equation: $\frac{x}{100}(32) = \frac{x(32)}{100} = \frac{32x}{100}$, which reduces to $\frac{8x}{25}$. Then multiply both sides by 25, and divide both sides by 8. Check your work by plugging in 75 for x.

7.   21   Plug the base and height into the area formula for a triangle: $A = \frac{1}{2}bh = \frac{1}{2}(7)(6) = 21$.

8.   14   Find the radius from a circle's area by getting rid of π and taking the square root of 49. Then multiply the radius by 2 to find the diameter.

9.   6   Find the radius from a circle's circumference ($C = 2\pi r$) by getting rid of π from both sides (they cancel out), which leaves $12 = 2r$. Divide both sides by 2. Check your work by plugging in 6 for the radius.

10. 25π Be careful not to just fill in a familiar formula with the given numbers. Here, you aren't given r. Instead, you're given the diameter. Since $d = 2r$, the radius is 5 ($10 = 2r$). Plug the radius into the area formula for a circle: $A = \pi r^2 = \pi(5)^2 = 25\pi$.

Part II
The Strategies

Chapter 5
ISEE Quantitative Reasoning & Mathematics Achievement

INTRODUCTION

This section will provide you with a review of the math strategy that you need to do well on the ISEE. When you get started, you may feel that the material is too easy. Don't worry. This test measures your basic math skills, so although you may feel a little frustrated reviewing things you have already learned, this type of basic review is important for ensuring that you don't make preventable mistakes.

Lose Your Calculator!

You will not be allowed to use a calculator on the ISEE. If you have developed a habit of reaching for your calculator whenever you need to add or multiply a couple of numbers, follow our advice: put your calculator away now, and don't take it out again until the test is behind you. Do your homework assignments without it, and complete the practice sections of this book without it. Trust us, you'll be glad you did.

Write It Down

Do not try to do math in your head. You are allowed to write in your test booklet if you're taking a paper-based test, and we recommend that you do so. If you are taking an online ISEE, use scratch paper. You'll need to provide your own at home, but test centers will provide it for you. You may have 4 pieces of scratch paper for the full test. Even when you are just adding a few numbers together, write them down and do the work on paper. Writing things down will not only help eliminate careless errors, but it will also give you something to refer back to if you need to check over your work.

One Pass, Two Pass

Within any math section, you can classify the questions into three categories:

- those you can answer easily in a short period of time
- those that you can do given enough time
- those that you have absolutely no idea how to tackle

When you work on a math section, start out with the first question. If it is one of the first type and you think you can do it without too much trouble, go ahead. If not, mark it in your test booklet or flag it on your screen and save it for later. Move on to the second question and decide whether or not to do that one.

Once you've made it all the way through the section, working slowly and carefully to answer all the questions that come easily to you, go back and try some of those that you think you can answer but will take you a little longer. You should pace yourself so that time will run out while you're finishing the second pass through the section. Make sure you save the last minute to fill in an answer for any question in the third category. Working this way, you'll know that you answered all the questions that were easy for you. Using a two-pass system is good, smart test-taking.

QUANTITATIVE REASONING QUESTION TYPES

While the Mathematics Achievement section will consist entirely of straightforward questions, a little more than half of the Quantitative Reasoning section will consist of Word Problems, and the remainder of the section will be Quantitative Comparisons, so it's worth giving those two question formats a little special attention.

WORD PROBLEMS—LOWER, MIDDLE, & UPPER LEVEL

A little more than half of the problems in the Quantitative Reasoning section are written in paragraph form with many words. The hard part is usually not the underlying math; the hard part is translating the words into math. So let's focus on translating.

Key Words and Phrases to Translate

Specific words and phrases show up repeatedly in word problems. You should be familiar with all of those on this page.

What You Read in English	What You Do in Math
and, more than, the sum of, plus	+
less than, the difference between, take away from	−
of, the product of, as much as	×
goes into, divided by, the quotient	÷
is, are, was, were, the result will be, has, have, earns, equals, is the same as	=
what, what number, a certain number	variable (x, y, z)
half of a number	$\dfrac{1}{2}x$
twice as much as, twice as old as	$2x$
% (percent)	$\dfrac{\quad}{100}$
how many times greater	divide the two numbers

Strategy: Bite-Sized Pieces

. Peyton is reading a book at a rate of 5 pages every 12 minutes. If he continues reading the book at this rate and finishes the book in 288 minutes, how many pages long is the book?

(A) 24
(B) 60
(C) 100
(D) 120

Remember that the units match on the top and on the bottom.

Start with some POE. Since Peyton reads 5 pages in 12 minutes, and 288 minutes is more than 10 times 12, it must take him longer than 50 minutes. Cross out (A). Now recognize that this is a proportion question because we have two sets of data we are comparing. Set up your fractions.

$$\frac{5 \text{ pages}}{12 \text{ minutes}} = \frac{\text{Number of pages in the book}}{288 \text{ minutes}}$$

Because we know that we must do the same thing to the top and the bottom of the first fraction to get the second fraction, and because $12 \times 24 = 288$, we must multiply $5 \times 24 = 120$.

$$\overset{\times 24}{\overbrace{\frac{5 \text{ pages}}{12 \text{ minutes}}}} = \frac{\text{Number of pages in the book}}{288 \text{ minutes}} \underset{\times 24}{}$$

So Peyton's book $5 \times 24 = 120$ pages long. Note that you could also use cross-multiplication to solve for the number of pages. The correct answer is (D).

Half of the crayons in a box of 40 have been used. Of these used crayons, $\frac{3}{4}$ of them are missing their paper wrapping labels. The rest of the used crayons still have their labels.

How many used crayons still have a label?

(A)   5
(B) 10
(C) 15
(D) 20

Work through tedious word problems one piece of information at a time. First, find half of the crayons: half of 40 is 20. Of the 20, $\frac{3}{4}$ of them are missing their wrappings, so $20 \times \frac{3}{4} = 15$. Therefore, 5 of the used crayons still have a label. The correct answer is (A).

Practice Drill 1—Word Problems (Lower, Middle, & Upper Levels)

1. There are 32 ounces in 1 quart. 128 ounces equals how many quarts?

    (A) 3
    (B) 4
    (C) 6
    (D) 32

2. Betty is twice as old as her daughter Fiona. Fiona is twice as old as her dog Rufus. If Rufus is 11, how old is Betty?

    (A) 11
    (B) 22
    (C) 44
    (D) 88

3. A clothing store sold 1,250 pairs of socks this year. Last year, the store sold 250 pairs of socks. This year's sales are how many times greater than last year's sales?

    (A)   4
    (B)   5
    (C)   50
    (D) 1,000

4. There are 500 students at Eisenhower High School. $\frac{2}{5}$ of the total students are first-years. $\frac{3}{5}$ of all the freshmen are girls.

    How many freshman girls are there?

    (A) 120
    (B) 200
    (C) 300
    (D) 380

When You Are Done
Check your answers in Chapter 9, page 232.

QUANTITATIVE COMPARISON—MIDDLE & UPPER LEVELS

Quant Comp: Same Book, Different Cover

Quantitative comparison (or "quant comp") is a type of question—one slightly different from the traditional multiple-choice questions that may be used—that tests exactly the same math concepts you have learned so far in this book. There is no new math for you to learn here, just a different approach for this type of question.

You will see a total of 17 quant comp questions, and only in the Quantitative Reasoning section (Section 2).

Lower Level Test-Takers
The ISEE's Primary and Lower Level tests do not include quantitative comparison questions, so you can skip this section.

The Rules of the Game

In answering a quant comp question, your goal is very simple: determine which column is larger and choose the appropriate answer. There are four possible answers.

(A) means that column A is always greater
(B) means that column B is always greater
(C) means that column A is always equal to column B
(D) means that the relationship between the columns is not consistent

To make it easier to use POE in quant comp, where there are no choices written out for you in the test booklet, we suggest that you write "A B C D" next to each question. Online test-takers will see the answer choices on the screen with each question. Regardless of modality, when you know you can eliminate an answer, cross it off.

Don't Do Too Much Work

They Look Different, But the Math Is the Same
This section will introduce you to quantitative comparison, a different type of question from the "regular" multiple-choice questions you're used to seeing. Don't worry—these questions test your knowledge of exactly the same math skills you have already learned in this book.

Quant comp is a strange new question type for most students. Don't let it intimidate you, however. Always keep your goal in mind: to figure out which column is larger. Do you care <u>how much</u> larger one column is? We hope not!

Here's a good example.

Column A	Column B
$2 \times 4 \times 6 \times 8$	$3 \times 5 \times 7 \times 9$

Test-takers who don't appreciate the beauty of quant comp look at this one and immediately start multiplying. Look carefully, however, and compare the numbers in both columns.

Of the first numbers in each column, which is larger, 2 or 3 ?

Next, look at the second number in each column. Which is larger, 4 or 5 ?

Now, look at the third numbers. Which is larger, 6 or 7 ?

Finally, look at the fourth numbers. Which is larger, 8 or 9 ?

In each case, column B contains larger numbers. Now, when you multiply larger numbers together, what happens? You guessed it—even larger numbers!

Which column is larger? Without doing a single bit of multiplication you know that (B) is the right answer. Good work!

(D) Means Different

Choice (D) is useful when the relationship between the columns can change. You may have to choose (D) when you have variables in a quant comp problem. For example:

Column A	Column B
$g + 12$	$h - 7$

Which column is larger here depends entirely on what g and h equal, and the problem doesn't give you that information. This is a perfect time to choose (D).

But be careful and don't be too quick to choose (D) when you see a variable.

Column A	Column B
$g + 12$	$g - 7$

With one small change, the answer is no longer (D). Because the variables are the same here, you can determine that no matter what number is represented by g, Column A will always be larger. So, in this case, the answer is (A).

Column A	Column B
$6 \times 3 \times 4$	$4 \times 6 \times 3$

When a quant comp question contains no variables and no unknown quantities, the answer cannot be (D).

Even if you somehow forget how to multiply (don't worry, you won't forget), someone somewhere knows how to multiply, so you can get rid of (D).

By the way, look quickly at the last example. First, you eliminate (D) because there are no variables. Do you need to multiply? Nope! The columns contain exactly the same numbers, just written in a different order. What's the answer? You got it: (C)!

Practice Drill 2—Quant Comp (Middle & Upper Levels)

(A) The quantity in Column A is greater.
(B) The quantity in Column B is greater.
(C) The two quantities are equal.
(D) The relationship cannot be determined from the information given.

Remember to time yourself during this drill!

	Column A	Column B
1.	17×3	$17 \times 2 + 17$

	Column A	Column B
2.	$\dfrac{1}{2}$	$\dfrac{3}{8}$

	Column A	Column B
3.	$b + 80$	$b + 82$

Robbie is two inches shorter than Maitri.

Jasper is four inches taller than Maitri.

	Column A	Column B`
4.	Robbie's height	Jasper's height

	Column A	Column B
5.	16^3	4^6

Karina lives two miles from school.

Jennifer lives four miles from school.

Column A	Column B
6. The distance from Karina's house to school	The distance from Karina's house to Jennifer's house

GLOBAL STRATEGIES

Guesstimating

Sometimes accuracy is important. Sometimes it isn't.

Which of the following fractions is less than $\frac{1}{4}$?

(A) $\frac{4}{18}$

(B) $\frac{4}{12}$

(C) $\frac{7}{7}$

(D) $\frac{12}{5}$

When You Are Done
Check your answers in Chapter 9, pages 232–233.

Some Things Are Easier Than They Seem
Guesstimating, or finding approximate answers, can help you eliminate wrong answers and save lots of time.

Without doing a bit of calculation, think about this question. It asks you to find a fraction smaller than $\frac{1}{4}$. Even if you're not sure which one is actually smaller, you can certainly eliminate some wrong answers.

Start simple: $\frac{1}{4}$ is less than 1, right? Are there any fractions in the choices that are greater than 1? Get rid of (D).

Look at (C). $\frac{7}{7}$ equals 1. Can it be less than $\frac{1}{4}$? Eliminate (C). Already, without doing any math, you have a 50 percent chance of guessing the right answer. If you have a few extra seconds, you can evaluate the remaining two answer choices. Which one's easier to work with? Look at (B). $\frac{4}{12}$ reduces to $\frac{1}{3}$, which is bigger than $\frac{1}{4}$. You might also think about the fact that $\frac{3}{12}$ would be $\frac{1}{4}$, so $\frac{4}{12}$ must be bigger. The answer is (A).

Here's another good example.

> A group of three people buys a one-dollar raffle ticket that wins $400. If the one dollar that they paid for the ticket is subtracted and the remainder of the prize money is divided equally among the group, how much will each person receive?
>
> (A) $62.50
> (B) $75.00
> (C) $100.00
> (D) $133.00

This isn't a terribly difficult question. To solve it mathematically, you would take $400, subtract $1, and then divide the remainder by three. But by using a little logic, you don't have to do any of that.

The raffle ticket won $400. If there were four people, each one would have won about $100 (actually slightly less because the problem tells you to subtract the $1 price of the ticket, but you get the idea). So far so good? However, there weren't four people; there were only three. This means fewer people among whom to divide the winnings, so each one should get more than $100, right?

Look at the choices. Eliminate (A), (B), and (C). What's left? The right answer!

Guesstimating also works very well with some geometry questions.

Working with Choices

In Chapter 3, Fundamental Math Skills for the ISEE, we reviewed the concepts that the ISEE will be testing. However, the questions in the practice drills were slightly different from those that you will see on your exam. The ones on the exam are going to give you four answers from which to choose. In this chapter, we'll look at how to apply test strategy to those math concepts.

There are many benefits to working with multiple-choice questions. For one, if you really mess up calculating the question, chances are your answer will not be among those given. Now you have a chance to go back and try that problem again more carefully. Another benefit, which this chapter will explore in more depth, is that you may be able to use the information in the choices to help you solve the problems.

NUMBERS & OPERATIONS

Math Vocabulary

1. Which of the following is the least odd integer greater than 26 ?

   (A) 29
   (B) 28
   (C) 27.5
   (D) 25

Notice that the choices are often in either ascending or descending numerical order.

The first and most important thing you need to do on this—and every—problem is to read and understand the question. What important vocabulary words did you see in the question? There is "odd" and "integer." You should always underline, highlight, or jot down (depending on your testing modality) important words from the questions so that you avoid careless errors. Eliminate (B) because 28 is even. 27.5 is not an integer, so eliminate (C) as well. 25 is odd, but it is not greater than 26, so eliminate (D). The correct answer is (A). Even though the least odd integer greater than 26 is 27, that's not an answer choice. The question is only asking about the numbers that are given to you.

2. Which of the following is NOT a factor of 36 and a multiple of 3 ?

   (A) 36
   (B) 18
   (C) 4
   (D) 3

Did you mark the words *factor* and *multiple*? Did you note that this is a NOT question? Eliminate the three answer choices that ARE factors of 36 and multiples of 3. A factor is a number that divides into a number, and a multiple is that number multiplied by something else. 36 is a factor of 36 since $36 \times 1 = 36$, and it is also a multiple of 3; eliminate (A). $18 \times 2 = 36$, so it is a factor of 36. $3 \times 6 = 18$, so it is a multiple of 3; eliminate (B). $4 \times 9 = 36$, so 4 is a factor of 36. However, 4 is not a multiple of 3. The correct answer is (C).

The Rules of Zero

3. If $ab = 16$ and $cd = 0$, and a, b, c, and d represent four distinct integers, which of the following must be true?

   (A) $a = 4$
   (B) $c = 0$
   (C) $d = 0$
   (D) $abcd = 0$

Remember the Rules of Zero
Zero is even. It's neither + nor −, and anything multiplied by $0 = 0$.

While a, c, and d each *could* equal what they do in the answer choices, they do not *have* to equal those amounts. However, if $cd = 0$, anything multiplied by 0 equals 0 as well. Therefore, $abcd$ must equal 0. The correct answer is (D).

Common Multiples

4. Which of the following is equal to $8 \times 4 \times 3$?

   (A) $96 \div 3$
   (B) $32 + 12$
   (C) $4 \times 4 \times 6$
   (D) 24×2

Solve $8 \times 4 \times 3$ from left to right. $8 \times 4 = 32$, and $32 \times 3 = 96$. Eliminate (A) because $96 \div 3$ is definitely less. $32 + 12$ is too small as well, so eliminate (B). 24×2 is also too small, so the correct answer must be (C). $4 \times 4 = 16$, and $16 \times 6 = 96$, but you didn't have to do that work thanks to POE!

> **Don't Do More Work Than You Have To**
> When looking at answer choices, start with what's easy for you; work through the harder ones only when you have eliminated all of the others.

Working with Negative Numbers

5. $10 - 12$ is equivalent to

   (A) $10 - (-12)$
   (B) $12 - 10$
   (C) $10 + (-12)$
   (D) $-10 - 12$

$10 - 12 = -2$. Remember that two negatives are the same as a positive, so (A) is the same as $10 + 12$. Eliminate (A). $12 - 10 = 2$, not -2, so eliminate (B) as well. Keep (C) because adding a negative number is the same as subtracting. Choice (D) equals -22, so eliminate this choice as well. The correct answer is (C).

Order of Operations

6. $14 + 18 \div 2 \times 3 - 7 =$

   (A) -483
   (B) -4
   (C) 34
   (D) 41

Remember PEMDAS and tackle multiplication and division before addition and subtraction. Work left to right within each group, so $18 \div 2 = 9$ and $9 \times 3 = 27$. Now the equation reads $14 + 27 - 7$. Do the addition and subtraction from left to right as well: $14 + 27 = 41$, and $41 - 7 = 34$. The correct answer is (C).

Factors and Multiples

7. What is the difference of the distinct prime factors of 54 ?

   (A) −5
   (B) 1
   (C) 3
   (D) 11

First, note the key words "difference" and "distinct." Then find the distinct prime factors by breaking down 54 into a factor tree. $54 = 9 \times 6$. Break 9 down into 3×3, and 6 into 2×3. Therefore, 2 and 3 are the distinct prime factors of 54. Now, find the difference: $3 − 2 = 1$. The correct answer is (B).

Factors Are Few; Multiples Are Many
The factors of a number are always equal to or less than that number and there's a limited quantity of them. The multiples of a number are always equal to or greater than that number and there are infinitely many of them. Be sure not to confuse the two!

Fractions

8. Which of the following is greater than $\frac{6}{8}$?

   (A) $\frac{3}{4}$

   (B) $\frac{4}{5}$

   (C) $\frac{5}{7}$

   (D) $\frac{6}{9}$

Eliminate (A) because $\frac{3}{4}$ is equivalent to $\frac{6}{8}$. Now try to eliminate others. Eliminate (D) because a larger denominator with the same numerator will be less, not greater. From here, either use the Bowtie method from Chapter 3 to find common denominators or convert the fractions to decimals. $\frac{6}{8}$ is equivalent to 0.75 and $\frac{4}{5}$ is equivalent to 0.8. Choice (B) is the correct answer.

Percents

9. A certain high school has 35 seniors, 40 juniors, 55 sophomores, and 70 first-years. What percent of the students at this high school are juniors?

   (A) 20%
   (B) 25%
   (C) 35%
   (D) 40%

Percent means *out of 100*, and the word *of* in a word problem tells you to multiply.

Start with some POE. There are 40 juniors, but more than 100 students, so the juniors are less than 40%. Eliminate (D). Now add all the students together to find the total, which will become the denominator of the fraction: 35 + 40 + 55 + 70 = 200. To find the percent of the juniors, or the part out of the whole, place the juniors in the numerator: $\frac{40}{200}$. Simplify $\frac{40}{200}$ to $\frac{20}{100}$, which is equal to 20%. The correct answer is (A).

Exponents—Middle & Upper Levels

10. Which of the following is NOT equal to 2^6 ?

    (A) $2^3 \times 2^3$
    (B) 4^3
    (C) 6^3
    (D) 8^2

Note the NOT. Three of your answers will be equivalent to 2^6 and to each other. This question is testing MADSPM. When multiplying the same base, add the exponents. A power raised to a power will result in multiplication. Choice (A) requires addition of the exponents since the bases are the same: 3 + 3 = 6, so $2^3 \times 2^3 = 2^6$, so eliminate (A). Choice (B) does not have the same base as 2, but it is related. $2^2 = 4$, and the expression can be rewritten $(2^2)^3 = 2^6$. Eliminate (B). Since 6 is not a perfect square or cube of 2, leave (C). Since 8 can be rewritten as 2^3, (D) can read $(2^3)^2 = 2^6$. Eliminate (D). The correct answer is (C).

Square Roots—Middle & Upper Levels

11. The square root of 40 falls between what two integers?

    (A) Between 4 and 5
    (B) Between 5 and 6
    (C) Between 6 and 7
    (D) Between 7 and 8

Think of perfect squares near 40. $\sqrt{36} = 6$ and $\sqrt{49} = 7$. Since 40 is between 36 and 49, $\sqrt{40}$ must be between 6 and 7. If you have trouble with this one, try working backwards. As we discussed in Chapter 3, a square root is just the opposite of squaring a number. Using the numbers in the answer choices, 4^2 is 16, 5^2 is 25, 6^2 is 36, and 7^2 is 49. You can stop there because 40 is between 36 and 49. The correct answer is (C).

Practice Drill 3—Numbers & Operations (Middle & Upper Levels)

Time yourself on this drill. When you are done, check your answers in Chapter 9.

1. How many distinct factors does the number 16 have?

   (A) 2
   (B) 4
   (C) 5
   (D) 6

Remember to time yourself and work in two passes during this drill!

2. Which of the following contains all the common factors of 12 and 48 ?

   (A) 1, 2, and 6
   (B) 12 and 24
   (C) 1, 2, 3, 4, and 6
   (D) 1, 2, 3, 4, 6, and 12

3. Which of the following is a multiple of 7 ?

   (A) 71
   (B) 87
   (C) 91
   (D) 104

4. Which of the following is NOT a multiple of 8 ?

   (A) 4
   (B) 16
   (C) 32
   (D) 56

5. If the final total of a dinner bill—after including a 25% tip—is $50, what was the cost of the dinner before including the tip?

   (A) $12.50
   (B) $25.00
   (C) $37.50
   (D) $40.00

6. The number 1,026 is NOT divisible by which of the following?

   (A) 2
   (B) 4
   (C) 6
   (D) 9

7. The sum of three consecutive, odd, positive integers is 21. What is the square of the smallest of the three integers?

   (A) 9
   (B) 25
   (C) 36
   (D) 49

8. One-third of the cars available for purchase at a used car dealership are silver. If there are 24 silver cars at the dealership, how many used cars are available for purchase?

   (A)   8
   (B) 24
   (C) 48
   (D) 72

9. Jake stands five-eighths of every day he works. In a four-day period, Jake stands the equivalent of how many full workdays?

   (A) 1.5
   (B) 2
   (C) 2.5
   (D) 3

10. $\dfrac{1}{2} + \dfrac{1}{3} + \dfrac{1}{4} - \dfrac{1}{2} + \dfrac{2}{3} + \dfrac{3}{4} =$

   (A) 2
   (B) $\dfrac{5}{2}$
   (C) 3
   (D) $\dfrac{7}{2}$

11. Which of the following is closest to 75% of $49.95 ?

   (A) $7.50
   (B) $12.50
   (C) $37.00
   (D) $40.00

12. The product of 0.027 and 10,000 is approximately

   (A)   2.7
   (B)   27
   (C)   270
   (D) 2,700

Column A	Column B
13. The total cost of 3 plants that cost $4 each	The total cost of 4 plants that cost $3 each

(A) The quantity in Column A is greater.
(B) The quantity in Column B is greater.
(C) The two quantities are equal.
(D) The relationship cannot be determined from the information given.

The product of 3 integers is 48.

Column A	Column B
14. The smallest of the 3 integers	1

Column A	Column B
15. $(7-4) \times 3 - 3$	0

The price of a pair of shoes is $100. The price is increased by 20%.

Nobody buys the shoes at the higher prices, so the price is then reduced by 20%.

Column A	Column B
16. The final price of the pair of shoes after reductions	$100

Column A	Column B
17. $\left(-\dfrac{5}{6}\right)^3$	$\left(-\dfrac{5}{6}\right)^5$

Column A	Column B
18. $\left(\dfrac{5}{6}\right)^4$	$\left(\dfrac{5}{6}\right)^6$

(A) The quantity in Column A is greater.
(B) The quantity in Column B is greater.
(C) The two quantities are equal.
(D) The relationship cannot be determined from the information given.

When You Are Done
Check your answers in Chapter 9, pages 233–235.

Remember to time yourself and work in two passes during this drill!

Column A	Column B
19. $\left(-\dfrac{5}{6}\right)^2$	$\left(-\dfrac{5}{6}\right)^4$

Column A	Column B
20. $\dfrac{3}{4} \times \dfrac{3}{4}$	$\dfrac{3}{4} + \dfrac{3}{4}$

Practice Drill 4—Numbers & Operations (Upper Level)

1. A company's profit was $95,000 in 2013. In 2023, its profit was $570,000. The profit in 2023 was how many times as great as the profit in 2013 ?

   (A)   4
   (B)   6
   (C)   8
   (D) 10

2. How many numbers between 1 and 100, inclusive, are both prime and a multiple of 4 ?

   (A)   0
   (B) 12
   (C) 20
   (D) 25

3. How many factors do the integers 24 and 81 have in common?

   (A) 1
   (B) 2
   (C) 3
   (D) 4

4. How many numbers between 10 and 150 inclusive are multiples of both 3 and 5 ?

   (A)   9
   (B) 10
   (C) 15
   (D) 20

5. $3^4 \times 3^4 \times 3^4 =$

   (A) 3^8
   (B) 3^{12}
   (C) 3^{64}
   (D) $3(3^4)$

6. Marie's garden contains 30 yellow roses, 50 red roses, and 40 white roses. Of the roses in her garden, what percent are NOT yellow?

   (A) 30%
   (B) 50%
   (C) 75%
   (D) 90%

7. A bookstore sells a signed copy of a particular book for $55 and an unsigned copy for $40. By approximately what percent is the signed copy marked up?

   (A) 27%
   (B) 30%
   (C) 38%
   (D) 45%

8. Candace normally scores 25 points in a basketball game. During the last game of her season, she scored only 15 points. What is the percent change in the number of points she scored?

   (A) 10%
   (B) 40%
   (C) 60%
   (D) 67%

9. The dues to enter a tournament are $24. A team with three participants will split the tournament dues evenly. If they add a fourth person to the team and still split the dues evenly, how much will each participant then pay?

   (A) $2
   (B) $6
   (C) $8
   (D) $32

10. In Jade's class, 14 of the 26 students have brown eyes. What is the ratio of the students in Jade's class with brown eyes to students with another eye color?

(A) 7:13
(B) 6:7
(C) 7:6
(D) 13:12

11. Casper runs 3 miles every day and swims 2 miles every day. When Casper has completed a total of 25 miles, how many miles did he swim?

(A) 5
(B) 10
(C) 12.5
(D) 15

12. What is the greatest common factor of $(3xy)^3$ and $3x^2y^5$?

(A) xy
(B) $3x^2y^5$
(C) $3x^2y^3$
(D) $27x^3y^3$

(A) The quantity in Column A is greater.
(B) The quantity in Column B is greater.
(C) The two quantities are equal.
(D) The relationship cannot be determined from the information given.

	Column A	Column B
13.	$\sqrt{25-9}$	$\sqrt{25} - \sqrt{9}$

	Column A	Column B
14.	4^{12}	64^4

	Column A	Column B
15.	The number of nonnegative even integers less than 10	4

When You Are Done
Don't forget to check your answers in Chapter 9, pages 235–237.

ALGEBRAIC CONCEPTS

Basic Algebraic Equations—Middle & Upper Levels

1. $-104 = 8n$. What is the value of n ?

   (A) -18
   (B) -13
   (C) 13
   (D) 18

Divide both sides by 8. Since a negative divided by a positive is negative, eliminate (C) and (D). $-\dfrac{104}{8} = -13$. If you find the equation confusing or you're better at multiplying than dividing, use the answer choices and work backward. Each of the answer choices is a possible value for x. $8 \times -13 = -104$. The correct answer is (B).

Solve for Variable–Upper Level Only

2. $5x - 14 = 8x + 4$. Find the value of x.

   (A) -6
   (B) -3
   (C) 4
   (D) 6

To isolate x, manipulate the expressions by always doing the same thing to both sides. Use the opposite operation to "undo" portions of the equation to get x by itself. Subtract $5x$ from both sides to yield $-14 = 3x + 4$. To get x by itself, subtract 4 from both sides: $-18 = 3x$. Now, divide by 3 on both sides to get $-6 = x$. The correct answer is (A). Just as in question 1, if you get stuck, use the answer choices to work backward.

Percent Algebra—Upper Level Only

3. 15% of 50% of what is equal to 24 ?

   (A) 36
   (B) 80
   (C) 160
   (D) 320

Use translation to turn English into math here. Need to review? Go back to Chapter 3! Percent translates to ÷100, of translates into multiplication, a what is an unknown value, so $\frac{15}{100}\left(\frac{50}{100}\right)(x) = 24$. Simplify to find that $\frac{15}{100}\left(\frac{1}{2}\right)(x) = 24$. Continue to simplify to find that $\frac{15}{200}(x) = 24$. Multiply both sides by 200 to find that $15x = 4,800$. Now, divide by 15 on both sides to get x by itself to find that $x = 320$. Remember that you can also use the choices and work backward. You might notice that (A) is too small, because 50% of 36 is 18, which is smaller than 24. So start with choice (C) in the middle. 50% of 160 is 80, and 15% of 80 is 12. Since that's still too small, cross out (B) and (C), leaving you with correct answer (D).

Practice Drill 5—Algebraic Concepts (Middle & Upper Levels)

1. If $18 = 3(3x - 6)$, then $x + 6 =$
   - (A)   4
   - (B)   6
   - (C)   10
   - (D)   26

(A) The quantity in Column A is greater.
(B) The quantity in Column B is greater.
(C) The two quantities are equal.
(D) The relationship cannot be determined from the information given.

Column A	Column B
2. $30(1 - 2n)$	$30 - 2n$

Column A	Column B
3. $(x + y)(x - y)$	$x^2 - y^2$

a and b are integers.
$a + b = 5$

Column A	Column B
4. a	b

$$a > 0$$
$$b < 0$$

Column A	Column B
5. $-(ab)$	$-ab$

When You Are Done
Don't forget to check your answers in Chapter 9, page 237.

Practice Drill 6—Algebraic Concepts (Upper Level)

1. For what integer value of x does $x^4 = 4x + 8$?

   (A) 1
   (B) 2
   (C) 3
   (D) 4

2. 25% of 40% of what is equal to 36?

   (A) 90
   (B) 144
   (C) 360
   (D) 650

3. $x^a = (x^3)^3$

   $y^b = \dfrac{y^{10}}{y^2}$

   What is the value of $a \times b$?

   (A) 17
   (B) 30
   (C) 48
   (D) 72

(A) The quantity in Column A is greater.
(B) The quantity in Column B is greater.
(C) The two quantities are equal.
(D) The relationship cannot be determined from the information given.

Column A	Column B
4. $\dfrac{x^2 x^5}{x^4}$	x^3

When You Are Done
Don't forget to check your answers in Chapter 9, page 238.

STRATEGY: PLUGGING IN—LOWER, MIDDLE, AND UPPER LEVELS

The ISEE will often ask you questions about real-life situations for which the numbers have been replaced with variables. One of the easiest ways to tackle these questions is with a powerful technique called *Plugging In*.

> Mark is two inches taller than John, who is four inches shorter than Bernal. If b represents Bernal's height in inches, then in terms of b, an expression for Mark's height is
>
> (A) $b + 6$
> (B) $b + 4$
> (C) $b + 2$
> (D) $b - 2$

The problem with this question is that we're not used to thinking of people's heights in terms of variables. Have you ever met someone who was b inches tall?

Whenever you see variables used in the question and in the choices, just plug in a number to replace the variable.

1. Choose a number for b.
2. Using that number, figure out Mark's and John's heights.
3. Draw a box around Mark's height, because that's what the question asked you for.
4. Plug your number for b into the choices and choose the one that gives you the number you found for Mark's height.

Here's How It Works

> Mark is two inches taller than John, who is four inches shorter than Bernal. If b represents Bernal's height in inches, then ~~in terms of b,~~ an expression for Mark's height is
>
> (A) $b + 6$
> (B) $b + 4$
> (C) $b + 2$
> (D) $b - 2$

Cross this out or ignore it on the screen! Because you are Plugging In, you don't need to pay any attention to "in terms of" any variable.

For Bernal's height, let's pick 60 inches. This means that $b = 60$. Remember, there is no right or wrong number to pick. 50 would work just as well.

If Bernal is 60 inches tall, now we can figure out that, because John is four inches shorter than Bernal, John's height must be $(60 - 4)$, or 56 inches.

The other piece of information we learn from the problem is that Mark is two inches taller than John. If John's height is 56 inches, that means Mark must be 58 inches tall.

So here's what we've got.

Bernal   60 inches = b

John   56 inches

Mark $\boxed{58}$ inches

Now, the question asks for Mark's height, which is 58 inches. The last step is to go through the choices substituting 60 for b, and choose the one that equals 58.

(A) $b + 6$ $60 + 6 = 66$ ELIMINATE

(B) $b + 4$ $60 + 4 = 64$ ELIMINATE

(C) $b + 2$ $60 + 2 = 62$ ELIMINATE

(D) $b - 2$ $60 - 2 = 58$ PICK THIS ONE!

> Don't forget to check every answer choice when Plugging In!

After reading this explanation, you may be tempted to say that Plugging In takes too long. Don't be fooled. The method itself is often faster and more accurate than regular algebra. Try it out. Practice. As you become more comfortable with Plugging In, you'll get even quicker and better results. You still need to know how to do algebra, but if you do only algebra, you may have difficulty improving your ISEE score. Plugging In gives you a way to break through whenever you are stuck. You'll find that having more than one way to solve ISEE math problems puts you at a real advantage.

Occasionally, you may run into a Plugging In question that doesn't contain variables. These questions usually ask about a percentage or a fraction of some unknown number or price. This is the one time that you should Plug In even when you don't see variables in the answer.

Also, be sure you plug in "good" numbers. Good doesn't mean right because there's no such thing as a right or wrong number to plug in. A good number is one that makes the problem easier to work with. If a question asks about minutes and hours, try 30 or 60, not 128. Also, whenever you see the word percent, plug in 100!

On Monday, Sarolta ate one-half of a fruit tart. On Tuesday, Sarolta then ate one-fourth of what was left of the tart. What fraction of the tart did Sarolta eat on Monday and Tuesday?

(A) $\dfrac{3}{8}$

(B) $\dfrac{1}{2}$

(C) $\dfrac{5}{8}$

(D) $\dfrac{3}{4}$

> Use the denominators of the fractions in the question stem and the answer choices to help you choose a good number to plug in.

There are no variables, but there is an unknown amount with fractions, so Plug In! Since the denominators of the fractions are 2 and 4, an easy number to work with would be 8 slices of tart. Plugging 8 into the information given, Sarolta ate 4 slices on Monday, leaving 4 slices remaining. On Tuesday, she ate 1 slice. Add the eaten slices together to get 5 out of the 8 slices. The answer is (C).

Practice Drill 7—Plugging In (Middle & Upper Levels)

Take the Algebra Away, and Arithmetic Is All That's Left
When you plug in for variables, you won't need to write equations and won't have to solve algebra problems. Doing simple arithmetic is always easier than doing algebra.

Don't worry about timing yourself on this drill. Focus on the strategy. Plug In for each question so you learn how to use the technique.

1. At a charity fundraiser, 200 people each donated x dollars. In terms of x, what was the total number of dollars that was donated?

   (A) $\dfrac{x}{200}$

   (B) $200x$

   (C) $\dfrac{200}{x}$

   (D) $200 + x$

2. If 10 magazines cost d dollars, how many magazines can be purchased for 3 dollars?

   (A) $\dfrac{3d}{10}$

   (B) $30d$

   (C) $\dfrac{d}{30}$

   (D) $\dfrac{30}{d}$

3. The zoo has four times as many monkeys as lions. There are four more lions than there are zebras at the zoo. If z represents the number of zebras in the zoo, then in terms of z, how many monkeys are there in the zoo?

   (A) $4z$
   (B) $z + 4$
   (C) $4z + 16$
   (D) $4z + 4$

4. If J is an odd integer, which of the following must be true?

   (A) $(J \div 3) > 1$
   (B) $(J - 2)$ is a positive integer.
   (C) $2 \times J$ is an even integer.
   (D) $J > 0$

5. The price of a suit is reduced by 20%, and then the resulting price is reduced by another 10%. The final price is what percent off of the original price?

(A) 20%
(B) 25%
(C) 28%
(D) 30%

6. If m is an even integer, n is an odd integer, and p is the product of m and n, which of the following is always true?

(A) p is a fraction.
(B) p is an odd integer.
(C) p is divisible by 2.
(D) p is greater than zero.

> Middle Level students can stop here and check their answers in Chapter 9. Upper Level students have more math fun ahead!

More Practice: Upper Level

7. If p is an odd integer, which of the following must be an odd integer?

(A) $p^2 + 3$
(B) $2p + 1$
(C) $p \div 3$
(D) $p - 3$

8. If m is the sum of two positive even integers, which of the following CANNOT be true?

(A) $m < 5$
(B) $3m$ is odd.
(C) m is even.
(D) m^3 is even.

9. Antonia has twice as many baseball cards as Krissi, who has one-third as many baseball cards as Ian. If Krissi has k baseball cards, how many baseball cards do Antonia and Ian have together?

(A) $\dfrac{3k}{2}$

(B) $\dfrac{6k}{2}$

(C) $\dfrac{8k}{2}$

(D) $\dfrac{10k}{2}$

10. The product of $\frac{1}{2}b$ and a^2 can be written as

(A) $(ab)^2$

(B) $\dfrac{a^2}{b}$

(C) $2a \times \dfrac{1}{2}b$

(D) $\dfrac{a^2b}{2}$

11. Hidden Glen Elementary school is collecting donations for a school charity drive. The total number of students in Mr. Greenwood's history class donates an average of y dollars each. The same number of students in Ms. Norris's science class donates an average of z dollars each. In terms of y and z, what is the average amount of donations for each student from both classes?

(A) $\dfrac{z}{y}$

(B) $\dfrac{(y + z)}{2}$

(C) $(y + z)$

(D) $2(y + z)$

	Column A	Column B
12.	$7(x - 3)$	$21 - 7x$

$$x > 0$$
$$y > 0$$

	Column A	Column B
13.	$\dfrac{xy}{2}$	$\sqrt{xy}$

When You Are Done
Don't forget to check your answers in Chapter 9, pages 238–242.

STRATEGY: PLUGGING IN THE ANSWERS (PITA)—LOWER, MIDDLE, & UPPER LEVELS

Plugging In the Answers (or PITA) is similar to Plugging In. When variables are in the choices, Plug In. When numbers are in the choices, Plug In the Answers.

Plugging In the Answers works because on a multiple-choice test, the right answer is always one of the choices. On this type of question, you can't plug in any number you want because only one number will work. Instead, you can plug in numbers from the choices, one of which must be correct. Here's an example.

> Jayden baked a batch of cookies. He gave half to his friend Imani and six to his mother. If he now has eight cookies left, how many did Jayden bake originally?
>
> (A) 8
> (B) 12
> (C) 20
> (D) 28

See what we mean? It would be hard to just start making up numbers of cookies and hope that eventually you guessed correctly. However, the number of cookies that Jayden baked originally must be either 8, 12, 20, or 28 (the four choices). So pick one—start in the middle with either (B) or (C)—and then work backward to determine whether you have the right choice.

Let's start with (C): Jayden baked 20 cookies. Now work through the events listed in the question. He had 20 cookies and he gave half to Imani. That leaves Jayden with 10 cookies. Then, he gave 6 to his mom. Now he's got 4 left.

Keep going. The problem says that Jayden now has 8 cookies left. But if he started with 20—(C)—he would have only 4 left. So is (C) right? No.

No problem. Pick another choice and try again. Be smart about which choice you pick. When we used the number in (C), Jayden ended up with fewer cookies than we wanted him to have, didn't he? So the right answer must be a number larger than 20, the number we took from (C).

The good news is that the choices in most Plugging In the Answers questions go in consecutive order, so it makes it easier to pick the next larger or smaller number, depending on which direction you've decided to go. We need a number larger than 20. So let's go to (D)—28.

Jayden started out with 28 cookies. The first thing he did was give half, or 14, to Imani. That left Jayden with 14 cookies. Then he gave 6 cookies to his mother. $14 - 6 = 8$. Jayden has eight cookies left over. Keep going with the question. It says, "If he now has eight cookies left…." He has 8 cookies left and, voilà—he's supposed to have 8 cookies left.

What does this mean? It means you've got the right answer!

Practice Drill 8—Plugging In the Answers (Middle & Upper Levels)

Remember to time your-
self during this drill!

1. Tina can read 60 pages per hour. Nick can read 45 pages per hour. If both Tina and Nick read at the same time, how many minutes will it take them to read a total of 210 pages?

   (A) 72
   (B) 120
   (C) 145
   (D) 180

2. Three people—Abigail, Emiko, and Diego—want to put their money together to buy a $90 radio. If Emiko agrees to pay twice as much as Diego, and Abigail agrees to pay three times as much as Emiko, how much must Emiko pay?

   (A) $10
   (B) $20
   (C) $30
   (D) $45

3. Four less than a certain number is two-thirds of that number. What is the number?

   (A) 1
   (B) 6
   (C) 8
   (D) 12

4. Anshuman is half as old as Brinda and three times as old as Cindy. If the sum of their ages is 40, what is Brinda's age?

   (A) 6
   (B) 12
   (C) 18
   (D) 24

5. If $70x + 33y = 4{,}233$, and x and y are positive integers, x could be which of the following values?

   (A) 42
   (B) 47
   (C) 55
   (D) 60

6. The sum of three positive integers is 9 and their product is 24. If the smallest of the integers is 2, what is the largest?

    (A) 4
    (B) 6
    (C) 8
    (D) 9

7. Lori is 15 years older than Carol. In 10 years, Lori will be twice as old as Carol. How old is Lori now?

    (A) 5
    (B) 12
    (C) 20
    (D) 25

8. A group of people are sharing equally the $30 cost of buying a video game. If an additional person joined the group, each person would owe $1 less. How many people are in the group currently?

    (A) 5
    (B) 6
    (C) 10
    (D) 12

When You Are Done
Don't forget to check your answers in Chapter 9, pages 242–244.

QUANT COMP PLUGGING IN—MIDDLE & UPPER LEVELS

Plugging In helps you deal with variables, which means it also works on quant comp questions with variables. There are some special rules you'll need to follow to make sure you can reap all the benefits that Plugging In has to offer you in the quant comp part of the Quantitative Reasoning section.

Column A	Column B
x	x^2

Follow these three simple steps, and you won't go wrong.

Step 1: If you're taking a paper-based test, write "A B C D" next to the problem. Online testers, get ready to use the strikeout tool.

Step 2: Plug in an "easy" number for x. By easy number, we mean a nice simple integer, such as 3. When you plug in 3 for x in the above example, column A is 3 and column B is 9, right? Think about the choices and what they mean. Column B is larger, so can the correct answer be (A)? No, eliminate it. Can the correct answer be (C)? No, you can get rid of that one too!

Weird Numbers
For your second Plug In, use ZONE F to remind yourself of "weird" options:
Zero
One
Negative
Extreme
Fraction

Step 3: Now plug in a "weird" number for *x*. A weird number might be a little harder to define, but it is something that most test-takers won't think of—for instance, zero, one, a fraction, or a negative number. In this case, try plugging in 1. Column A is 1 and column B is also 1. So the columns can be equal. Now look at the choices you have left. Choice (B) means that column B is always greater. Is it? No. Cross off (B) and pick (D).

Remember, if you get one result from plugging in a number and you get a different result by plugging in another number, you have to pick (D). But don't think too much about these questions or you'll end up spending a lifetime looking for the perfect "weird" number. Just remember that you always have to plug in **twice** on quant comp questions with variables.

Practice Drill 9—Quant Comp Plugging In (Middle & Upper Levels)

(A) The quantity in Column A is greater.
(B) The quantity in Column B is greater.
(C) The two quantities are equal.
(D) The relationship cannot be determined from the information given.

Remember to time yourself during this drill!

$$x > 1$$

	Column A	Column B
1.	x	x^2

b is an integer and $-1 < b < 1$.

	Column A	Column B
2.	$\dfrac{b}{2}$	$\dfrac{b}{8}$

	Column A	Column B
3.	*p* gallons	*m* quarts

x is a positive integer.

	Column A	Column B
4.	$\dfrac{x}{4}$	$\dfrac{x}{5}$

w is an integer less than 4.

p is an integer greater than 10.

	Column A	Column B
5.	pw	w

	Column A	Column B
6.	$4c + 6$	$3c + 12$

When You Are Done
Don't forget to check your answers in Chapter 9, pages 244-245.

FUNCTIONS—MIDDLE & UPPER LEVELS

Remember that functions are just a set of directions. Since they often involve variables, look for opportunities to Plug In! Need to review? Go back to Chapter 3!

Practice Drill 10—Functions

1. Let $b* = 2b + 7$. What is the value of $5*$?
   (A) -1
   (B) 6
   (C) 14
   (D) 17

2. If $¿n¿ = 4n - 4$ and $¿n¿ = 20$, what is the value of n ?
   (A) 4
   (B) 6
   (C) 20
   (D) 76

3. If $a\Delta b = 4a + 3b$, then $3\Delta b =$
   (A) $4a + 9$
   (B) $7 + 3b$
   (C) $12 + b^2$
   (D) $12 + 3b$

Remember to time yourself during this drill!

4. In the three-digit number, 3*H*8, *H* represents a digit. If 3*H*8 is divisible by 3, which of the following could be *H* ?

(A) 2
(B) 3
(C) 5
(D) 7

5. For any integer *c*, let $\langle c \rangle = 2c + c(c + 3)$

What is $\langle 10 \rangle - \langle 3 \rangle$?

(A) 24
(B) 84
(C) 126
(D) 150

When You Are Done
Don't forget to check your answers in Chapter 9, page 245.

GEOMETRY & MEASUREMENT—LOWER, MIDDLE, & UPPER LEVELS

BCDE is a rectangle with an area of 45. If the length of *BC* is 15, what is the perimeter of *BCDE* ?

(A) 120
(B) 90
(C) 60
(D) 36

If the area of the rectangle is 45 and one of its sides is 15, find the other side by using the area formula $l \times w = A$. Therefore, $15 \times w = 45$, which means that *w* equals 3. Find the perimeter by adding all the sides: 15 + 15 + 3 + 3 = 36. The correct answer is (D).

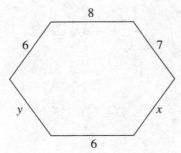

If the perimeter of the polygon is 42, what is the value of $x + y$?

(A)   6
(B)   13
(C)   14
(D)   15

Use the figure to guesstimate that x and y aren't dramatically smaller than the other sides, so cross out (A). Add all the sides to find the perimeter: $6 + 8 + 7 + x + 6 + y = 42$. Simplify to find that $27 + x + y = 42$. Subtract 27 from both sides to find that $x + y = 15$. The correct answer is (D).

Maddie has a bag of 24 marbles. She divides the marbles into 2 piles. Maddie keeps 1 pile and gives the other pile to her sister. If her sister's pile has half as many marbles as Maddie's pile, how many marbles does Maddie have?

(A)   6
(B)   8
(C)   12
(D)   16

Let the answer choices help! If Maddie has the bigger pile, she has more than half of the 24 marbles. $\frac{1}{2}(24) = 12$, so Maddie must have more than 12. Cross out answer choices (A), (B), and (C). That leaves answer choice (D). If Maddie has 16 marbles, her sister would have 8, and $16 + 8 = 24$. The correct answer is (D).

Guesstimating: A Second Look
Guesstimating worked well when we were just using it to estimate the size of a number, but geometry problems are undoubtedly the best place to guesstimate whenever you can.

Let's try the next problem. Remember, unless a particular question tells you otherwise, you can safely assume that figures are drawn to scale.

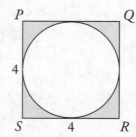

A circle is inscribed in square *PQRS*. What is the area of the shaded region?

(A) $16 - 6\pi$
(B) $16 - 4\pi$
(C) $16 - 3\pi$
(D) $16 - 2\pi$

Wow, a circle inscribed in a square—that sounds tough!

Not necessarily. Look at the picture. What fraction of the square looks like it is shaded? Half? Three-quarters? Less than half? It looks like about one-quarter of the area of the square is shaded. You've just done most of the work necessary to solve this problem.

Now, let's just do a little math. The length of one side of the square is 4, so the area of the square is 4×4 or 16.

So the area of the square is 16, and we said that the shaded region was about one-fourth of the square. One-fourth of 16 is 4, right? So we're looking for a choice that equals about 4. Let's look at the choices.

(A) $16 - 6\pi$
(B) $16 - 4\pi$
(C) $16 - 3\pi$
(D) $16 - 2\pi$

This becomes a little complicated because the answers include π. For the purposes of guesstimating, and in fact for almost any purpose on the ISEE, you should just remember that π is a little more than 3.

Let's look back at those answers.

(A) $16 - 6\pi$ is roughly equal to $16 - (6 \times 3) = -2$
(B) $16 - 4\pi$ is roughly equal to $16 - (4 \times 3) = 4$
(C) $16 - 3\pi$ is roughly equal to $16 - (3 \times 3) = 7$
(D) $16 - 2\pi$ is roughly equal to $16 - (2 \times 3) = 10$

Now let's think about what these answers mean.

Choice (A) is geometrically impossible. A figure cannot have a negative area. Eliminate it.

Choice (B) means that the shaded region has an area of about 4. Sounds pretty good.

Choice (C) means that the shaded region has an area of about 7. The area of the entire square was 16, so that would mean that the shaded region was almost half the square. Possible, but doubtful.

Choice (D) means that the shaded region has an area of about 10. That's more than half the square and in fact, almost three-quarters of the entire square. No way; cross it out.

At this point you are left with only (B), which we feel pretty good about, and (C), which seems a little large. What should you do?

Pick (B) and pat yourself on the back because you chose the right answer without doing a lot of unnecessary work. Also, remember how useful it was to guesstimate and make sure you do it whenever you see a geometry problem, unless the problem tells you that the figure is <u>not</u> drawn to scale!

Weird Shapes

Whenever the test presents you with a geometric figure that is not a square, rectangle, circle, or triangle, draw a line or lines to divide that figure into the shapes that you do know. Then you can easily work with shapes you know all about.

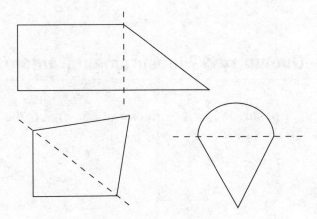

Shaded Regions—Middle & Upper Levels

Sometimes geometry questions show you one figure inscribed in another and ask you to find the area of a shaded region inside the larger figure and outside the smaller figure (like the problem at the beginning of this section). To find the areas of these shaded regions, find the area of the outside figure and then subtract the area of the figure inside. The difference is what you need.

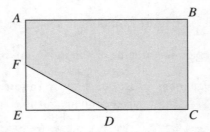

ABCE is a rectangle with a length of 10 and a width of 6.
Points F and D are the midpoints of AE and EC, respectively.
What is the area of the shaded region?

(A) 25.5
(B) 30
(C) 45
(D) 52.5

Start by labeling your figure with the information given if you're working in a test booklet, or by drawing the figure on your scratch paper. The next step is to find the area of the rectangle. Multiply the length by the width and find that the area of the rectangle is 60. Now we need to find the area of the triangle that we are removing from the rectangle. Because the height and base of the triangle are parts of the sides of the rectangle, and points D and F are the midpoints of the length and width of the rectangle, we know that the height of the triangle is half the rectangle's width, or 3, and the base of the triangle is half the rectangle's length, or 5. Using the formula for the area of a triangle, we find the area of the triangle is 7.5. Now we subtract the area of the triangle from the area of the rectangle: 60 − 7.5 = 52.5. The correct answer is (D).

Practice Drill 11—Geometry & Measurement (Middle & Upper Levels)

1. If a regular pentagon has a perimeter of 65, what is the length of each side?

   (A) 5
   (B) 11
   (C) 13
   (D) 16

2. What is the perimeter of a right triangle with legs that measure 3 cm and 4 cm?

   (A) 12 cm
   (B) 10 cm
   (C)   5 cm
   (D)   4 cm

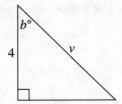

NOTE: Figure NOT drawn to scale.

3. If $b = 60$, then $v =$

    (A) 8
    (B) 5
    (C) $4\sqrt{2}$
    (D) 4

4. What is one-fourth of the difference between the number of degrees in a rectangle and the number of degrees in a triangle?

    (A)   45
    (B)   90
    (C) 120
    (D) 180

5. If one-half the perimeter of a square is equal to its area, what is the length of one side?

    (A) 1
    (B) 2
    (C) 4
    (D) 8

6. The area of a circle with a radius of 3 is equal to the circumference of a circle with a diameter of

    (A) 2
    (B) 4
    (C) 6
    (D) 9

7. Two right circular cylinders have equal volumes. The formula for the volume of a cylinder is $V = \pi r^2 h$, where r is the radius of the cylinder and h is its height. The cylinder has a radius of 3 and a height of 4. If the other cylinder has a radius of 6, what is its height?

    (A) 1
    (B) 2
    (C) 4
    (D) 8

8. If the perimeter of a square is $36n^2$, what is the length of one side?

   (A) $6n$
   (B) $9n$
   (C) $6n^2$
   (D) $9n^2$

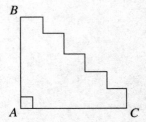

NOTE: Figure NOT drawn to scale.

9. If $AB = 12$ and $AC = 20$, what is the perimeter of the figure above?

   (A) 32
   (B) 44
   (C) 52
   (D) 64

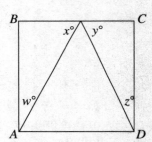

10. If $ABCD$ is a rectangle, and $x = 70$, what is the value of $y° + z° - w°$?

   (A) 20°
   (B) 70°
   (C) 90°
   (D) 110°

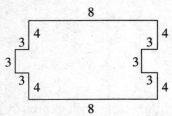

NOTE: Figure NOT drawn to scale.

11. What is the area of the figure above if all the angles shown are right angles?

    (A) 38
    (B) 42
    (C) 50
    (D) 88

12. How many meters of fencing are needed to surround a yard that measures 32 meters wide by 28 meters long?

    (A)   60 meters
    (B) 120 meters
    (C) 448 meters
    (D) 896 meters

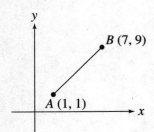

13. What is the slope of a line that is perpendicular to line segment *AB* ?

    (A) $-\dfrac{4}{3}$

    (B) $-\dfrac{3}{4}$

    (C) $\dfrac{3}{4}$

    (D) $\dfrac{4}{3}$

14. *PO* and *QO* are radii of the circle with center *O*. What is the value of *x* ?

    (A) 30°
    (B) 45°
    (C) 60°
    (D) 90°

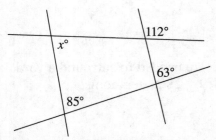

NOTE: Figure NOT drawn to scale.

15. What is the value of $x°$?

    (A) 117°
    (B) 100°
    (C) 95°
    (D) 46°

16. What is the perimeter of this figure if *ABC* is an equilateral triangle?

    (A) $6 + 3\pi$
    (B) $6 + 6\pi$
    (C) $12 + 3\pi$
    (D) $12 + 6\pi$

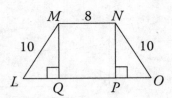

17. If *MNPQ* is a square, what is the area of the trapezoid?
    (A) 48
    (B) 64
    (C) 88
    (D) 112

Line *m* is the graph of $y = x + 4$.

Column A	Column B

18. Slope of line *m*   Slope of line *l* that is perpendicular to line *m*

(A) The quantity in Column A is greater.
(B) The quantity in Column B is greater.
(C) The two quantities are equal.
(D) The relationship cannot be determined from the information given.

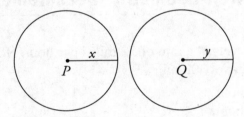

Note: Figure not drawn to scale.

Column A	Column B

19. Circumference of Circle *P*   Area of Circle *Q*

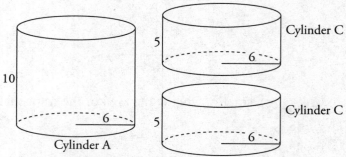

Note: Volume of a right cylinder: $V = \pi r^2 h$

Column A	Column B
20. Volume of Cylinder A	Total Volume of Cylinders B and C

When You Are Done
Don't forget to check your answers in Chapter 9, pages 245–248.

Practice Drill 12—Non-Geometric Measurement

1. A car travels at a rate of 50 miles per hour. How long will it take to travel 300 miles?

    (A) 1 hour
    (B) 5 hours
    (C) 6 hours
    (D) 30 hours

Luke travels from Providence to Boston at an average speed of 50 miles per hour without stopping.
He returns to Providence along the same route at an average speed of 60 miles per hour without stopping.

Column A	Column B
2. Luke's average speed for the entire trip	55 miles per hour

When You Are Done
Don't forget to check your answers in Chapter 9, page 248.

DATA ANALYSIS & PROBABILITY

Guesstimating: A Third Look

Guesstimating can often be a powerful tool on Probability questions, particularly those with answer choices. Before you dive into calculations, think about whether the thing the question is asking about is likely to happen (more than 50% probability) or not very likely to happen (less than 50% probability). Are there lots of different ways to get what the question wants or are there very few ways? Use Process of Elimination accordingly!

A box contains 6 purple, 3 green, 2 blue, and 1 black pen. If those are the only pens in the box and 1 pen is to be randomly chosen from the box, what is the probability that the chosen pen will be blue?

(A) $\frac{1}{12}$

(B) $\frac{1}{6}$

(C) $\frac{1}{2}$

(D) $\frac{5}{6}$

Start with some Guesstimating. Are there lots of ways to get a blue pen or only a few? There are only 2 blue pens and lots of pens of other colors, so the probability should be less than 50%: eliminate (C) and (D). Now, even if you forget how to calculate probability, you have a 50% chance of getting the question right. There are 2 blue pens and a total of 12 pens, so the probability is $\frac{2}{12}$, which reduces to $\frac{1}{6}$. The answer is (B).

Practice Drill 13—Data Analysis & Probability

1. After playing 15 games, Michelle assesses her performance in her candlepin bowling league. She calculates several statistical measures and puts the data in the following table.

Measure	Value
Lowest Score	60
Highest Score	94
Mean	76
Median	76
Mode	77
Range	34

Michelle then realizes that she forgot to include a frame from her best game, and the score for that game was actually 109 rather than 94. If she recalculates the data, which of her statistics would change the most?

(A) Mean
(B) Median
(C) Mode
(D) Range

A 6-sided number die, numbered 1 to 6, is rolled.

(A) The quantity in Column A is greater.
(B) The quantity in Column B is greater.
(C) The two quantities are equal.
(D) The relationship cannot be determined from the information given.

	Column A	Column B
2.	Probability that the number rolled is prime	$\dfrac{3}{6}$

Set A: {all prime numbers}

Set B: {all positive multiples of 5 less than 50}

Set C: intersection of Sets A and B

	Column A	Column B
3.	Number of elements in Set C	1

Set *A*: {1, 3, 8, 11, 15}

Set *B*: {2, 4, 8, 9, 10, 20}

(A) The quantity in Column A is greater.
(B) The quantity in Column B is greater.
(C) The two quantities are equal.
(D) The relationship cannot be determined from the information given.

<u>Column A</u>	<u>Column B</u>
4. Median of Set *A*	Median of Set *B*

<u>Column A</u>	<u>Column B</u>
5. Probability of a fair penny having heads face up on two consecutive flips	Probability of a fair penny having heads face up on three consecutive flips

<u>Column A</u>	<u>Column B</u>
6. The average (arithmetic mean) of 4, 6, 8, and 10	The median of 4, 6, 8, and 10

Meredith has 7 pairs of purple shoes, 2 pairs of red shoes, and 1 pair of white shoes. She chooses one pair of shoes at random.

<u>Column A</u>	<u>Column B</u>
7. Probability of <u>not</u> picking a red pair of shoes	$\dfrac{8}{10}$

When You Are Done
Don't forget to check your answers in Chapter 9, pages 248–250.

Chapter 6
ISEE Verbal

INTRODUCTION

The Verbal section of the ISEE is the first thing you'll encounter on test day and it consists of 40 questions (34 for the Lower Level). The Upper Level ISEE has 19 synonym questions and 21 sentence completion questions. The Middle Level ISEE has 17–23 synonym questions and 17–23 sentence completion questions. The Lower Level ISEE has 17 synonym questions and 17 sentence completion questions. The set of synonym questions always comes before the set of sentence completion questions.

40 questions in only 20 minutes? Should you try to spend 30 seconds on each question to get them all done? **No!**

Primary Level Students

There is no Verbal section on the Primary Levels, so you can skip this chapter!

You Mean I Don't Have to Answer All the Questions?

Nope. You'll actually improve your score by working on fewer questions, as long as you're still using all of the allotted time. Even though you shouldn't work on all of the questions, you should still answer any skipped questions with your favorite letter because there is no penalty for a wrong answer!

Remember, this test is designed for students in two to four different grade levels. There will be vocabulary on some of these questions that is aimed at students older than you, and almost no one in your grade will get those questions right. The ISEE score you receive will compare you only with students in your own grade. The younger you are in your test level, the fewer questions you are expected to complete. Sixth graders are expected to complete the fewest questions on the Middle Level test. Eighth graders are expected to do the fewest questions on the Upper Level test.

"Allotted Time"?

If you can't define *allotted*, make a flashcard for it! Look in Chapter 2 for ideas on how to make and use flashcards to learn new words.

So, why rush through the questions you can get right to get to the really tough ones that almost nobody gets? That approach only ensures that you will make hasty, careless errors. Work slowly on the questions that have vocabulary that you know to make sure you get them right. Then try the ones that have some unfamiliar words in them.

If you pace yourself, you'll have much more time for each question than students who think they have to get them all done.

Guess?

Yes. Fill in an answer even for the questions you don't read. Why? Because there is no penalty for a wrong answer on the ISEE, so you've got nothing to lose (and plenty to gain when you happen to be right!).

Which Questions Should I Work on?

Everybody's different. You know some words that your friends don't, and vice versa. Some verbal questions are harder for certain people than they are for others. Given this variability, this chapter's questions have not been separated by level, with the exception of the Two Blank Sentences Completions that appear only on the Upper Level test and the Text Complete questions that appear only on the Lower Level test. Lower Level students who are voracious readers might be surprised by how many questions they can answer, even questions that are of Upper Level difficulty!

So, here's the plan: Do the sentence completions part of the section first; you'll spend more than half the time on those questions, but you don't want to rush them and make mistakes. Flip past the synonyms in your test booklet or use the review screen to jump to Part Two in the online test. Then head back to the synonyms. Work on all the synonyms that are easy for you first. Those are the questions for which you know the definitions of the words involved. Then, go back through and answer the questions with words that sound familiar, even if you are not sure of their dictionary definition—these are words you sort of know. Remember to skip a number on the answer sheet or click the flag on the screen when you skip a question—but do fill it in at some point!

Knowing your own vocabulary is the key to deciding if you can answer a question easily.

Know Yourself

Categorize the words you see in ISEE questions into:

- words you know
- words you sort of know
- words you really don't know

Be honest with yourself when it comes to deciding if you know a word or not, so you apply the techniques that are best for the questions on which you are working. Keep your idea of the word's meaning flexible, because the test-writers sometimes use the words in ways that you and I do not! (They claim to use dictionary definitions, but lots of words have multiple dictionary definitions.)

Of course, the easiest way to get a verbal question right is by making sure all the words in it fall into the first category—words you know. The best way to do this is by learning new vocabulary words *every day*. Check out the Vocabulary chapter (Chapter 2) for the best ways to do this.

You can raise your verbal score moderately just by using the techniques we teach in this chapter. But if you want to see a substantial rise in your score, you need to build up your vocabulary too.

Eliminate Choices

With math questions, there's always one *correct* answer. The other answers are simply wrong. In a verbal question, however, things are not that simple. Words are much more slippery than numbers. So verbal questions have *best* answers, not *correct* answers. The other answers aren't necessarily wrong, but the people who score the ISEE think they're not as good as the *best* one. This means that—even more so than on the Quantitative sections—in the Verbal and Reading sections you should always try to eliminate choices. Get used to looking for *worse* answers. There are many more of them than there are *best* answers, so *worse* answers are easier to find!

When you find them, cross them out in the question booklet or use the online strikeout feature to make sure you don't spend any more time looking at them. No matter which other techniques you use to answer a question, first eliminate wrong answers instead of trying to magically pick out the best answer right away.

One thing to remember for the Verbal section: you should not eliminate choices that contain words you don't know. It doesn't matter that *you* don't know what a word means—it could still be the answer.

**Cross Out
the Bad Ones**
Even when none of the answers look particularly right, you can usually eliminate at least one.

Shop Around
Check every choice in a verbal question to be sure you're picking the *best* answer there.

Don't Rule It Out
Don't eliminate answers that use words you don't know.

What If I Can't Narrow It Down to One Answer?

Should you guess? Yes. Even if you can't eliminate any choices, you should still guess. We mentioned before that you should leave a minute or two at the end of the section to fill in an answer for any questions you did not get to. Why? *Because there's no guessing penalty on the ISEE.* Nothing is subtracted from your score for a wrong answer, and because there are four choices, you'll get approximately 25 percent of the questions on which you guess randomly correct.

That means that you should *never* leave a question blank. Pick a letter (A, B, C, or D) to fill in for your random guesses. It doesn't matter which letter you use, but stick with one letter-of-the-day so you don't have to think about it.

Of course, the number of questions you get right will increase if you can eliminate some choices before you guess, so we'll teach you techniques to do this.

Where Do I Start?

Jump over to sentence completions first. They take longer to read and work through, but they have more context to help you get the question right, even if you don't know all the words involved. If you get stuck on a sentence completion, simply fill in the letter-of-the-day and move on.

You'll be answering the questions in the following order:

- sentence completions
- synonyms with words you know
- synonyms with words you sort of know

> **Bubble Practice**
>
> If you're take a paper-based test, whenever you do a practice test, use the sample answer sheet so you get used to skipping around and making sure you're always on the same number on the test booklet and answer sheet.

REVIEW—THE VERBAL PLAN

Pacing and Verbal Strategy

What's the order in which I answer questions in the Verbal section?

1. _____

2. _____

3. _____

How long should I spend on sentence completions? _____

What's the technique I'll be using all the time, regardless of whatever

else I'm using to answer a question? _____

How many choices must I have eliminated to guess

productively? _____

Can I eliminate choices that contain words I don't know?

_____

If you had trouble with any of these questions, just review this part of the chapter before moving on.

When You Are Done
Don't forget to check your answers in Chapter 9, page 250.

Knowing My Vocabulary

Look at each of the following words and decide if it's a word that you know, sort of know, or really don't know. If you know it, write down its definition.

insecticide (noun) _____

trifle (verb) _____

repugnant (adjective) _____

mollify (verb) _____

camouflage (verb) _____

historic (adjective) _____

Check the ones you thought you knew or sort of knew. Look them up in the dictionary and make flashcards for them.

Be Honest
Do you <u>really</u> know the definition of the word? The ISEE uses dictionary definitions, and these may differ from your own sometimes. If you're not positive, you may want to use the techniques for when you sort of know the word.

SYNONYMS

What Is a Synonym?

On the ISEE, a synonym question asks you to choose the answer that comes closest in meaning to the stem word (the word in capital letters). Often, the best answer won't mean the exact same thing as the stem word, but it will be closer than any of the other choices.

You need to decide which vocabulary category the synonym stem word falls into for you, so you know which technique to use. First, find all the synonyms for which you know the stem word, and then go back and find the ones with stem words you sort of know.

When You Know the Stem Word

Don't Waste Time
Make sure you cross out answers you've eliminated, so you don't look at them again.

Write Down Your Own Definition

Come up with a simple definition—a word or a phrase. Write it next to the stem word or on your scratch paper. Then look at the answers, eliminate the ones that are furthest from your definition, and choose the closest one.

It's very simple. Don't let the test-writers put words into your mouth. Make sure you're armed with your own definition before you look at their choices. They often like to put in a word that is a close second to the best answer; if you've got your own synonym ready, you'll be able to make the distinction.

When you're practicing on paper, cover the answers with your hand so you get used to ignoring them and coming up with your own definition. Eventually, you may not have to write down your definitions, but you should start out that way so that you are not influenced by the choices they give you.

As you compare the choices with your definition, cross out the wrong ones with your pencil or the online strikeout tool. Crossing out choices is something you should *always* do—it saves you time because you don't go back to choices you've already decided were not the best.

As always, don't eliminate words you don't know. Try this one. Write your definition of WITHER before you look at the choices.

WITHER: _____

(A) play
(B) spoil
(C) greatly improve
(D) wilt

The stem word means "shrivel" or "dry up." Which answer is closest? Choice (D). You may have been considering (B), but (D) is closer.

Practice Drill 1—Write Your Own Definition

Write your definition—just a word or two—for each of these stem words. The definition doesn't have to be fancy; the key is to understand the meaning.

1. BIZARRE: _____

2. PREFACE: _____

3. GENEROUS: _____

4. MORAL: _____

5. ALTER: _____

6. REVOLVE: _____

7. HOPEFUL: _____

8. LINGER: _____

9. ASSIST: _____

10. CONSTRUCT: _____

11. STOOP: _____

12. CANDID: _____

13. TAUNT: _____

14. COARSE: _____

15. VAIN: _____

16. SERENE: _____

17. UTILIZE: _____

18. VIGOROUS: _____

19. PROLONG: _____

20. BENEFIT: _____

When You Are Done
Don't forget to check your answers in Chapter 9, page 250.

Write Another Definition

Why would you ever need to change your definition? Let's see.

MANEUVER:

- (A) avoidance
- (B) deviation
- (C) find
- (D) contrivance

Your definition may be something like *move* or *control* if you know the word from hearing it applied to cars. But that definition isn't in the choices. The problem is that you're thinking about *maneuver* as a verb. However, *maneuver* can also be a noun. It means "a plan, scheme, or trick." Now go back and eliminate. The answer is (D).

The ISEE sometimes uses secondary definitions, which can be the same part of speech or a different part of speech from the primary definition. Just stay flexible in your definitions, and you'll be fine.

Practice Drill 2—Write Another Definition

Write down as many definitions as you can think of for the following words. Your definitions may be the same part of speech or different. If you have a hard time thinking of different meanings, look up the word.

1. POINT: _____ _____

2. INDUSTRY: _____ _____

3. FLAG: _____ _____

4. FLUID: _____ _____

5. CHAMPION: _____ _____

6. TABLE: _____ _____

7. SERVICE: _____ _____

When You Are Done
Don't forget to check your answers in Chapter 9, page 251.

Practice Drill 3—Basic Synonym Techniques

Try these synonyms.

- Use the definition for the stem word that you wrote down before.
- Look at the choices, and eliminate the ones that are furthest from your definition.
- If there are stem words that you don't know well enough to define, just skip and mark them and come back after you've learned techniques for stem words you sort of know.

1. BIZARRE:
   (A) lonely
   (B) unable
   (C) odd
   (D) found

2. PREFACE:
   (A) introduce
   (B) state
   (C) propose
   (D) jumble

3. GENEROUS:
   (A) skimpy
   (B) faulty
   (C) ample
   (D) unusual

4. MORAL:
   (A) imitation
   (B) full
   (C) real
   (D) upright

5. ALTER:
   (A) sew
   (B) make up
   (C) react
   (D) change

6. REVOLVE:
   (A) push against
   (B) go forward
   (C) leave behind
   (D) turn around

7. HOPEFUL:
   (A) discouraging
   (B) promising
   (C) fulfilling
   (D) deceiving

8. LINGER:
   (A) hurry
   (B) abate
   (C) dawdle
   (D) attempt

9. ASSIST:
   (A) work
   (B) discourage
   (C) hinder
   (D) help

10. CONSTRUCT:
    (A) build
    (B) type
    (C) live in
    (D) engage

11. STOOP:
    (A) raise
    (B) elevate
    (C) condescend
    (D) realize

12. CANDID:
    (A) picture
    (B) honest
    (C) prepared
    (D) unfocused

13. TAUNT:

    (A) delay
    (B) stand
    (C) show
    (D) tease

14. COARSE:

    (A) smooth
    (B) crude
    (C) polite
    (D) furious

15. VAIN:

    (A) conceited
    (B) beautiful
    (C) talented
    (D) helpless

16. SERENE:

    (A) helpful
    (B) normal
    (C) calm
    (D) disastrous

17. UTILIZE:

    (A) pass on
    (B) resort to
    (C) rely on
    (D) make use of

18. VIGOROUS:

    (A) slothful
    (B) aimless
    (C) energetic
    (D) glorious

19. PROLONG:

    (A) affirmative
    (B) lengthen
    (C) exceed
    (D) assert

20. BENEFIT:

    (A) cooperate
    (B) struggle
    (C) assist
    (D) appeal

When You Are Done
Don't forget to check your answers in Chapter 9, page 251.

When You Sort of Know the Stem Word

Why should you answer synonym questions quickly? Why can they seem harder than sentence completions, even though you should do them faster?

Synonyms can be harder to beat than sentence completions because the ISEE gives you no context with which to figure out words that you sort of know. But that doesn't mean you're done after the easy synonyms. You can get the medium ones too. You just need to create your own context to figure out words you don't know very well.

Also, keep in mind that your goal is to eliminate the worst answers and make educated guesses. You'll be able to do this for every synonym that you sort of know. Even if you eliminate just one choice, you've increased your chances of guessing correctly. You'll gain points overall.

Make Your Own Context

You can create your own context for the word by figuring out how you've heard it used before. Think of the other words you've heard used with the stem word. Is there a certain phrase that comes to mind? What does that phrase mean?

If you still can't come up with a definition for the stem word, just use the context in which you've heard the word to eliminate answers that wouldn't fit at all in that same context.

How about this stem word?

ABOMINABLE:

Where have you heard *abominable*? The Abominable Snowman, of course. Think about it—you know it's a monster-like creature. Which choices can you eliminate?

ABOMINABLE:

(A)	enormous	the enormous snowman? maybe
(B)	terrible	the terrible snowman? sure
(C̸)	rude	the rude snowman? probably not
(D̸)	talkative	the talkative snowman? only Frosty!

You can throw out everything except (A) and (B). Now you can guess, with a much better shot at getting the answer right than guessing from four choices. Or you can think about where else you've heard the stem word. Have you ever heard something called an *abomination*? Was it something terrible or was it something enormous? Choice (B) is the answer.

Try this one. Where have you heard this stem word? Try the answers in that context.

SURROGATE:

(A) requested
(B) paranoid
(C) numerous
(D) substitute

Have you heard the stem word in *surrogate mother*? If you have, you can definitely eliminate (A), (B), and (C). A surrogate mother is a substitute mother.

Try one more.

ENDANGER:

(A) rescue
(B) frighten
(C) confuse
(D) threaten

Everyone's associations are different, but you've probably heard of *endangered species* or *endangered lives*. Use either of those phrases to eliminate choices that can't fit into it. Rescued species? Frightened species? Confused species? Threatened species? Choice (D) works best.

Practice Drill 4—Making Your Own Context

Write down the phrase in which you've heard each word.

1. COMMON: _____

2. COMPETENT: _____

3. ABRIDGE: _____

4. UNTIMELY: _____

5. HOMOGENIZE: _____

6. DELINQUENT: _____

7. INALIENABLE: _____

8. PALTRY: _____

9. AUSPICIOUS: _____

10. PRODIGAL: _____

When You Are Done
Don't forget to check
your answers in
Chapter 9, page 251.

Practice Drill 5—Using Your Own Context

1. COMMON:

   (A) beautiful
   (B) novel
   (C) typical
   (D) constant

2. COMPETENT:

   (A) angry
   (B) peaceful
   (C) well-written
   (D) capable

3. ABRIDGE:

   (A) complete
   (B) span
   (C) reach
   (D) shorten

4. UNTIMELY:

   (A) late
   (B) punctual
   (C) inappropriate
   (D) continuous

5. HOMOGENIZE:

   (A) make the same
   (B) send away
   (C) isolate
   (D) enfold

6. DELINQUENT:

   (A) underage
   (B) negligent
   (C) superior
   (D) advanced

7. INALIENABLE:

   (A) misplaced
   (B) universal
   (C) assured
   (D) democratic

8. PALTRY:

   (A) meager
   (B) colored
   (C) thick
   (D) abundant

9. AUSPICIOUS:

   (A) supple
   (B) minor
   (C) favorable
   (D) ominous

10. PRODIGAL:

   (A) wasteful
   (B) amusing
   (C) disadvantaged
   (D) lazy

When You Are Done
Don't forget to check
your answers in
Chapter 9, page 251.

Use Word Parts to Piece Together a Definition

Prefixes, roots, and suffixes can help you figure out what a word means. You should use this technique in addition to word association, because not all word parts retain their original meanings.

You may never have seen this stem word before, but if you've been working on your Vocabulary chapter, you know that the root *pac* or *peac* means "peace." You can see the same root in *Pacific*, *pacifier*, and the word *peace* itself. So which answer matches this synonym?

PACIFIST:

(A) innocent person
(B) person opposed to war
(C) warmonger
(D) wanderer of lands

It's (B). In the following stem word, we see *cred*, a word part that means "belief" or "faith." You can see this word part in *incredible*, *credit*, and *credibility*. The answer is now simple.

CREDIBLE:

(A) obsolete
(B) believable
(C) fabulous
(D) mundane

Choice (B) again. What are the word parts in the following stem word?

MONOTONOUS:

(A) lively
(B) educational
(C) nutritious
(D) repetitious

Mono means "one." *Tone* has to do with sound. If something keeps striking one sound, how would you describe it? Choice (D) is the answer.

The only way you'll be able to use word parts is if you know them. Get cracking on the Vocabulary chapter!

Words You Really Don't Know

Don't spend time on a synonym with a stem word you've never seen if you don't know any of its word parts. Simply make sure you fill in your letter-of-the-day for that question.

Practice Drill 6—All Synonyms Techniques

Directions: Each of the following questions consists of one word followed by four words or phrases. You are to select the one word or phrase whose meaning is closest to the word in capital letters.

1. PRINCIPLE:

    (A) leader
    (B) established
    (C) theory
    (D) chief

2. CAPTURE:

    (A) secure
    (B) lose
    (C) bargain
    (D) halt

3. BEFRIEND:

    (A) sever ties
    (B) close down
    (C) connect with
    (D) enjoy

4. AUTOMATIC:

    (A) involuntary
    (B) enjoyable
    (C) forceful
    (D) hapless

5. APTITUDE:

    (A) difficulty
    (B) reason
    (C) mistake
    (D) ability

6. CAPITAL:

    (A) primary
    (B) regressive
    (C) capable
    (D) central

7. REPRESS:

    (A) defy
    (B) faithful
    (C) ruling
    (D) prevent

8. ENDURE:

    (A) take in
    (B) stick with
    (C) add to
    (D) run from

9. TRANSMIT:

    (A) eliminate
    (B) watch
    (C) send
    (D) annoy

10. DIALOGUE:

    (A) speak
    (B) conversation
    (C) monologue
    (D) sermon

11. EULOGY:

    (A) attack
    (B) tribute
    (C) complement
    (D) encouragement

12. BAN:

    (A) remove
    (B) impose
    (C) forbid
    (D) specify

13. APATHY:

   (A) involvement
   (B) compassion
   (C) contempt
   (D) indifference

14. OMNISCIENT:

   (A) agile
   (B) logical
   (C) knowledgeable
   (D) invulnerable

15. TRANSGRESS:

   (A) transport
   (B) eradicate
   (C) include
   (D) violate

16. VIVACIOUS:

   (A) nimble
   (B) lively
   (C) easily amused
   (D) direct

17. HYPERBOLE:

   (A) isolation
   (B) identification
   (C) exaggeration
   (D) sharp curve

18. CONGENITAL:

   (A) innocent
   (B) inborn
   (C) graceful
   (D) acquired

19. SUCCINCT:

   (A) subterranean
   (B) confusing
   (C) blatant
   (D) direct

20. CRAFTY:

   (A) apt
   (B) sly
   (C) agile
   (D) wicked

When You Are Done
Don't forget to check
your answers in
Chapter 9, page 251.

SENTENCE COMPLETIONS

What Is a Sentence Completion?

On an ISEE sentence completion, you need to pick the answer that best fills the blank in the sentence you're given. Just like with synonym problems, you have to choose the best word from the choices, and sometimes it's not a perfect fit. On the Upper Level test, some questions will have two blanks. On the Lower Level test, some questions will ask for a phrase.

Often, however, you'll actually find more than one choice that could fit in the blank. How do you decide which is best to choose?

Just like on the synonym questions, you need to make sure the ISEE test-writers don't get to put words into your mouth. That's how they confuse you, especially on the medium and hard questions. You need to have your own answer ready before you look at theirs.

Come Up with Your Own Word

The easiest way to make sure you don't get caught up in the ISEE's tricky answers is to ignore them until you've thought of your own word for the blank. When you're working on paper, cover them up with your hand! Why waste your time plugging all their answers into the sentence, anyway? Let's look at one.

> Quite ------- conditions continue to exist in many
> mountain towns in America where houses do not have
> running water or electricity.

> **Just Use the Sentence**
> Don't try to use outside knowledge to fill in the blank. Use only what the sentence tells you.

What word would you put in the blank? Something like *basic* or *old-fashioned* or *harsh*? Write down any words that occur to you. Which part of the sentence lets you know which words could fit? "Where houses do not have running water or electricity" gives you the clue.

When you've come up with one or two words you would put in the blank, write them down. (You may not always have to write them, but during practice you should, so you can compare your answers with the answers in this book.) Then, uncover the answers.

> (A) common
> (B) primitive
> (C) orderly
> (D) lively

Which looks most like your words? Choice (B). Any of the other words could appear in this sentence in real life, right? However, because the only context you have is the sentence itself, you have to use what the sentence gives you to get the *best* answer for the ISEE.

Use the Clue

Try this one.

> Museums are good places for students of ------.

What word did you come up with? Art? History? Science? Those words are all different! Don't worry, you will not get a sentence completion like this because there's not enough information to go on—any choice could be defended! There will always be a clue to tell you what can go in the blank.

> Museums that house paintings and sculptures are good
> places for students of -------.

What's your word? Something like "art." What told you it was art, and not history or science? Underline the part of the sentence that gave you the clue when you're working on paper. If you're working online, use the highlight tool! The clue is the most important part of the sentence—the part that tells you what to put in the blank.

Try another one. Underline or highlight the clue and fill in the blank.

> The businessman was ------- because sales were down
> and costs were up, and his demeanor showed his
> unhappiness.

Recycle
Often you can use the very same word(s) you see in the clue—or something close!

Don't be afraid to just reuse the clue in the blank—the clue is *unhappiness* and the word *unhappy* would go well in the blank! When it fits, use the clue itself. Now eliminate answers.

(A) despondent
(B) persuasive
(C) indifferent
(D) unresponsive

Even if you're not sure what *despondent* means, do the other words mean *unhappy*? No. Choice (A) must be the answer.

Cover the answers, underline or highlight the clue, and fill in the blank before looking at the choices.

> To join the soccer team, a student absolutely had to be
> able to practice two hours a day; however, buying the
> uniform was -------.

(A) obligatory
(B) universal
(C) natural
(D) optional

Your word was probably something like "not required" or "unnecessary." (Don't worry if you're using a short phrase instead of a word—anything that expresses the meaning of what should go in the blank is fine.) But the clue was "absolutely had to," and your words are the opposite of that. What's going on?

Up until now, all the sentences we've seen have had a clue that was pretty much the same as the word in the blank. But sometimes the word in the blank is actually different from the clue—in fact, an opposite. How can you tell when this is true? Well, which word in the sentence told you? *However. However* lets you know that the word in the blank would be the opposite of the clue (the clue was "absolutely had to").

There are many little words that can tell you if the blank is the same as the clue or different.

Use Direction Words

Direction words tell you if the blank continues in the same direction as the clue or if it changes direction.

Which of these responses do you want to hear when you've just asked someone to the prom?

I really like you, *but* _____.

I really like you, *and* _____.

Why is the first one so awful to hear? *But* lets you know that the sentence is going to suddenly change direction and not be about liking you anymore. Why is the second one so much better? *And* lets you know that the sentence is going to continue in the same direction and continue to be all about liking you. Some other direction words are below. If you can think of any others, add them here.

Different Direction	**Same Direction**
but	and
however	thus
although	therefore
rather	so
instead	because
despite	in addition
yet	consequently

Now, cover the answers, underline or highlight the clue, circle or highlight the direction words, and fill in your own word.

When people first began investigating the human brain they were unscientific in their methods, but eventually they began to develop methods that were -------.

(A) objective
(B) inconclusive
(C) lucrative
(D) widespread

Going Thataway
Be careful when you see a direction word—make sure you know which way you need to go. Try plugging in opposites as a test.

Which choice is closest to yours? If you underlined *unscientific* and circled *but*, then you could have written *scientific* in the blank. Choice (A) is closest.

Practice Drill 7—Coming Up with Your Own Word

Underline or highlight the clues, circle or highlight the direction words, and come up with one or two words for each of these sentences.

1. The leading actor's rehearsals were so _____ that the director and producer were already imagining what a hit the movie would be.

2. Once very _____, computers are now found in almost every home.

3. After playing more than a dozen different concert halls, the orchestra was praised by critics for its _____ rendition of Beethoven's famous *Fifth Symphony*.

4. Although Miles had been unable to sleep the night before, he seemed remarkably _____ when he gave his presentation.

5. Julie was _____ to have been in the right place at the right time; the drama coach gave her the lead in our class play.

6. Mr. Jones is an intelligent and _____ teacher; his knowledge is matched only by his concern for his students.

7. To the casual observer, all fingerprints may appear to be _____, but in fact each individual's prints are unique.

8. Hardly one to _____, Josh tackled every project as soon as he got it.

9. In Charles Dickens's *A Christmas Carol*, Scrooge is a particularly _____ character, refusing to give a raise to his assistant, Bob Cratchit, despite his enormous wealth.

10. Alfred Wegener's theory that the continents are slowly drifting apart has recently been confirmed by instruments that measure very small _____ in land masses.

11. Despite their seemingly _____ architecture, the pyramids of Giza are actually intricate marvels of ancient engineering.

12. Unlike animals, which must seek sustenance in their surrounding environments, plants are able to _____ their own food.

13. Great variations in successive layers of polar ice make it possible for scientists to determine how the climate has _____ over the past millennium.

14. Because of the rigors of mountain climbing, the team needs equipment that is both _____ enough to support the members and completely reliable.

15. For a student to qualify for the foreign study program, good language skills are absolutely necessary; however, prior travel to the host country is _____.

16. The task was very _____ because certain parts needed to be carried out over and over again.

17. Because the ground there was steep and dangerous, the mountain guide told us that it was _____ to approach the edge.

18. Most members of the drama club, though reserved in real life, are quite _____ once they get on stage.

19. Physicians offer recommendations about food groups and eating habits to help their patients follow a more _____ diet.

20. Fundraising is only effective when _____ individuals are available, showing their concern by their readiness to give.

21. Not one to be easily intimidated, the corporal remained _____ while the opposing army pressed toward his troop's position.

22. Unlike her confident companion, she tended to be _____ when she found herself among strangers.

23. Although the rest of the class laughed at her antics, the teacher was _____ by Shelly's constant interruptions.

24. To avoid being penalized for tardiness, you should be _____ with your assignments.

25. Carpentry and cabinet-making are such difficult trades that they require great _____ with woodworking tools.

26. One of the most ecologically diverse places on Earth, the tropical rain forests of Brazil are home to an incredible _____ of insect species.

27. Higher math is a _____ discipline; it requires just as much imagination and insight as do any of the arts.

28. Many tribes in New Guinea are known for their _____ societies; all property belongs to all members of the tribe.

29. Because their roots are external and their leaf bases clasp, palm trees are rigid and upright, yet _____ enough to bend in strong winds.

30. Though some assert that all behavior is learned, there are others who hold that some behaviors are _____, existing before any learning occurs.

31. A very outgoing and _____ individual, the mayor loved to talk to her fellow citizens.

32. Staring wide eyed, the crowd was _____ by the magician's amazing feats of illusion.

When You Are Done
Don't forget to check your answers in Chapter 9, page 252.

Practice Drill 8—Eliminating Answers Based on Your Word

Using what you wrote in the sentences above, eliminate answers that cannot fit.

1. The leading actor's rehearsals were so ------- that the director and producer were already imagining what a hit the movie would be.

   (A) indignant
   (B) overacted
   (C) trite
   (D) imaginative

2. Once very -------, computers are now found in almost every home.

   (A) common
   (B) unusual
   (C) obtainable
   (D) simple

3. After playing more than a dozen different concert halls, the orchestra was praised by critics for its ------- rendition of Beethoven's famous *Fifth Symphony*.

   (A) unimaginative
   (B) typical
   (C) moving
   (D) loud

4. Although Miles had been unable to sleep the night before, he seemed remarkably ------- when he gave his presentation.

   (A) worn
   (B) tired
   (C) presentable
   (D) alert

5. Julie was ------- to have been in the right place at the right time; the drama coach gave her the lead in our class play.

   (A) fortunate
   (B) inspired
   (C) dramatic
   (D) impressive

6. Mr. Jones is an intelligent and ------- teacher; his knowledge is matched only by his concern for his students.

   (A) caring
   (B) experienced
   (C) unusual
   (D) original

7. To the casual observer, all fingerprints may appear to be -------, but in fact, each individual's prints are unique.

   (A) different
   (B) complicated
   (C) personal
   (D) similar

8. Hardly one to -------, Josh tackled every project as soon as he got it.

   (A) strive
   (B) volunteer
   (C) procrastinate
   (D) disagree

9. In Charles Dickens's *A Christmas Carol*, Scrooge is a particularly ------- character, refusing to give a raise to his assistant, Bob Cratchit, despite his enormous wealth.

   (A) circumspect
   (B) miserly
   (C) generous
   (D) demure

10. Alfred Wegener's theory that the continents are slowly drifting apart has recently been confirmed by instruments that measure very small ------- in land masses.

   (A) locomotion
   (B) adhesion
   (C) punishment
   (D) erosion

11. Despite their seemingly ------- architecture, the pyramids of Giza are actually intricate marvels of ancient engineering.

   (A) revolutionary
   (B) complex
   (C) archaic
   (D) simplistic

12. Unlike animals, which must seek sustenance in their surrounding environment, plants are able to ------- their own food.

   (A) find
   (B) digest
   (C) gather
   (D) manufacture

13. Great variations in successive layers of polar ice make it possible for scientists to determine how the climate has ------- over the past millennium.

   (A) migrated
   (B) altered
   (C) tended
   (D) petrified

14. Because of the rigors of mountain climbing, the team needs equipment that is both ------- enough to support two members and completely reliable.

   (A) weighty
   (B) consistent
   (C) sturdy
   (D) innovative

15. For a student to qualify for the foreign study program, good language skills are absolutely necessary; however, prior travel to the host country is -------.

   (A) inevitable
   (B) mandatory
   (C) plausible
   (D) optional

16. The task was very ------- because certain parts needed to be carried out over and over again.

   (A) standard
   (B) enjoyable
   (C) tiresome
   (D) common

17. Because the ground there was steep and dangerous, the mountain guide told us that it was ------- to approach the edge.

   (A) encouraged
   (B) forbidden
   (C) important
   (D) possible

18. Most members of the drama club, though reserved in real life, are quite ------- once they get on stage.

(A) dynamic
(B) quarrelsome
(C) threatening
(D) behaved

19. Physicians offer recommendations about food groups and eating habits in order to help their patients follow a more ------- diet.

(A) total
(B) hearty
(C) balanced
(D) fulfilling

20. Fundraising is effective only when ------- individuals are available, showing their concern by their readiness to give.

(A) popular
(B) famous
(C) selfless
(D) meaningful

21. Not one to be easily intimidated, the corporal remained ------- while the opposing army pressed toward his troop's position.

(A) commanding
(B) composed
(C) aggressive
(D) communicative

22. Unlike her confident companion, she tended to be ------- when she found herself among strangers.

(A) lively
(B) friendly
(C) crowded
(D) bashful

23. Although the rest of the class laughed at her antics, the teacher was ------- by Shelly's constant interruptions.

(A) irked
(B) amused
(C) consoled
(D) confused

24. To avoid being penalized for tardiness, you should be ------- with your assignments.

(A) original
(B) punctual
(C) precise
(D) thorough

25. Carpentry and cabinet-making are such difficult trades that they require great ------- with woodworking tools.

(A) adeptness
(B) alertness
(C) awareness
(D) assertiveness

26. One of the most ecologically diverse places on Earth, the tropical rain forests of Brazil are home to an incredible ------- of insect species.

(A) size
(B) collection
(C) range
(D) group

27. Higher math is a very ------- discipline; it requires just as much imagination and insight as do any of the arts.

(A) logical
(B) creative
(C) new
(D) surprising

28. Many tribes in New Guinea are known for their ------- societies; all property belongs to all members of the tribe.

    (A) primitive
    (B) communal
    (C) ancient
    (D) savage

29. Because their roots are external and their leaf bases clasp, palm trees are rigid and upright, yet ------- enough to bend in strong winds.

    (A) tropical
    (B) vibrant
    (C) elastic
    (D) flamboyant

30. Though some assert that all behavior is learned, there are others who hold that some behaviors are -------, existing before any learning occurs.

    (A) ostentatious
    (B) innate
    (C) durable
    (D) cultural

31. A very outgoing and ------- individual, the mayor loved to talk to her fellow citizens.

    (A) garrulous
    (B) majestic
    (C) classy
    (D) rambunctious

32. Staring wide eyed, the crowd was ------- by the magician's amazing feats of illusion.

    (A) rewarded
    (B) conjoined
    (C) stupefied
    (D) pleased

When You Are Done
Don't forget to check your answers in Chapter 9, page 252.

Use "Positive/Negative"

Sometimes you'll have trouble coming up with a word of your own. Don't sweat it; you can still eliminate answers.

Gregor was a gifted violinist who was ------- about practicing, showing a dedication to his art that even surpassed his talent.

If you can't come up with an exact word, decide if it's good or bad. In the sentence above, is Gregor good about practicing or is he bad about practicing? Underline or highlight the clue that tells you, and put a little "+" sign if the word is good, and a "–" sign if the word is bad. (You can put an "n" if it's neither.) Gregor is good about practicing, so which of the following choices can you eliminate? We've marked whether they're positive or negative, so cross out the ones you know are wrong.

    (A) diligent   +
    (B) ornery   –
    (C) practical   +
    (D) ambivalent   n

Choices (B) and (D) cannot fit because they don't match what we know about the word in the blank (it's positive). So between (A) and (C), which best expresses the same thing as the clue? Choice (A). If you're not sure what *diligent* means, make a flashcard for it. (And if you're not sure what to do with the flashcard, get cracking on the Vocabulary chapter!)

Practice Drill 9—Using Positive/Negative

Decide if the blank is positive, negative, or neutral. Try to come up with a word of your own, if you can.

1. Our manager was normally so _____ that it surprised everyone when he failed so badly on the test.

2. Frozen vegetables, though perhaps not as nutritious as fresh ones, can be a _____ way to get vitamins into a dietary plan.

3. The five-person team of adventurers almost _____ after ten grueling days in stormy weather.

4. David enjoyed the Matisse exhibit at the museum; Matisse is one of his _____ artists.

5. Petra was so _____ while giving her speech in front of the class that her stomach began to ache.

6. The Neanderthals of Krapina were _____ hunters, possessing great strength and prowess.

7. Mr. Lambert _____ the class for not studying enough for the science exam.

8. The two knights engaged in a _____ fight; it would not end until one of them lay dead on the ground.

9. If Wanda had a better sense of her accomplishments, she would stop making such _____ remarks about herself.

10. As their diet became enriched by energy-laden fat, the populations of early hunters _____ and spread throughout the plains.

When You Are Done
Don't forget to check your answers in Chapter 9, page 252.

Practice Drill 10—Eliminating Based on Positive/Negative

Use your judgment on the sentences below to eliminate answers that cannot fit.

1. Our manager was normally so ------- that it surprised everyone when he failed so badly on the test.

    (A) successful
    (B) conceited
    (C) hateful
    (D) spiteful

2. Frozen vegetables, though perhaps not as nutritious as fresh ones, can be a ------- way to get vitamins into a dietary plan.

    (A) poor
    (B) inadequate
    (C) convenient
    (D) lenient

3. The five-person team of adventurers almost ------- after ten grueling days in stormy weather.

    (A) struggled
    (B) perished
    (C) paused
    (D) lapsed

4. David enjoyed the Matisse exhibit at the museum; Matisse is one of his ------- artists.

    (A) unusual
    (B) respected
    (C) unknown
    (D) cherished

5. Petra was so ------- while giving her speech in front of the class that her stomach began to ache.

    (A) loud
    (B) calm
    (C) anxious
    (D) relaxed

6. The Neanderthals of Krapina were ------- hunters, possessing great strength and prowess.

    (A) formidable
    (B) unsuitable
    (C) unstable
    (D) researched

7. Mr. Lambert ------- the class for not studying enough for the science exam.

    (A) congratulated
    (B) warned
    (C) chastised
    (D) corrected

8. The two knights engaged in a ------- fight; it would not end until one of them lay dead on the ground.

    (A) divided
    (B) humiliating
    (C) tenuous
    (D) perilous

9. If Wanda had a better sense of her accomplishments, she would stop making such ------- remarks about herself.

    (A) deprecating
    (B) indelicate
    (C) rebellious
    (D) fertile

10. As their diet became enriched by energy-laden fat, the populations of early hunters ------- and spread throughout the plains.

    (A) divided
    (B) congregated
    (C) thrived
    (D) restored

When You Are Done
Don't forget to check your answers in Chapter 9, page 252.

Two-Blank Sentences—Upper Level Only

Two-blank sentences are usually longer than one-blank sentences. Does that mean they're harder? Nope. Actually, if you take two-blank sentences slowly, one blank at a time, they can be easier to get right! Check it out.

> Since Europe has been polluting its rivers, the ------- of
> many species of fish has been severely -------.

Cover your answers, and look for the clues and direction words. Which blank do you try first? Whichever is easier for you or whichever you have more information for in the form of clues and direction words. For this example, let's go with the second blank, because we know something bad has been happening to the fish. How do we know? The clues are *polluting its rivers* and *severely*, and the direction word is *Since*, which keeps everything moving in the same direction. We can at least put a "–" sign next to the second blank. Now, when you uncover the answers to check them, uncover only the words for the blank you're working on. Don't even look at the words for the first blank here! You're going to eliminate answers based only on what cannot fit in the second blank.

(A) XXXX . . . augmented
(B) XXXX . . . observed
(C) XXXX . . . approached
(D) XXXX . . . threatened

You can eliminate (B) and (C), because they're not negative enough. Cross them out so you don't look at them again. Do you know what (A) means? If not, you can't eliminate it. Never eliminate words you don't know.

Now look back at the sentence and fill in a word or two for the first blank. What is it that can be negatively affected by pollution? Once you've got a word or two, look at the choices that are left for the first blank.

(A)   acceptance … augmented
(B)   ~~audacity … observed~~
(C)   ~~equanimity … approached~~
(D)   habitat … threatened

Which fits better? You may have had a word like *environment* or *survival* filled in. Choice (D) definitely fits better than (A). Notice that if you didn't know what *augmented*, *audacity*, or *equanimity* meant, you could still get this question right. That's because on two-blank sentence completions, as soon as you eliminate a choice based on one of its words, the whole thing is gone—you never have to look at it again, and it doesn't matter what the other word in it is. (However, if *augmented*, *audacity*, or *equanimity* comes up in a one-blank sentence, you do need to know it to eliminate it—so make some flashcards for those words.)

Think of all the time you'd waste if you tried plugging the words for each choice into the sentence. You'd be reading the sentence four or five times! Plus, you'd find more than one choice that sounded okay, and you'd have nothing with which to compare them.

Two-blank sentence completions are your friends on the ISEE. Treat your friends right—do them one blank at a time, coming up with your own words.

Practice Drill 11—Two-Blank Sentence Completions (Upper Level Only)

Cover the answers, underline or highlight the clues, circle or highlight the direction words, and come up with a word for one of the blanks. Eliminate answers based on that blank alone, and then go back up to the sentence to work on the other blank. Then, eliminate again.

1. Psychologists have long ------- the connection between violence on television and actual crime; the wealth of different ------- makes it very hard to reach a consensus.

   (A) found . . . facts
   (B) debated . . . opinions
   (C) agreed . . . articles
   (D) argued . . . criminals

2. Jason felt quite ------- about his ability to score well; he had studied ------- the night before.

   (A) frightened . . . thoroughly
   (B) happy . . . poorly
   (C) confident . . . diligently
   (D) resistant . . . lately

3. Although the pilot checked all his instruments before takeoff, the ------- of one of them almost caused the plane to -------.

   (A) malfunction . . . crash
   (B) misuse . . . land
   (C) safety . . . abort
   (D) refusal . . . fly

4. Her treatment of the subject was so ------- that the class was convinced she had only ------- the material the night before.

   (A) spotty . . . skimmed
   (B) thorough . . . misunderstood
   (C) partial . . . memorized
   (D) confused . . . learned

5. Communities need to work not -------, but -------; as a group, they can solve problems more easily.

   (A) in groups . . . communally
   (B) at home . . . detached
   (C) always . . . constantly
   (D) in isolation . . . together

6. Despite the best efforts of his coach, Josh remained ------- in his ------- streak.

   (A) mired . . . losing
   (B) upbeat . . . winning
   (C) free . . . consistent
   (D) taken . . . sportsman

7. Due to the author's ------- handwriting, the typist had a difficult time ------- the manuscript.

   (A) perfect . . . transcribing
   (B) careful . . . reading
   (C) illegible . . . deciphering
   (D) readable . . . translating

8. The maid, while appropriately ------- to the guests of the hotel, was ------- with her employers.

   (A) indifferent . . . curt
   (B) submissive . . . pleasant
   (C) obsequious . . . obstinate
   (D) reliable . . . obedient

9. The owner is difficult to work for, less for her critical and ------- nature than for her -------.

(A) exacting . . . procrastination
(B) perfect . . . assistance
(C) meticulous . . . encouragement
(D) carefree . . . complaints

10. Smithers hoped that the committee would not ------- a course of action that would ------- an already bad situation in the workplace.

(A) relate . . . assist
(B) formulate . . . amend
(C) recommend . . . exacerbate
(D) present . . . mediate

When You Are Done
Don't forget to check your answers in Chapter 9, page 253.

Guess Aggressively When You've Worked on a Sentence

When you've narrowed a sentence completion down to two or three answers, it's probably because you don't know the vocabulary in some of those answers. Just take a guess and move on—you're not going to be able to divine the meanings of the words (and trust us, the proctor will not let you pull out a dictionary). You've increased your chances of getting the question right by eliminating one or two choices, and there's no guessing penalty, so fill in a bubble and move on.

Which Letter Should I Use?
No matter what you may have heard, it doesn't matter which letter you use to fill in answers for questions you don't work on. ERB tries to use letters in equal amounts.

When to Take a Guess

What if you come across a sentence that is so confusing that you can't even decide if the blank(s) should be positive or negative, much less come up with a word of your own? Don't waste your time on it. Just make sure you fill in your letter-of-the-day and move on.

If you have only a minute left, and you're not yet done, make sure you fill in your letter-of-the-day on all remaining questions.

Review—The Sentence Completions Plan

One-Blank Sentence Completions

For each and every sentence completion, the first thing I do is _____ the answers.

I look for the _____, and I mark it by _____ it.

I look for any _____ words, and I _____ them.

Then I _____.

If I have trouble coming up with a word for the blank, I decide if the blank is _____ or _____ (or neither).

Then I _____ choices and _____.

Two-Blank Sentence Completions—Upper Level Only

For each and every sentence completion, the first thing I do is _____ the answers.

I look for the _____, and I mark it by _____ it.

I look for any _____ words, and I _____ them.

If the sentence completion has two blanks, I do them _____.

Which blank do I try first? _____

I come up with a word for one of the blanks, and when I uncover the choices, I uncover only _____ and I eliminate based on those.

Then I go back to the sentence and _____ for the other blank, uncover the choices that are left, and eliminate.

Eliminating Choices and Guessing

Can I eliminate choices just because they contain words I do not know?

_____

What do I do if I can eliminate only one or two choices? _____

_____

What do I do if the sentence or the vocabulary looks so difficult that I can't come up with a word or decide if the blank is positive or negative? _____

_____

What do I spend my last minute on? _____

_____

Why should I never leave a question unanswered, even if I did not work on that question at all?

_____

If you have trouble answering any of these questions, go back and review the appropriate section of this chapter before going on.

When You Are Done
Don't forget to check your answers in Chapter 9, page 253.

Practice Drill 12—All Sentence Completion Techniques

Upper Level test-takers should complete the entire drill. Others should stop after question 13.

1. One of the simple guidelines of public speaking is that good presentations require ------- preparation.

   (A) thorough
   (B) fretful
   (C) partial
   (D) solitary

2. Franklin D. Roosevelt was an effective -------, taking time out each week to speak to the people of the United States by radio in casual "fireside chats."

   (A) writer
   (B) warrior
   (C) communicator
   (D) legislator

3. Compared with Asia, the huge continent to its east, Europe is actually quite ------- in size, though not in its impressive and numerous cultural contributions.

   (A) mammoth
   (B) modest
   (C) irregular
   (D) predictable

4. Even though she was known to be quite outgoing, Janet could be ------- if she didn't know everyone in the room.

   (A) timid
   (B) extroverted
   (C) diverse
   (D) separate

5. Unlike the convex lens, which brings light rays together, the concave lens actually ------- light rays.

   (A) merges
   (B) dissolves
   (C) assists
   (D) spreads out

6. Usually cool and collected, the coach grew ------- when he saw his best player needlessly injured in the illegal play.

   (A) indifferent
   (B) furious
   (C) realistic
   (D) impatient

7. The ruler of the kingdom was known to be quite a -------; he was domineering and cruel to all his subjects.

   (A) leader
   (B) tyrant
   (C) democrat
   (D) highbrow

8. Most house fires can be avoided through such simple ------- as proper education and a well-placed fire extinguisher.

   (A) previews
   (B) presentations
   (C) precautions
   (D) preventions

9. The dishonest employee ------- his company, absconding with more than two thousand dollars' worth of supplies.

   (A) relieved
   (B) reported
   (C) swindled
   (D) demoted

10. Almost worse than the cast that covered it, the scar on Noor's leg was quite -------.

    (A) pleasant
    (B) ghastly
    (C) beneficial
    (D) ingenious

11. Theories of the origin of the universe are far from -------; after all, no one was around to witness the event.

    (A) hypothetical
    (B) plausible
    (C) credible
    (D) definitive

12. The situation called for ------- measures; the solution would not be simple and straightforward.

    (A) complex
    (B) unique
    (C) elementary
    (D) firsthand

13. The day was hardly a ------- one; everything that could possibly go wrong did.

    (A) reluctant
    (B) facile
    (C) resistant
    (D) frenetic

14. Known for their ------- skills at goldsmithing, the Incas produced some of the most beautiful and ------- gold figurines of all time.

    (A) primitive . . . expensive
    (B) early . . . religious
    (C) expert . . . intricate
    (D) novice . . . strong

15. It is hard to imagine that so much modern machinery, from huge oil tankers, cars, and jet engines all the way down to ------- nuts, bolts, and screws, is made from ------- material: steel.

    (A) minuscule . . . the same
    (B) tremendous . . . the common
    (C) countless . . . the perfect
    (D) flimsy . . . the unique

16. Once a common and important means of -------, sailing has become more of a sport and a ------- than a primary way of getting around.

    (A) conveyance . . . profession
    (B) transportation . . . hobby
    (C) relaxation . . . business
    (D) socialization . . . vocation

17. Because she was the best at spelling, Zaila was ------- to be our ------- at the county spelling bee.

    (A) assigned . . . principal
    (B) picked . . . treasurer
    (C) chosen . . . representative
    (D) elected . . . washout

18. Martha could no longer keep -------;
with unusual -------, she spoke out
passionately against the injustices at
her school.

(A) pace . . . speed
(B) quiet . . . timidity
(C) up . . . facility
(D) silent . . . vigor

19. With a multitude of nationalities
present, this campus is one of the
most ------- and ------- in the whole
country.

(A) diverse . . . fascinating
(B) uniform . . . tremendous
(C) multifaceted . . . bland
(D) homogeneous . . . ethnic

20. Standing on their feet and applauding,
the audience was ------- the actor's
------- performance of Abe Lincoln in
Illinois.

(A) rebellious at . . . fanatic
(B) thrilled by . . . weak
(C) impressed with . . . uninspired
(D) electrified by . . . marvelous

When You Are Done
Don't forget to check
your answers in
Chapter 9, page 254.

Chapter 7
ISEE Reading

AN OPEN-BOOK TEST

Keep in mind when you approach the Reading Section of the ISEE that *it is an open-book test.* But you can't read the passages in advance of the test to prepare and you have a limited amount of time to get through the passages and questions. What does this all mean? You will be much better served to take a *strategic* approach.

Read with a Purpose

When you read for school, you have to read everything—carefully. Not only is there no time for such an approach on the ISEE, but reading carefully at the outset does not even make sense. Each passage has only six questions (five for Lower Level), and all you need to read and process is the information that will provide answers to those questions. As only questions can generate points, your goal is to get to the questions as quickly as possible.

Even so, it does help to have a high-level overview of the passage before you attack the questions. There are two ways to accomplish this goal.

- If you are a fairly fast reader, get through the passage quickly, ignoring the nitty-gritty and focusing on the overall point of each paragraph.
- If you don't read quickly enough to read the entire passage in a way that will provide you with the overall point of the paragraphs, read the first sentence of each paragraph.

Once you have identified the point of each paragraph, those points will flow into the overall purpose of the passage and also provide a map of where to find detailed information. Once you have established the purpose and map, you should go right to the questions.

Answering Questions

By reading more quickly up front, you have more time to spend on finding the answer to a particular question.

Some questions are about particular parts of a passage, while others are about the passage as a whole. Depending on how well you understood the purpose of the passage, you may be able to answer big picture questions quite easily. Detail questions, on the other hand, will require some work; after all, you didn't get lost in the details when you got through the passage quickly!

For a particular detail question, you will need to go back to the passage with the question in mind and *find the answer in the passage.* Let's repeat that last part: you should *find the answer in the passage.* If you know what the answer should look like, it is much easier to evaluate the choices. True, some questions cannot be answered in advance, such as "Which one of the following questions is answered in the passage?" But the general rule is *find the answer* before you go to the choices.

In all cases, you should use effective Process of Elimination. Correct answers are fully supported by the text of the passage. There is no reading between the lines, connecting the dots, or getting inside the author's head. If you are down to two answers, determine which one is not supported by the text of the passage. It takes only one word to doom an otherwise good answer.

In short, follow this process for detail questions:

- Read and understand the question.
- Go to the passage and *find the answer* (unless the question is too open-ended).
- Use Process of Elimination, getting rid of any answer that is not consistent with the answer you found and/or is not fully supported by the text of the passage.

We will look at some specific question types shortly, but if you follow the general approach outlined here, you will be able to answer more questions accurately.

Pacing

Let's amend that last statement: you will be able to answer more questions accurately if you have a sound pacing plan. While reading up front more quickly will generate more time for the questions, getting through all the passages and all the questions in the time allotted is difficult for almost all students.

There are six passages on the Middle and Upper Level exams, five on the Lower Level, four on Primary 3 and 4, and three on Primary 2. Some passages are short and some quite long. Some might seem like fairly quick reads, and some might seem a bit dense. They cover a broad array of topics, from history to science to fiction. You may relate to some passages but not to others. On top of that, if you are rushing through the section to make sure you answer every single question, you are likely making a lot of mistakes. Slow down to increase your accuracy.

How many passages should you do? That depends on you. You should attack as many passages as you can while still maintaining a high degree of accuracy. If, for example, dropping to five passages allows you to answer all but one or two questions correctly, while rushing through six creates a lot of silly mistakes, do five.

> Doing fewer passages accurately can generate more points than rushing through more passages.

Always pick your passages wisely. You don't get extra credit for answering questions on a more complex passage correctly. If you begin a passage and are thinking "Uh, what?" move on to another passage. You might end up coming back to the passage, or you may never look at it again. What is most important is that you nail the easier passages before you hit the more complicated ones.

A Note to Primary and Lower Students

The strategies in this chapter are applicable to all levels, but the passages are geared toward the Middle and Upper levels. Unless you are already reading chapter books, you will likely find them too difficult.

STEP ONE: READING THE PASSAGE
Let's put the new reading approach into practice.

Label the Paragraphs
After you read each paragraph, ask yourself what you just read. Put it into your own words—just a couple of words—and label the side of the paragraph or your scratch paper with your summary. This way you'll have something to guide you back to the relevant part of the passage when you answer a question. The key to labeling the paragraphs is practice—you need to do it quickly, coming up with one or two words that accurately remind you of what's in the paragraph.

If the passage has only one paragraph, come up with a single label.

State the Main Idea
After you have read the entire passage, ask yourself two questions.

- **"What?"** What is the passage about?

- **"So what?"** What's the author's point about this topic?

The answers to these questions will show you the main idea of the passage. Scribble down this main idea in just a few words. The answer to "What?" is the thing that was being talked about: "bees" or "weather forecasting." The answer to "So what?" gives you the rest of the sentence: "Bees do little dances that tell other bees where to go for pollen" or "Weather forecasting is complicated by many problems."

Don't assume you will find the main idea in the first sentence. While often the main idea is in the beginning of the passage, it is not always in the first sentence. The beginning may just be a lead-in to the main point.

Practice Drill 1—Getting Through the Passage

As you quickly read each paragraph, label it. When you finish the passage, answer "What?" and "So what?" to get the main idea.

Line

1   Contrary to popular belief, the first European known to lay eyes
2   on America was not Christopher Columbus or Amerigo Vespucci
3   but a little-known Viking by the name of Bjarni Herjolfsson.
4   In the summer of 986, Bjarni sailed from Norway to Iceland,
5   heading for the Viking settlement where his father, Heriulf,
6   resided.
7   When he arrived in Iceland, Bjarni discovered that his father
8   had already sold his land and estates and set out for the latest
9   Viking settlement on the subarctic island called Greenland.
10   Discovered by a notorious murderer and criminal named Erik the
11   Red, Greenland lay at the limit of the known world. Dismayed,
12   Bjarni set out for this new colony.
13   Because the Vikings traveled without chart or compass, it was
14   not uncommon for them to lose their way in the unpredictable
15   northern seas. Beset by fog, the crew lost their bearings. When
16   the fog finally cleared, they found themselves before a land that
17   was level and covered with woods.
18   They traveled farther up the coast, finding more flat, wooded
19   country. Farther north, the landscape revealed glaciers and rocky
20   mountains. Though Bjarni realized this was an unknown land, he
21   was no intrepid explorer. Rather, he was a practical man who had
22   simply set out to find his father. Refusing his crew's request to
23   go ashore, he promptly turned his bow back out to sea. After four
24   days' sailing, Bjarni landed at Herjolfsnes on the southwestern tip
25   of Greenland, the exact place he had been seeking all along.

"What" is this passage about? _____

"So what?" What's the author's point? _____

What type of passage is this? _____

When You Are Done
Don't forget to check your answers in Chapter 9, page 254.

STEP TWO: ANSWERING THE QUESTIONS

Now, we're getting to the important part of the Reading Comprehension section. This is where you need to spend time to avoid careless errors. After reading a passage, you'll have a group of questions that are in no particular order. The first thing you need to decide is whether the question you're answering is general or specific.

General Questions

General questions are about the passage as a whole. They come in a variety of forms but ideally all can be answered based on your initial read.

Main idea

- Which of the following best expresses the main point?
- The passage is primarily about
- The main idea of the passage is
- The best title for this passage would be

Purpose

- The purpose of the passage is
- The author wrote this passage to

Tone/attitude

- The author's tone is
- The attitude of the author is one of

Organization and Structure

- Which one of the following best describes the organization of the passage as a whole?
- Which one of the following best describes the organization of the second paragraph?

Notice that all of these questions require you to know the main idea, but the ones at the beginning of the list don't require anything else, and the ones toward the end require you to use your map.

Answering a General Question

Keep your answers to "What? So what?" in mind. The answer to a general question will concern the main idea. If it helps, you can go back to your paragraph labels. The labels will allow you to look at the passage again without getting bogged down in the details.

- For a straight **main idea** question, just ask yourself, "What was the 'What? So what?' for this passage?"

- For a **general purpose** question, ask yourself, "Why did the author write this?"

- For a **tone/attitude question**, ask yourself, "How did the author feel about the subject?"

- For an **organization and structure question**, use your map for questions about the entire passage, and use Process of Elimination for questions about a paragraph.

Answer the question in your own words before looking at the choices. Eliminate answers that are not consistent with your predicted answer, as well as those that are too broad or too narrow. They should be "just right."

Practice Drill 2—Answering a General Question

Use the passage about Vikings that you just read and labeled. Reread your main idea and answer the following questions. Use the questions above to help you paraphrase your own answer before looking at the choices. When you're done, check your answers in Chapter 9.

1. This passage is primarily about
   (A) the Vikings and their civilization
   (B) the waves of Viking immigration
   (C) sailing techniques of Bjarni Herjolfsson
   (D) one Viking's glimpse of the New World

2. What was the author's purpose in writing this passage?
   (A) To turn the reader against Italian adventurers
   (B) To show his disdain for Erik the Red
   (C) To demonstrate the Vikings' nautical skills
   (D) To correct a common misconception about the European discovery of America

> What was the answer to "What? So what?" for this passage?

When You Are Done
Don't forget to check your answers in Chapter 9, page 254.

Specific Questions

Specific questions are about a detail or section of the passage. While the questions can be presented in a number of different ways, they boil down to questions about WHAT the author said, WHY the author said something, and Vocab-in-Context.

What?

- According to the passage/author
- The author states that
- Which of these questions is answered by the passage?
- The author implies in line X
- It can be inferred from paragraph X
- The most likely interpretation of X is

Why?

> Which answer is closest to what the author said overall?

- The author uses X to
- Why does the author say X?

Vocab-in-Context

- What does the passage mean by X?
- X probably represents/means
- Which word best replaces the word X without changing the meaning?
- As it is used in _____ , X most nearly means

Specific interpretation

> Why did the author write this passage? Think about the main idea.

- The author would be most likely to agree with which one of the following?
- Which one of the following questions is answered in the passage?

Once you have read and understood the question, go to the passage to find the answer. You should be able to find the answer quickly:

- Use your **paragraph labels** to go straight to the information you need.
- Use the **line or paragraph reference**, if there is one, but be careful. With a line reference ("In line 10…"), be sure to read the whole surrounding paragraph, not just the line. If the question says, "In line 10…," then you need to read lines 5 through 15 to actually find the answer.
- Use words that stand out in the question and passage. Names, places, and long words will be easy to find back in the passage. We call these **lead words** because they lead you back to the right place in the passage.

Once you're in the right area, answer the question in your own words. Then look at the choices and eliminate any that aren't like your answer or are not supported by the text of the passage.

For Vocab-in-Context questions, be sure to come up with your own word based on the surrounding sentences. It does not matter if you do not know the word being tested, as long as you can figure it out from context. Even if you do know the word, it may be used in an unusual way. So, always ignore the word and come up with your own before using Process of Elimination.

EXCEPT/LEAST/NOT Questions

These are other types of confusing questions. The test-writers are reversing what you need to look for, asking you which answer is false.

> All of the following can be inferred from the passage EXCEPT

Here again, writing things down is key. Before you go any further, cross out "EXCEPT" if you're working on paper. Now you have a much more positive question to answer. Of course, as always, you will go through all the choices, but for this type of question you will put a "T" or "F" next to the answers as you check them out. Let's say we've checked out these answers. Here's what a test booklet would look like:

T   (A)   Americans are patriotic.
T   (B)   Americans have great ingenuity.
F   (C)   Americans love war.
T   (D)   Americans do what they can to help one another.

And here's what your scratch paper would look like:

A   T

B   T

C   F

D   T

Which one stands out? The one with the "F." That's your answer. You made a confusing question much simpler than the test-writers wanted it to be. If you don't go through all the choices and mark them, you run the risk of accidentally picking one of the choices that you know is true because that's what you usually look for on reading comp questions.

You should skip an EXCEPT/LEAST/NOT question if you're on your last passage and there are other questions you can try instead—just fill in your letter-of-the-day on your answer sheet.

Practice Drill 3—Answering a Specific Question

Use the passage about Vikings that you just read and labeled. Use your paragraph labels and the lead words in each question to get to the part of the passage you need, and then put the answer in your own words before going back to the choices.

What's the lead word here? *Norway. Norway* should also be in one of your labels.

1. According to the passage, Bjarni Herjolfsson left Norway to

   (A) found a new colony
   (B) open trading lanes
   (C) visit a relative
   (D) map the North Sea

What's the lead word here? *Iceland.* Again, this should be in one of your labels. Go back and read this part.

2. Bjarni's reaction upon landing in Iceland can best be described as

   (A) disappointed
   (B) satisfied
   (C) amused
   (D) indifferent

Go back and read this part. Replace the words they've quoted with your own.

3. "The crew lost their bearings" probably means that

   (A) the ship was damaged beyond repair
   (B) the crew became disoriented
   (C) the crew decided to mutiny
   (D) the crew went insane

What's the lead word here? *Greenland.* Is it in one of your labels? What does that part of the passage say about Greenland? Paraphrase before looking at the answers!

4. It can be inferred from the passage that, prior to Bjarni Herjolfsson's voyage, Greenland

   (A) was covered in grass and shrubs
   (B) was overrun with Vikings
   (C) was rich in fish and game
   (D) was as far west as the Vikings had traveled

5. With which of the following statements about Viking explorers would the author most probably agree?

   (A) Greenland and Iceland were the Vikings' final discoveries.
   (B) Viking explorers were cruel and savage.
   (C) The Vikings' most startling discovery was an accidental one.
   (D) Bjarni Herjolfsson was the first settler of America.

When You Are Done
Don't forget to check your answers in Chapter 9, page 254.

STEP THREE: PROCESS OF ELIMINATION

Before you ever look at a choice, you've come up with your own answer, in your own words. What do you do next?

Well, you're looking for the closest answer to yours, but it's much easier to eliminate answers than to try to magically zoom in on the best one. Work through the answers using Process of Elimination. As soon as you eliminate an answer, cross off the letter in your test booklet or use the strikeout feature online so that you no longer think of that choice as a possibility.

How Do I Eliminate Choices?

On a General Question

Eliminate an answer that is:

- Too small. The passage may mention it, but it's only a detail—not a main idea.
- Not mentioned in the passage.
- In contradiction to the passage—it says the opposite of what you read.
- Too big. The answer tries to say that more was discussed than really was.
- Too extreme. An extreme answer is one that is too negative or too positive, or uses absolute words like *all*, *every*, *never*, or *always*. Eliminating extreme answers makes tone/attitude questions especially quick.
- Going against common sense. The passage is not likely to back up answers that just don't make sense at all.

On a Specific Question

Eliminate any choice that is:

- too extreme
- in contradiction to passage details
- not mentioned in the passage
- against common sense

If you look back at the questions you did for the Viking passage, you'll see that many of the wrong choices fit into the categories above.

On a Tone Question

Eliminate any choice that is:

- too extreme
- opposite in meaning
- against common sense: answers that make the author seem confused or uninterested (an ISEE author won't be either)

What Kinds of Answers Do I Keep?

Best answers are likely to be:

- paraphrases of the words in the passage
- traditional and conservative in their outlook
- moderate, using words like *may*, *can*, and *often*

When You've Got It Down to Two

If you've eliminated all but two answers, don't get stuck and waste time. Keep the main idea in the back of your mind and step back.

- Reread the question.
- Look at what makes the two answers different.
- Go back to the passage.
- Which answer is worse? Eliminate it.

REVIEW—THE READING PLAN

The Passages

After I read each paragraph, I _____ it.

After I read an entire passage, I ask myself _____? and _____?

The Questions

The four main types of general questions, and the questions I can ask myself to answer them, are:

_____   _____

_____   _____

_____   _____

_____   _____

To find the answer to a specific question, I can use three clues.

_____

_____

_____

If the question says "in line 22," where do I begin reading for the answer?

_____

_____

The Answers

On a general question, I eliminate answers that are:

_____

_____

_____

_____

_____

On a specific question, I eliminate answers that are:

_____

_____

_____

When I've got it down to two possible answers, I should:

_____

_____

_____

If you had any trouble with these questions, reread this section of the chapter before going further.

When You Are Done
Don't forget to check your answers in Chapter 9, page 255.

Practice Drill 4—All Reading Techniques—Middle & Upper Levels

Line

1   Immediately following the dramatic end of World War II came
2   a realization that the United States now had to turn its attention
3   inward. Years of fighting battles around the globe had drained the
4   country of important resources. Many industries (such as housing)
5   suffered, as both materials and workers were used elsewhere in the
6   war effort. Once the soldiers began returning, it became clear that
7   new jobs and new homes were among their biggest needs. The
8   homes needed to be affordable, since few people had the time or
9   ability to save much during the war.
10   It was in this situation that many house developers saw a
11   business opportunity. Amid such a pressing demand for new
12   homes, developer William Levitt realized the need for a new
13   method of building. He sought a way to build homes cheaper and
14   faster than ever before.
15   He wasn't the only developer to realize this, but he was one of
16   the best in making it happen. He applied the same ideas to homes
17   that Henry Ford had used 50 years earlier in making cars. Levitt
18   did not build a factory with an assembly line of fully formed
19   homes rolling out of some giant machine. Instead, he adapted
20   the assembly line formula into a system in which the workers,
21   rather than the product, moved for a streamlined, efficient building
22   process.
23   Previously, a developer who completed four homes a year had
24   been moving at a good pace. Levitt planned to do that many each
25   week, and succeeded. He created specialized teams that focused
26   on only one job each and moved up and down the streets of new
27   homes. Teams of foundation-builders, carpenters, roofers, and
28   painters worked faster by sticking to just one task as they moved,
29   factory-style, from house to house. The time and money saved
30   allowed Levitt to build cheap homes of good value.
31   With this new approach, Levitt oversaw the building of some of
32   the first towns that would eventually be called suburbs—planned
33   communities outside the city. Some critics blame developers like
34   Levitt for turning farmland into monotonous, characterless towns.
35   However, most agree that his contribution to the country following
36   a bitter war was mostly positive. He did vary the style of home
37   from street to street, and his work on simpler home features was
38   influenced by the work of architecture great Frank Lloyd Wright.
39   In the end, Levitt's success speaks for itself. After his first
40   success—building thousands of homes in Long Island, New

41   York—he went on to found several more "Levittowns" in
42   Pennsylvania, New Jersey, and elsewhere. Levitt gave home
43   buyers what they wanted: nice pieces of land with nice homes
44   on top. In a way, by creating houses that so many families
45   could afford, William Levitt made the American dream a more
46   affordable reality.

1. The primary purpose of the passage is to

   (A) discuss the final days of World War II
   (B) suggest that suburban housing is unaffordable
   (C) describe one person's contribution to an industry
   (D) prove that the economy changed after World War II

2. Which of the following statements about William Levitt is best supported by the passage?

   (A) He invented the word "suburb."
   (B) He was unconcerned with the appearance of the homes he built.
   (C) His homes were built in Ford-style factories.
   (D) His efficient methods helped make homes more affordable.

3. Which of the following best describes Levitt?

   (A) Courageous patriot
   (B) Strict businessman
   (C) Ground-breaking entrepreneur
   (D) Financial mastermind

4. It can be inferred from the passage that

   (A) Levitt was the only developer working in New York following World War II
   (B) Levitt and Henry Ford created homes the same way
   (C) other developers did not know how to use the concept of assembly line construction
   (D) Levitt built homes much faster than was customary before World War II

5. The passage mentions all of the following as reasons for the postwar housing demand EXCEPT the

   (A) destruction of American homes during the war
   (B) difficulty of saving money during the war
   (C) search for new jobs and new homes by returning soldiers
   (D) use of home-building materials elsewhere during the war

6. The passage suggests that a potential drawback to "assembly-line style" houses is that they can be

   (A) hard to sell
   (B) not very sturdy
   (C) similar-looking
   (D) horrible for the environment

When You Are Done
Don't forget to check your answers in Chapter 9, page 255.

Practice Drill 5—All Reading Techniques—Middle & Upper Levels

Line

1 Etymology, the study of words and word roots, may sound like
2 the kind of thing done by boring librarians in small, dusty rooms.
3 Yet etymologists actually have a uniquely interesting job. They
4 are, in many ways, just like archaeologists digging up the physical
5 history of people and events. The special aspect of etymology is
6 that it digs up history, so to speak, through the words and phrases
7 that are left behind.

8 The English language, in particular, is a great arena in which
9 to explore history through words. As a language, English has an
10 extraordinary number of words. This is in part due to its ability
11 to adapt foreign words so readily. For example, "English" words
12 such as *kindergarten* (from German), *croissant* (from French), and
13 *cheetah* (from Hindi) have become part of the language with little
14 or no change from their original sounds and spellings. So English
15 language etymologists have a vast world of words to explore.

16 Another enjoyable element of etymology for most word experts
17 is solving word mysteries. No, etymologists do not go around
18 solving murders, cloaked in intrigue like the great fictional
19 detective Sherlock Holmes. What these word experts solve are
20 mysteries surrounding the origin of some of our most common
21 words.

22 One of the biggest questions English language experts have
23 pursued is how English came to have the phrase *OK*. Though it
24 is one of the most commonly used slang expressions, its exact
25 beginning is a puzzle even to this day. Even its spelling is not
26 entirely consistent—unless you spell it *okay*, it's hard even to call
27 it a word.

28 Etymologists have been able to narrow *OK*'s origin down to
29 a likely, although not certain, source. It became widely used
30 around the time of Martin Van Buren's run for president in
31 1840. His nickname was Old Kinderhook. What troubles word
32 experts about this explanation is that the phrase appeared in some
33 newspapers before Van Buren became well known. As a result, it's
34 unlikely that Van Buren could be called its primary source. Like
35 bloodhounds following a faint scent, etymologists will doubtless
36 keep searching for the initial source. However, it is clear that
37 *OK*'s popularity and fame have exceeded those of the American
38 president to whom it has been most clearly linked.

1. It can be inferred from the second paragraph that English vocabulary

    (A) is easy to learn for speakers of other languages
    (B) can claim many sources
    (C) has a longer history than that of many other languages
    (D) affects American politics

2. The author mentions the words "kindergarten," "croissant," and "cheetah" most likely because

    (A) they are words with unknown origins
    (B) etymologists dispute words like these
    (C) they represent words that are similarly spelled and spoken in two languages
    (D) English speakers find them difficult to pronounce

3. According to the passage, etymologists are

    (A) investigators of word history
    (B) lovers of vocabulary words
    (C) scientists of the five senses
    (D) archaeologists of extinct languages

4. Which of the following best states the purpose of the fourth and fifth paragraphs?

    (A) To illustrate another non-English word
    (B) To define the phrase "OK"
    (C) To show an interesting aspect of etymology
    (D) To compare American phrases

5. The primary purpose of the passage is to

    (A) provide information about the English language
    (B) discuss enjoyable aspects of the study of words
    (C) show that language plays an important role in politics
    (D) describe the origin of the phrase "OK"

When You Are Done
Don't forget to check your answers in Chapter 9, page 256.

Practice Drill 6—All Reading Techniques—Middle & Upper Levels

Line

1   It is easy to lose patience with science today. The questions
2   are pressing: How dangerous is dioxin? What about low-level
3   radiation? When will that monstrous earthquake strike California?
4   And why can't we predict weather better? But the evidence is
5   often described as "inconclusive," forcing scientists to base their
6   points of view almost as much on intuition as on science.

7   When historians and philosophers of science listen to these
8   questions, some conclude that science may be incapable of
9   solving all these problems any time soon. Many questions seem
10   to defy the scientific method, an approach that works best when
11   it examines straightforward relationships: If something is done to
12   variable A, what happens to variable B? Such procedures can, of
13   course, be very difficult in their own ways, but for experiments,
14   they are effective.

15   With the aid of Newton's laws of gravitational attraction, for
16   instance, ground controllers can predict the path of a planetary
17   probe—or satellite—with incredible accuracy. They do this by
18   calculating the gravitational tugs from each of the passing planets
19   until the probe speeds beyond the edge of the solar system. A
20   much more difficult task is to calculate what happens when two or
21   three such tugs pull on the probe at the same time. The unknowns
22   can grow into riddles that are impossible to solve. Because of
23   the turbulent and changing state of the Earth's atmosphere, for
24   instance, scientists have struggled for centuries to predict the
25   weather with precision.

26   This spectrum of questions—from simple problems to those
27   impossibly complex—has resulted in nicknames for various fields
28   of study. "Hard" sciences, such as astronomy and chemistry, are
29   said to yield precise answers, whereas "soft" sciences, such as
30   sociology and economics, admit a great degree of uncertainty.

1. Which of the following best tells what this passage is about?

   (A) How the large variety of factors some scientists deal with makes absolute scientific accuracy impossible

   (B) How Newton solved the problem of accuracy and science

   (C) How "hard" science is more important than "soft" science

   (D) Why science now uses less and less conclusive evidence

2. According to the passage, it can be inferred that the scientific method would work best in which of the following situations?

   (A) Predicting public reactions to a set of policy decisions

   (B) Identifying the factors that will predict a California earthquake

   (C) Predicting the amount of corn that an acre will yield when a particular type of fertilizer is used

   (D) Calculating how much a cubic centimeter of water will weigh when cooled under controlled conditions

3. The author suggests that accurately predicting the path of a planetary probe is more difficult than

   (A) forecasting the weather

   (B) determining when an earthquake will occur

   (C) predicting economic behavior

   (D) determining the gravitational influence of one planet

4. According to the passage, "hard" science can be distinguished from "soft" science by which of the following characteristics?

   (A) Finding precise answers to its questions

   (B) Identifying important questions that need answers

   (C) Making significant contributions to human welfare

   (D) Creating debates about unresolved issues

5. The author implies that when confronted with complex questions, scientists base their opinions

   (A) on theoretical foundations

   (B) more on intuition than on science

   (C) on science and intuition, in varying degrees

   (D) on experimental procedures

When You Are Done
Don't forget to check your answers in Chapter 9, page 256.

Practice Drill 7—All Reading Techniques—Upper Level

Line

1   Bob Dylan was born on May 24, 1941 in Duluth, Minnesota, but
2   his name wasn't Dylan. He was born Robert Allen Zimmerman,
3   one of two sons born to Abraham and Betty Zimmerman.
4   Nineteen years later, he moved to New York City with his new
5   name and a passion to pursue his dream of becoming a music
6   legend.

7   Bob Dylan's career began like those of many musicians.
8   He began to play in New York City at various clubs around
9   Greenwich Village. He began to gain public recognition as a
10   singer/songwriter and was even reviewed by *The New York Times*
11   his first year in New York. He signed his first record deal with
12   Columbia Records a mere ten months after moving to New York.
13   From that point on, his career skyrocketed.

14   What is unique about Bob Dylan, given his huge success, is
15   his vocal quality. Dylan's singing voice was untrained and had
16   an unusual edge to it. Because of this, many of his most famous
17   early songs first reached the public through versions by other
18   performers who were more immediately palatable. Joan Baez was
19   one of these musicians who performed many of Dylan's early
20   songs. She furthered Dylan's already rising performance career
21   by inviting him onstage during her concerts, and many credit her
22   with bringing Dylan to his vast level of national and international
23   prominence.

24   In his career, which spans more than four decades, Dylan has
25   produced 500 songs and more than 40 albums. This king of songs
26   has thirteen songs on *Rolling Stone* magazine's Top 500 Songs
27   of All Time, including his most famous song, "Like a Rolling
28   Stone," which tops the list. In 2004, Bob Dylan was ranked second
29   in *Rolling Stone* magazine's 100 Greatest Artists of All Time,
30   surpassed only by the Beatles.

31   In a recent television interview, Bob Dylan was asked why he
32   became a musician. He replied that from a very early age, he
33   knew it was his destiny to become a music legend. Certainly, that
34   destiny has been realized!

1. Which of the following best states the main idea of the passage?

   (A) The beginning of Bob Dylan's music career is similar to the beginnings of the careers of most other musicians.

   (B) It is extremely important to follow your dreams.

   (C) Bob Dylan never really knew what he wanted to be in life.

   (D) Bob Dylan had great success despite his unusual style of singing.

2. The word "prominence" at the end of the third paragraph most nearly means

   (A) perception

   (B) status

   (C) obviousness

   (D) protrusion

3. The passage most strongly supports which of the following statements about Joan Baez?

   (A) She was jealous of Bob Dylan's superior vocal training.

   (B) She grew up in Minnesota.

   (C) She has performed more of Bob Dylan's songs than of her own.

   (D) She helped Bob Dylan to become a music legend.

4. The phrase "king of songs" near the beginning of the fourth paragraph refers to

   (A) Bob Dylan's prolific nature as a singer/songwriter

   (B) Bob Dylan's ownership of *Rolling Stone* magazine

   (C) how most musicians regarded Bob Dylan as a king

   (D) Bob Dylan's perception of himself

5. Which of the following is best supported by the passage?

   (A) Bob Dylan has two brothers.

   (B) Bob Dylan was reviewed by Columbia Records his first year in New York.

   (C) "Like a Rolling Stone" is considered by some to be the best song of all time.

   (D) Without Joan Baez, Bob Dylan would never have succeeded.

When You Are Done
Don't forget to check your answers in Chapter 9, page 256.

Chapter 8
ISEE Writing

HOW IS THE ESSAY USED?

While the essay is not graded and does not affect your score, a copy is sent to the schools to which you apply. For this reason, you want to take the essay seriously and use it to show yourself to be organized and thoughtful.

LOWER, MIDDLE, & UPPER LEVELS

The Lower, Middle, and Upper Level tests ask you to "write an essay" on an assigned prompt. You will have close to two pages on which to write and 30 minutes to complete your essay.

Primary Levels

The Primary 2 ISEE and Primary 3 ISEE each have an untimed writing sample with a picture prompt. The directions will tell you to "write a story." The Primary 4 ISEE has an untimed writing sample with a written prompt. The Primary Level writing samples are typed. You will be able to cut, copy, paste, indent, undo, redo, and change the font size.

Here are sample prompts.

Primary 2 & 3

> **Look at the picture. Write a story about what you see in the picture. Type your story in the box below.**

Primary 4

Identify a person you admire or respect. Explain why you admire or respect that person. Then describe one thing you would do to show this person your admiration or respect.

Lower Level

Who is your favorite teacher? Why have you chosen this person?

Middle Level

If you could solve one problem in the world today, what would you choose and how would you solve the problem?

Upper Level

Name someone you consider to be a success, and describe what it is about that person that makes the person successful.

PLANNING AND WRITING YOUR ESSAY

When you read your prompt, do not start writing immediately! It is important that you spend a few minutes thinking about what you want to say and how you will organize your thoughts. A planned essay reads much better than a rambling, free-association essay. Also, the time you spend organizing your thoughts will enable you to write your essay more quickly once you get started. You just need to follow your outline and express the ideas you have already developed.

Your essay should be a traditional essay with an introduction, body paragraphs, and a conclusion. Your introduction will summarize the topic and explain your position, and your body paragraphs will include examples or reasons for your position. Thus, you want to spend your planning time deciding how you want to answer the prompt and what examples or reasons you will use to support your point of view. If you are used to providing three examples in essays at school, there is no need for that here. You don't have the space or the time. Rather, having one or two well-developed examples or reasons will be fine.

Grammar Boost
If you need a grammar boost, check out *Grammar Smart, 4th Edition.*

Be sure to avoid spelling, grammar, and punctuation errors. It is easier to avoid these errors if you have planned your essay in advance. Also, write neatly; again, this is easier if you plan your essay before you write it. Be sure to clearly indent each new paragraph as well. It is a good idea to leave yourself a bit of time at the end to review what you have written, so you can make sure you've written your best possible essay.

You should write one or two practice essays and show them to a parent, teacher, or other adult who can give you feedback. Tell that person that your goal is to provide an organized and thoughtful reply to the prompt, with a minimum of spelling and grammar errors.

On scrap paper, write an essay using the prompts on pages 227 and 229. If you will be testing online rather than on paper, type your essay or writing sample on a computer. Older students may wish to write a second practice essay after getting feedback.

Are you ready for another prompt?

Lower Level

Describe something you wish you could change about the city or town in which you live.

Middle Level

If you could spend one week anywhere in the world, where would you go? What would you do there?

Upper Level

Describe a book or work of art that had an effect on you. What about it affected you?

Chapter 9
ISEE Practice
Drills: Answers and
Explanations

ISEE Math

QUANTITATIVE REASONING QUESTION TYPES

WORD PROBLEMS

Practice Drill 1—Word Problems (Lower, Middle, & Upper Levels)

1. **B** Set up a proportion: $\dfrac{\text{ounces}}{\text{quarts}} = \dfrac{32}{1} = \dfrac{128}{x}$. Then cross-multiply to get $32(x) = 128$. Divide both sides by 32, and $x = 4$. The correct answer is (B).

2. **C** Start with the given age: Rufus's. If Rufus is 11, then find Fiona's age. *Fiona is twice as old as Rufus* translates to Fiona = 2(Rufus) or $F = 2(11)$, so Fiona is 22. Next find Betty's age. *Betty is twice as old as Fiona* translates to Betty = 2(Fiona) or $B = 2(22)$. Therefore, Betty is 44. The correct answer is (C).

3. **B** Translate the parts of the question. *This year's sales* = 1,250, *how many times greater than* means to divide, and *last year's sales* = 250. Thus, $\dfrac{1,250}{250} = 5$. The correct answer is (B).

4. **A** Translate the first part of the problem: *of* means to multiply and *the total students* = 500. So, the number of freshman is $\dfrac{2}{5}(500) = \dfrac{2 \times 500}{5} = \dfrac{1,000}{5} = 200$. Now, translate the second part of the problem: *of* means to multiply and *all the freshmen* = 200. Therefore, the number of freshmen girls is $\dfrac{3}{5}(200) = \dfrac{3 \times 200}{5} = \dfrac{600}{5} = 120$. The correct answer is (A).

QUANTITATIVE COMPARISON

Practice Drill 2—Quant Comp (Middle & Upper Levels)

1. **C** Both columns have actual values, so eliminate answer choice D, and then look at Column B. $17 \times 2 + 17$ is the same as $17 + 17 + 17$, or 17×3. Thus, the two columns are equal. The correct answer is (C).

2. **A** Both columns have actual values, so eliminate (D), and then get a common denominator to compare the fractions. You can even use the Bowtie method! Multiply the numerator in Column A by 8 (the denominator in Column B) to get $1 \times 8 = 8$. Multiply the numerator in Column B by 2 (the denominator in Column A) to get $3 \times 2 = 6$. The common denominator is 16 (2×8), but that doesn't actually matter since you only need to compare the numerators. 8 is bigger than 6, so Column A is greater, and the correct answer is (A).

3. **B** There are variables in the columns, so plug in twice. For instance, try $b = 10$. $10 + 80 = 90$, and $10 + 82 = 92$. In this case, column B is greater, so eliminate (A) and (C). Try another number, perhaps a negative number: –10. Perform the necessary calculations: $-10 + 80 = 70$ and $-10 + 82 = 72$. Column B is still greater, so the correct answer is (B).

4. **B** Plug in a value here. Say that Maitri is 60 inches tall, making Robbie 58 inches tall since *Robbie is two inches shorter than Maitri*. The question stem also states that *Jasper is four inches taller than Maitri*, so Jasper must be 64 inches tall. This makes Jasper taller than Robbie, so column B is greater. The correct answer is (B).

5. **C** Both columns have actual values, so first eliminate (D). When dealing with exponents, write it out! Column A can be rewritten as $16 \times 16 \times 16$. Column B can be rewritten as $4 \times 4 \times 4 \times 4 \times 4 \times 4$. Notice that 16 is the same as 4×4. Therefore, column A can also be written as $(4 \times 4) \times (4 \times 4) \times (4 \times 4)$. Since each column contains 6 fours, the two columns are equal. The correct answer is (C).

6. **D** The information given does not indicate the direction or orientation of either girl's house. However, the information does state that *Karina lives two miles from school*, so column A is 2. However, Jennifer could live another two miles past Karina's house, four miles in the other direction from the school (making the two houses 6 miles apart), or she could even live 4 miles north or south of the school (making the distance between their houses yet another value). Since there is no way to determine the distance between their houses without more information, the solution cannot be determined. The correct answer is (D).

NUMBERS & OPERATIONS

Practice Drill 3—Numbers & Operations (Middle & Upper Levels)

1. **C** List all the factors of 16: 1 and 16, 2 and 8, 4 and 4. Since 4 and 4 are not distinct from each other, count 4 only once. There are 5 distinct factors of 16. The correct answer is (C).

2. **D** List the factors of 12: 1 and 12, 2 and 6, 3 and 4. All of these are factors of 48. The correct answer is (D).

3. **C** A multiple of a number is that number multiplied by another number. Since $7 \times 13 = 91$, 91 is a multiple of 7. The correct answer is (C).

4. **A** A multiple of a number is that number multiplied by another number. 4 is a factor of 8, not a multiple of 8. The correct answer is (A).

5. **D** Guesstimate and let the answer choices help here. If the final bill after 25% tip is $50, $12.50 and $25 are way too small. The tip would be either the same amount as or more than the cost! Eliminate (A) and (B). Try one of the two remaining answer choices. $40 looks easiest to work with, so let's start there. If the cost is $40, 25% of 40 is calculated by multiplying $\frac{25}{100}(40) = 10$. $40 + $10 = $50, so that's our answer. The correct answer is (D).

6. **B** The question asks what is *NOT* a divisor of 1,026. Since 1,026 is even, eliminate (A). Do division or use rules of divisibility to test the other answer choices. $1 + 0 + 2 + 6 = 9$, so 1,026 is divisible by both 3 (because 9 is a multiple of 3) and 9 (because 9 is a multiple of 9). Since 1,026 is divisible by

both 2 and 3, it is divisible by 6. 26 is not divisible by 4, so 1,026 is not divisible by 4. The correct answer is (B).

7. **B** Use the answer choices to help here. Since the three integers are odd, the square of the smallest integer will also be odd. Eliminate (C) because 36 is even. If the sum of the three is 21, the smallest integer can't be 7 because 7 + 7 + 7 = 21. Eliminate (D) because 49 is the square of 7. Try one of the remaining two. Let's look at (B): The square root of 25 is 5, and 5 + 7 + 9 = 21, so that works.

8. **D** The question states that $\frac{1}{3}$ of the cars are silver and that there are 24 silver cars. Therefore, 24 × 3 equals the total number of cars, or 72. The correct answer is (D).

9. **C** To find the total amount of time Jake stands over the course of all four days, add $\frac{5}{8}$ for every day he works. $\frac{5}{8} + \frac{5}{8} + \frac{5}{8} + \frac{5}{8} = \frac{20}{8}$. This reduces to $\frac{10}{4}$, $\frac{5}{2}$, or 2.5. The correct answer is (C).

10. **A** Remember your order of operations and work left to right. Since the equation contains only addition and subtraction, find a common denominator. One possible common denominator of 2, 3, and 4 is 12, so $\frac{1}{2} + \frac{1}{3} + \frac{1}{4} - \frac{1}{2} + \frac{2}{3} + \frac{3}{4} = \frac{6}{12} + \frac{4}{12} + \frac{3}{12} - \frac{6}{12} + \frac{8}{12} + \frac{9}{12}$. Now, add all the numerators: 6 + 4 + 3 − 6 + 8 + 9 = 24, and $\frac{24}{12}$ = 2. The correct answer is (A).

11. **C** Guesstimate here. 75% is more than half, and 49.95 is essentially 50. Eliminate (A) and (B) since those are both less than half. $\frac{40}{50}$ is $\frac{4}{5}$, which is larger than $\frac{3}{4}$, so eliminate (D). The correct answer is (C).

12. **C** When multiplying by a multiple of 10, move the decimal to the right by however many 0s there are. Since this question contains multiplying by 10,000, move the decimal to the right four places. The correct answer is (C).

13. **C** Find the total cost in each of the columns. Column A contains the statement *The total cost of 3 plants that cost $4 each*, so 3($4) = $12. Column B contains the statement *The total cost of 4 plants that cost $3 each*, so 4($3) = $12. The columns are equal, so the correct answer is (C).

14. **D** You are given the statement The *product of 3 integers is 48*. There are many ways to reach a product of 48. For instance, 2 × 3 × 8 = 48. Of the three integers, the smallest is 2, so column A is 2. Compared to column B, column A is greater. Eliminate (B) and (C). However, this is not the only way to multiply integers to get a product of 48. For example, 1 × 2 × 24 = 48. In this case, the smallest of the three integers is 1, which means the two columns are equal. Since column A is not always greater nor are the two columns always equal, the correct answer is (D).

15. **A** Use correct PEMDAS to evaluate the expression in column A. First, work within the parentheses: (7 − 4) × 3 − 3 = (3) × 3 − 3. There are no exponents, so the next step is to do the multiplication and division from left to right: (3) × 3 − 3 = 9 − 3. Finally, add and subtract from left to right: 9 − 3 = 6. Since 6 is greater than 0, column A is greater. The correct answer is (A).

16. **B** Work through the information provided to find the value of column A. If the shoes are $100 and *the price is increased by 20%*, find 20% of $100 and add that result to the total. $\frac{20}{100}$(100) reduces to

$\frac{1}{5}(100) = \frac{100}{5} = 20$. The price increased $20, so $100 + $20 = $120. The shoes are now $120. However, *the price was reduced by 20%*. Find 20% of 120 and subtract that result from the total. $\frac{20}{100}(120)$ reduces to $\frac{1}{5}(120) = \frac{120}{5} = 24$. The price decreased $24, so $120 − $24 = $96. The final price of the shoes is $96, so column A is $96. Since column B is $100, it is greater. The correct answer is (B).

17. **B** Remember, a negative sign will stay negative with an odd exponent. Both columns contain negative numbers and odd exponents, so both columns will remain negative. With negative numbers, the value that is *closer to* zero will be the greater value (e.g., −1 > −4). When working with fractions, remember that as the denominator gets larger, the fraction will get smaller (e.g., $\frac{1}{2} > \frac{1}{4}$). However, with negative fractions, the one that is "less negative" will be greater (e.g., $-\frac{1}{4} > -\frac{1}{2}$). In column B, the exponent is greater, so the denominator in column B will be larger and thus the value of the fraction will be smaller. Since the fraction in column B will be less negative than the fraction in column A, the value in column B is greater. The correct answer is (B).

18. **A** Both fractions are positive and both are being raised to a positive, even power. However, be careful when working with fractions less than 1. When those numbers are raised to a positive power, they become smaller since the denominator increases. Remember, as the denominator gets larger, the fraction will get smaller (e.g., $\frac{1}{2} > \frac{1}{4}$). Thus, the denominator in column A (6^4) will be smaller than the denominator in column B (6^6), which means the value in column A will be greater. The correct answer is (A).

19. **A** The negative sign in both columns will become positive since both columns are being raised to an even power. With fractions less than 1, the larger the denominator, the smaller the fraction. Since the denominator in column A (6^2) will be smaller than the denominator in column B (6^4), the value in column A will be greater. The correct answer is (A).

20. **B** When multiplying fractions, multiply the numerators across and the denominators across. Therefore, the value of column A is $\frac{3}{4} \times \frac{3}{4} = \frac{3 \times 3}{4 \times 4} = \frac{9}{16}$. When adding fractions with a common denominator, add the numerators. Thus, the value of column B is $\frac{3}{4} + \frac{3}{4} = \frac{3+3}{4} = \frac{6}{4} = 1\frac{1}{2}$. Column B is greater. The correct answer is (B).

Practice Drill 4—Numbers & Operations (Upper Level)

1. **B** If the question asks *how many times as great*, that translates to division. Divide the profit in 2023 by the profit in 2013. $\frac{\$570,000}{\$95,000} = 6$ The correct answer is (B).

2. **A** Since 4 is not a prime number and no multiple of 4 will be prime either, there will not be any numbers in common. Therefore, the correct answer is (A).

3. **B** First, list all the factors of 24: 1 and 24, 2 and 12, 3 and 8, 4 and 6. Next, list all the factors of 81: 1 and 81, 3 and 27, 9 and 9. The only factors that 24 and 81 have in common are 1 and 3, so there are two factors in common. The correct answer is (B).

4. **B** List all the numbers from 10 to 150, inclusive, that are multiples of 3 and 5: 15, 30, 45, 60, 75, 90, 105, 120, 135, and 150. Inclusive means to include the ends of the range, so 150 should be included in this list. There are 10 numbers listed, so the correct answer is (B).

5. **B** When multiplying by the same base, add the exponents together. $4 + 4 + 4 = 12$, so the answer should be 3^{12}. The correct answer is (B).

6. **C** Add all the roses up to find that 30 yellow roses + 50 red roses + 40 white roses = 120 total roses. The roses that are not yellow are the 50 red and 40 white, which makes 90. $\frac{90}{120} = \frac{3}{4}$ or 75%. The correct answer is (C).

7. **C** To find the percent difference, find the difference and divide by the original value. The difference in price is \$15, and the original value is \$40, since \$55 is a markup, which is approximately 38%. The correct answer is (C).

8. **B** To find the percent change, find the difference in points and divide that by the original value, 25. $25 - 15 = 10$. Next, divide 10 by 25, which is $\frac{2}{5}$, or 0.4, which equals 40%. The correct answer is (B).

9. **B** If the team adds a fourth person and splits the dues evenly, $\frac{\$24}{4}$ = \$6 per person. The correct answer is (B).

10. **C** If 14 of the 26 students have brown eyes, then 12 students have another eye color. Thus, the ratio of students with brown eyes to students with another eye color is 14 to 12, which, when reduced, is 7 to 6. The correct answer is (C).

11. **B** When the question asks about ratios, make a Ratio Box. Place the given information into a Ratio Box:

	RUN	SWIM	TOTAL
Ratio	3	2	
Multiplier			
Actual			25

Add the two ratio portions to find the ratio total, which is 5. Next determine what times 5 equals 25, which is 5. Finally, multiply 2 by 5 to find the actual number of miles Casper swam, which is 10. The correct answer is (B).

12. **C** First, simplify the first expression: $(3xy)^3 = 3^3x^3y^3 = 27x^3y^3$. While comparing it to the other expression, $3x^2y^5$, you can work with one aspect of the expression at a time. Start with the coefficients: the greatest common factor of 3 and 27 is 3. Eliminate (A) and (D) since neither contains 3. Both of

the remaining answers contain x^2, so compare y in the two expressions. One has $y^3 = y \times y \times y$ and the other has $y^5 = y \times y \times y \times y \times y$. The greatest common factor is y^3 since both expressions have at least 3 ys. Eliminate (B). The correct answer is (C).

13. **A** Evaluate the expressions, using order of operations. Column A is $\sqrt{25 - 9} = \sqrt{16} = 4$, and column B is $\sqrt{25} - \sqrt{9} = 5 - 3 = 2$. Therefore, column A is greater. The correct answer is (A).

14. **C** Remember, with exponents, you can always write it out. However, this is a common trick on the ISEE. Another way to evaluate these expressions is to rewrite them with the same base. In column B, 64 is the same as 4^3, so the whole expression can be rewritten as $(4^3)^4$. Using the exponent rules (MADSPM), you can further simplify: $\left(4^3\right)^4 = 4^{3 \times 4} = 4^{12}$. Since the value in column B is the same as the value of column A, the correct answer is (C).

15. **A** First, list the nonnegative even integers less than 10. Don't forget about zero! The list should contain 0, 2, 4, 6, and 8. Therefore, column A is 5. Since this is greater than the value of column B, the correct answer is (A).

ALGEBRAIC CONCEPTS

Practice Drill 5—Algebraic Concepts (Middle & Upper Levels)

1. **C** First, distribute 3 on the right-hand side of the equation. Since $3(3x - 6) = 9x - 18$, $18 = 9x - 18$. Add 18 to both sides to isolate x: $36 = 9x$. Divide both sides by 9 to find that $x = 4$. Not so fast! Remember the question asks for $x + 6$, so $4 + 6 = 10$. The correct answer is (C).

2. **D** First, simplify the expression in column A. Distribute the 30 in the expression $30(1 - 2n)$ to get $30 - 60n$. The value of each column varies depending on the value of n, so test some values to see if there's a consistent relationship—this is a strategy that will be discussed in more detail later in this chapter. If $n = 2$, then column A, $30 - 60(2) = -90$. In column B, $30 - 2(2) = 26$. Column B is greater, so eliminate (A) and (C). But what if $n = -3$? Column A will now read $30 - 60(-3) = 210$, and column B will read $30 - 2(-3) = 36$. Column A is greater in this case. Since neither column is always greater, the correct answer is (D).

3. **C** First, simplify column A: $(x + y)(x - y)$ can be FOILed out to be $x^2 + xy - xy - y^2$. The two middle values cancel each other out, so the expression reads $x^2 - y^2$, which is the same as the expression in column B. Since the two columns are equal, the correct answer is (C). Note that you can also plug in values for x and y and solve the problem this way. You should try more than one set of numbers to check for other possible outcomes.

4. **D** While there are some constraints on the values of a and b (namely that they have to add up to 5), there are an infinite number of values that a and b could each be. If a were 2, b would be 3. But if a were 57, b would be –52. Since neither column is always greater, the correct answer is (D).

5. **C** The columns will always be equal because the negative signs will always cancel out and the same numbers are being multiplied in each column, so the result will not vary. The correct answer is (C).

Practice Drill 6—Algebraic Concepts (Upper Level)

1. **B** Let the answer choices help here. Remember that exponents mean multiplying a number by itself, so the numbers on the right side of the equation are going to have the same factors as x. Since 4 and 8 are not multiples of 3, eliminate (C). 1 is too small, since 1 to any power is 1 and the right side of the equation has to be at least 8. Eliminate (A). Try one of the remaining two answer choices. Smaller numbers are easier to use with exponents, so try (B). $2^4 = 2 \times 2 \times 2 \times 2 = 16$ and $4(2) + 8 = 16$, so that works. The correct answer is (B).

2. **C** Use translation! "Percent" translates to ÷ 100, "of" translates into multiplication, and a "what" is an unknown value. So $\frac{25}{100} \times \frac{40}{100} \times x = 36$. Reduce the fractions to get $\frac{1}{4} \times \frac{2}{5} \times x = 36$, then $\frac{1}{10} \times x = 36$. Multiply both sides by 10 to get $x = 360$. You might also notice that 25% is $\frac{1}{4}$, and $\frac{1}{4}$ of 40% would be 10%, and taking 10% of a number just moves the decimal point one place to the left.

3. **D** Use MADSPM to simplify the exponents in the equations first. When raising a power to a power, multiply the exponents together. For the first equation, $\left(x^3\right)^3 = x^{3\times3} = x^9$, so $a = 9$. When dividing by the same base, subtract the exponents. For the second equation, $\frac{y^{10}}{y^2} = y^{10-2} = y^8$, so $b = 8$. The question asks to find $a \times b$, so $9 \times 8 = 72$. The correct answer is (D).

4. **C** Remember, if you see exponents, you can always write it out! You could also plug in since there are variables in the columns. However, another way to find the values of the two columns is to use the exponent rules (MADSPM). For column A, $\frac{x^2 x^5}{x^4} = \frac{x^{2+5}}{x^4} = \frac{x^7}{x^4} = x^{7-4} = x^3$. Column B is also x^3. Since the two columns are equal, the correct answer is (C).

STRATEGY: PLUGGING IN

Practice Drill 7—Plugging In (Middle & Upper Levels)

1. **B** This is a Plugging In question because there are variables in the choices and the question stem contains the phrase *in terms of*. Plug in a value, work through the problem to find a target answer, and then check each of the choices to see which yields the target answer. For instance, plug in $x = \$3$. The question asks for the total amount of money donated, so $3 \times 200 = 600$. \$600 is the target answer. Now, plug 3 into the choices for x to see which choice matches your target answer (600). Eliminate (A) because $\frac{3}{200}$ is way too small. Choice (B) works because $200(3) = 600$. Eliminate (C) because $\frac{200}{3}$ is too small. Eliminate (D) because $200 + 3$ or $203 \neq 600$. The correct answer is (B).

2. **D** This is a Plugging In question because there are variables in the choices. Plug in a value, work through the problem to find a target answer, and then check each of the choices to see which yields the target answer. For instance, plug in 6 for d dollars. If 10 magazines cost $6, then $3 would buy 5 magazines—you spend half as much money, so you can get only half as many magazines. So 5 is the target answer. Now, plug 6 into the choices to see which answer yields 5, the target answer. Eliminate (A) because $\frac{3 \times 6}{10} = \frac{18}{10} = 1.8$ does not equal 5. Eliminate (B) because 30(6) is way too large. Choice (C) is a fraction, $\frac{6}{30} = \frac{1}{5}$, so it will not equal 5. Choice (D) works, as $\frac{30}{6} = 5$, so keep this choice. The correct answer is (D).

3. **C** This is a Plugging In question because there are variables in the choices and the question stem contains the phrase *in terms of*. Plug in a value, work through the problem to find a target answer, and then check each of the choices to see which yields the target answer. *The zoo has four times as many monkeys as lions*, so, for instance, plug in 40 for the monkeys, which translates to 4 × lions = 40, so there are 10 lions. *There are four more lions than zebras*, which means that 10 − 4 = 6 zebras, so $z = 6$. The question asks *how many monkeys are there in the zoo*, so the target answer is 40. Now, plug 6 into the choices for z to see which choice matches your target answer (40). Eliminate (A) because 4 × 6 = 24 is not equal to 40. Eliminate (B) because 6 + 4 = 10 is still too small. Since 4(6) + 16 = 40, keep (C). Remember to try all four choices when plugging in, so check (D) as well. 4(6) + 4 = 28, which is too small, so eliminate (D). The correct answer is (C).

4 **C** In this question, J is an odd integer, so plug in an odd integer for J. Since this is a *must be* question, see if there is a number that would make the answer untrue. Plug in 1 for J to make (A) untrue, since $\frac{1}{3}$ is not greater than 1. This number for J will also eliminate (B) since 1 − 2 = −1, which is not a positive integer. Choice (C) is true since 2 × 1 = 2, which is an even integer. Eliminate (D) since J could be negative. For example, if $J = -3$, −3 is not greater than 0. Check that value for (C) to be sure it always works. Again, if $J = -3$, then 2 × −3 = −6, which is still an even integer. Since it always works, the correct answer is (C).

5. **C** When there are percents or fractions without a starting or ending value in the question stem, feel free to use Plugging In. For instance, plug in $100 for the starting price of the suit. It is *reduced by 20%*, so 20% of $100 is equal to $\frac{1}{5}(100) = \frac{100}{5} = 20$. That is the amount the suit is reduced. Subtract that from $100 to find the resulting price: $100 − $20 = $80. The suit is then *reduced by 10%*, so 10% of $80 is $\frac{10}{100}(80) = \frac{1}{10}(80) = \frac{80}{10} = 8$. Subtract this from $80 to find the final price of the suit: $80 − $8 = $72. The final price is $72. The *final price is what percent off of the original* is another way of asking the *final price is what percent less than the original*. So, use the percent change

formula: % change $= \dfrac{\text{difference}}{\text{original}} \times 100$. The difference is $\$100 - \$72 = 28$. The original price was $\$100$. Therefore, $\dfrac{28}{100}(100) = 28$. The correct answer is (C).

6. **C** Try plugging in values that satisfy the question stem and eliminate choices. It may be necessary to plug in twice on *must be true* or *always true* questions. If m is an even number, let $m = 2$, and let $n = 3$ since it must be an odd integer. If p is the product of m and n, then $p = (2)(3) = 6$. Now check the choices. Eliminate (A) because p is not a fraction. Eliminate (B) as well since p is not an odd integer. Keep (C) because 6 is divisible by 2. Finally, keep (D) because 6 is greater than zero. Plug in again to compare the remaining choices. Perhaps keep one number the same, so $n = 3$, but make $m = -2$ instead of 2. Now $p = (-2)(3) = -6$. Choice (C) still works since -6 is divisible by 2, but (D) no longer works since p is less than zero. Since it is always true, the correct answer is (C).

More Practice: Upper Level

7. **B** Since there are variables in the choices, plug in a value for p, paying attention to the restrictions in the question. If p is an odd integer, make sure to plug in an odd integer, for instance $p = 3$. Now, test the choices to see which one can be eliminated. Cross off (A) because $(3)^2 + 3 = 9 + 3 = 12$, which is not odd. Choice (B) works since $2(3) + 1 = 6 + 1 = 7$, which is odd. Choice (C) works since $\dfrac{3}{3} = 1$. Choice (D) does not work since $3 - 3 = 0$. Remember 0 is even, not odd. Plug in a second time for the remaining choices. Try $p = 5$. Choice (B) still works because $2(5) + 1 = 10 + 1 = 11$, but eliminate (C) because $\dfrac{5}{3}$ is no longer an integer. The correct answer is (B).

8. **B** The wording on this problem is tricky: it asks for which CANNOT be true, so try to find examples that COULD be true to eliminate choices. Pay attention to the restrictions in the problem, and plug in two positive even integers: say 4 and 6. Thus, $4 + 6 = 10 = m$. Next, eliminate choices that WORK. Choice (A) does not work since 10 is greater than 5. Keep it. Choice (B) does not work because $3(10) = 30$, which is even, not odd. Keep it. Eliminate (C) because $m = 10$, which is even, so it works. Eliminate (D) as well because 10^3 ends in a zero, which is also even, so this statement works. Now, plug in a second time for the remaining choices. Try new numbers, and remember that the numbers do not have to be distinct from one another. Try plugging in 2 for both positive even integers. Thus, $2 + 2 = 4 = m$. Check the remaining answers and eliminate the choices that WORK. For (A), 4 is less than 5. That works, so eliminate (A). For (B), $3(4) = 12$, which does not work since it's even, so keep it. The only choice left is (B), which is the correct answer.

9. **D** This is a Plugging In question because there are variables in the choices. Plug in a value, work through the problem to find a target answer, and then check each of the choices to see which yields the target answer. For instance, plug in 20 for Antonia. Since Antonia has *twice as many baseball cards as Krissi*, Krissi has $\dfrac{1}{2}$ the number of cards that Antonia has. Therefore, Krissi must have 10 cards, and $k = 10$. Krissi has *one-third as many baseball cards as Ian*, so Ian has 3 times as many as Krissi has: $10 \times 3 = 30$, or 30 cards. Together, Antonia and Ian have $20 + 30 = 50$, so 50 is the

target answer. Now, plug in 10 for k to find which choice yields 50, your target answer. Eliminate (A) because $\frac{3 \times 10}{2} = \frac{30}{2} = 15$, not 50. Eliminate (B) because $\frac{6 \times 10}{2} = \frac{60}{2} = 30$ is still too small. Choice (C) is still too small, as $\frac{8 \times 10}{2} = \frac{80}{2} = 40$. Choice (D) works because $\frac{10 \times 10}{2} = \frac{100}{2} = 50$. The correct answer is (D).

10. **D** This is a Plugging In question because there are variables in the choices. Plug in a value, work through the problem to find a target answer, and then check each of the choices to see which yields the target answer. Let $b = 4$ and $a = 3$. Finding the *product* means multiply, so $\frac{1}{2}(4) \times 3^2 = 2 \times 9 = 18$. The target answer is 18. Now, plug in your values for b and a into the choices to find the choice that equals your target answer (18). Eliminate (A) since $(3 \times 4)^2 = (12)^2 = 144$, which is too big. Eliminate (B) since $\frac{3^2}{4} = \frac{9}{4}$ and is not equal to 18. Also eliminate (C) since $2(3) \times \frac{1}{2}(4) = 6 \times 2 = 12$, which does not equal 18. Choice (D) works: $\frac{3^2 \times 4}{2} = \frac{9 \times 4}{2} = \frac{36}{2} = 18$. Keep it. The correct answer is (D).

11. **B** Since the question involves averages, use $T = AN$. However, save yourself some time by reading carefully! Notice that the classes have an equal number of students donating money. Because of this, simply plug in values for the averages since it doesn't matter how many actual students are donating money from each class. You only need values for the average of each class, so start there. Those two averages will become the numbers for your *Total* in the next part of the problem. For instance, plug in $3 as the average, y, for Mr. Greenwood's class, and $5 for z, the average for Ms. Norris's class. Add these two numbers to find the total amount of money donated $(3 + 5 = 8)$, and put 8 in the *Total* spot. There are 2 classes donating money, so the *Number of items* is 2. Find the average by dividing: $\frac{8}{2} = 4$. The target answer is 4. Now, plug in 3 for y and 5 for z to find which choice yields 4, the target answer. Eliminate (A) because $\frac{5}{3} \neq 4$. Choice (B) works because $\frac{3+5}{2} = \frac{8}{2} = 4$. Eliminate (C) because $3 + 5 \neq 4$. Finally, eliminate (D) because $2(3 + 5) = 2(8) = 16$, which is way too large. The correct answer is (B).

12. **D** Since there are variables in the columns, plug in. First, simplify column A: $7(x - 3) = 7x - 21$. Now, plug in a value for x. For instance, let $x = 3$. Plug in 3 to column A to find that $7(3) - 21 = 21 - 21 = 0$. Now, do the same for column B: $21 - 7(3) = 21 - 21 = 0$. The columns are equal, so eliminate (A) and (B). Remember, plug in a second time to see if a different outcome is possible. This time let $x = 2$. In column A, the expression will read $7(2) - 21$, which simplifies to $14 - 21 = -7$. In column B, the expression will read $21 - 7(2)$, which simplifies to $21 - 14 = 7$. Now column B is greater. Since the columns are not always equal nor is column B always greater, the correct answer is (D).

13. **D** Since there are variables in the columns, plug in values for the variables and evaluate the expressions. For instance, let $x = 3$ and $y = 5$ since x and y must be positive numbers. Column A is

$\dfrac{3 \times 5}{2} = \dfrac{15}{2} = 7.5$, whereas column B is $\sqrt{3 \times 5} = \sqrt{15}$, which is a little bit less than 4 since $\sqrt{16} = 4$. Since column A is greater, eliminate (B) and (C). Now, plug in a second time to see if a different outcome is possible. Let $x = 1$ and $y = 1$. Column A is $\dfrac{1 \times 1}{2} = \dfrac{1}{2}$, and column B is $\sqrt{1 \times 1} = \sqrt{1} = 1$. This time, column B is greater. Since neither column is always greater, the correct answer is (D).

STRATEGY: PLUGGING IN THE ANSWERS (PITA)

Practice Drill 8—Plugging In the Answers (Middle & Upper Levels)

1. **B** The question is asking for a specific value and there are real numbers in the choices, so use PITA to solve. Tina can read 60 pages per hour, which is 60 pages in 60 minutes, and Nick can read 45 pages in 60 minutes. Combined, they can read 105 pages (60 + 45) in 60 minutes. Now, start with one of the middle choices to see which answer will yield a total of 210 pages. Try (B): if they read for 120 minutes, they will read double the amount they did in 60 minutes. That will make the math easy. In 60 minutes they read 105 pages, so $105 \times 2 = 210$. This satisfies the question, so (B) is correct.

2. **B** The question is asking for a specific value and there are real numbers in the choices, so use PITA to solve, starting with (C). The choices represent how much Emiko pays. If Emiko pays $30 and she pays twice as much as Diego, then Diego would have paid $15 since $\dfrac{1}{2} \times 30 = 15$. Abigail paid three times as much as Emiko, so he would have paid $3 \times 30 = 90$. This added together is more than $90, so eliminate (C) and (D), as these will amount to a total that is too much. Try (B): if Emiko paid $20, Diego would have paid $10 since $\dfrac{1}{2} \times 20 = 10$. Abigail paid $3 \times 20 = 60$. Add these amounts together to find that $20 + $10 + $60 = 90, which satisfies the question. The correct answer is (B).

3. **D** First, translate the English into math and then use PITA to test the choices. *Four less than a certain number* translates to $n - 4$, and two-thirds of a number translates to $\dfrac{2}{3} \times n$. So the equation is $n - 4 = \dfrac{2}{3} \times n$. Now, use PITA to find the one that satisfies the equation, starting with (C). If $n = 8$, then the equation will read $8 - 4 = \dfrac{2}{3}(8)$. Since $4 \neq \dfrac{16}{3}$, eliminate (C) and try another choice. Try (D): if $n = 12$, then $12 - 4 = \dfrac{2}{3}(12)$, which is $8 = \dfrac{24}{3}$ or $8 = 8$. Since 12 works, stop here. The correct answer is (D).

4. **D** The question is asking for a specific value and there are real numbers in the choices, so use PITA to solve. The question asks for Brinda's age, so label the choices "B" and create 2 additional columns next to it, one labeled as A and the other as C. Now, follow the steps of the question and test the choices, starting with (C). If Brinda is 18, then Anshuman must be 9 because *Anshuman is half as old as Brinda*.

It is also stated that *[Anshuman] is three times as old as Cindy* (remember, Anshuman is the subject of the sentence), so Cindy must be 3 since $\frac{9}{3} = 3$. Find the total of their ages: $18 + 9 + 3 = 30$, which is too small. Eliminate (A), (B), and (C). Choice (D) is the only answer left, so it must be correct. Stop work and move on! If you have time later to check, you'll see that if Brinda is 24, then Anshuman must be 12 and Cindy is 4, which makes the total $24 + 12 + 4 = 40$. The correct answer is (D).

5. **D**   The question is asking for a specific value and there are real numbers in the choices, so use PITA to solve. The question asks for a possible value of x. So, plug in for x and see if there is an integer that would work to make the rest of the equation balance. Start with one of the middle choices. Try (C): if $x = 55$, then $70(55) = 3{,}850$. Solve the rest of the equation: $3{,}850 + 33y = 4{,}233$ to see if y is an integer. Subtract 3,850 from both sides to find that $33y = 383$. You can try dividing, but you could also guesstimate: $33 \times 11 = 363$ and $33 \times 12 = 396$, so 383 is not divisible by 33. Therefore, eliminate (C) and try another choice. Try (D): $70(60) + 33y = 4{,}233$ simplifies to $4{,}200 + 33y = 4{,}233$. Subtract 4,200 from both sides to find that $33y = 33$. Divide each side by 33 to find that $y = 1$. Since 1 is an integer, this satisfies the question. The correct answer is (D).

6. **A**   This question gives a fair amount of information in the question, that the smallest of the three integers is 2, the sum of $2 + x + y = 9$, and the product of $2xy = 24$. Simplify these equations first and then use PITA to solve. Subtract 2 from either side of the sum to find that $x + y = 7$, and divide by 2 in the second equation to find that $xy = 12$. Now Plug In, starting with the largest number to find the largest number as efficiently as possible. Eliminate (C) and (D) right away since 8 or 9 added to another positive integer cannot equal 7. Try (B): plug in 6 to get $6 + y = 7$, so y would have to equal 1. This cannot be true, however, since the smallest integer has to be 2. Eliminate (B). Choice (A) is the only answer left, so it must be correct. Stop work and move on! If you have time later to check, you'll see that if you plug in 4 that $4 + y = 7$ means that $y = 3$. These are both larger than 2, the smallest number. Do these numbers work in the second equation? Yes! $3 \times 4 = 12$. The correct answer is (A).

7. **C**   Be sure to label the choices very carefully to stay visually organized. The question asks for Lori's age now, so label the choices "L," and create another column to the right and label it "C" for Carol's age. Next, create two more columns and label them as "L + 10" and "C + 10" for their respective ages in 10 years. Now, plug in, starting with (C): if Lori is 20 years now, Carol must be 5 because *Lori is 15 years older than Carol*. This means that in 10 years, Lori will be 30 ($20 + 10 = 30$), and Carol will be 15 ($5 + 10 = 15$). The question states that *in 10 years, Lori will be twice as old as Carol*. $30 = 2 \times 15$, so this satisfies the statement. The correct answer is (C).

8. **A**   Let the choices help here. The choices represent the number of people currently in the group. Eliminate (D) immediately since 30 cannot be divided 12 ways (hopefully there aren't partial people in the group!). Try (B), which is the middle answer of the remaining choices: if there are 6 people buying the game now, the cost would be $5 each since $\frac{30}{6} = 5$. If a seventh person joined, the cost per person would be $\frac{30}{7}$, which is not an integer. Since the problem stated that adding 1 person to the group would result in each person owing $1 less, this does not satisfy the question, so eliminate (B) and try another choice. Try (A): if there are 5 people buying the game, they will each pay $6 since $\frac{30}{5} = 6$. If a sixth person joins, they will each pay $5 because $\frac{30}{6} = 5$. Since $5 is exactly one dollar less than $6, this satisfies the question stem. Choice (A) is correct.

QUANT COMP PLUGGING IN

Practice Drill 9—Quant Comp Plugging In (Middle & Upper Levels)

1. **B** Since there are variables in the columns, plug in a number. Pay attention to the restriction given: plug in a number greater than 1 for x. Let $x = 4$. Column A is equal to 4, and column B is equal to 4^2, or 16. Since column B is greater, eliminate (A) and (C). Try a different number to see if column A could be greater or if the quantities could be equal. Since $x > 1$, x cannot be negative, zero, or one. Try a very large number. $1{,}000^2$ is much larger than 1,000, so column B is still greater. You could also try a decimal, like 2.5. In this case, column B is still greater since $2.5^2 = 6.25$, which is greater than 2.5. Therefore, since column B is always greater, the correct answer is (B).

2. **C** Read the question carefully: *b is an integer and –1 < b < 1*. There is only one integer between –1 and 1. Therefore, b must be 0. Plug 0 in for b into each of the columns. Column A is $\frac{0}{2} = 0$. Column B is $\frac{0}{8} = 0$. The quantities are equal, so (C) is the correct answer.

3. **D** Since there are variables in the columns, plug in values for p and m. For instance, let $p = 16$ and $m = 3$. Since it takes 4 quarts to make one gallon, column B is less than 1 gallon while column A is 16 gallons. This makes column A greater. However, the question does not state anything about requirements for these numbers, and the values could easily be reversed, that $p = 3$ and $m = 16$. The 16 quarts in column B is equal to 4 gallons, which is greater than the 3 gallons in column A. Since this could be true as well, it cannot be determined which quantity is larger. The correct answer is (D).

4. **A** Since there are variables in the columns, plug in a number. Pay attention to the restriction given: if x must be a positive integer, plug in a positive integer for x. For example, let $x = 3$. Column A is $\frac{3}{4}$ while column B is $\frac{3}{5}$. If you're not sure which value is greater, draw a picture. You can also use Bowtie to compare fractions. Column A becomes $\frac{15}{20}$, and column B becomes $\frac{12}{20}$. Thus, column A is greater. Eliminate (B) and (C). Try plugging in another value for x to see if another outcome is possible. Remember the restriction given, so x cannot be negative or zero, so try a large integer. Make $x = 100$. Column A is $\frac{100}{4} = 25$, and column B is $\frac{100}{5} = 20$. Column A is still greater. You could also try $x = 1$, but you will get the same result. Column A will be greater since $\frac{1}{4} = 0.25$ is greater than $\frac{1}{5} = 0.20$. The correct answer is (A).

5. **D** Since there are variables in the columns, plug in values for p and w, according to the information given: *w is an integer less than 4*, so let $w = 3$. You are also given that *p is an integer greater than 10*, so let $p = 11$. Therefore, column A is $(3)(11) = 33$, while column B is equal to 3. In this case, column A is greater. Eliminate (B) and (C). Now, try plugging in different numbers to see if another outcome is possible. Let $w = 0$ and $p = 12$. In column A, $(12)(0) = 0$. This is equal to column B since $w = 0$. Since column A isn't always greater nor are the two columns always equal, the correct answer is (D).

6. **D** Since there are variables in the columns, plug in a value for *c*. Let *c* = 2. In column A, 4(2) + 6 = 8 + 6 = 14. Do the same for column B: 3(2) + 12 = 6 + 12 = 18. In this case, column B is greater, so eliminate (A) and (C). Now, try a different number, perhaps a negative number. Let *c* = –10. Now column A will read 4(–10) + 6 = –40 + 6 = –34. Do the same to column B: 3(–10) + 12 = –30 + 12 = –18. In this case, –18 > –34, so column A is now greater. Since neither column is always greater, the correct answer is (D).

FUNCTIONS

Practice Drill 10—Functions

1. **D** In this equation, 5 will replace *b*. Thus, 2(5) + 7 = 10 + 7 = 17. The correct answer is (D).

2. **B** Since the function is equal to 20, it can be rewritten as 20 = 4*n* – 4. Solve for *n*. Add 4 to both sides of the equation to get 24 = 4*n*. Divide both sides by 4 to get *n* = 6. The correct answer is (B).

3. **D** The value in front of Δ is *a*, and the value after Δ is *b*. Therefore, 3Δ*b* can be rewritten as 4(3) + 3*b* or 12 + 3*b*. The correct answer is (D).

4. **D** Use PITA to evaluate the expression and then determine if the resulting 3-digit number is divisible by 3. The numbers 328, 338, and 358 are not divisible by 3. The number 378 is divisible by 3. The correct answer is (D).

5. **C** In this equation, the numerical value inside the $\diamondsuit$ will replace *c* where it appears in the equation. Thus, $\langle 10 \rangle$ = 2(10) + 10(10 + 3) = 20 + 10(13) = 150. Next find $\langle 3 \rangle$, which is 2(3) + 3(3 + 3) = 6 + 3(6) = 24. Finally, find $\langle 10 \rangle - \langle 3 \rangle$, which is 150 – 24 = 126. The correct answer is (C). Note: $\langle 10 \rangle - \langle 3 \rangle$ is not equivalent to $\langle 7 \rangle$, which is (B).

GEOMETRY & MEASUREMENT

Practice Drill 11—Geometry & Measurement (Middle & Upper Levels)

1. **C** A regular figure means that all the sides are equal. A pentagon has 5 sides, so to find each individual side, divide the perimeter by the number of sides: 65 ÷ 5 = 13. The correct answer is (C).

2. **A** To find the perimeter of a shape, add all the sides together. First, find the hypotenuse by recognizing this is a special right triangle (3-4-5) or using the Pythagorean Theorem: $3^2 + 4^2 = c^2$, which simplifies to 9 + 16 = 25 = c^2, and $\sqrt{25}$ = 5. Add 3 + 4 + 5 to find the perimeter of the triangle is 12. The correct answer is (A).

3. **A** If $b° = 60°$, the other angle must be 30 since $180° − 90° − 60° = 30°$, which is a special right triangle. In a 30-60-90 triangle, the sides measure x, $x\sqrt{3}$, and $2x$, respectively. The side across from the 30° angle is x, which we know is 4. Therefore, v, the hypotenuse, is twice that value. $4(2) = 8$, so $v = 8$. The correct answer is (A).

4. **A** Translate this question very carefully into math. *What* translates to the unknown x, *is* to =, *of* to multiplication, and *difference* to subtraction. There are 360 degrees in a rectangle and 180 degrees in a triangle. Therefore, the equation should read $x = \frac{1}{4}(360 − 180)$. Remember PEMDAS and work inside the parentheses first. $x = \frac{1}{4}(180)$, so $x = 45$. The correct answer is (A).

5. **B** The perimeter of a square is $= 4s$ and the area of a square is $= s^2$. Since one-half the perimeter is equal to the area, $\frac{1}{2}(4s) = s^2$. Now solve for s. $2s = s^2$. Divide both sides by s to get $s = 2$. The correct answer is (B).

6. **D** Use your formulas. Area of a circle $= \pi r^2$ and Circumference of a circle $= 2\pi r = \pi d$. So the area of a circle with radius 3 is $\pi(3^2) = 9\pi$. That means the circumference of the other circle is 9π. Since $9\pi = \pi d$, the diameter is equal to 9. The correct answer is (D).

7. **A** Use the formula given to find the volume of the first cylinder: $V = \pi r^2 h = \pi(3)^2(4) = 36\pi$. If the other cylinder is equal in volume to the first cylinder, then plug in the volume and radius of the other cylinder to find its height: $36\pi = \pi(6)^2 h$ simplifies to $36\pi = \pi(36)h$. Divide both sides by 36 to get $1 = h$. The correct answer is (A).

8. **D** Use your formula. Since the perimeter of a square is 4 times the length of one side, you can divide the perimeter by 4 to get the length of one side. $\frac{36n^2}{4} = 9n^2$ The correct answer is (D).

9. **D** The length of AB is the same as all the different heights added together on the right-hand side of the figure. Therefore, the perimeter will contain two lengths of 12. Similarly, the length of AC is the same as all the different lengths added together that are across the figure (in this case, above AC), so there will be two lengths of 20. To find the perimeter, add all the sides: $P = 12 + 12 + 20 + 20 = 64$. The correct answer is (D).

10. **B** Notice the three triangles that have been created within the rectangle. Look at the two right angles that surround the larger triangle in the middle. For the right triangle on the left, the value of x is given (70); therefore, to find w, simply subtract 90 and 70 from 180 to get $w = 20$. For the right triangle on the right, y and z must add up to 90 since a triangle has 180°. Finally, plug in these values into the equation given: $y° + z° − w° = 90 − 20 = 70$. The correct answer is (B).

11. **D** Notice that the part that juts out on the left side of the shape would fit into the indented part on the right side of the shape. Filling in the hole would make a rectangle with a length of 8 and a width of $4 + 3 + 4 = 11$. To find the area of a rectangle, use the formula: $A = l \times w$. Therefore, $A = 8 \times 11 = 88$. The correct answer is (D).

12. **B** The length of fencing needed to surround a yard is the same as the perimeter. Draw a rectangle and label the length as 28 and the width as 32. Remember, in a rectangle, opposite sides are equal to each other. Calculate the perimeter by adding all the sides: $28 + 28 + 32 + 32 = 120$. The correct answer is (B).

13. **B** The slope of a line is found using the formula $\frac{rise}{run}$ or $\frac{y_2 - y_1}{x_2 - x_1}$. Therefore, the slope of line segment AB is $\frac{9-1}{7-1} = \frac{8}{6} = \frac{4}{3}$. To find the slope of the line perpendicular to this line segment, take the negative reciprocal. The reciprocal of $\frac{4}{3}$ is $\frac{3}{4}$. Change the sign to get $-\frac{3}{4}$. The correct answer is (B).

14. **B** Even though the length of the radius is unknown, it is still possible to find the angle measurements. There is a 90° angle in the center of the circle, and both OQ and OP are radii of the circle, which means they are the same length. Therefore, this is an isosceles right triangle, meaning the two smaller angles are congruent. All triangles have 180°, so 180º – 90° = 90°. The two smaller angles add up to 90°, so $\frac{90°}{2} = 45°$. The correct answer is (B).

15. **D** Notice that the four intersecting lines form a quadrilateral. All quadrilaterals contain 360°, so keep a tally of the vertices and find the missing angle x. Since 85 is already provided, 360° – 85° = 275°. All straight lines add up to 180°, so use the exterior angles to find the interior angles. For example, if one of the exterior angles is 63°, the supplementary angle must be 117°. Subtract this from 275° to find that 275° – 117° = 158°. The other exterior angle, 112°, is opposite the interior vertex. Since opposite angles are equal, the interior vertex must also be 112°. Subtract this from the current total to find that 158° – 112° = 46°. The missing angle x is 46°. The correct answer is (D).

16. **C** Since ABC is an equilateral triangle, all 3 sides are equal to 6. Label AC as 6 and BC as 6. The question asks for the perimeter of the figure. There are two sides of the triangle that are part of the figure's perimeter, so add them together: $AB + AC = 6 + 6 = 12$. Eliminate (A) and (B) since the answer must have a 12 in it. Now find the rounded portion, which is half of the circumference (i.e., a semicircle). Since BC is 6, note that the diameter of the semicircle is also 6. If $C = \pi d$, then half of the circumference is $\frac{1}{2}\pi d$. Plug in the value for the diameter and simplify: $\frac{1}{2}\pi(6) = 3\pi$. The full expression for the perimeter will then read $12 + 3\pi$. The correct answer is (C).

17. **D** Break the trapezoid into two triangles and a square. Next, figure out the missing segment lengths. If $MN = 8$ and $MNQP$ is a square, then NP, QP, and MQ also equal 8. Next find LQ and PO. You may notice that these are 6-8-10 right triangles. Otherwise, use the Pythagorean Theorem to find the base of the triangles: $a^2 + 8^2 = 10^2$. Solve for a: $a^2 + 64 = 100$. Subtract 64 from both sides to get $a^2 = 36$. Then take the square root of both sides, and $a = 6$. To find the areas of the triangles, plug the base and the height into the formula $A = \frac{1}{2}bh = \frac{1}{2}(6)(8) = 24$. There are two triangles, so $24 + 24 = 48$. To find the area of square $MNQP$, plug the side length into the formula $A = s^2 = 8^2 = 64$. Finally, add the areas: 2 triangles + 1 square = 48 + 64 = 112. The correct answer is (D).

18. **A** Since line m is equal to $y = x + 4$, the slope of line m is equal to 1. Remember, the slope is the coefficient of x in linear equations. Therefore, column A is 1. Perpendicular lines will have slopes that are negative reciprocals of one another. Therefore, line l, which is perpendicular to line m, will have

a slope of –1 since the negative reciprocal of $\frac{1}{1}$ is $-\frac{1}{1}$. Thus, column B is –1. Since 1 is greater than –1, column A is greater. The correct answer is (A).

19. **D** There are no instructions as to the values of x and y, so use Plugging In. For instance, x and y could be equal. Let both x and y equal 4. Column A would be $C = 2(4)\pi$, or 8π, and column B would be $A = \pi(4)^2 = 16\pi$. In this case, column B is greater, so eliminate (A) and (C). Since x and y do not have to be equal, plug in a second time to see if a different outcome is possible. Say that $x = 2$ and $y = 1$. Then column A will be $C = 2(2)\pi = 4\pi$, and column B will be $A = \pi(1)^2 = \pi$. Now, column A is greater. Since neither column is always greater, the correct answer is (D).

20. **C** Use the formula given to find the areas of each figure. In column A, the height of Cylinder A is 10 and the radius is 6. Plug these values into the volume formula to find that $V = \pi(6)^2(10) = \pi(36)(10) = 360\pi$. This means column A is 360π. For column B, you can find the volumes of Cylinder B and Cylinder C separately and then add the results together. Alternatively, since the two figures have the same dimensions, you can multiply the volume formula by 2 to find the total volume. Thus, column B is $V = 2\pi(6)^2(5) = 2\pi(36)(5) = 2\pi(180) = 360\pi$. Since the columns are equal, the correct answer is (C).

Practice Drill 12—Non-Geometric Measurement

1. **C** Set up a proportion: $\frac{\text{miles}}{\text{hours}} = \frac{50}{1} = \frac{300}{x}$. Then cross-multiply to get $50x = 300$. Divide both sides by 50, and $x = 6$. The correct answer is (C).

2. **C** Remember, if you see the word average, you can use $T = AN$. Luke made two trips, so the *Number of items* is 2. Column A represents the average speed for the entire trip, so to find the total speed, add the speeds from both parts of the trip: $50 + 60 = 110$. Put that value in the *Total* spot. Finally, divide to find the average: $\frac{50 + 60}{2} = \frac{110}{2} = 55$. Thus, column A is 55, which is the same as column B. Since the two columns are equal, the correct answer is (C).

DATA ANALYSIS & PROBABILITY

Practice Drill 13—Data Analysis & Probability

1. **D** Michelle's new range is 46 (109 – 60 = 49), which is 15 more than her previous range. Since the new highest score is 15 points higher than the old highest score, the mean (average) can be calculated using $T = AN$. The old Total = 76(15) = 1,140. So the new total is 1,140 + 15 = 1,155. Use $T = AN$ again to calculate the new average: 1,155 = A(15). The new mean (average) would be 77, only a 1-point difference. The median and mode would not change, since they are unaffected by a change in the largest number (given that the largest number was not the mode).

2. **C** List the prime numbers on the 6-sided die: 2, 3, and 5 (Note! 1 is not a prime number). Since there are 6 sides on the die, the probability of rolling a prime number is $\frac{3}{6}$, so column A is $\frac{3}{6}$. This is the same value listed in column B. Since the columns are equal, the correct answer is (C).

3. **C** Start with Set B, since it is a finite set. Set B consists of 5, 10, 15, 20, 25, 30, 35, 40, and 45. Set A contains all prime numbers. The only prime number contained in Set B is 5, so the intersection of these two sets (i.e., Set C) will contain only the number 5. There is only one number in Set C, so the columns are equal. The correct answer is (C).

4. **B** This question is testing math vocabulary. The median of a set is the middle number when the numbers are listed in order from least to greatest. In Set A, the numbers are already in order, so find the middle number: 8. Thus, column A is 8. In Set B, the numbers are also already in order. However, there is an even number of items in this set, so the median will be found by taking the average of the two middle numbers. The two middle numbers are 8 and 9, so the median is $\frac{8+9}{2} = \frac{17}{2} = 8.5$. The value in column B is 8.5. Since column B is greater, the correct answer is (B).

5. **A** The probability of getting heads on any single flip is $\frac{1}{2}$, since there are two sides of a coin and only one of those is heads. Column A is the probability of getting heads on 2 consecutive flips, so you need to multiply the probability of the first flip by the probability of the second flip (i.e., Event 1 $\times$ Event 2): $\frac{1}{2} \times \frac{1}{2} = \frac{1 \times 1}{2 \times 2} = \frac{1}{4}$. To find column B, include the probability of a getting heads on the third flip (i.e., Event 1 $\times$ Event 2 $\times$ Event 3): $\frac{1}{2} \times \frac{1}{2} \times \frac{1}{2} = \frac{1 \times 1 \times 1}{2 \times 2 \times 2} = \frac{1}{8}$. Since column A is greater, the correct answer is (A). Note: If you know that the probability of getting the same result (in this case, heads) on consecutive flips of a coin diminishes with each subsequent flip, you can find the correct answer quickly!

6. **C** Remember, if you see the word *average*, you can use $T = AN$. First, find the sum: $4 + 6 + 8 + 10 = 28$. That number goes in the *Total* place. There are 4 numbers, so put 4 in the *Number of items* spot. Divide to get $\frac{28}{4} = 7$. Column A is 7. Remember that the median of a set is the middle number when the numbers are listed in order from least to greatest. Since there is an even number of items in this set, the median will be found by taking the average of the two middle numbers, 6 and 8. The average of 6 and 8 is $\frac{6+8}{2} = \frac{14}{2} = 7$, so the value in column B is 7. Since the two columns are equal, the correct answer is (C).

7.   **C**   First, find the probability of *not* picking red shoes, which is the same as picking purple or white shoes, and then compare the result to column B's value. There are 10 total pairs to pick from, and there are 8 pairs of shoes that are purple or white (i.e., not red), so the probability is $\frac{\text{not red}}{\text{total}} = \frac{8}{10}$. Column A is $\frac{8}{10}$ which is the value of column B. Since the columns are equal, the correct answer is (C).

ISEE Verbal

REVIEW—THE VERBAL PLAN

Pacing and Verbal Strategy

I will do the verbal questions in this order.

1.   Sentence completions

2.   Synonyms with words I sort of know

3.   Synonyms with words I know

I should spend 10–15 minutes on sentence completions.

I will always eliminate wrong (or "worse") answers.

If possible, I will eliminate choices before I guess, but even if I can't eliminate any, I will still guess productively.

No, I cannot eliminate choices that contain words I do not know.

SYNONYMS

Practice Drill 1—Write Your Own Definition

Possible Definitions

1.   weird
2.   introduction
3.   giving
4.   lesson found in a fable or tale
5.   change
6.   circle around
7.   optimistic
8.   stick around
9.   help
10.   build
11.   bend down
12.   honest
13.   tease
14.   rough
15.   self-centered
16.   calm
17.   use
18.   full of life
19.   stretch out
20.   help

Practice Drill 2—Write Another Definition

Look up these seven words in a dictionary to see how many different meanings they can have.

Practice Drill 3—Basic Synonym Techniques

1.	**C**	5.	**D**	9.	**D**	13.	**D**	17.	**D**
2.	**A**	6.	**D**	10.	**A**	14.	**B**	18.	**C**
3.	**C**	7.	**B**	11.	**C**	15.	**A**	19.	**B**
4.	**D**	8.	**C**	12.	**B**	16.	**C**	20.	**C**

Practice Drill 4—Making Your Own Context

Possible Contexts (Answers Will Vary)

1. Common cold; common sense
2. Competent to stand trial
3. Abridged dictionary
4. Untimely demise; untimely remark
5. Homogenized milk
6. Juvenile delinquent; delinquent payments
7. Inalienable rights
8. Paltry sum
9. Auspicious beginning; auspicious occasion
10. Prodigal son

Practice Drill 5—Using Your Own Context

1.	**C**	3.	**D**	5.	**A**	7.	**C**	9.	**C**
2.	**D**	4.	**C**	6.	**B**	8.	**A**	10.	**A**

Practice Drill 6—All Synonyms Techniques

1.	**C**	5.	**D**	9.	**C**	13.	**D**	17.	**C**
2.	**A**	6.	**A**	10.	**B**	14.	**C**	18.	**B**
3.	**C**	7.	**D**	11.	**B**	15.	**D**	19.	**D**
4.	**A**	8.	**B**	12.	**C**	16.	**B**	20.	**B**

SENTENCE COMPLETIONS

Practice Drill 7—Coming Up with Your Own Word

These words are just to give you an idea of what you could use. Any words that accurately fill the blank, based on the clue and the direction word, will do.

1. good	8. waste time	15. not necessary	22. intimidated; shy	28. sharing
2. rare	9. frugal	16. repetitive	23. annoyed	29. flexible
3. remarkable	10. movement	17. risky	24. on time	30. inborn
4. awake	11. simple	18. outgoing	25. skill	31. affable; talkative
5. lucky	12. produce	19. balanced	26. variety	32. awestruck
6. thoughtful	13. changed	20. generous	27. creative	
7. alike	14. strong	21. steadfast		

Practice Drill 8—Eliminating Answers Based on Your Word

Below are the correct answers to the problems. You should have eliminated the other choices.

1. **D**	8. **C**	15. **D**	22. **D**	29. **C**
2. **B**	9. **B**	16. **C**	23. **A**	30. **B**
3. **C**	10. **A**	17. **B**	24. **B**	31. **A**
4. **D**	11. **D**	18. **A**	25. **A**	32. **C**
5. **A**	12. **D**	19. **C**	26. **C**	
6. **A**	13. **B**	20. **C**	27. **B**	
7. **D**	14. **C**	21. **B**	28. **B**	

Practice Drill 9—Using Positive/Negative

1. +	3. –	5. –	7. –	9. –
2. +	4. +	6. +	8. –	10. +

Practice Drill 10—Eliminating Based on Positive/Negative

1. **A**	3. **B**	5. **C**	7. **C**	9. **A**
2. **C**	4. **D**	6. **A**	8. **D**	10. **C**

Practice Drill 11—Two-Blank Sentence Completions (Upper Level Only)

1. **B**	3. **A**	5. **D**	7. **C**	9. **A**
2. **C**	4. **A**	6. **A**	8. **C**	10. **C**

Review—The Sentence Completions Plan

One-Blank Sentence Completions

For each and every sentence completion, the first thing I do is *ignore* the answers.

I look for the *clue*, and I mark it by *underlining or highlighting* it.

I look for any *direction* words, and I *circle or highlight* them.

Then I *come up with my own word for the blank*. If I have trouble coming up with a word for the blank, I decide if the blank is *positive* or *negative* (or neither).

Then I *eliminate* choices, and *I guess from the remaining choices.*

Two-Blank Sentence Completions—Upper Level Only

For each and every sentence completion, the first thing I do is *ignore* the answers.

I look for the *clue*, and I mark it by *underlining or highlighting* it.

I look for any *direction* words, and I *circle or highlight* them.

If the sentence completion has two blanks, I do them *one at a time.*

I do the blank that is easier first—the one that has the better clue.

I come up with a word for one of the blanks, and when I uncover the choices, I uncover only *the words for the blank that I am working on*, and I eliminate based on those.

Then, I go back to the sentence and *come up with a word* for the other blank, uncover the choices that are left, and eliminate.

Eliminating Choices and Guessing

No, I cannot eliminate choices that contain words I do not know.

If I can eliminate only one or two choices, then I guess from the remaining choices.

If the sentence or vocabulary looks so difficult that I can't come up with a word or decide if the blank is positive or negative, then I fill in my "letter-of-the-day."

I spend my last minute filling in the "letter-of-the-day" for any questions I have not gotten around to answering.

I should never leave a question unanswered because there is no penalty for guessing.

Practice Drill 12—All Sentence Completion Techniques

1. **A**	5. **D**	9. **C**	13. **B**	17. **C**
2. **C**	6. **B**	10. **B**	14. **C**	18. **D**
3. **B**	7. **B**	11. **D**	15. **A**	19. **A**
4. **A**	8. **C**	12. **A**	16. **B**	20. **D**

ISEE Reading

READING COMPREHENSION

Practice Drill 1—Getting Through the Passage

You should have brief labels like the following:

1st Label:	Norway → Iceland	What?	A Viking
2nd Label:	Iceland → Greenland	So What?	Found America early
3rd Label:	Lost	Passage type?	History of an event—social studies
4th Label:	Saw America; landed Greenland		

Practice Drill 2—Answering a General Question

1. **D**

2. **D**

Practice Drill 3—Answering a Specific Question

1. **C**	2. **A**	3. **B**	4. **D**	5. **C**

Review—The Reading Plan

After I read each paragraph, I label it either on the page or on my scratch paper.

After I read an entire passage, I ask myself: What? and So what?

The five main types of general questions, and the questions I can ask myself to answer them, are:

- Main idea: What was the "What? So what?" for this passage?
- Tone/attitude: How did the author feel about the subject?
- General interpretation: Which answer stays closest to what the author said and how he said it?
- General purpose: Why did the author write this?
- Prediction: How was the passage arranged? What will come next?

To find the answer to a specific question, I can use three clues.

- Paragraph labels
- Line or paragraph reference
- Lead words

If the question says "In line 22," then I begin reading at approximately line 17.

On a general question, I eliminate answers that are:

- Too small
- Not mentioned in the passage
- In contradiction to the passage
- Too big
- Too extreme
- Against common sense

On a specific question, I eliminate answers that are:

- Too extreme
- Contradicting passage details
- Not mentioned in the passage
- Against common sense

When I've got it down to two possible answers, I should:

- Reread the question
- Look at what makes the two answers different
- Go back to the passage
- Eliminate the answer that is worse

Practice Drill 4—All Reading Techniques—All Levels

What? William Levitt

So what? Built homes efficiently

1. **C**	3. **C**	5. **A**
2. **D**	4. **D**	6. **C**

Practice Drill 5—All Reading Techniques—All Levels

What? Etymology

So what? Has many words to explore

1.	**B**	3.	**A**	5.	**B**
2.	**C**	4.	**C**		

Practice Drill 6—All Reading Techniques—Middle & Upper Levels

What? Science

So what? Doesn't have all the answers

1.	**A**	3.	**D**	5.	**C**
2.	**D**	4.	**A**		

Practice Drill 7—All Reading Techniques—Upper Level

What? Bob Dylan

So what? Was destined to be a musician

1.	**D**	3.	**D**	5.	**C**
2.	**B**	4.	**A**		

Part III
Practice Tests

See the *Get More (Free) Content* page after the Table of Contents for instructions on how to register this book to access an online version of each test at PrincetonReview.com.

HOW TO TAKE A PRACTICE TEST

Here are some suggestions for taking your practice test.

- Find a quiet place to take the test where you won't be interrupted or distracted, and make sure you have enough time to take the entire test.

- Time yourself strictly. The online test has a built-in timer, but if you're testing on paper, use a timer, watch, or stopwatch that will ring, and do not allow yourself to go over time for any section.

- Take a practice test in one sitting, allowing yourself breaks of no more than two minutes between sections.

- If you're preparing for an online test, take your practice test online as well. Don't forget to use scratch paper!

- If you're preparing for a paper-based test, use the attached answer sheets to bubble in your choices.

- Each bubble you choose should be filled in thoroughly, and no other marks should be made in the answer area.

- Make sure to double-check that your bubbles are filled in correctly!

Chapter 10
Upper Level ISEE
Practice Test

 This test is also available in an online format when you register this book at PrincetonReview.com. See the *Get More (Free) Content* page after the Table of Contents for instructions.

Upper Level ISEE Practice Test

Be sure each mark *completely* fills the answer space.

SECTION 1 - Verbal Reasoning

1 Ⓐ Ⓑ Ⓒ Ⓓ	9 Ⓐ Ⓑ Ⓒ Ⓓ	17 Ⓐ Ⓑ Ⓒ Ⓓ	25 Ⓐ Ⓑ Ⓒ Ⓓ	33 Ⓐ Ⓑ Ⓒ Ⓓ
2 Ⓐ Ⓑ Ⓒ Ⓓ	10 Ⓐ Ⓑ Ⓒ Ⓓ	18 Ⓐ Ⓑ Ⓒ Ⓓ	26 Ⓐ Ⓑ Ⓒ Ⓓ	34 Ⓐ Ⓑ Ⓒ Ⓓ
3 Ⓐ Ⓑ Ⓒ Ⓓ	11 Ⓐ Ⓑ Ⓒ Ⓓ	19 Ⓐ Ⓑ Ⓒ Ⓓ	27 Ⓐ Ⓑ Ⓒ Ⓓ	35 Ⓐ Ⓑ Ⓒ Ⓓ
4 Ⓐ Ⓑ Ⓒ Ⓓ	12 Ⓐ Ⓑ Ⓒ Ⓓ	20 Ⓐ Ⓑ Ⓒ Ⓓ	28 Ⓐ Ⓑ Ⓒ Ⓓ	36 Ⓐ Ⓑ Ⓒ Ⓓ
5 Ⓐ Ⓑ Ⓒ Ⓓ	13 Ⓐ Ⓑ Ⓒ Ⓓ	21 Ⓐ Ⓑ Ⓒ Ⓓ	29 Ⓐ Ⓑ Ⓒ Ⓓ	37 Ⓐ Ⓑ Ⓒ Ⓓ
6 Ⓐ Ⓑ Ⓒ Ⓓ	14 Ⓐ Ⓑ Ⓒ Ⓓ	22 Ⓐ Ⓑ Ⓒ Ⓓ	30 Ⓐ Ⓑ Ⓒ Ⓓ	38 Ⓐ Ⓑ Ⓒ Ⓓ
7 Ⓐ Ⓑ Ⓒ Ⓓ	15 Ⓐ Ⓑ Ⓒ Ⓓ	23 Ⓐ Ⓑ Ⓒ Ⓓ	31 Ⓐ Ⓑ Ⓒ Ⓓ	39 Ⓐ Ⓑ Ⓒ Ⓓ
8 Ⓐ Ⓑ Ⓒ Ⓓ	16 Ⓐ Ⓑ Ⓒ Ⓓ	24 Ⓐ Ⓑ Ⓒ Ⓓ	32 Ⓐ Ⓑ Ⓒ Ⓓ	40 Ⓐ Ⓑ Ⓒ Ⓓ

SECTION 2 - Quantitative Reasoning

1 Ⓐ Ⓑ Ⓒ Ⓓ	9 Ⓐ Ⓑ Ⓒ Ⓓ	17 Ⓐ Ⓑ Ⓒ Ⓓ	25 Ⓐ Ⓑ Ⓒ Ⓓ	33 Ⓐ Ⓑ Ⓒ Ⓓ
2 Ⓐ Ⓑ Ⓒ Ⓓ	10 Ⓐ Ⓑ Ⓒ Ⓓ	18 Ⓐ Ⓑ Ⓒ Ⓓ	26 Ⓐ Ⓑ Ⓒ Ⓓ	34 Ⓐ Ⓑ Ⓒ Ⓓ
3 Ⓐ Ⓑ Ⓒ Ⓓ	11 Ⓐ Ⓑ Ⓒ Ⓓ	19 Ⓐ Ⓑ Ⓒ Ⓓ	27 Ⓐ Ⓑ Ⓒ Ⓓ	35 Ⓐ Ⓑ Ⓒ Ⓓ
4 Ⓐ Ⓑ Ⓒ Ⓓ	12 Ⓐ Ⓑ Ⓒ Ⓓ	20 Ⓐ Ⓑ Ⓒ Ⓓ	28 Ⓐ Ⓑ Ⓒ Ⓓ	36 Ⓐ Ⓑ Ⓒ Ⓓ
5 Ⓐ Ⓑ Ⓒ Ⓓ	13 Ⓐ Ⓑ Ⓒ Ⓓ	21 Ⓐ Ⓑ Ⓒ Ⓓ	29 Ⓐ Ⓑ Ⓒ Ⓓ	37 Ⓐ Ⓑ Ⓒ Ⓓ
6 Ⓐ Ⓑ Ⓒ Ⓓ	14 Ⓐ Ⓑ Ⓒ Ⓓ	22 Ⓐ Ⓑ Ⓒ Ⓓ	30 Ⓐ Ⓑ Ⓒ Ⓓ	
7 Ⓐ Ⓑ Ⓒ Ⓓ	15 Ⓐ Ⓑ Ⓒ Ⓓ	23 Ⓐ Ⓑ Ⓒ Ⓓ	31 Ⓐ Ⓑ Ⓒ Ⓓ	
8 Ⓐ Ⓑ Ⓒ Ⓓ	16 Ⓐ Ⓑ Ⓒ Ⓓ	24 Ⓐ Ⓑ Ⓒ Ⓓ	32 Ⓐ Ⓑ Ⓒ Ⓓ	

SECTION 3 - Reading Comprehension

1 Ⓐ Ⓑ Ⓒ Ⓓ	9 Ⓐ Ⓑ Ⓒ Ⓓ	17 Ⓐ Ⓑ Ⓒ Ⓓ	25 Ⓐ Ⓑ Ⓒ Ⓓ	33 Ⓐ Ⓑ Ⓒ Ⓓ
2 Ⓐ Ⓑ Ⓒ Ⓓ	10 Ⓐ Ⓑ Ⓒ Ⓓ	18 Ⓐ Ⓑ Ⓒ Ⓓ	26 Ⓐ Ⓑ Ⓒ Ⓓ	34 Ⓐ Ⓑ Ⓒ Ⓓ
3 Ⓐ Ⓑ Ⓒ Ⓓ	11 Ⓐ Ⓑ Ⓒ Ⓓ	19 Ⓐ Ⓑ Ⓒ Ⓓ	27 Ⓐ Ⓑ Ⓒ Ⓓ	35 Ⓐ Ⓑ Ⓒ Ⓓ
4 Ⓐ Ⓑ Ⓒ Ⓓ	12 Ⓐ Ⓑ Ⓒ Ⓓ	20 Ⓐ Ⓑ Ⓒ Ⓓ	28 Ⓐ Ⓑ Ⓒ Ⓓ	36 Ⓐ Ⓑ Ⓒ Ⓓ
5 Ⓐ Ⓑ Ⓒ Ⓓ	13 Ⓐ Ⓑ Ⓒ Ⓓ	21 Ⓐ Ⓑ Ⓒ Ⓓ	29 Ⓐ Ⓑ Ⓒ Ⓓ	
6 Ⓐ Ⓑ Ⓒ Ⓓ	14 Ⓐ Ⓑ Ⓒ Ⓓ	22 Ⓐ Ⓑ Ⓒ Ⓓ	30 Ⓐ Ⓑ Ⓒ Ⓓ	
7 Ⓐ Ⓑ Ⓒ Ⓓ	15 Ⓐ Ⓑ Ⓒ Ⓓ	23 Ⓐ Ⓑ Ⓒ Ⓓ	31 Ⓐ Ⓑ Ⓒ Ⓓ	
8 Ⓐ Ⓑ Ⓒ Ⓓ	16 Ⓐ Ⓑ Ⓒ Ⓓ	24 Ⓐ Ⓑ Ⓒ Ⓓ	32 Ⓐ Ⓑ Ⓒ Ⓓ	

SECTION 4 - Mathematics Achievement

1 Ⓐ Ⓑ Ⓒ Ⓓ	11 Ⓐ Ⓑ Ⓒ Ⓓ	21 Ⓐ Ⓑ Ⓒ Ⓓ	31 Ⓐ Ⓑ Ⓒ Ⓓ	41 Ⓐ Ⓑ Ⓒ Ⓓ
2 Ⓐ Ⓑ Ⓒ Ⓓ	12 Ⓐ Ⓑ Ⓒ Ⓓ	22 Ⓐ Ⓑ Ⓒ Ⓓ	32 Ⓐ Ⓑ Ⓒ Ⓓ	42 Ⓐ Ⓑ Ⓒ Ⓓ
3 Ⓐ Ⓑ Ⓒ Ⓓ	13 Ⓐ Ⓑ Ⓒ Ⓓ	23 Ⓐ Ⓑ Ⓒ Ⓓ	33 Ⓐ Ⓑ Ⓒ Ⓓ	43 Ⓐ Ⓑ Ⓒ Ⓓ
4 Ⓐ Ⓑ Ⓒ Ⓓ	14 Ⓐ Ⓑ Ⓒ Ⓓ	24 Ⓐ Ⓑ Ⓒ Ⓓ	34 Ⓐ Ⓑ Ⓒ Ⓓ	44 Ⓐ Ⓑ Ⓒ Ⓓ
5 Ⓐ Ⓑ Ⓒ Ⓓ	15 Ⓐ Ⓑ Ⓒ Ⓓ	25 Ⓐ Ⓑ Ⓒ Ⓓ	35 Ⓐ Ⓑ Ⓒ Ⓓ	45 Ⓐ Ⓑ Ⓒ Ⓓ
6 Ⓐ Ⓑ Ⓒ Ⓓ	16 Ⓐ Ⓑ Ⓒ Ⓓ	26 Ⓐ Ⓑ Ⓒ Ⓓ	36 Ⓐ Ⓑ Ⓒ Ⓓ	46 Ⓐ Ⓑ Ⓒ Ⓓ
7 Ⓐ Ⓑ Ⓒ Ⓓ	17 Ⓐ Ⓑ Ⓒ Ⓓ	27 Ⓐ Ⓑ Ⓒ Ⓓ	37 Ⓐ Ⓑ Ⓒ Ⓓ	47 Ⓐ Ⓑ Ⓒ Ⓓ
8 Ⓐ Ⓑ Ⓒ Ⓓ	18 Ⓐ Ⓑ Ⓒ Ⓓ	28 Ⓐ Ⓑ Ⓒ Ⓓ	38 Ⓐ Ⓑ Ⓒ Ⓓ	
9 Ⓐ Ⓑ Ⓒ Ⓓ	19 Ⓐ Ⓑ Ⓒ Ⓓ	29 Ⓐ Ⓑ Ⓒ Ⓓ	39 Ⓐ Ⓑ Ⓒ Ⓓ	
10 Ⓐ Ⓑ Ⓒ Ⓓ	20 Ⓐ Ⓑ Ⓒ Ⓓ	30 Ⓐ Ⓑ Ⓒ Ⓓ	40 Ⓐ Ⓑ Ⓒ Ⓓ	

Section 1
Verbal Reasoning

| **40 Questions** | **Time: 20 Minutes** |

This section is divided into two parts that contain two different types of questions. As soon as you have completed Part One, answer the questions in Part Two. You may write in your test booklet. For each answer you select, fill in the corresponding circle on your answer document.

Part One – Synonyms

Each question in Part One consists of a word in capital letters followed by four answer choices. Select the one word that is most nearly the same in meaning as the word in capital letters.

SAMPLE QUESTION:
    GENERIC:

        (A) effortless
        (B) general
        (C) strong
        (D) thoughtful

<u>Sample Answer</u>
Ⓐ ● Ⓒ Ⓓ

Go on to the next page. ⟶

VR

Part Two – Sentence Completion

Each question in Part Two is made up of a sentence with one or two blanks. One blank indicates that a word is missing. Two blanks indicate that two words are missing. Each sentence is followed by four answer choices. Select the one word or pair of words that best completes the meaning of the sentence as a whole.

SAMPLE QUESTIONS:

Always ------, Edgar's late arrival surprised his friends.

<u>Sample Answer</u>
Ⓐ Ⓑ ● Ⓓ

(A)   entertaining
(B)   lazy
(C)   punctual
(D)   sincere

After training for months, the runner felt ------ that she would win the race, quite different from her ------ attitude initially.

<u>Sample Answer</u>
Ⓐ Ⓑ ● Ⓓ

(A)   confident . . . excited
(B)   indifferent . . . concern
(C)   secure . . . apprehensive
(D)   worried . . . excited

STOP. Do not go on until told to do so.

Part One – Synonyms

Directions: Select the word that is most nearly the same in meaning as the word in capital letters.

1. GRAVE:

    (A) deadly
    (B) final
    (C) open
    (D) solemn

2. FOMENT:

    (A) articulate
    (B) dissemble
    (C) instigate
    (D) praise

3. INARTICULATE:

    (A) creative
    (B) friendly
    (C) overly sensitive
    (D) tongue-tied

4. AMELIORATE:

    (A) enjoy
    (B) hinder
    (C) improve
    (D) restrain

5. THESIS:

    (A) belief
    (B) paper
    (C) report
    (D) study

6. DEBUNK:

    (A) build
    (B) discredit
    (C) impress
    (D) justify

7. DISDAIN:

    (A) annoy
    (B) contempt
    (C) find
    (D) hope

8. RETICENT:

    (A) anxious
    (B) aware
    (C) informed
    (D) reserved

9. PREVALENT:

    (A) fascinating
    (B) minority
    (C) old-fashioned
    (D) predominant

10. SATIATE:

    (A) deny
    (B) fill
    (C) serve
    (D) starve

Go on to the next page. ➜

11. CANDID:

   (A) defiant
   (B) dejected
   (C) frank
   (D) stingy

12. EMULATE:

   (A) brush off
   (B) imitate
   (C) perplex
   (D) permit

13. TAINT:

   (A) annoy
   (B) handle
   (C) infect
   (D) master

14. ENIGMA:

   (A) effort
   (B) mystery
   (C) struggle
   (D) tantrum

15. DETRIMENTAL:

   (A) considerate
   (B) desolate
   (C) emphatic
   (D) injurious

16. METICULOUS:

   (A) favorable
   (B) finicky
   (C) gigantic
   (D) maddening

17. JUXTAPOSE:

   (A) keep away
   (B) place side by side
   (C) put behind
   (D) question

18. CONGENIAL:

   (A) friendly
   (B) impressive
   (C) inborn
   (D) magical

19. MITIGATE:

   (A) bend
   (B) ease
   (C) harden
   (D) untangle

20. ELUSIVE:

   (A) real
   (B) slippery
   (C) treacherous
   (D) unhappy

Go on to the next page. ➝

Part Two – Sentence Completion

Directions: Select the word or word pair that best completes the sentence.

21. Jane felt ------- about whether to go to the party or not; on one hand it seemed like fun, but on the other, she was very tired.

    (A) ambivalent
    (B) apathetic
    (C) happy
    (D) irritated

22. Like the more famous Susan B. Anthony, M. Carey Thomas ------- feminism and women's rights.

    (A) championed
    (B) defaced
    (C) found
    (D) gained

23. Morality is not -------; cultures around the world have different ideas about how people should be treated.

    (A) debatable
    (B) helpful
    (C) realistic
    (D) universal

24. Although Ms. Sanchez ------ the student that he needed a good grade on the final exam, he did not study at all.

    (A) admonished
    (B) congratulated
    (C) criticized
    (D) ridiculed

25. Thomas Jefferson was a man of ------- talents: he was known for his skills as a writer, a musician, an architect, and an inventor as well as a politician.

    (A) abundant
    (B) frugal
    (C) mundane
    (D) overblown

26. Monica could remain ------- no longer; the injustices she witnessed moved her to speak up.

    (A) active
    (B) furious
    (C) helpful
    (D) reticent

27. Louisa May Alcott's *Little Women* is largely -------; much of the story is based on her experiences as a young woman growing up in Concord, Massachusetts.

    (A) autobiographical
    (B) fictional
    (C) moving
    (D) visual

Go on to the next page. ➞

28. Though his lectures could be monotonous, Mr. Cutler was thankfully rather ------- when he spoke to students in small, informal groups.

    (A) amiable
    (B) pious
    (C) prosaic
    (D) vapid

29. Craig had ------- that the day would not go well, and just as he'd thought, he had two pop quizzes.

    (A) an antidote
    (B) an interest
    (C) a premonition
    (D) a report

30. Far from shedding light on the mystery, Jason's ------- response left people unsure.

    (A) impartial
    (B) opaque
    (C) risky
    (D) systematic

31. Although Marie was a talented and ------- performer, her gifts were often ------- because she didn't know how to promote herself.

    (A) faithful . . . supported
    (B) insulting . . . overlooked
    (C) promising . . . satisfied
    (D) versatile . . . ignored

32. Although she was the daughter of a wealthy slaveholder, Angelina Grimke ------- slavery and ------- her whole life for the cause of abolition.

    (A) desired . . . picketed
    (B) detested . . . dedicated
    (C) hated . . . wasted
    (D) represented . . . fought

33. Rhubarb is actually quite -------, requiring a large amount of sugar to make it -------.

    (A) bitter . . . palatable
    (B) flavorful . . . fattening
    (C) nutritious . . . sickening
    (D) unpopular . . . sticky

34. Because Martha was naturally -------, she would see the bright side of any situation, but Jack had a ------- personality and always waited for something bad to happen.

    (A) cheerful . . . upbeat
    (B) frightened . . . mawkish
    (C) optimistic . . . dreary
    (D) realistic . . . unreasonable

35. Although Edgar was not telling the truth, his ------- succeeded: it ------- the crowd to demand that Edgar's competitor be rejected.

    (A) antipathy . . . questioned
    (B) condone . . . encouraged
    (C) fallacy . . . incited
    (D) lie . . . permitted

Go on to the next page. ➡

36. Even though the critics praised the author's ------- use of words, they found the text ------- at a mere 100 pages.

(A) hackneyed . . . threadbare
(B) improper . . . laconic
(C) precise . . . short
(D) sure . . . banal

37. Erica's mother could not ------- why Erica would study a subject as ------- as the culture of 13th century French winemakers.

(A) fathom . . . esoteric
(B) intend . . . bizarre
(C) respond . . . gruesome
(D) understand . . . interesting

38. The threat of the storm did not ------- Ernie's excitement for the race; he had no ------- running in even the most unpleasant of weather.

(A) diminish . . . reservations about
(B) improve . . . concerns about
(C) lessen . . . inclination to go
(D) understate . . . abilities for

39. Always -------, Mr. Sanford refused to spend any money on anything unnecessary; to him, even a meal at a restaurant was a ------- excess.

(A) parsimonious . . . gratuitous
(B) penurious . . . useful
(C) spendthrift . . . respectable
(D) stingy . . . selective

40. To her -------, Margie was given the unfair label of -------, even though her love of the arts was far from superficial.

(A) chagrin . . . dilettante
(B) frustration . . . adversary
(C) irritation . . . performer
(D) surprise . . . mentor

STOP. If there is time, you may check your work in this section only.

QR

Section 2
Quantitative Reasoning

---

37 Questions

Time: 35 Minutes

This section is divided into two parts that contain two different types of questions. As soon as you have completed Part One, answer the questions in Part Two. You may write in your test booklet. For each answer you select, remember to fill in the corresponding circle on your answer document.

Any figures that accompany the questions in this section may be assumed to be drawn as accurately as possible EXCEPT when it is stated that a particular figure is not drawn to scale. Letters such as *x, y,* and *n* stand for real numbers.

Part One – Word Problems

Each question in Part One consists of a word problem followed by four answer choices. You may write in your test booklet; however, you may be able to solve many of these problems in your head. Next, look at the four answer choices given and select the best answer.

EXAMPLE 1:

What is the value of the expression

$5 + 3 \times (10 - 2) \div 4$?

(A)   5
(B)   9
(C)   11
(D)   16

The correct answer is 11, so circle C is darkened.

Sample Answer

Ⓐ Ⓑ ● Ⓓ

Go on to the next page. ⟶

Part Two – Quantitative Comparisons

All questions in Part Two are quantitative comparisons between the quantities shown in Column A and Column B. Using the information given in each question, compare the quantity in Column A to the quantity in Column B, and choose one of these four answer choices:

(A)   The quantity in Column A is greater.
(B)   The quantity in Column B is greater.
(C)   The two quantities are equal.
(D)   The relationship cannot be determined from the information given.

EXAMPLE 2:	Column A	Column B	Sample Answer
	50% of 40	20% of 100	Ⓐ Ⓑ ● Ⓓ

The quantity in Column A (20) is the same as the quantity in Column B (20), so circle C is darkened.

EXAMPLE 3:

y is any real nonzero number

Column A	Column B	Sample Answer
y	$\dfrac{1}{y}$	Ⓐ Ⓑ Ⓒ ●

Since y can be any real number (including an integer or a fraction), there is not enough information given to determine the relationship, so circle D is darkened.

STOP. Do not go on until told to do so. STOP

NO TEST MATERIAL ON THIS PAGE

Part One – Word Problems

Directions: Choose the best answer from the four choices given.

1. Which of the following is greatest?

   (A) 0.0100
   (B) 0.0099
   (C) 0.1900
   (D) 0.0199

2. Which of the following is NOT the product of two prime numbers?

   (A) 33
   (B) 35
   (C) 45
   (D) 91

3. If x, y, and z are consecutive even integers, then what is the difference between x and z ?

   (A) 0
   (B) 1
   (C) 2
   (D) 4

Questions 4–5 refer to the following chart.

Clothing Close-out		
Dresses	Originally $120	Now $90
Coats	Originally $250	Now $180
Shoes	Originally $60	Now $40
Hats	Originally $40	Now $20

4. Which of the items for sale has the greatest percent discount?

   (A) Dresses
   (B) Coats
   (C) Shoes
   (D) Hats

5. Purchasing which item will save the buyer the most dollars?

   (A) Dresses
   (B) Coats
   (C) Shoes
   (D) Hats

Go on to the next page. ➔

6. Amy is three years older than Beth and five years younger than Jo. If Beth is b years old, how old is Jo, in terms of b ?

   (A) $2b + 3$
   (B) $2b - 3$
   (C) $b + 4$
   (D) $b + 8$

7. If x is divided by 5, the remainder is 4. If y is divided by 5, the remainder is 1. What is the remainder when $(x + y)$ is divided by 5 ?

   (A) 0
   (B) 1
   (C) 2
   (D) 3

8. If x is a factor of p and y is a factor of q, then which of the following is true?

   (A) pq is a factor of xy.
   (B) pq is a multiple of x.
   (C) p is a factor of xy.
   (D) p is a multiple of xy.

9. Find the maximum value of y when $y = 3x^2 + 2$ and $-3 \le x \le 2$.

   (A) 2
   (B) 14
   (C) 29
   (D) 50

10. If b is a positive integer and $(x + 5)^2 = x^2 + bx + 25$, then b is equal to what value?

    (A) 5
    (B) 10
    (C) 20
    (D) 25

11. J is a whole number divisible by 4. J is also divisible by 3. Which of the following is NOT a possible value for J ?

    (A) 12
    (B) 24
    (C) 30
    (D) 36

12. The product of 0.48 and 100 is approximately

    (A) 0.5
    (B) 4.8
    (C) 5
    (D) 50

Go on to the next page. ➡

13. If the length of a rectangle is increased by 20% and the width of the rectangle is decreased by 10%, what is the percent increase of the area of the rectangle?

    (A)   8%
    (B)   9%
    (C)   10%
    (D)   12%

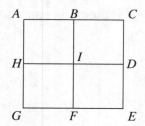

14. Square *ACEG* shown above is composed of 4 squares with sides of 1 meter each. Traveling only on the lines of the squares, how many different routes from *A* to *D* that are exactly 3 meters long are possible?

    (A)   2
    (B)   3
    (C)   4
    (D)   5

15. If, in triangle *ABC*, the measure of angle *B* is greater than 90°, and *AB = BC*, what is a possible measure for angle *C* in degrees?

    (A)   35
    (B)   45
    (C)   60
    (D)   It cannot be determined from the information given.

16. Chumway Motors discounts the cost of a car by 10% and then runs another special one-day deal offering an additional 20% off the discounted price. What discount does this represent from the original price of the car?

    (A)   28%
    (B)   30%
    (C)   40%
    (D)   72%

17. David scored 82, 84, and 95 on his first three math tests. What score does he need on his fourth test to bring his average up to a 90 ?

    (A)   90
    (B)   92
    (C)   96
    (D)   99

Go on to the next page. ➞

18. Howard has a coin jar filled with only quarters and nickels. If he has a total of 23 coins that equal $2.15, which of the following could be the number of nickels Howard has in the jar?

(A)   5
(B)   10
(C)   18
(D)   20

19. If $p^2 + q^2 = 25$ and $2pq = 10$, what is the value of $(p - q)^2$?

(A)   250
(B)   100
(C)   50
(D)   15

20. The ratio of yellow paint to red paint to white paint needed to make a perfect mixture of orange paint is 3 to 2 to 1. If 36 gallons of orange paint are needed to paint a cottage, how many gallons of red paint will be needed?

(A)   2
(B)   6
(C)   12
(D)   15

Go on to the next page. ➡️

Part Two – Quantitative Comparisons

Directions: Using all information given in each question, compare the quantity in Column A to the quantity in Column B. All questions in Part Two have these answer choices:

(A) The quantity in Column A is greater.
(B) The quantity in Column B is greater.
(C) The two quantities are equal.
(D) The relationship cannot be determined from the information given.

	Column A	Column B
21.	25% of 50	50% of 25

A piggy bank is filled with nickels and pennies, totaling $2.10, and the number of pennies is double the number of nickels. (Note: 1 nickel = $0.05 and 1 penny = $0.01.)

	Column A	Column B
22.	The total value of the nickels	$1.75

360 is the product of 4 consecutive integers.

	Column A	Column B
23.	The greatest of the 4 consecutive integers	6

	Column A	Column B
24.	x^2	x^3

	Column A	Column B
25.	$8 - 20 \div 2 \times 5 + 3$	20

Go on to the next page. ➞

QR

②

Answer choices for all questions on this page.

(A) The quantity in Column A is greater.
(B) The quantity in Column B is greater.
(C) The two quantities are equal.
(D) The relationship cannot be determined from the information given.

$$(x + 2)(x - 2) = 0$$

	Column A	Column B
26.	x	2

	Column A	Column B
27.	$\sqrt{36} + \sqrt{16}$	$\sqrt{52}$

	Column A	Column B
28.	3^{12}	9^6

The volume of a solid cube is 27.

	Column A	Column B
29.	The height of the cube	3

$$\frac{x + 2}{y + 2} = \frac{x}{y}$$

	Column A	Column B
30.	x	$y + 2$

	Column A	Column B
31.	The sum of the integers from 1 to 100, inclusive	The sum of the even integers from 1 to 200, inclusive

$$\frac{x}{4} = 1.5$$

	Column A	Column B
32.	x	5

Go on to the next page. ➡

Answer choices for all questions on this page.

(A) The quantity in Column A is greater.
(B) The quantity in Column B is greater.
(C) The two quantities are equal.
(D) The relationship cannot be determined from the information given.

Column A	Column B
33. $\left(\dfrac{1}{5}\right)^{-\frac{1}{2}}$	$\left(\dfrac{1}{5}\right)^{4}$

A card is drawn from a standard deck and a 6-sided number cube, numbered 1 to 6, is rolled.

Column A	Column B
34. If a king is drawn from the deck, the probability of rolling an even number	If a spade is drawn from the deck, the probability of rolling a number less than 4

When they are in season, a farmer sells turnips for $1.80 per bunch. At the beginning of the off-season, this farmer increases the price per bunch by 10%; however, at the end of the off-season, the farmer decreases by 10% the price of turnips per bunch.

Column A	Column B
35. The price of turnips per bunch at the end of the off-season	$1.80

A box contains 4 cookies, 5 brownies, and 6 doughnuts. Two items are removed from the bag.

Column A	Column B
36. The probability that both items are brownies	The probability that one item is a cookie and the other is a doughnut

A triangle has two sides measuring 4 and 6, respectively.

Column A	Column B
37. The greatest possible area of the triangle	12

STOP. If there is time, you may check your work in this section only.

3

Section 3
Reading Comprehension

This section contains six short reading passages. Each passage is followed by six questions based on its content. Answer the questions following each passage on the basis of what is <u>stated</u> or <u>implied</u> in that passage. You may write in the test booklet.

**STOP. Do not go on
until told to do so.** STOP

Questions 1–6

Line

1 New Orleans was the site of the last
2 major battle during the War of 1812,
3 a lengthy conflict between British and
4 American troops. The Battle of New
5 Orleans in January 1815 was one of the
6 greatest victories in American military
7 history. However, the great success of this
8 battle did not actually bring about the end of
9 the war. Surprisingly, the Treaty of Ghent,
10 which declared the end of the war, had
11 already been signed by both sides a month
12 earlier.
13 How was that possible? There were two
14 major reasons. The first is that New Orleans
15 was relatively isolated and communication
16 in the growing United States was not as
17 simple as it is today. Thus, it is possible that
18 the British commanders and the American
19 general, Andrew Jackson, did not realize a
20 treaty had been signed before they started
21 their battle. A second reason is that there is
22 a difference between a signed treaty and a
23 ratified treaty. Even if all soldiers fighting in
24 and around New Orleans had known of the
25 treaty, it had not yet been ratified by the U.S.
26 Senate. Thus, though the Treaty of Ghent
27 took place in December prior to the Battle of
28 New Orleans, the war did not officially end
29 until February 1815, when the Senate ratified
30 the treaty.

31 Had the combatants in New Orleans
32 known of the treaty, they might have
33 avoided a tough battle, especially the
34 British. In the battle, a force of about 4,000
35 American troops decisively defeated an
36 enemy of nearly twice its size. At stake for
37 the soldiers was control of the waterways of
38 the Mississippi, and the fighting was fierce.
39 A combination of tactical mistakes and bad
40 weather doomed the British attack, costing
41 them nearly 2,000 soldiers injured or killed.
42 The Americans lost fewer than 200. But
43 was the terrible battle all for nothing? Some
44 historians suggest that victory that day was
45 crucial for the American military in order
46 to enforce and help quickly ratify the peace
47 treaty. Potentially, with an American loss in
48 New Orleans, the British could have found
49 hope to continue the conflict.

Go on to the next page. ➡

1. The primary purpose of the passage is to

   (A) blame the British for fighting an unnecessary war
   (B) celebrate the tactical military maneuvers of Andrew Jackson
   (C) convince readers that peace treaties are often worthless
   (D) provide greater details about the end of a historical conflict

2. The passage suggests that all of the following occurred near the end of the War of 1812 EXCEPT

   (A) Andrew Jackson ignored the orders of President Madison
   (B) communication with the battle line commanders was slow
   (C) the Treaty of Ghent was signed
   (D) weather conditions hurt the efforts of the British soldiers

3. Which of the following is implied by the passage?

   (A) Andrew Jackson did not know the difference between a signed treaty and a ratified treaty.
   (B) President Madison did not realize the Battle of New Orleans was possible.
   (C) The British may have had a chance for victory with better conditions and preparation.
   (D) The British troops knew of the treaty but attacked anyway.

4. According to the passage, New Orleans was a strategic battle site because

   (A) it was the only location where American forces were better supplied than the British forces
   (B) the American forces would be trapped in the swamplands if they lost
   (C) the British were attempting to defeat a more numerous force
   (D) the Mississippi River was nearby and control of it was important

5. After which of the following was the War of 1812 officially at an end?

   (A) both armies signing the Treaty of Ghent
   (B) British retreat from the Mississippi
   (C) the Battle of New Orleans
   (D) the Senate's ratification of the Treaty of Ghent

6. According to the passage, a treaty

   (A) cannot be signed by the president without the consent of the Senate
   (B) has sometimes been ignored by those in battle
   (C) is always used to end a war
   (D) is not effective until it is ratified by the Senate

Go on to the next page. ➡️

Questions 7–12

Line

1　　According to game maker Hasbro,
2　approximately 750 million people have
3　played the well-known game *Monopoly*
4　since it was invented in the 1930s. Charles
5　Darrow is typically credited as the inventor
6　of the world's most famous board game.
7　However, he likely derived his version of
8　*Monopoly* from one of several other games
9　similarly involving realty buying and selling
10　that were already in existence prior to the
11　1930s when he got his patent for the game.
12　　A probable reason that Darrow's
13　*Monopoly* became the hugely successful
14　game that still exists today is that he took
15　a diligent approach to producing it. Other
16　similar games existed, but some of them
17　had no board or regulation pieces. With
18　help from his wife and son who adorned the
19　sets with detail, Darrow personally created
20　the pieces and boards that became the first
21　*Monopoly* game sets. His extra work in
22　creating the entire environment that players
23　needed gave his game something extra that
24　other variations did not have.

25　　Darrow had marginal success selling
26　his games in various parts of the country.
27　Several Philadelphia area stores were
28　the first to carry his game and sell it in
29　large quantities. Despite this, Darrow had
30　difficulty selling his game to the major game
31　manufacturer of the time, Parker Brothers.
32　He was told that his game was too complex
33　and had fundamental errors in its design
34　that would limit its appeal. Ultimately, the
35　continued sales he managed on his own
36　forced Parker Brothers to reassess the
37　worth of his game. Eventually, the company
38　agreed to produce the game and shortly
39　thereafter it became the bestselling game in
40　the country.
41　　That success turned Charles Darrow
42　into a millionaire, which is the ultimate
43　irony. Darrow initially began work on
44　*Monopoly* to help support himself and his
45　family following the financial troubles tied
46　to the stock market crash of 1929.
47　　Thus, Charles Darrow became a
48　millionaire by producing a game that allows
49　"regular" people to feel like they are buying
50　and selling homes and real estate like
51　millionaires.

Go on to the next page. ⟶

7. The best title for this passage would be

   (A) "A Comparison of Several Early Real Estate Board Games"
   (B) "How Hasbro Introduced *Monopoly* to the World"
   (C) "The Early History of Charles Darrow's *Monopoly*"
   (D) "Two Views of Charles Darrow's Life"

8. It is suggested by the passage that

   (A) Darrow decided to make his game less complex after initially meeting with Parker Brothers
   (B) Darrow had no other skills to use after the stock market crash of 1929
   (C) Parker Brothers probably doubted that a complex game could sell well
   (D) Philadelphia was the only major city where he could sell his game

9. As used in line 49, "regular" refers to people who

   (A) rent rather than own property
   (B) are in the top 1% of wealthiest people
   (C) love to play board games
   (D) are in a lower economic class than millionaires

10. With which of the following would the author be LEAST likely to agree?

    (A) Charles Darrow chose to continue to sell his game despite criticisms.
    (B) Charles Darrow is not the first person to conceive of a board-based real estate game.
    (C) Charles Darrow preferred to achieve his goals without the help of others.
    (D) Some of the things Darrow chose to do helped make his game sell better than other games.

11. Which of the following was NOT mentioned by the author as contributing to the ultimate success of *Monopoly*?

    (A) Darrow's efforts to initially sell the game on his own
    (B) the addition of specific pieces and a playing board in each set
    (C) the adjustments Parker Brothers made to the game
    (D) the enjoyment people get in pretending to be millionaires

12. The author suggests in the third paragraph that

    (A) certain errors in *Monopoly* served to limit its appeal
    (B) Charles Darrow sold his game in Philadelphia because he knew it would be popular there
    (C) *Monopoly* was initially too complex to be popular
    (D) some people doubted that *Monopoly* would be popular

Go on to the next page. ➞

Questions 13–18

Line

1   Every year, hundreds of hopeful
2   students arrive in Washington, D.C., in
3   order to compete in the National Spelling
4   Bee. This competition has been held
5   annually since 1925 and is sponsored by
6   E.W. Scripps Company. The sponsors
7   provide both a trophy and a monetary award
8   to the champion speller. In the competition,
9   students under 16 years of age take turns
10 attempting to properly spell words as
11 provided by the moderator. The champion
12 is the sole remaining student who does not
13 make a mistake.
14   Most American students are familiar
15 with the concept of a spelling bee because
16 it is practiced in many schools throughout
17 the country. The National Spelling Bee,
18 however, is a much bigger setting and
19 showcases only the best spellers from all
20 parts of the nation. Students who appear
21 at the National Spelling Bee have already
22 won competitions at local and state levels.
23 Winning the competition nowadays requires
24 the ability to perform under intense pressure
25 against very talented students in front
26 of a large audience. A student who wins
27 the event in the twenty-first century will
28 experience a much different challenge than
29 the first winner, Frank Neuhauser, did in
30 1925 when he defeated only nine other
31 competitors.

32   Clearly, the 95 years of the National
33 Spelling Bee's existence attests to the
34 importance of spelling in the English
35 language. However, struggles with spelling
36 English words go back much more than
37 95 years. The captivating thing about
38 spelling correctly in English is that it is in
39 many ways without rules. English language
40 has a powerful capacity to absorb new
41 words from other languages and in doing so
42 make them "English" words. As a result of
43 this ability to borrow from other languages,
44 the sheer number of words in English is
45 much higher than any other language. Thus,
46 spelling in many other languages involves
47 fewer words, fewer rules, and fewer odd
48 exceptions to those rules. It turns out that a
49 spelling bee in most other languages would
50 be a waste of time. Why is that? Well,
51 without the myriad exceptions to common
52 vocabulary, there would be very few words
53 that everyone didn't already know.

Go on to the next page. ➞

13. The author mentions "other languages" in line 41 in order to point out that

    (A) English-language spelling bees are unnecessarily complex
    (B) one challenge in English-language spelling bees is the number of words that can be tested
    (C) spelling bees are at least 95 years old
    (D) words are harder to spell in English than in any other language

14. According to the passage, what is a major difference between the first National Spelling Bee and today's competition?

    (A) Spellers in the past did not expect the competition to grow so large.
    (B) The competition no longer focuses on only English words.
    (C) There are more competitors.
    (D) The words used today are significantly harder.

15. In line 51, the word "myriad" most nearly means

    (A) confusing
    (B) dangerous
    (C) linguistic
    (D) numerous

16. Which of the following can be inferred from the passage?

    (A) A competitor at the National Spelling Bee has already won at least one smaller spelling bee.
    (B) E.W. Scripps Company desires to eliminate poor spelling in America.
    (C) Frank Neuhauser would not do well in today's competition.
    (D) The competition has grown too large.

17. The author of the passage intends to

    (A) compare the presentation of the current National Spelling Bee with the structure in the past
    (B) contrast the English language with other languages
    (C) investigate the role that vocabulary plays in our lives
    (D) review the history and current form of the National Spelling Bee

18. The author's attitude toward winners of the National Spelling Bee is

    (A) admiring
    (B) critical
    (C) indifferent
    (D) questioning

Go on to the next page. ⟶

Questions 19–24

Line

1   The idea of black holes was developed
2 by Karl Schwarzschild in 1916. Since then,
3 many different scientists have added to the
4 theory of black holes in space. A black hole
5 is usually defined as a very dense celestial
6 body from which nothing, not even light,
7 can escape. But from what do black holes
8 originate?
9   A black hole begins as a star. A star
10 burns hydrogen, and this process, called
11 fusion, releases energy. The energy released
12 outward works against the star's own
13 gravity pulling inward and prevents the star
14 from collapsing. After millions of years
15 of burning hydrogen, the star eventually
16 runs out of fuel. At this point, the star's
17 own gravity and weight cause it to start
18 contracting.
19   If the star is small and not very heavy,
20 it will shrink just a little and become a white
21 dwarf when it runs out of fuel. White dwarf
22 stars do not emit much energy, so they are
23 usually not visible without a telescope.

24   If the star is bigger and heavier, it will
25 collapse very quickly in an implosion. If the
26 matter that remains is not much heavier than
27 our Sun, it will eventually become a very
28 dense neutron star. However, if the matter
29 that remains is more than 1.7 times the
30 mass of our Sun, there will not be enough
31 outward pressure to resist the force of
32 gravity, and the collapse will continue. The
33 result is a black hole.
34   The black hole will have a boundary
35 around it called the horizon. Light and
36 matter can pass over this boundary to enter,
37 but they cannot pass back out again—this is
38 why the hole appears black. The gravity and
39 density of the black hole prevent anything
40 from escaping.
41   Scientists are still adding to the black
42 hole theory. They think they may have
43 found black holes in several different
44 galaxies, and as they learn more about them,
45 scientists will be able to understand more
46 about how black holes are formed and what
47 happens as the holes change.

Go on to the next page. ➞

19. The purpose of the question in the first paragraph is to

    (A) illustrate how little we know about black holes
    (B) indicate the source of the facts quoted in the passage
    (C) interest the reader in the topic of the passage
    (D) set a goal for independent research

20. According to the passage, which of the following causes a collapsing star to become a neutron star?

    (A) mass greater than 1.7 times that of our Sun
    (B) mass less than 1.7 times that of our Sun
    (C) remaining fuel that can be used in fusion
    (D) slow, brief shrinkage process

21. The passage suggests that if we were to send a satellite to the horizon of a black hole, it would probably

    (A) begin spinning uncontrollably and fly apart
    (B) be immediately repelled from the black hole
    (C) be pulled into the black hole and not come back out
    (D) enter, and then immediately exit, the black hole

22. According to the passage, which of the following is an effect of the process of fusion?

    (A) The star does not immediately collapse.
    (B) The star generates hydrogen.
    (C) The star survives millions of years longer than average.
    (D) The white dwarf fails to produce light.

23. Black holes appear black because

    (A) only a little energy escapes them
    (B) only one galaxy contains them
    (C) they are extraordinarily large
    (D) they do not eject light they have absorbed

24. Which of the following best describes the organization of the passage?

    (A) It discusses the biggest, heaviest celestial bodies before moving on to the smaller, lighter ones.
    (B) It introduces the topic and then narrates chronologically the process by which stars become black holes.
    (C) It uses a personal story to introduce the topic, and then compares and contrasts black holes.
    (D) It uses the example of one specific black hole in order to generalize.

Go on to the next page. ➞

Questions 25–30

Line

1　　　The midterm elections of 2014 had
2　the lowest voter turnout of any American
3　election cycle since World War II, with only
4　36.4 percent of the eligible voting public
5　casting a ballot. What is most disturbing
6　about this number is that it was less than
7　100 years ago that 200 women marched on
8　the White House, incurring public scorn,
9　arrest, and even torture, to secure the vote
10　for half the American public.
11　　　Women's Suffrage, the movement
12　dedicated to securing women's right to
13　vote in the United States, began in earnest
14　in the 1840s. Several Women's Rights
15　Conventions were held throughout the 19th
16　century, beginning with the Seneca Falls
17　Convention of 1848, during which attendees
18　officially passed a resolution in favor of
19　Women's Suffrage. Over the next 70 years,
20　many brave women fought for the cause of
21　basic gender equality.
22　　　This fight came to a head in 1917, when
23　members of the National Women's Party,
24　led by Alice Paul, picketed outside the
25　White House in order to influence President
26　Wilson and Congress to pass an amendment
27　to the United States Constitution that
28　would enfranchise women and guarantee
29　their voting rights. This was the first time
30　in the history of the United States that the
31　White House was picketed, and it was

32　done so in an orderly and peaceful fashion.
33　After months of nonviolent protest, police
34　arrested over 200 women for blocking a
35　public sidewalk in July 1917.
36　　　Paul and many of her followers
37　underwent a hunger strike during their
38　incarceration to protest the deplorable
39　conditions of the prison, which resulted
40　in many women being force-fed and Paul
41　herself being moved to the psychiatric
42　ward of the hospital. The rest were sent
43　to the Occoquan Workhouse. It was at
44　this workhouse that the most terrible and
45　significant event of the Women's Suffrage
46　movement would occur. Dubbed the "Night
47　of Terror," 44 guards armed with clubs
48　attacked 33 women protesters as they
49　returned to the house. They were brutally
50　beaten, choked, and one was stabbed to
51　death. These events infuriated the nation
52　when they were exposed, and within two
53　weeks a judge had ordered the prisoners
54　released and cleared of all charges.
55　　　Due to the widespread gain of support
56　these women earned through their peaceful
57　protest and physical endurance, as well as
58　the work of countless men and women of
59　the previous 70 years, the 19th Amendment
60　was added to the Constitution three years
61　later, on August 20, 1920.

Go on to the next page. ⟶

3

25. The main purpose of the passage is to

    (A) portray Alice Paul as an integral figure of the Women's Suffrage movement

    (B) attribute the adoption of the 19th Amendment solely to the Night of Terror

    (C) describe the actions taken by part of the American public to secure equal voting rights

    (D) demonstrate the terrible actions of guards against women's rights protestors

26. The word "exposed" as used in line 52 most closely means

    (A) unprotected
    (B) bare
    (C) revealed
    (D) buried

27. Which of the following best expresses the author's attitude toward the percentage of voter turnout mentioned in the first paragraph?

    (A) shock
    (B) reassurance
    (C) pessimism
    (D) terror

28. According to the author, the most probable legacy of the Night of Terror is

    (A) President Wilson's pardon of the protestors

    (B) the imprisonment of the 44 guards who attacked the protesters

    (C) the desired delay of the 19th amendment for several years

    (D) the right to vote for women

29. Which of the following does the passage imply was a reason for the protesters' hunger strike?

    (A) They were attempting to improve the environment of their captivity.

    (B) They were resisting being force-fed at the prison.

    (C) They wanted to be able to use the sidewalk for peaceful protest.

    (D) They were unable to eat after being choked during the Night of Terror.

30. The author believes that the National Women's Party's tactics are best described as

    (A) calm but pointless
    (B) disorderly but successful
    (C) violent and immediate
    (D) nonviolent and effective

Go on to the next page. ➞

Questions 31–36

Line

1   He was one of the greatest scientists of
2 this age. In fact, he was perhaps one of the
3 greatest scientists of any age. Yet he owed
4 much of his success not to mathematics
5 or physics or any other science but to a
6 disease. He was Stephen Hawking.
7   Born in 1942, three hundred years after
8 the death of Galileo, Stephen Hawking
9 had an unimpressive start to his scholarly
10 pursuits. At his revered English primary
11 school, St. Albans, he was considered by
12 his teachers a good, but not exceptional,
13 student. It was not evident at the time that
14 he would become internationally acclaimed
15 as a leader in several scientific fields.
16 He continued this moderately successful
17 academic trend at University College in
18 Oxford. Again, his professors thought him
19 to be intelligent, but not extraordinary in
20 his efforts. Both his cleverness and lack
21 of diligence were noticed by some of his
22 instructors.
23   After graduating from Oxford, he
24 continued to Cambridge, another excellent
25 school. Clearly, Hawking was moving
26 forward into a good science career.
27 However, it was at this time that he
28 encountered a life-changing challenge. He
29 was diagnosed with a disease that affects
30 and damages the nervous system. That

31 meant that he was eventually going to lose
32 control of his muscles and spend his life in
33 a wheelchair. Surprisingly though, Hawking
34 credited this event with making his outlook
35 on life strong again. He claimed that until
36 then, he was often bored by life. For a man
37 with such a powerful mind, that makes
38 sense. He was talented, but he saw little use
39 for his talent and felt no pressure to work
40 hard. His diagnosis and impending physical
41 problems forced him to start living life to
42 the fullest.
43   Most of Stephen Hawking's
44 contributions to science came after learning
45 of his disease. His work in the field of
46 physics has influenced the greatest scientists
47 alive. Though he passed away before the
48 technology became possible, he had hoped
49 to take a trip into space with the help of
50 influential friends. Though he moved only
51 with a special wheelchair and spoke only
52 with the help of a computerized speech
53 enhancer for the last several decades of his
54 life, he still had the ability to contribute
55 to the world. He credited his disease
56 with forcing him to face the limited time
57 available in one lifetime. Stephen Hawking
58 made a crippling disease the source of one
59 of the greatest scientific careers the world
60 has known. Through his misfortune, he
61 learned to reach his greatest potential.

Go on to the next page. ⟶

31. The author's tone is best described as

    (A) remorseful
    (B) admiring
    (C) pitying
    (D) scornful

32. The purpose of the last line of the first paragraph ("He was Stephen Hawking") is to

    (A) reveal an answer to a riddle
    (B) specify a subject who has already been introduced
    (C) answer a question the author asked earlier
    (D) name the greatest scientist of all time

33. Which of the following describes Stephen Hawking's attitude toward his disease?

    (A) actively nonchalant
    (B) bitterly irate
    (C) ironically appreciative
    (D) unreservedly giddy

34. According to the second paragraph, Stephen Hawking was seen by some as

    (A) often disrespectful
    (B) particularly brilliant
    (C) somewhat lazy
    (D) uniquely energetic

35. The passage does all of the following EXCEPT

    (A) demonstrate a connection between Stephen Hawking's disease and his success as a physicist
    (B) describe a goal Hawking wanted to achieve
    (C) note particular theories developed by Hawking
    (D) set forth educational institutions attended by Hawking

36. The passage can best be described as focusing primarily on

    (A) biographical details
    (B) medical diagnoses
    (C) scientific discoveries
    (D) technological advancements

STOP. If there is time, you may check your work in this section only. STOP

Section 4
Mathematics Achievement

Each question is followed by four suggested answers. Read each question and then decide which one of the four suggested answers is best.

Find the row of spaces on your answer document that has the same number as the question. In this row, mark the space having the same letter as the answer you have chosen. You may write in your test booklet.

SAMPLE QUESTION:

Sample Answer

Ⓐ ● Ⓒ Ⓓ

What is the perimeter of an isosceles triangle with two sides of 4 cm and one side of 6 cm?

(A)   10 cm
(B)   14 cm
(C)   16 cm
(D)   24 cm

The correct answer is 14 cm, so circle B is darkened.

STOP. Do not go on
until told to do so.

STOP

NO TEST MATERIAL ON THIS PAGE

1. Which one of the following pairs of numbers identifies the two different prime factors of 36 ?

    (A) 2 and 3
    (B) 3 and 4
    (C) 3 and 12
    (D) 4 and 9

2. For what nonzero value of x will the expression $\dfrac{x-3}{4x}$ be equal to 0 ?

    (A) −3
    (B) −2
    (C)   1
    (D)   3

3. Two positive whole numbers are in a ratio of 3 to 4. If the smaller of the two numbers is 9, what is the average of the two numbers?

    (A)   4
    (B) 10
    (C) 10.5
    (D) 12

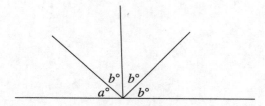

4. The four angles in the figure above share a common vertex on a straight line. What is the value of b when a equals 42 ?

    (A) 38
    (B) 40
    (C) 42
    (D) 46

5. What is 85% of 50 ?

    (A) 150.75
    (B) 135
    (C) 42.5
    (D) 39

6. A set of three positive integers has a sum of 11 and a product of 36. If the smallest of the three numbers is 2, what is the largest?

    (A) 2
    (B) 4
    (C) 6
    (D) 9

Go on to the next page. ⟶

7. What is two-thirds of one-half?

    (A) $\dfrac{1}{3}$

    (B) $\dfrac{7}{6}$

    (C) $\dfrac{1}{2}$

    (D) $\dfrac{2}{3}$

8. If the distance around an oval-shaped track is 400 meters, how many laps does a runner have to run to cover a distance of 4 kilometers?
   (1 kilometer = 1,000 meters)

    (A)   4
    (B)   10
    (C)   15
    (D)   1,000

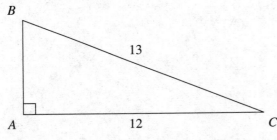

9. In triangle *ABC* shown above, the length of side *AB* is

    (A)   5
    (B)   7
    (C)   11
    (D)   14

10. Find the value of $\dfrac{2.7 \times 10^7}{3.0 \times 10^{-3}}$.

    (A) 9.0×10^{10}
    (B) 9.0×10^9
    (C) 9.0×10^4
    (D) 9.0×10^3

11. MegaMusic decides to decrease the price of a digital song from \$1.60 to \$1.20. The percent decrease for this digital song is

    (A)   20%

    (B)   25%

    (C) $33\dfrac{1}{3}\%$

    (D)   40%

12. There are *x* students in Mrs. Sproul's class, 4 fewer than twice as many as are in Mrs. Puccio's class. If there are *y* students in Mrs. Puccio's class, then what is the value of *y* in terms of *x* ?

    (A) $\dfrac{x}{2} + 2$

    (B) $2x + 4$

    (C) $2x - 4$

    (D) $\dfrac{x}{2} - 4$

Go on to the next page. ➡

Questions 13–14 refer to the following definition.

For all real numbers x,

$\#x = x^2$ if x is negative;
$\#x = 2x$ if x is positive.

13. $\#(-6) - \#(6) =$

   (A)   −24
   (B)   16
   (C)   24
   (D)   30

14. What is the value of $\#[\#x - \#y]$ when $x = 3$ and $y = -4$?

   (A)   −10
   (B)   12
   (C)   32
   (D)   100

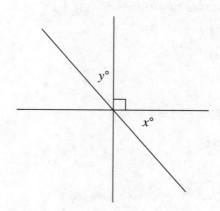

15. In the figure above, what is the value of x in terms of y ?

   (A) y
   (B) $90 - y$
   (C) $90 + y$
   (D) $180 - y$

16. $\dfrac{4a^4 b^6 c^3}{2a^3 b^5 c^2} =$

   (A) $\dfrac{2ac}{b}$

   (B) $\dfrac{ac}{b}$

   (C) $\dfrac{2b}{c}$

   (D) $2abc$

Go on to the next page.   →

4

17. In Mr. Johanessen's class, $\frac{1}{4}$ of the students failed the final exam. Of the remaining students in the class, $\frac{1}{3}$ scored an A. What fraction of the whole class passed the test but scored below an A?

(A) $\frac{1}{4}$

(B) $\frac{5}{12}$

(C) $\frac{1}{2}$

(D) $\frac{7}{12}$

18. When buying new clothes for school, Rena spends $20 more than Karen and $50 more than Lynn does. If Rena spends r dollars, then what is the cost of all three of their purchases in terms of r?

(A) $r + 70$

(B) $\frac{r + 70}{3}$

(C) $3r - 70$

(D) $r + 210$

19. In a group of 100 children, all of whom are either left-handed or right-handed, there are 34 more right-handed children than there are left-handed. How many left-handed children are in the group?

(A) 33
(B) 37
(C) 67
(D) 68

20. Samantha made a chart of her students' favorite types of books.

FAVORITE TYPE OF BOOK

Type of Book	Number of Students
Mystery	8
Fantasy	20
Sci-Fi	10
Other	2

A circle graph is made using the data. What is the central angle of the portion of the graph representing Sci-Fi?

(A) 10°
(B) 25°
(C) 45°
(D) 90°

Go on to the next page. ➞

21. At Nicholas's Computer World, computers usually sold for $1,500 are now being sold for $1,200. What fraction of the original price is the new price?

(A) $\frac{1}{10}$

(B) $\frac{1}{5}$

(C) $\frac{3}{4}$

(D) $\frac{4}{5}$

22. If $\frac{3}{x} = \frac{y}{4}$, then

(A) $xy = 12$

(B) $3y = 4x$

(C) $\frac{x}{y} = \frac{4}{3}$

(D) $3x = 4y$

23. The ratio of juniors to seniors at Kennett High School is 3 to 2. If there is a total of 600 juniors and seniors at the school, how many are seniors?

(A) 120
(B) 240
(C) 360
(D) 400

24. 150% of 40 is

(A) 30
(B) 40
(C) 50
(D) 60

25. Jane studied for her math exam for 4 hours last night. If she studied $\frac{3}{4}$ as long for her English exam, how many hours did she study all together?

(A) 3

(B) $4\frac{3}{4}$

(C) 6

(D) 7

26. $\frac{0.966}{0.42} =$

(A) 0.23
(B) 2.3
(C) 23
(D) 230

Go on to the next page. ➔

27. Nicole was able to type 35 words per minute. If she increased her speed to 42 words per minute, what was the percent increase in her typing speed?

   (A) $16\frac{2}{3}\%$

   (B) 20%

   (C) 70%

   (D) 71%

28. The first term in a series of numbers is 50. Each subsequent term is one-half the term before it if the term is even, or one-half rounded up to the next whole number if the term is odd. What is the third term in this sequence?

   (A) 13
   (B) 24
   (C) 30
   (D) 40

29. Sophia recorded the number of siblings each student in her class has in the table below.

SIBLINGS OF EACH STUDENT

Number of Siblings	Number of Students with that Number of Siblings
0	6
1	10
2	8
3	6
4	1
5	1

What is the mode of the data?

   (A) 1
   (B) 2
   (C) 6
   (D) 10

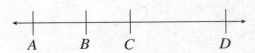

30. On the number line shown above, if segment BD has a length of 18, segment AB has a length of 5, and segment CD has a length of 12, then segment AC has a length of

   (A) 6
   (B) 11
   (C) 17
   (D) 23

Go on to the next page. ➡️

31. The decimal representation of $2 + 40 + \frac{1}{100}$ is

    (A) 24.1
    (B) 24.01
    (C) 42.1
    (D) 42.01

32. What is the least possible integer divisible by 2, 3, 4, and 5 ?

    (A) 30
    (B) 40
    (C) 60
    (D) 90

33. If a car travels at x miles per hour, in terms of x and y, how long does it take it to travel y miles?

    (A) $\dfrac{2x}{y}$

    (B) xy

    (C) $\dfrac{y}{x}$

    (D) $\dfrac{x}{y}$

34. Triangles ABC and PQR are similar. The length of $\overline{BC}$ is 4 and the length of $\overline{QR}$ is 12. If the area of ABC is 6, what is the area of PQR ?

    (A) 54
    (B) 24
    (C) 18
    (D) 15

35. James buys one halibut steak and two salmon steaks for $30.00. Dave buys two halibut steaks and four salmon steaks for $60.00. If halibut steaks cost x dollars each and salmon steaks cost y dollars each, what is the value of x ?

    (A) $5.00
    (B) $8.00
    (C) $10.00
    (D) It cannot be determined from the information given.

Question 36 refers to the following definition.

For all positive integer values of x,

$(x) = \frac{1}{2}x$ if x is even;

$(x) = 2x$ if x is odd.

36. $(1 + 5) =$

    (A) 2
    (B) 3
    (C) 4
    (D) 6

37. Which of the following equals $2(4z + 1)$?

    (A) $2z + \dfrac{1}{2}$

    (B) $2z + 1$

    (C) $4z + 2$

    (D) $8z + 2$

Go on to the next page. ⟶

MA

38. The stem-and-leaf plot shown represents the length, in minutes, of movies that Janet watched over the summer.

Stem	Leaf
10	8 9
11	1 2 2 5 5 6 7
12	0 3 4 8
13	2 4 6 6 7 7 9
14	2 3 3 8 9 9
15	7

What is the median length, in minutes, of the movies Janet watched?

(A)   130
(B)   132
(C)   133
(D)   136

39. Zoo A has 3 monkeys. Zoo B has 8 monkeys. Zoo C has 16 monkeys. What is the average number of monkeys at the three zoos?

(A)   3
(B)   7
(C)   9
(D)   27

40. A steak costs $4 more than a hamburger, and a hamburger costs $4 more than a grilled cheese sandwich. If six grilled cheese sandwiches cost $2x$ dollars, how much will 4 steaks and 2 hamburgers cost?

(A) $2x + 40$
(B) $2x + 48$
(C) $6x + 34$
(D) $12x + 40$

41. What is the solution set to the inequality $|3 - 2x| > 9$?

(A) $-3 < x < 6$
(B) $-6 < x < 3$
(C) $x < -3$ or $x > 6$
(D) $x < -6$ or $x > 3$

42. $100xy$ is what percent of xy ?

(A)   10
(B)   100
(C)   1,000
(D)   10,000

43. If Ismail's home is four miles from school and Lakshmi's home is eight miles from school, then the distance from Ismail's home to Lakshmi's home is

(A)   4 miles
(B)   8 miles
(C)   12 miles
(D)   It cannot be determined from the information given.

44. Two partners divide a profit of $2,000 so that the difference between the two amounts is half of their average. What is the ratio of the larger to the smaller amount?

(A)   6:1
(B)   5:3
(C)   4:1
(D)   2:1

Go on to the next page. ➡

45. What is the total value, in cents, of j coins worth 10 cents each and $j + 5$ coins worth 25 cents each?

   (A) $35j + 125$
   (B) $35j + 5$
   (C) $10j + 130$
   (D) $2j + 5$

46. A box of coins has 6 pennies, 3 nickels, 4 dimes, and 5 quarters. If two coins are selected at random, what is the probability that the first coin is a penny and the second coin is a quarter?

   (A) $\dfrac{11}{18}$

   (B) $\dfrac{17}{18}$

   (C) $\dfrac{6}{18} \times \dfrac{5}{18}$

   (D) $\dfrac{6}{18} \times \dfrac{5}{17}$

47. The formula for the volume of a cone is $\frac{1}{3}\pi r^2 h$, where r is the radius of the circular base and h is the height of the cone.

   What is the radius of a cone with a volume of 12π and a height of 4 ?

   (A) 3
   (B) 4
   (C) 8
   (D) 9

STOP. If there is time, you may check your work in this section only. STOP

Essay

You will have 30 minutes to plan and write an essay on the topic printed on the other side of this page. **Do not write on another topic. An essay on another topic is not acceptable.**

The essay is designed to give you an opportunity to show how well you can write. You should try to express your thoughts clearly. How well you write is much more important than how much you write, but you need to say enough for a reader to understand what you mean.

You will probably want to write more than a short paragraph. You should also be aware that a copy of your essay will be sent to each school that will be receiving your test results. You are to write only in the appropriate section of the answer sheet. Please write or print so that your writing may be read by someone who is not familiar with your handwriting.

You may make notes and plan your essay on the reverse side of the page. Allow enough time to copy the final form onto your answer sheet. You must copy the essay topic onto your answer sheet, on page 3, in the box provided.

Please remember to write only the final draft of the essay on pages 3 and 4 of your answer sheet and to write it in blue or black pen. Again, you may use cursive writing or you may print. Only pages 3 and 4 will be sent to the schools.

Directions continue on next page.

REMINDER: Please write this essay topic on the first few lines of page 3 of your answer sheet.

Essay Topic

If you could change one thing about your country, what would you change and why?

- Only write on this essay question
- Only pages 3 and 4 will be sent to the schools
- Only write in blue or black pen

NOTES

_____

_____

_____

_____

_____

_____

_____

_____

_____

_____

_____

_____

STUDENT NAME_____**GRADE APPLYING FOR**_____

You must write your essay topic in this space.

_____

_____

_____

Use specific details and examples in your response.

_____

_____

_____

_____

_____

_____

_____

_____

_____

_____

_____

_____

_____

_____

_____

Page 3

Chapter 11
Upper Level ISEE
Practice Test:
Answers and
Explanations

ANSWER KEY

ISEE UL Verbal Reasoning 1

1. D	5. A	9. D	13. C	17. B	21. A	25. A	29. C	33. A	37. A
2. C	6. B	10. B	14. B	18. A	22. A	26. D	30. B	34. C	38. A
3. D	7. B	11. C	15. D	19. B	23. D	27. A	31. D	35. C	39. A
4. C	8. D	12. B	16. B	20. B	24. A	28. A	32. B	36. C	40. A

ISEE UL Quantitative Reasoning 2

1. C	5. B	9. C	13. A	17. D	21. C	25. B	29. C	33. A	37. C
2. C	6. D	10. B	14. B	18. C	22. B	26. D	30. B	34. C	
3. D	7. A	11. C	15. A	19. D	23. C	27. A	31. B	35. B	
4. D	8. B	12. D	16. A	20. C	24. D	28. C	32. A	36. B	

ISEE UL Reading Comprehension 3

1. D	5. D	9. D	13. B	17. D	21. C	25. C	29. A	33. C
2. A	6. D	10. C	14. C	18. A	22. A	26. C	30. D	34. C
3. C	7. C	11. C	15. D	19. C	23. D	27. C	31. B	35. C
4. D	8. C	12. D	16. A	20. B	24. B	28. D	32. B	36. A

ISEE UL Mathematics Achievement 4

1. A	6. C	11. B	16. D	21. D	26. B	31. D	36. B	41. C	46. D
2. D	7. A	12. A	17. C	22. A	27. B	32. C	37. D	42. D	47. A
3. C	8. B	13. C	18. C	23. B	28. A	33. C	38. B	43. D	
4. D	9. A	14. D	19. A	24. D	29. A	34. A	39. C	44. B	
5. C	10. B	15. B	20. D	25. D	30. B	35. D	40. A	45. A	

EXPLANATIONS

Section 1 Verbal Reasoning

1. **D** Grave is defined as "serious" or "sober." An example phrase is "a grave silence," which would be a serious or sober silence. This makes (D) solemn the correct answer choice.

2. **C** To foment is defined as "to foster" or "to promote." An example phrase is to "foment trouble," which would be to promote or cause trouble. This makes (C) instigate the correct answer choice.

3. **D** Inarticulate is the opposite of articulate. Articulate can be defined as "well expressed" or "clearly spoken." Since inarticulate is the opposite of articulate, it is defined as unclear, or not well understood or expressed. None of the first three choices, creative, friendly, or overly sensitive, are related to being well spoken or not. Choices (A), (B), and (C) can be eliminated. This makes (D) tongue-tied the best answer.

4. **C** One clue to finding the definition of ameliorate is the root "amo," which is Latin for love. In Spanish this is "amor" and in Italian it is "amore." This root establishes that the correct word will be a positive word, which means that (B) hinder and (D) restrain can be eliminated. Ameliorate is defined as making something better, which makes (C) improve the correct answer.

5. **A** Thesis is another word for theory. A theory is best defined as "an idea or belief," which best matches (A). One common use of the word "thesis" is to refer to the overarching piece of written work produced in a degree program, which might make (B), (C), or (D) appear to be likely answer choices. However, a written thesis is called a thesis because its aim is to explain or support the idea behind it, matching the true definition of the word thesis. Choice (A) is the correct answer.

6. **B** To debunk is defined as "to disprove." An example phrase is to "debunk a popular theory," which would be to disprove a popular theory. This makes (B) discredit the correct answer choice.

7. **B** Disdain contains the root word "dis," which means "apart," "asunder," "away," or "having a negative force." Since this is a negative root the answer choice should be negative as well, which eliminates (C) find and (D) hope. Since disdain is defined as a lack of respect, (B) contempt is the correct answer.

8. **D** Reticent is defined as "withdrawn" or "introverted." An example phrase is "she was reticent about giving her answer aloud in class." This makes (D) reserved the best answer.

9. **D** Prevalent is defined as "widespread." An example phrase would be "acronyms have become prevalent in text message and email communications." This makes (D) predominant the correct answer.

10. **B**   Satiate comes from the root "sat" or "satis," which means "to satisfy" or "enough." Other words with this root include satisfaction, satisfactory, and satiable. All of these words have definitions related to being satisfied or having enough. Satiate is defined as "being full, having a desire or appetite fulfilled." This makes (B) fill the correct answer.

11. **C**   Candid is defined as "truthful" or "straightforward." An example phrase would be "to speak candidly," which would be to speak truthfully. This makes (C) frank the correct answer.

12. **B**   Emulate is related to the similar sounding word imitate. Emulate is defined as "attempting to copy or imitate" another's actions. This makes (B) imitate the correct answer.

13. **C**   Taint is defined as "to contaminate or pollute." An example phrase would be "the case involved tainted evidence, which resulted in a mistrial." This makes (C) infect the correct answer.

14. **B**   Enigma is defined as "a puzzle" or "a mystery." An example sentence is "The unsolved disappearance of Amelia Earhart is one of the great enigmas of our time." This makes (B) mystery the correct answer.

15. **D**   Detrimental is defined as "harmful" or "resulting in a loss." It is the adjective form of the noun detriment, which is defined as a loss or harm. Loss or harm best matches (D) injurious, which is the correct answer.

16. **B**   Meticulous is defined as "overly attentive to detail," "exact," or "precise." An example sentence would be "The doctor was meticulous; she ran every test and examined her patient inch by inch." This makes (B) finicky the correct answer.

17. **B**   Juxtapose comes from the Latin root juxta, which means "next to." To juxtapose is defined as "to place two items close to one another," in order to establish a contrast between them. The best match for this definition is (B) place side by side, which is the correct answer.

18. **A**   Congenial has two main roots: con and gen. Con means "with;" examples of words with this root and meaning are connect, contract, congregate. Gen means "race" or "kind of;" in other words "relation." Examples of words with this root are genealogy, genetics, genes. Congenial is defined as something or someone pleasant due to being well-suited to a certain situation. This best matches answer (A) friendly, the correct answer.

19. **B**   To mitigate is defined as "to soften." An example sentence is "The seriousness of Amy's injuries was mitigated by the immediate medical attention she received." This makes (B) ease the correct answer.

20. **B**   Elusive is directly related to the word elude, which means "to avoid or escape." This makes (B) slippery the correct answer.

21. **A** Pay attention to the clues in the sentence. The second half of the sentence indicates that Jane is torn between two feelings or sides, so the missing word should mean the same thing as torn. Choice (A), ambivalent, means "to have conflicted feelings," which matches the word you are looking for. Choice (B), apathetic, means "to not care at all," so it can be eliminated. Neither happy nor irritated means "torn," so (C) and (D) can be eliminated as well. Choice (A) is the correct answer.

22. **A** Pay attention to the clues in the sentence. The sentence states that M. Carey Thomas was like Susan B. Anthony, the famous women's rights activist. This indicates that Thomas also supported women's rights, and so the missing word must mean "supported." Choice (A), championed, is a synonym for supported. Choice (B) means "to desecrate or vandalize," so eliminate it. Neither (C) nor (D) means supported, so they can be eliminated as well. Choice (A) is the correct answer.

23. **D** Pay attention to the clues in the sentence. The second half of the sentence states that different cultures have different ideas about how people should be treated. This indicates that morality is not the same everywhere, since there's a "not" in front of the blank so the missing word must mean "the same" or "standardized." Choice (A), debatable, is the opposite meaning of the blank, so it can be eliminated. Neither (B) nor (C) mean not related or not standardized, so they can be eliminated as well. Only (D), universal, matches the meaning of the blank.

24. **A** Pay attention to the clues in the sentence and the direction words. The sentence starts with although, and ends with the fact that the student did not study at all. This indicates that the opposite happened earlier in the sentence: Ms. Sanchez warned or advised the student that he should study. Since neither (B), (C), nor (D) means "advised" or "warned," the only possible answer is (A).

25. **A** Pay attention to the clues in the sentence. The sentence tells you that Thomas Jefferson was skilled at many things. This indicates that Jefferson was a man of many talents, so the missing word must mean "many." The only choice that matches this answer choice is (A), abundant.

26. **D** Pay attention to the clues in the sentence. The second part of the sentence states that Monica was moved to speak up. This indicates that Monica could no longer remain silent or quiet. Neither (A), (B), nor (C) means "silent" or "quiet," which makes (D) the only possible answer choice.

27. **A** Pay attention to the clues in the sentence. The second part of the sentence states that *Little Women* was based on Louisa May Alcott's own life. This indicates that the missing word will mean "personal." While the other three answer choices may seem related to a writing style or a novel, only (A), autobiographical, matches personal.

28. **A** Pay attention to the clues in the sentence and the direction words. The sentence starts with "Though his lectures could be monotonous... ." "Though" is an opposite direction word, so the missing word will mean the opposite of monotonous. Look for a word that means interesting or captivating. Choice (A), amiable, matches this meaning. Choice (B) means "religious" or "reverential," so it can be eliminated. Choices (C) and (D) are synonymous with boring or dull; eliminate those as well. Choice (A) is the correct answer.

29. **C** Pay attention to the clues in the sentence. The second part of the sentence states "…just as Craig had thought, he had two pop quizzes." Since having pop quizzes is generally considered a negative occurrence, the missing word most likely means he "felt" or had "known" the day would go badly right from the start. The only answer choice that is related to feeling or knowing how things would turn out is (C), a premonition.

30. **B** Pay attention to the clues in the sentence. The first part of the sentence says "Far from shedding light on the mystery," and the second part says Jason's response "left people unsure." This indicates that Jason's response was unclear, so the missing word must match that meaning. Choice (A), impartial, means "to be unbiased," which does not match unclear. Eliminate it. Choice (B), opaque, means "to be unclear" or "not transparent." Choice (C), risky, means to have "the possibility of danger," which does not match unclear and so can be eliminated. Choice (D), systematic, means to be "thorough or methodical," which is also incorrect. Choice (B) is the correct answer.

31. **D** On two-blank sentence completions, always start with one blank to work with first and eliminate answer choices based on that. The first blank matches the word "talented" in the sentence, so look for a word that means "talented" or "skilled." Neither "faithful" in (A) nor "insulting" in (B) matches this meaning, so both choices should be completely eliminated. The rest of the sentence says that although Marie was talented, she didn't know how to promote herself. This indicates that her talents were overlooked, so the second word should match that meaning. Between (C) and (D), only "ignored" in (D) matches that meaning. Choice (D) is the correct answer.

32. **B** Pay attention to the clues in the sentence and the direction words. The first part of the sentence states that "Although she was the daughter of a wealthy slaveholder… ." Since "although" is an opposite direction word, the remainder of the sentence most likely explains that Angelina Grimke was against slavery. If you start with the first word, the answer should match "against." Since (A) and (D) are the opposite of "against," those choices can be eliminated. The second blank most likely means "fought" or "dedicated," since she would have been for abolition. Only "dedicated" in (B) matches this meaning, making it the best answer choice.

33. **A** On two-blank sentence completions, always start with one blank to work with first and eliminate answer choices based on that. The second part of the sentence says that a great deal of sugar is required when cooking with rhubarb, indicating that it takes sugar to make the rhubarb taste "good" or "edible" for the second blank. Since neither fattening, sickening, nor sticky matches this meaning, (A) is most likely the correct answer. However, you should still check the other blank. Since the second part of the sentence discusses how much sugar is needed when cooking rhubarb, rhubarb must be the opposite of sweet. Check (A)'s first word to make sure it means the opposite of sweet. Since "bitter" is the opposite of sweet, (A) is the correct answer.

34. **C** On two-blank sentence completions, always start with one blank to work with first and eliminate answer choices based on that. The first half of the sentence states that Martha would see the bright side of any situation, so the missing blank would mean she is naturally "happy" or "cheerful."

Neither (B) nor (D) matches this meaning, so those answer choices can be eliminated. The remainder of the sentence begins with the opposite direction word "but" and states that Jack was always waiting for something bad to happen. This indicates that the second blank means "negative" or "depressed." Choice (A) is the opposite meaning of negative, so it can be eliminated. Only (C) works for both blanks.

35.   **C**   On two-blank sentence completions, always start with one blank to work with first and eliminate answer choices based on that. The first half of the sentence says that Edgar was not telling the truth, indicating that the missing word means "lies" or "falsehoods." Only (C) and (D) match this meaning, eliminating (A) and (B). The second part of the sentence indicates that Edgar's lies encouraged the crowd to reject Edgar's competitor, so the second blank must match "encouraged." Between "incited" and "permitted," "incited" is the best match. Choice (C) is the correct answer.

36.   **C**   On two-blank sentence completions, always start with one blank to work with first and eliminate answer choices based on that. The second part of the sentence refers to the text as being "a mere 100 pages." The word "mere" indicates that the missing word must mean "short." Choices (A), (B), and (C) all match this meaning. "Banal" means "lacking depth" and is not related to length, and so (D) can be eliminated. The first part of the sentence discusses the critics praise for the author's use of words, so the first blank must mean something positive. Hackneyed means "trite" or "overused," and improper means "out of the norm or standard," neither of which is a positive meaning. The only positive answer is (C), precise. Choice (C) is the correct answer.

37.   **A**   On two-blank sentence completions, always start with one blank to work with first and eliminate answer choices based on that. The sentence starts by saying Erica's mother could not do something, followed by the word "why." Usually when someone does not know "why" something is happening or has happened, it means they do not understand. Look for the answer choices that match "understand" for the first word. Only (A) and (D) match; eliminate (B) and (C). The entire sentence is saying that Erica's mother couldn't understand why she would study the culture of thirteenth century French winemakers. Compare (A) and (D) to see which one makes the most sense in the context of the sentence. If this were an interesting subject, would Erica's mother not be able to understand why she wanted to study it? No; eliminate (D). The fact that the subject is very obscure, or esoteric, does make it more difficult to understand as a subject choice. Choice (A) is the correct answer.

38.   **A**   On two-blank sentence completions, always start with one blank to work with first and eliminate answer choices based on that. The first part of the sentence states that Ernie was still excited about the race despite the storm. The missing word most likely means that the storm did not diminish or reduce Ernie's excitement. Only (A) and (C) match this meaning; eliminate (B) and (D) completely. Since Ernie remained excited about the race, he was not afraid of running it in bad weather. The second blank must mean he had no concerns or reservations about running in the storm. Since inclination is the opposite of concern or reservation, (C) cannot be correct. Choice (A) is the correct answer.

39. **A** On two-blank sentence completions, always start with one blank to work with first and eliminate answer choices based on that. The entire sentence is discussing how stingy Mr. Sanford is, and says "even a restaurant meal" was an excess. What kind of excess? Most likely an unnecessary or a wasteful expense. The only word in the answer choices that matches this meaning is (A), gratuitous. Ideally, you should check to make sure that the first word in (A) works as well. The sentence makes it clear that Mr. Sanford doesn't like to spend money, or is stingy. Parsimonious does mean stingy, so (A) is the correct answer. However, if you were unsure of what parsimonious meant you should feel confident in (A) due to process of elimination.

40. **A** Pay attention to clues and direction words in the sentence. The second part of the sentence starts with "even though," an opposite direction phrase. It continues to state that her love of art was far from superficial. Since the opposite direction phrase comes in front of this description, the missing second word must mean a superficial love of art. Neither mentor, performer, nor adversary matches that meaning, and so (B), (C), and (D) can be eliminated. This leaves (A) as the most likely answer based on process of elimination. The first word describes how Margie felt about being told she has a superficial love of art, which is not true, so that word will most likely mean "unhappiness" or "frustration." Chagrin matches this meaning, making (A) the correct answer.

Section 2 Quantitative Reasoning

1. **C** Since all of the answers are decimals between 0 and 1, the greatest number will be the one closest to 1. Choice (A) is equivalent to $\frac{1}{100}$, (B) is equivalent to $\frac{99}{10,000}$, (C) is equivalent to $\frac{19}{100}$, and (D) is equivalent to $\frac{199}{10,000}$. Thus, the correct answer is (C) since it is the closest to 1.

2. **C** Pay careful attention to the word *NOT*. Choice (A) is the product of two prime numbers: 3 and 11. Choice (B) is the product of two prime numbers: 5 and 7. Choice (D) is the product of two prime numbers: 7 and 13. Choice (C) is the product of 5 and 9, 3 and 15, or 1 and 45. Since 45 is not the product of 2 prime numbers, the correct answer is (C).

3. **D** Since the values of x, y, and z are not given, plug in. Let $x = 2$, $y = 4$, and $z = 6$. The difference between x and z is 4 since $z - x = 6 - 2 = 4$. The correct answer is (D).

4. **D** Use the chart to determine each amount. To find percent change, use the formula: % change = $\frac{\text{difference}}{\text{original}} \times 100$. For (A), the difference of the two prices is \$30, so the percent discount is $\frac{120 - 90}{120} \times 100 = \frac{30}{120} \times 100 = 25$. For (B), the difference of the two prices is \$70, so the percent discount is $\frac{250 - 180}{250} \times 100 = \frac{70}{250} \times 100 = 28$. For (C), the difference of the two prices is \$20, so the percent discount is $\frac{60 - 40}{60} \times 100 = \frac{20}{60} \times 100 \approx 33$. For (D), the difference of the two

prices is \$20, so the percent discount is $\dfrac{40-20}{40} \times 100 = \dfrac{20}{40} \times 100 = 50$. Since 50% is the greatest discount, the correct answer is (D).

5. **B** Use the chart to determine each amount. The buyer will save \$30 on dresses, \$70 on coats, \$20 on shoes, and \$20 on hats. Therefore, purchasing coats will save the buyer the most dollars, so the correct answer is (B).

6. **D** Since there are variables in the question and answers, plug in a value for b (Beth's age). If $b = 7$, then Amy is 10 years old and Jo is 15 years old. The correct answer will be the one that equals 15, so plug 7 in for b and check each answer choice. Choice (A) is $2(7) + 3 = 17$. Choice (B) is $2(7) - 3 = 11$. Choice (C) is $7 + 4 = 11$. Choice (D) is $7 + 8 = 15$. Since it is the only one that matches the target value, (D) is the correct answer.

7. **A** Since there are variables in the question, plug in values for x and y that will fit the restrictions of the problem. If $x = 9$, then $5\overline{)9}$ with a remainder of 4. If $y = 6$, then $5\overline{)6}$ with a remainder of 1. Plug in the values of x and y to get $x + y = 9 + 6 = 15$. 5 divides into 15 exactly three times (i.e., the remainder is 0), so the correct answer is (A).

8. **B** Since there are variables in the question and answers, plug in values for x, p, y, and q. If $x = 2$, then let $p = 6$. If $y = 5$, then let $q = 15$. Next, test these values in each answer choice to find the true statement. For (A), $pq = 6 \times 15 = 90$ and $xy = 2 \times 5 = 10$. Since 90 is not a factor of 10, eliminate (A). In (B), $pq = 6 \times 15 = 90$ and $xy = 2 \times 5 = 10$. Since 90 is a multiple of 10, keep (B). For (C), $p = 6$ and $xy = 2 \times 5 = 10$. Since 6 is not a factor of 10, eliminate (C). In (D), $p = 6$ and $xy = 2 \times 5 = 10$. Since 6 is not a multiple of 10, eliminate (D). Only (B) contains a true statement, so it is the correct answer.

9. **C** The range of x is given ($-3 \le x \le 2$), so test the highest and lowest values of x in the equation given to see what the maximum value of y is. If $x = 2$, then $3(2)^2 + 2 = 3(4) + 2 = 12 + 2 = 14$. Eliminate (A) because (B) contains a possible value of y that is higher than 2. If $x = -3$, then $3(-3)^2 + 2 = 3(9) + 2 = 27 + 2 = 29$. Eliminate (B) since (C) contains a greater value of y. There is not a value of x that will yield a higher value of y in this equation since the outermost values of x have been tested, so the correct answer is (C).

10. **B** To determine the value of b, FOIL (first, outer, inner, last) the left side of the equation: $(x + 5)^2 = (x + 5)(x + 5) = x^2 + 5x + 5x + 25 = x^2 + 10x + 25$. Since $x^2 + 10x + 25 = x^2 + bx + 25$, then $10x = bx$. Therefore, $b = 10$. The correct answer is (B).

11. **C** Pay careful attention to the word *NOT*. Since the answer choices represent possible values of J, plug in the answer choices (PITA). In choices (A), (B), and (C), J can equal 12, 24, or 36 since each one is divisible by both 4 and 3. However, in (C), while 30 is divisible by 3, it is not divisible by 4. Thus, J cannot equal 30, and the correct answer is (C).

12. **D** Estimation is a good way to solve this problem, since the question is asking for an approximation. 0.48 is close to 0.5 or $\frac{1}{2}$. The product of $\frac{1}{2}$ and 100 is 50 ($\frac{1}{2} \times 100 = 50$), so the correct answer is (D).

13. **A** Since the length and width of the rectangle are not provided, plug in values. Let $l = 20$ and $w = 10$. If the length is increased by 20%, then the new length of the rectangle is 24 since $0.2 \times 20 = 4$ and $20 + 4 = 24$. If the width is decreased by 10%, then the new width of the rectangle is 9 since $0.1 \times 10 = 1$ and $10 - 1 = 9$. To find the area of a rectangle, use the formula $A = l \times w$. The area of the original rectangle is $20 \times 10 = 200$, and the area of the new rectangle is $24 \times 9 = 216$. Next, to determine percent change, use the formula: % change $= \dfrac{\text{difference}}{\text{original}} \times 100$. The difference of the areas is 16 since $216 - 200 = 16$, and the original area is 200. Thus, $\dfrac{216 - 200}{200} \times 100 = \dfrac{16}{200} \times 100 = 8$. Therefore, the correct answer is (A).

14. **B** Since each segment is 1 meter and each route must be exactly 3 meters long, the only possible routes are $AH \rightarrow HI \rightarrow ID$, $AB \rightarrow BI \rightarrow ID$, and $AB \rightarrow BC \rightarrow CD$. With only 3 different routes possible, the correct answer is (B).

15. **A** There are 180° in a triangle. If angle B is greater than 90°, then the remaining two angles must have a sum less than 90°. The remaining two angles must also be equal to each other since the question states that $AB = BC$. Since the answer choices represent possible values of angle C, test the answer choices (PITA). If angle C is 35°, then angle A is 35°, and angle B would equal 110°. Since 35° is a possible value of angle C, (A) is the correct answer. Note the remaining choices are incorrect because angle B must be greater than 90°. Choice (B) is incorrect because if angle C is 45°, then angle A is 45°, and angle B would equal 90°. Choice (C) is incorrect because if angle C is 60°, then angle A is 60°, and angle B would equal 60°.

16. **A** Since the price of the car is not given, plug in. If the car costs $100, then a 10% discount is $10 since $0.1 \times 100 = 10$. The discounted price is $90 ($100 - 10 = 90$). After the one-day deal, the car is discounted another 20%, which is $18 since $0.2 \times 90 = 18$. The total amount of the discounts is $28 since $10 + 18 = 28$. The discount off the original price is 28% $\left(\dfrac{\text{discount}}{\text{original}} = \dfrac{28}{100} \right)$, so the correct answer is (A).

17. **D** Use $T = AN$. For this problem, write two $T = AN$ equations. The first $T = AN$ will represent David's first three tests. The *Total* can be determined by adding his first three test scores: 82 + 84 + 95 = 261. The *Number of items* is the number of tests, which is 3. The second $T = AN$ will represent David's average for all four tests. The *Average* (90) and the *Number of items* (4) are given. Multiply to find the *Total* of all four tests: $4 \times 90 = 360$. To find the score needed on his fourth test, subtract the two totals from the two $T = AN$ equations. Therefore, in order to bring his average up to 90, David must get a 99 on his fourth test (360 – 291 = 99). The correct answer is (D).

18. **C** Since the answer choices represent possible values for the number of nickels, use the answer choice (PITA). If Howard has 10 nickels, he would have 50 cents since $10 \times 0.05 = 0.5$. He has 23 coins, so he would have 13 quarters, which would equal $3.25 since $13 \times 0.25 = 3.25$. Therefore, he would have well over $2.15, so (B) is too big. To bring the total down, he needs more nickels. Eliminate (A) and (B). If Howard has 18 nickels, he would have 90 cents since $18 \times 0.05 = 0.9$. He has 23 coins, so he would have 5 quarters, which would equal $1.25 since $5 \times 0.25 = 1.25$. Therefore, he would have $2.15 since $0.9 + 1.25 = 2.15$. Thus, the correct answer is (C).

19. **D** Remember that $(p - q)^2 = (p - q)(p - q) = p^2 - pq - pq + q^2 = p^2 - 2pq + q^2$. Notice that the question stated that $p^2 + q^2 = 25$ and $2pq = 10$. Thus, $p^2 - 2pq + q^2$ can be rewritten as $25 - (10)$ which equals 15. The correct answer is therefore (D).

20. **C** Use a ratio box. The numbers for the ratio row are provided. Remember to add the 3 numbers to get the total. The total amount of orange paint needed is also given, so add that value to the ratio box.

	Yellow	Red	White	Total (Orange)
Ratio	3	2	1	6
Multiplier				
Real Value				36

What number does 6 need to be multiplied by to get 36? 6. Therefore, 6 goes in all the cells for the multiplier row.

	Yellow	Red	White	Total (Orange)
Ratio	3	2	1	6
Multiplier	6	6	6	6
Real Value		12		36

The question asks for the amount of red paint needed. Since $2 \times 6 = 12$, the correct answer is (C).

21. **C** To determine the value of Column A, multiply 0.25 and 50, which equals 12.5. For Column B, multiply 0.5 and 25, which equals 12.5. Since the two columns are equal, the correct answer is (C).

22. **B** Since Column B provides a specific value and the total value of nickels is not given, plug in $1.75 in for Column A (i.e., the total value of the nickels) to see if that could be the value of Column A. If $1.75 were the total value of the nickels, then there would be 35 nickels since $\frac{1.75}{.05} = \frac{175}{5} = 35$. The problems says that the number of pennies is double the number of nickels, so if there are 35 nickels, then there are 70 pennies, which is a total value of $0.70 since $0.01 \times 70 = 0.7$. Add the 2 totals to get $2.45 (1.75 + 0.7 = 2.45). However, the total amount of money inside the piggy bank was actually $2.10. Since $2.45 is greater than $2.10 and a smaller overall total is needed, then the value of the nickels must be smaller than $1.75. Therefore, the value of Column B is greater, and the correct answer is (B).

23. **C** Since Column B provides a specific value and the greatest of the 4 consecutive integers is not given, plug 6 in for Column A to see if 6 could work. If 6 were the greatest, then the other 3 integers would be 5, 4, and 3. The product of the four integers would be 360 since $6 \times 5 \times 4 \times 3 = 360$, which is what the problem stated. Therefore, since 6 is the greatest of the 4 consecutive integers and the two columns are equal, the correct answer is (C).

24. **D** Since the value of x is not given, plug in. If $x = 2$, then Column A would be $(2)^2 = 4$ and Column B would be $(2)^3 = 8$. Currently, Column B is greater. However, since the value of x was not given, remember to plug in more than once! If $x = -2$, then Column A would be $(-2)^2 = 4$ and Column B would be $(-2)^3 = -8$. This time Column A is greater. Since neither column is always greater, the correct answer is (D).

25. **B** Remember order of operations (PEMDAS). For Column A, multiplication and division should be performed in order from left to right: $80 - 20 \div 2 \times 5 + 3 \rightarrow 8 - 10 \times 5 + 3 \rightarrow 8 - 50 + 3$. Next, addition and subtraction should be performed in order from left to right: $8 - 50 + 3 \rightarrow -42 + 3 = -39$. Since $20 > -39$, Column B is greater, and the correct answer is (B).

26. **D** According to the equation given, x will be equal to whatever will make the equation equal to zero. Since the equation is already factored, set each binomial equal to zero: $(x + 2) = 0$ and $(x - 2) = 0$. Next, solve for x. For the first binomial, $x = -2$. For the second one, $x = 2$. Thus, Column A will equal -2 and 2, which is sometimes less than Column B and sometimes equal to Column B. Since Column B is not always greater, nor are the two columns always equal, the correct answer is (D).

27. **A** The value of Column A is 10 since $\sqrt{36} = 6$ and $\sqrt{16} = 4$ and $6 + 4 = 10$. Column B cannot be simplified since 52 is not a perfect square; therefore, the value of $\sqrt{52}$ will have to be approximated. Since $\sqrt{49} = 7$ and $\sqrt{64} = 8$, then the value of $\sqrt{52}$ is between 7 and 8. Since that range is less than 10, Column A is greater. The correct answer is (A).

28. **C** When exponents do not have a common base, see if it is possible to rewrite the bases so they are the same. For example, in Column B, 9 can be rewritten as 3^2. Therefore, Column B can be rewritten as $(3^2)^6$. Remember MADPSM. Since there is an exponent being raised to another power, multiply. Thus, $(3^2)^6 = 3^{2 \times 6} = 3^{12}$. Therefore, the two columns are equal, and the correct answer is (C). Note that when in doubt with exponents, expand them out. Column A can be rewritten as $3 \times 3 \times 3 \times 3 \times 3 \times 3 \times 3 \times 3 \times 3 \times 3 \times 3 \times 3$, and Column B can be rewritten as $9 \times 9 \times 9 \times 9 \times 9 \times 9$. Each 9 is the same as 3×3, so $9 \times 9 \times 9 \times 9 \times 9 \times 9 = 3 \times 3 \times 3 \times 3 \times 3 \times 3 \times 3 \times 3 \times 3 \times 3 \times 3 \times 3$. As before, the two columns are equal, so (C) is the correct answer.

29. **C** All sides of a cube are equal, so to find the height of the cube, you need the side measure. The formula for the volume of a cube is $V = s \times s \times s$ or $V = s^3$. The volume of the cube is given as $V = 27$, so $s = 3$ since the $\sqrt[3]{27} = 3$. Therefore, the two columns are equal, and the correct answer is (C). Note that if you do not know cube roots, you should use the value in Column B to plug in for the height in Column A. If the height were 3, then the volume of the cube would be $3 \times 3 \times 3$ which equals 27. Since 27 is the volume of the cube, 3 is the correct height of the cube, so the columns are equal.

30. **B** Since the values of x and y are not given, plug in. If $x = 2$, then y would also need to equal 2 to make the equation true: $\frac{x+2}{y+2} = \frac{2+2}{2+2} = \frac{4}{4}$ and $\frac{4}{4} = \frac{2}{2}$. Therefore, Column A is 2 and Column B is 4 ($y + 2 = 2 + 2 = 4$). Currently, Column B is greater. Remember to plug in more than once since the values of the variables are not given. Try "weird" numbers like 0, 1, or fractions. However, x and y will always be equal to each other in order for the left and right sides of the equation to be equal. Since Column B will always be 2 greater than Column A, the correct answer is (B).

31. **B** One method for solving problems like these is to look for a pattern. For Column A, notice that if you pair up the numbers from either end, they all add up to 101: $1 + 100 = 101$, $2 + 99 = 101$, $3 + 98 = 101$, $4 + 97 = 101$, $5 + 96 = 101$, etc. Next, find the number of pairs. To do this, divide the biggest number (in this case 100) by 2: $\frac{100}{2} = 50$. Thus, there will be 50 pairs that add up to 101. Multiply to find the sum of the set of integers: $101 \times 50 = 5{,}050$. Column A is equal to 5,050. You can use the same method for Column B, but remember that this set is *even* integers. The pattern in Column B is the numbers add up to 202: $2 + 200 = 202$, $4 + 198 = 202$, $6 + 196 = 202$, $8 + 194 = 202$, $10 + 192 = 202$, $10 + 192 = 202$, etc. There will be 100 pairs that add up to 202 since $\frac{200}{2} = 100$. Remember to multiply to find the sum of this set of numbers: $202 \times 100 = 20{,}200$. Thus, Column B equals 20,200. Since Column B is greater than Column A, the correct answer is (B).

32. **A** Since the value of x can be determined, solve the equation to find the value of Column A. If $\frac{x}{4} = 1.5$, then multiply both sides by 4 to get $x = 6$. Column A is equal to 6. Since 6 is greater than 5, Column A will always be greater, and the correct answer is (A).

33. **A** Use the exponent rules to simplify Column A. To simplify a negative exponent, rewrite as a positive exponent and take the reciprocal: $\left(\frac{1}{5}\right)^{-\frac{1}{2}} \Rightarrow \left(\frac{1}{\frac{1}{5}}\right)^{\frac{1}{2}}$. Next simplify inside the parentheses: $\left(\frac{1}{\frac{1}{5}}\right) = 1 \times \frac{5}{1} = 5$. Simplified, the equation looks a lot less intimidating: $(5)^{\frac{1}{2}}$. Finally, a fractional exponent can be rewritten as a root. In this case, a number to the $\frac{1}{2}$ power is the same as the square root. Therefore, $(5)^{\frac{1}{2}} = \sqrt{5}$. Since 5 is not a perfect square, $\sqrt{5}$ will be between 2 and 3 because $\sqrt{4} = 2$ and $\sqrt{9} = 3$. Thus, Column A is between 2 and 3. In Column B, $\left(\frac{1}{5}\right)^4 = \left(\frac{1^4}{5^4}\right) = \left(\frac{1 \times 1 \times 1 \times 1}{5 \times 5 \times 5 \times 5}\right) = \frac{1}{625}$. Since Column B is less than 1, Column A is greater, and the correct answer is (A).

34. **C** To find the probability of an event, find the total of what is wanted out of the total possible outcomes: Probability $= \dfrac{\text{the number of what you want}}{\text{the total number}}$. In Column A, all that is wanted is to roll an even number. (Note the problem is NOT asking for the probability of both events, so the fact that a king is drawn from the deck of cards is extra information.) From 1 to 6, there are 3 even numbers: 2, 4, and 6. Therefore, the probability is $\dfrac{\text{even}}{\text{total}} = \dfrac{3}{6} = \dfrac{1}{2}$. Column A is equal to $\dfrac{1}{2}$. In Column B, all that is wanted is to roll a number less than 4 (again, note that drawing a spade from the deck is extra information). From 1 to 6, there are 3 numbers less than 4: 1, 2, and 3. Therefore, the probability is $\dfrac{\text{less than 4}}{\text{total}} = \dfrac{3}{6} = \dfrac{1}{2}$, and Column B is equal to $\dfrac{1}{2}$. Since the two columns are equal, the correct answer is (C).

35. **B** Break word problems into bite-sized pieces. To find the value of Column A, work through the information provided. If, in season, turnips are $1.80, then the increase at the beginning of the off-season will be $0.18 since 10% of 1.80 = 0.1 × 1.8 = 0.18. The new price is $1.98 since

1.8 + 0.18 = 1.98. When the farmer decreases the price at the end of the off-season, the discount amount is about $0.20 since 10% of 1.98 = 0.1 × 1.98 = 0.198. The final price is $1.78 since 1.98 − 0.2 = 1.78. Thus, Column A is equal to 1.78. This value is less than $1.80, so Column B is greater. The correct answer is (B).

36.   **B**   To find the probability of an event, find the total of what is wanted out of the total possible outcomes: Probability = $\dfrac{\text{the number of what you want}}{\text{the total number}}$. In Column A, choosing a brownie the first time would be $\dfrac{\text{brownie}}{\text{total}} = \dfrac{5}{15}$. On the second selection, there will be one brownie fewer and one item fewer overall, so the probability of choosing a brownie the second time would be $\dfrac{4}{14}$. To find the probability of BOTH events, multiply the fractions together: $\dfrac{5}{15} \times \dfrac{4}{14} = \dfrac{20}{210}$. (Note you can reduce prior to multiplying if you choose.) The value of Column A is $\dfrac{20}{210}$. For Column B, choosing a cookie the first time would be $\dfrac{\text{cookie}}{\text{total}} = \dfrac{4}{15}$. Making a second selection means that there is one fewer item overall to choose from, so the total decreases by 1. The probability of choosing a doughnut the second time is $\dfrac{\text{doughnut}}{\text{total}} = \dfrac{6}{14}$. To find the probability of BOTH events, multiply the fractions together: $\dfrac{4}{15} \times \dfrac{6}{14} = \dfrac{24}{210}$. (Note you can reduce prior to multiplying if you choose.) The value of Column B is $\dfrac{24}{210}$. Since the value of Column B is greater, the correct answer is (B).

37.   **C**   To find the area of a triangle, use the formula $A = \left(\dfrac{1}{2}\right) bh$. Since the problem provides two of the three sides lengths of the triangle, plug those values in for the base and height of the triangle. After all, if the triangle were a right triangle, the legs could be 4 and 6. Therefore, $A = \left(\dfrac{1}{2}\right)(4)(6) = 12$, and Column A could equal 12. This would be equal to Column B. How do you know if this is the greatest possible area? If the triangle were not a right triangle (i.e., the angle between sides 4 and 6 were less than 90° or greater than 90°), then the height would decrease. Making the triangle a right triangle allows for the greatest possible height. Therefore, the two columns are equal, and the correct answer is (C).

Section 3 Reading Comprehension

1. **D**   For general purpose questions, ask yourself "Why did the author write this?" The passage describes a battle that took place between the Americans and the British, after a treaty was signed but before it was ratified. The author explains the different possible reasons the timing worked out that way, and what the timing of those events actually meant in historical context. The author at no point casts blame on the British, nor does he say the war was unnecessary. Eliminate (A). The author does state that the British made tactical errors, but never mentions the tactical maneuvers of Andrew Jackson, eliminating (B). The author does not indicate that peace treaties are worthless, only that there are several steps to finalizing them, so eliminate (C). The author does explain the confusing way the War of 1812 ended, which supports (D).

2. **A**   On Except/Not/Least questions, cross check each answer choice and write a "T" for true and an "F" for false for each answer choice, based on the passage. The false answer will be the correct choice. This question asks about what is mentioned in the passage as occurring near the end of the war. President Madison is never mentioned in the passage, so (A) is false. Lines 14–17 state that communication was more complicated at this time, so (B) is true. Lines 9–12 state that the Treaty of Ghent was signed, so (C) is true. Lines 39–41 state that bad weather doomed the British, so (D) is true. Choice (A) is the correct answer.

3. **C**   On specific questions, make sure you are going back to the passage to find the answer. Since this is an open-ended question, take the answer choices one by one. Although Andrew Jackson is mentioned in the passage, it only says that it is possible he was unaware a treaty was signed, not that he didn't understand the difference between a signed and a ratified treaty. Eliminate (A). President Madison is never mentioned in the passage, eliminating (B). Lines 39–41 state that tactical mistakes and bad weather were the reason for the loss by the British, so it may have been that more time and better conditions would have resulted in a different outcome of the battle. Keep (C). The passage never states one way or the other if it was known to the British that the treaty was signed. Eliminate (D). Choice (C) is the correct answer.

4. **D**   On specific questions, go find the answer! The question asks why New Orleans was a strategic battle point. Lines 36–38 state that the battle would determine who controlled the waterways of the Mississippi. This best supports (D). There is no mention of the American being better supplied, so eliminate (A). There is no mention of anyone being trapped if they lost, eliminating (B). It was the Americans who were attempting to defeat a more numerous force, not the British, so eliminate (C). Choice (D) is the correct answer.

5. **D**   On specific questions, go find the answer! Lines 26–30 state that the war ended after the Treaty of Ghent was ratified by the Senate in February 1815. This best supports (D). Although all the other answers contain information mentioned in the passage, they are not the answer to this question.

6. **D** On specific questions, make sure you are going back to the passage to find the answer. Since this is an open-ended question, take the answer choices one by one. The President is never mentioned in the passage, eliminating (A). Since the author does not know if the commanders ignored the treaty or were unaware of its existence, (B) is not necessarily true. Eliminate it. Choice (C) contains extreme language; this passage discusses only one war a treaty played a part in, not that treaties are always used. Eliminate (C). Choice (D) is supported by lines 21–30, which explain that a treaty is not officially effective until it is ratified, not after it is signed. Choice (D) is the correct answer.

7. **C** This question is a "main idea" question in disguise. Ask yourself the "so what?" of the story. This story is about Charles Darrow, and the history of how he created and sold the board game *Monopoly*. Although other realty-based board games are mentioned, (A) is much too specific for a main idea answer. Eliminate it. Hasbro is mentioned only casually in line 1. It is not related to the main idea. Eliminate (B). The passage is focused on Charles Darrow's creation of *Monopoly*, not his life in general, and there is only one view presented in the passage. This eliminates (D). Only (C) supports the main idea, which is a review of Charles Darrow's development of *Monopoly*.

8. **C** On specific questions, make sure you are going back to the passage to find the answer. Since this is an open-ended question, take the answer choices one by one. The passage never mentions Darrow changing his game, which eliminates (A). There is also no mention of Charles Darrow's lack of skills, so eliminate (B). Lines 29–34 state that Parker Brothers thought Darrow's game was too complex to become widely popular, which supports (C). Although Philadelphia is mentioned in lines 27–29, the passage states that it was the first city to have stores carry the game, not the only city, eliminating (D). Choice (C) is the correct answer.

9. **D** On specific questions, make sure you are going back to the passage to find the answer. This question asks about what kind of people the word "regular" refers to. The people in this sentence are those who buy a game that lets them feel as though they are behaving like "millionaires." It can be inferred then that these regular people are not in fact millionaires. This best supports answer (D). There is no mention of renting versus owning, the 1%, or the love of playing board games in this part of the passage. The only possible answer is (D).

10. **C** On Except/Not/Least questions, cross check each answer choice and write a "T" for true and an "F" for false for each answer choice, based on the passage. The false answer will be the correct choice. Lines 35–37 clearly state that Charles Darrow continued to sell his game, so (A) is true. Lines 7–10 state that Darrow most likely based his game on already existing realty-based games, so (B) is true. Choice (C) is false; the third paragraph states that he made multiple attempts to sell his game to a larger company. Choice (D) is true, the second paragraph describes the extra details Darrow created to make his game more successful compared to others. As (C) is the false answer, it is the correct answer.

11.   **C**   On Except/Not/Least questions, cross check each answer choice and write a "T" for true and an "F" for false for each answer choice, based on the passage. The false answer will be the correct choice. Choice (A) is mentioned in the second paragraph, so it is true. Choice (B) is mentioned at the end of the second paragraph, so it is true. Choice (D) is mentioned in lines 47–51, so it is true. At no point are any adjustments to the game by Parker Brothers mentioned, making (C) false. Therefore, (C) is the correct answer.

12.   **D**   This question asks what the author suggests in the third paragraph, so make sure to check the answers with that part of the passage. The author does not believe that *Monopoly* had limited appeal, either for complexity or errors, but Parker Brothers did. Eliminate (A) and (C). Although Philadelphia is mentioned in this paragraph, the author does not say why Darrow sold his games there. Eliminate (B). Choice (D) is supported by the passage in that the author says the Parker Brothers were not convinced the game would be popular. Choice (D) is the correct answer.

13.   **B**   This question asks why the author mentions "other languages" in line 41; go back to the passage and find the answer. In this sentence, the author is explaining that the English language is adept at absorbing words from other languages. The other languages are likely mentioned in order to stress the pool of words that the English language draws from when absorbing new words. This best supports (B). This sentence does not discuss the complexity of spelling bees, only the complexity of the English language, so eliminate (A). This sentence does not mention time at all, eliminating (C). And there is no mention of spelling in this sentence, eliminating (D). Choice (B) is the correct choice.

14.   **C**   On specific questions, make sure you are going back to the passage to find the answer. This question asks what the major difference is between the first National Spelling Bee and those of today. The first National Spelling Bee is mentioned only in lines 26–31. The only major detail discussed about the first Spelling Bee in these lines is that the winner only had to beat nine other contestants. This most strongly supports (C), that there are more competitors now than originally. There is no mention of what the expectations for the spelling bee were, eliminating (A). The words that were included in the original spelling bee were not discussed, eliminating (D). And there is no mention that the spelling bee has switched to testing a different language than English, eliminating (B). The correct answer is (C).

15.   **D**   When asked a vocabulary in context question, focus on what the word means in the sentence. In line 47, the author states that other languages have fewer rules than English. In lines 50–53, the author states that without all these rules there wouldn't be a point in having a spelling bee at all. This implies that the English language has many spelling rules, so myriad must mean many. The only answer choice that matches this meaning is (D), numerous.

16.   **A**   This is a very open-ended question, so make sure to check each answer choice with the passage. According to lines 20–22, students who reach the National Spelling Bee have won other lower-level spelling bees first. This supports (A), so keep it. There is no discussion of the motivation behind the sponsors of the spelling bee, so eliminate (B). The passage states that Frank Neuhauser

would have a very different experience in today's spelling bee than he had in the original, not that he would do poorly. Eliminate (C). And the author never states that the spelling bee has grown too large, only that it is larger today than the original event, eliminating (D). Choice (A) is the correct answer.

17.   **D**   This is a general purpose question in disguise. Why did the author write this passage, what point are they trying to make? The author focuses on two main points: the evolution of the spelling bee and why the English language makes the spelling bee interesting. Choice (A) is not supported by the passage; the author does not focus on the presentation or structure of the spelling bee. Choice (B) is too specific; the author does much more than merely contrast English with other languages. The role of vocabulary in our lives is never mentioned, so (C) is also incorrect. Choice (D) touches both on the history and the form of the spelling bee, making it the correct answer.

18.   **A**   On tone questions, eliminate answer choices that are too extreme or don't make sense based on the passage. The author is most likely interested in the spelling bee if they are writing about it, so (C), indifferent, cannot be correct. The author is neither questioning nor critical of the spelling bee, eliminating (B) and (D). This leaves (A), admiring, as the best answer choice.

19.   **C**   In order to answer this question, ask yourself "Why does the author include this question? What purpose does this question serve in the passage?" The question, from what does a black hole originate, is asked at the end of the first paragraph. The beginning of the next paragraph discusses the origins of a black hole, a description which is continued through the remainder of the passage. This best supports (C). The details presented in the passage indicate we know a great deal about black holes, eliminating (A). This question does not include a source, eliminating (B). There is no mention of independent research, so (D) is also incorrect. Choice (C) is the correct answer.

20.   **B**   This is a specific question, so go back to the passage and find the answer. The question asks what causes a collapsing star to become a neutron star. This process is discussed at the beginning of the fourth paragraph, which states that a collapsing star will become a neutron star if it is big, heavy, and collapses very quickly in an implosion. It goes on to say that the mass matters; it will only become a neutron star if it is not much heavier than our sun, but if it is more than 1.7 times that it will become a black hole. This best supports (B). Choice (A) is the opposite of what is stated in the passage, and (C) and (D) are not mentioned in this part of the passage.

21.   **C**   This is a specific question, so go back to the passage and find the answer. The horizon of a black hole is discussed in the fifth paragraph. It states that matter can pass over the horizon of a black hole, but it cannot pass back out. This suggests that a satellite would pass into a black hole but not come back out. The only answer that matches this is (C).

22.   **A**   This is a specific question, so go back to the passage and find the answer. The question asks what is a mentioned effect of the process of fusion. According to lines 9–11, fusion is the result of a star burning hydrogen. The energy this creates prohibits the star from collapsing. This supports (A). Although (B) may seem correct at first, it is a deceptive answer choice. Fusion is the result of a star

burning hydrogen; a star burning hydrogen is not the result of fusion. Eliminate (B). There is no mention of the average life of a star or a white dwarf in these lines, so (C) and (D) cannot be correct. Choice (A) is the correct answer.

23.   **D**   This is a specific question, so go back to the passage and find the answer. The question asks why a black hole appears black, which is discussed in lines 35–38. The passage states that a black hole appears black because no light or matter can escape from it. The only choice that matches this answer is (D).

24.   **B**   This question asks about the organization of the passage, so go back and examine the main idea of each paragraph and how they connect. At the beginning, the topic of black holes is introduced; the next three paragraphs discuss the process of stars changing into other forms of matter, ending with black holes. This best supports (B). Choice (A) is too general, so it can be eliminated. There is no personal story, only a historical reference, and no black holes are compared and contrasted, so eliminate (C). No single black hole is used in the story to generalize, eliminating (D). Choice (B) is the correct answer.

25.   **C**   For general purpose questions, ask yourself "Why did the author write this?" The passage describes the fight of the Women's Suffrage movement to earn the right to vote. This best matches (C). Choice (A) is too specific: Although Alice Paul is mentioned in the passage the focus is not solely on her. Choice (B) is too extreme; it was not solely the Night of Terror that prompted the Nineteenth Amendment. And while the deplorable actions of the guards are mentioned in the passage, they are also too specific to be the correct answer, eliminating (D). Choice (C) is correct.

26.   **C**   When asked a vocabulary in context question, focus on what the word means in the sentence. This sentence discusses how outraged the public was over the events of the Night of Terror. In this context, "exposed" most nearly means "made known to the public." The only choice that matches this meaning is (C), revealed.

27.   **C**   This question is asking what the author's attitude is toward a specific event, low voter turnout. In the first paragraph, after the author discusses the low voter turnout, they then refer to that number as "disturbing," since so many fought so hard to secure voting rights for all. This is certainly a negative attitude, which eliminates (B). Although (A) and (D) are negative, they are too extreme for this story. Only (C), pessimism, matches the tone of the passages.

28.   **D**   This is a specific question, so go back to the passage and find the answer. The passage describes the Night of Terror, and then goes on to say that these events infuriated the nation when they were discovered. The following paragraph then discusses how this new support eventually helped in the creation of the Nineteenth Amendment. This best supports (D). There is no mention of either President Wilson or the punishment of the guards in this part of the passage, eliminating (A) and (B), and (C) is the opposite of what was stated in the passage. Choice (D) is the correct answer.

29. **A** This is a specific question, so go back to the passage and find the answer. The hunger strike is discussed in lines 37–43, where it is stated that the women went on a hunger strike led by Alice Paul to protest the deplorable conditions of the prison. This best matches (A), they were trying to make the prison better. Choice (B) may seem correct, but it is deceptive. The prisoners were not force fed until after they began the strike, not before. Choices (C) and (D) also contain deceptive wording as they are on subjects mentioned in the passage, but neither is the answer to this question. The correct answer is (A).

30. **D** This is an attitude question in disguise; you are being asked what the author thought of the women's tactics. Ask yourself how the author described the women and the activities they engaged in. Look through the passage for descriptive phrases. The author states in lines 29–36 that the women protested in an orderly and peaceful fashion. In the last paragraph, the women's peacefulness and physical endurance are noted. Not only should the answer touch on these topics, but the answer should be generally positive, as the author's attitude is positive. This eliminates all choices but (D), since only (D) does not contain any negative ideas in it.

31. **B** On tone questions, eliminate answer choices that are too extreme or don't make sense based on the passage. The passage opens by saying that Stephen Hawking was one of the greatest scientists of this age, and then goes on to discuss how he overcame physical hardship to excel in his field. This eliminates (C) and (D), as they are too negative. The author is not displaying any sadness about the past, which eliminates (A). Only admiring, (B), works with the passage.

32. **B** When asked the purpose of a sentence or phrase in the passage, ask yourself "Why is this included? What point does the author make with this line?" Up until this point, it is unclear what scientist the author is discussing. At this point the author makes it clear whom they have been talking about. This best supports (B). There is no riddle or question prior to this, only a description, eliminating (A) and (C). Choice (D) is deceptive and extreme; the passage says Hawking was one of the greatest living, not the greatest. The correct answer is (B).

33. **C** This is a specific question, so go back to the passage and find the answer. Hawking's attitude towards his disease is discussed in lines 55–61, where it states he credited his disease with forcing him to face the limitations of his life and time. According to the last lines of the passage, because of his disease he reached his greatest potential. This best supports (C), that he was appreciative of his disease, which is somewhat ironic. He was not giddy, irate, or uncaring about his disease, eliminating (A), (B), and (D).

34. **C** This is a specific question, so go back to the passage and find the answer. The second paragraph discusses Hawking as a child and young man, and includes the descriptions "lack of diligence," "moderately successful," "not extraordinary," etc. This best supports (C). There is no mention of Hawking being disrespectful or energetic, eliminating (A) and (D). And it was not until later that he became considered brilliant, which makes (B) incorrect. Choice (C) is the correct answer.

35.   **C**   On Except/Not/Least questions, cross check each answer choice and write a "T" for true and an "F" for false for each answer choice, based on the passage. The false answer will be the correct choice. The last paragraph does discuss the connection between Hawking's disease and his success in science, so (A) is true. The last paragraph also includes the goal of Hawking to travel to space, so (B) is true as well. No specific theory of Hawking's is ever mentioned, making (C) false. The educational institutions Hawking attended are reviewed in the second and third paragraphs of the passage, so (D) is true. Only (C) is false, and therefore the correct answer.

36.   **A**   This question is a "main idea" question in disguise. Ask yourself the "so what?" of the story. This story is reviewing biographical details of Stephen Hawking, and focusing on the role his disease played in his life. There are no scientific discoveries discussed in the passage, eliminating (C). Although the author mentions Hawking's medical diagnosis and the technology he used with his disease, these answers are much too specific for this question. Only (A) matches the biographical description of the passage. Choice (A) is the correct answer.

Section 4 Mathematics Achievement

1.   **A**   Draw a factor tree of 36.

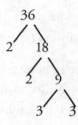

The prime factorization of 36 is $2 \times 2 \times 3 \times 3$ or $2^2 \times 3^2$. The two different prime factors of 36 are 2 and 3, so the correct answer is (A). Note that (B), (C), and (D) contain numbers that are not prime (4, 12, and 9).

2.   **D**   Use the answer choices (PITA) to find a value of x that will make the expression equal to 0. If $x = 3$, as in (D), then $\dfrac{x-3}{4x} = \dfrac{3-3}{4(3)} = \dfrac{0}{12} = 0$. No other answer choice contains a value of x that will make the expression equal 0. Thus, the correct answer is (D).

3.   **C**   If the numbers are in a ratio of 3 to 4 and the smaller of the two numbers is 9, then $\dfrac{3}{4} = \dfrac{9}{x}$. Cross-multiply and solve for x, and $x = 12$. Therefore, the larger number is 12. (Note you can also use a ratio box to find the larger number.) To find the average, use $T = AN$.

The *Total* will be the sum of the two integers: $9 + 12 = 21$. There are 2 numbers, so the *Number of items* is 2. Divide to find the *Average*: $\dfrac{21}{2} = 10.5$. Thus, the average is 10.5, and the correct answer is (C).

4. **D** There are 180° in a straight line. If $a = 42°$, then the remaining angles ($b + b + b$) will equal 138° since $180 - 42 = 138$. Since the remaining three angles are all equal, divide to find the value of b: $\frac{138}{3} = 46°$. The correct answer is (D).

5. **C** 85% of 50 will be greater than 25 (50% of 50) but less than 50 (100% of 50). Therefore, eliminate (A) and (B). One way to find 85% of 50 is to find the product: $0.85 \times 50 = 42.5$. Therefore, the correct answer is (C).

6. **C** To find the largest of the three numbers, use the answer choices (PITA). Start with (B) or (C), assigning variables to the numbers. Say $x = 2$, y is the middle number and z is the largest number. If the largest number is 6, then $x = 2$ and $z = 6$. Thus, y would have to be 3 since $2 + y + 6 = 11 \Rightarrow 8 + y = 11 \Rightarrow y = 3$. Check the other equation: $xyz = 2 \times 3 \times 6 = 36$. This works, so the largest number is 6, and the correct answer is (C).

7. **A** Translate the words into their math equivalents: two-thirds of one-half is the same as $\frac{2}{3} \times \frac{1}{2}$. Multiply the numerators together and multiply the denominators together to get $\frac{2}{6}$. Reduce to $\frac{1}{3}$. Therefore, the correct answer is (A).

8. **B** If there is 1 km in 1,000 m and the runner wants to run 4 km, then set up a proportion to solve for the total number of meters: $\frac{1 \text{ km}}{1,000 \text{ m}} = \frac{4 \text{ km}}{x}$. Cross-multiply to get $x = 4,000$. The question asks for the number of laps, so if 1 lap equals 400 m, then $\frac{1 \text{ lap}}{400 \text{ m}} = \frac{x}{4,000 \text{ m}}$. Cross-multiply and solve for x to get $x = 10$. Therefore, 4,000 m is equal to 10 laps, so the correct answer is (B).

9. **A** Use the figure provided. Since this is a right triangle and side BC is the hypotenuse, eliminate (D) since the hypotenuse is the longest side of a right triangle. Use the Pythagorean Theorem to solve for the missing side: $a^2 + b^2 = c^2$, where c is the hypotenuse. Thus, $a^2 + 12^2 = 13^2 \Rightarrow a^2 + 144 = 169 \Rightarrow a^2 = 25 \Rightarrow a = 5$. Side AB is 5, so the correct answer is (A). Note: this is a 5-12-13 right triangle. Memorizing the Pythagorean triples can make questions like these faster.

10. **B** When in doubt with exponents, expand them out. $\frac{2.7 \times 10^7}{3.0 \times 10^{-3}}$ can be rewritten as $\frac{27,000,000}{0.003}$. To get rid of the decimals in the denominator, move the decimal in the numerator and denominator to the right 3 spaces to get $\frac{27,000,000,000}{3}$. Divide to get 27,000,000,000 divided by $3 = 9,000,000,000$. To rewrite 9,000,000,000 in scientific notation, move the decimal 9 places to the left. The result is 9.0×10^9, or answer (B).

11. **B** To determine percent change, use the formula: % change = $\dfrac{\text{difference}}{\text{original}} \times 100$. The difference between the two prices is $0.40 since 1.6 − 1.2 = 0.4, and the original price of the digital song was $1.60. Therefore, $\dfrac{0.4}{1.6} \times 100 = \dfrac{40}{1.6} = \dfrac{400}{16} = 25$. The digital song decreased in price by 25%, so the correct answer is (B).

12. **A** Since there are variables in the question and answers, plug in a value for y (the number of students in Mrs. Puccio's class). If $y = 10$, then twice as many would be 20, and 4 less than 20 would be 16. Therefore, $x = 16$ (the number of students in Mrs. Sproul's class). Since the question asks for the value of y, the correct answer will be the one that equals 10. Plug 16 in for x and check each answer choice. Choice (A) is $\dfrac{16}{2} + 2 = 8 + 2 = 10$. Choice (B) is $2(16) + 4 = 32 + 4 = 36$. Choice (C) is $2(16) − 4 = 32 − 4 = 28$. Choice (D) is $\dfrac{16}{2} − 4 = 8 − 4 = 4$. Since it is the only one that matches the target value, (A) is the correct answer.

13. **C** Don't be intimidated by weird symbols! Use the definitions provided and plug in the given values for x. For the first part of the equation, #(−6), $x = −6$ so use the definition for when x is negative: #$(x) = x^2$. Thus, #(−6) $= (−6)^2 = 36$. For the second part of the equation, #(6), $x = 6$ so use the definition for when x is positive: #$(x) = 2x$. Thus, #(6) $= 2(6) = 12$. Now replace #(−6) with 36 and #(6) with 12, so the equation looks like 36 − 12 =, which is 24. The correct answer is (C).

14. **D** Don't be intimidated by weird symbols! Use the definitions provided and plug in the given values for x and y. #[#x − #y] can be rewritten as #[#(3) − #(−4)]. Start inside the brackets. For #(3), $x = 3$ so use the definition for x is positive #$(x) = 2x$. Thus, #(3) $= 2(3) = 6$. For #(−4), $x = −4$ so use the definition for x is negative: #$(x) = x^2$. (Don't let the different variables confuse you. Remember now the number inside the parentheses is an x value according to the definitions.) Thus, #(−4) $= (−4)^2$. Now the equation looks like #[6 − 16]. Simplify inside the brackets (6 − 16 = −10) to get #(−10). Since $x = −10$, use the definition for x is negative. Thus, #(−10) $= (−10)^2 = 100$. The final answer is 100, so the correct answer is (D).

15. **B** Since there are variables in the question and answers, plug in a value for x or y. If $x = 45$ and $x + 90 + y = 180$, then $y = 45$. The question asks for the value of x, so the correct answer will be the one that equals 45. Plug 45 in for y and check each answer choice. Choices (A) and (B) equal 45. Choice (C) equals 135 (90 + 45 = 135), and (D) equals 135 (180 − 45 = 135). Eliminate (C) and (D). Since two answers worked, plug in another value for x. If $x = 50$ and $x + 90 + y = 180$, then $y = 40$. The correct answer will be the one that equals 50 since $x = 50$. Plug in 40 for y and check the two remaining answer choices. Choice (A) equals 40; eliminate it. Choice (B) equals 50 (90 − 40 = 50). Since it is the only option that still works, the correct answer is (B).

16. **D** First, start by dividing the integers: $\frac{4}{2} = 2$. Eliminate (B) since it does not contain 2. Next, simplify the exponents using the exponent rules (MADSPM). Since the bases are being divided, subtract the exponents. $\frac{a^4}{a^3} = a^{4-3} = a^1 = a$. Eliminate (C) since it does not contain a. $\frac{b^6}{b^5} = b^{6-5} = b^1 = b$. Eliminate (A) since it does not contain b in the numerator. Note that b in the denominator is equal to b^{-1}. Therefore, the correct answer is (D).

17. **C** Since the number of students in the class is not provided, plug in. If there were 12 students in the class, then $\frac{1}{4}$ of 12 is 3 $\left(\frac{1}{4} \times 12 = 3\right)$, which means that 3 students failed the exam. The remaining number of students in the class (those who passed the exam) is 9 since $12 - 3 = 9$. Of those 9 passing students, $\frac{1}{3}$ scored an A. Thus, 3 students scored an A: $\left(\frac{1}{3} \times 9 = 3\right)$. The number of students who passed the exam but scored below an A is 6 ($9 - 3 = 6$). Therefore, the fraction of the whole class that passed but scored below an A is $\frac{6}{12} = \frac{1}{2}$. The correct answer is (C).

18. **C** Since there are variables in the question and answers, plug in a value for r. If $r = 100$, then Karen spends $80 since Rena spends $20 more than Karen ($100 - 20 = 80$). If Rena spends $100, then Lynn spends $50 since $100 - 50 = 50$. The question asks for the total cost of their purchases, which is $230: $100 + 80 + 50 = 230$. The question asks for the total cost, so the correct answer will be the one that equals 230. Plug 100 in for r and check each answer choice. Choice (A) equals $100 + 70 = 170$. Choice (B) equals $\frac{100 + 70}{3} = \frac{170}{3}$. Choice (C) equals $3(100) - 70 = 300 - 70 = 230$. Choice (D) equals $100 + 210 = 310$. Since it is the only one that matches the target value, (C) is the correct answer.

19. **A** Since the answer choices represent possible values for the number of left-handed children in the group, use the answer choices (PITA). If there are 37 left-handed children in the group, then there are 71 right-handed children in the group since $37 + 34 = 71$. Thus, there would be 108 children in the group since $37 + 71 = 108$, which is too big. Eliminate (B), (C), and (D) because a smaller number is needed for the number of left-handed children. Therefore, (A) is the correct answer. Note that if there were 33 left-handed children in the group, there would be 67 right-handed children ($33 + 34 = 67$) and 100 total children in the group ($33 + 67 = 100$).

20. **D** Use the chart provided to find the total number of students and the number of students whose favorite type of book is Sci-Fi. There are 40 students (8 + 20 + 10 + 2 = 40) and 10 chose Sci-Fi. Thus, 10 out of the 40 students, or $\frac{1}{4}\left(\frac{10}{40} = \frac{1}{4}\right)$, like Sci-Fi books the best. If this information were presented in a pie graph, then the central angle would be $\frac{1}{4}$ out of 360° since circles have 360°. $\frac{1}{4} \times 360 = \frac{360}{4} = 90$, so the central angle would be 90°. The correct answer is (D).

21. **D** To find what fraction the new price is compared to the original price, set up a fraction: $\frac{\text{new price}}{\text{old price}} = \frac{1,200}{1,500} = \frac{12}{15} = \frac{4}{5}$. Therefore, the correct answer is (D).

22. **A** Since there are variables in the question and answers, plug in a value for x or y. If $x = 3$, then $y = 4$ since $\frac{3}{3} = \frac{4}{4}$. Plug 3 in for x and 4 for y and check each answer choice to see which statement is true. Choice (A) equals 3(4) = 12. Choice (B) equals 3(4) = 4(3), or 12 = 12. Choice (C) equals $\frac{3}{4} = \frac{4}{3}$, which is not true. Choice (D) equals 3(3) = 4(4), or 9 = 16, which is not true. Since there are two answer choices that work, plug in again. This time if $x = 4$, then $y = 3$ since $\frac{3}{4} = \frac{3}{4}$. Now plug 4 in for x and 3 for y to see which of the remaining two answer choices is true. Choice (A) equals 4(3) = 12. Choice (B) equals 3(3) = 4(4), or 9 = 16, which is not true. Since it is the only option that is still true, the correct answer is (A). Another way to solve this problem would be to cross-multiply: $\frac{3}{x} = \frac{y}{4} \rightarrow x(y) = 3(4) \rightarrow xy = 12$. This matches (A), which is the correct answer.

23. **B** Use a ratio box. The numbers for the ratio row are provided. Remember to add the 2 numbers to get the total. The total number of juniors and seniors at the school is also given, so add that value to the ratio box.

	Juniors	Seniors	Total
Ratio	3	2	5
Multiplier			
Real Value			600

What number does 5 need to be multiplied by to get 600? 120. Therefore, 120 goes in all the cells for the multiplier row.

	Juniors	Seniors	Total
Ratio	3	2	5
Multiplier	120	120	120
Real Value		240	600

The question asks for the number of seniors. Since 2 × 120 = 240, the correct answer is (B).

24. **D** 150% of 40 will be greater than 40 since 100% of 40 is 40 ($1 \times 40 = 40$). Eliminate (A) and (B). Since 50% of 40 is 20 ($0.5 \times 40 = 20$), then 150% of 40 will equal 60. The correct answer is (D).

25. **D** The question is asking for the number of hours she studied all together. Eliminate (A) since the time she spent studying math alone was 4 hours. To find the number of hours she spent studying English, find $\frac{3}{4}$ of 4, which is $\frac{3}{4}(4) = \frac{12}{4} = 3$. If she spent 4 hours studying math and 3 hours of studying English, she spent a total of 7 hours studying. Therefore, the correct answer is (D).

26. **B** Long division is one way to approach division with decimals. $\frac{0.966}{0.42}$ can be written as $0.42\overline{)0.966}$. Move the decimal to the right three times to get rid of the decimal in the divisor and the dividend: $420\overline{)966}$. The result is $420\overline{)966.0}$ (with 2.3 above), so the correct answer is (B). Another option is to use the answer choices (PITA). Multiply the answer choices by 0.42 to see which one equals 0.966. Choice (B) is the only option that works.

27. **B** To determine percent change, use the formula: % change $= \dfrac{\text{difference}}{\text{original}} \times 100$. The difference between her two typing speeds is 7 since $42 - 35 = 7$, and her original speed was 35 words per minute. Therefore, $\dfrac{42 - 35}{35} \times 100 = \dfrac{7}{35} \times 100 = \dfrac{700}{35} = 20$. Her typing speed increased by 20%, so the correct answer is (B).

28. **A** The first term in the series is given: 50. To find the second number (which is an even term), multiply the first term by $\frac{1}{2}$. Thus, the second term equals 25 ($\frac{1}{2} \times 50 = 25$). To find the third number (which is an odd term), multiply the second term by $\frac{1}{2}$ and round to the nearest whole number. The third term equals 13 since $\frac{1}{2} \times 25 = 12.5$ and 12.5 rounds up to 13. Therefore, the correct answer is (A).

29. **A** Use the table provided to determine the mode of the data. The mode of a list of numbers is the number that appears most frequently. Note that the information is presented in a deceptive manner. Note that (D) is a trap. For example, 0 should be listed 6 times, since the number of students who have 0 siblings is 6. If the list were written out like this {0, 0, 0, 0, 0, 0, 1, 1, 1, 1, 1, 1, 1, 1, 1, 1, 1, 2, 2, 2, 2, 2, 2, 2, 2, 3, 3, 3, 3, 3, 3, 4, 5}, it would be easier to see that the mode is 1 since the number of students who have 1 sibling occurs the most times (10). The correct answer is (A).

30. **B** Mark the given lengths on the figure provided to see what other lengths can be determined. Segment *BC* is not provided; however, if segment *BD* = 18 and segment *CD* = 12, then *BC* = 6 since $18 - 12 = 6$. Segment *AB* is also given (5), so add it to the value found for segment *BC* to get the length of segment *AC*: $5 + 6 = 11$. The correct answer is (B).

31. **D** Eliminate (A) and (B) since 2 + 40 = 42, not 24. $\frac{1}{100}$ = 0.01. Eliminate (C) because 0.1 = $\frac{1}{10}$. Therefore, (D) is the correct answer.

32. **C** Since the question asks for a specific value, use the answer choices (PITA). Start with (A) because the *least* possible value is wanted. Choice (A) is incorrect because it is not divisible by 4. Choice (B) is incorrect because it is not divisible by 3. Choice (C) is divisible by all 4 numbers: $\frac{60}{2}$ = 30, $\frac{60}{3}$ = 20, $\frac{60}{4}$ = 15, and $\frac{60}{5}$ = 12. Since there is not a smaller possible integer, the correct answer is (C).

33. **C** Since there are variables in the question and answers, plug in values for x and y. If x = 30, then the car travels 30 mph. If y = 90, then find the time it will take a car traveling 30 mph to go 90 mph. Set up a proportion to solve: $\frac{30 \text{ miles}}{1 \text{ hour}} = \frac{90 \text{ miles}}{x}$. Cross-multiply and solve for x to get $30x = 90 \Rightarrow$ x = 3. It will take 3 hours, so the correct answer will be the one that equals 3. Plug 30 in for x and 90 in for y and check each answer choice. Choice (A) equals $\frac{2(30)}{90} = \frac{60}{90} = \frac{2}{3}$. Choice (B) equals 30×90 = 2,700. Choice (C) equals $\frac{90}{30} = 3$. Choice (D) equals $\frac{30}{90} = \frac{1}{3}$. Since it is the only one that matches the target value of 3, (C) is the correct answer.

34. **A** Similar triangles are triangles that have the same angle measures and corresponding sides have the same ratio. Thus, if in triangle ABC, side BC has a side measure of 4 and the side QR of triangle PQR has a side measure of 12, those sides correspond and have a ratio of 4:12. Therefore, the sides of triangle PQR will all be 3 times the size of the sides in triangle ABC. To find the area of a triangle, use the formula $A = \frac{1}{2}(b)(h)$. The area of triangle ABC is given (6), and any side can be the base, so let side BC (4) be the base. Therefore, $\frac{1}{2}(4)(h) = 6$. Simplify to get $2h = 6$, and divide to get h = 3. The height of triangle ABC is 3. The height of triangle PQR is not given; however, it will be 3 times the height of triangle ABC, so it will be 9 (3 × 3 = 9). Let the base of triangle PQR be side QR (12). Therefore, $A = \frac{1}{2}(12)(9) = 6(9) = 54$. The area of triangle PQR is 54, so the correct answer is (A).

35. **D** The answer choices represent possible values of x (i.e., the cost of each halibut steak), so plug in (PITA). If $x = 5$, then one halibut steak ($5) plus 2 salmon steaks cost $30, which means that each salmon steak (y) costs $12.50: $5 + 2y = 30 \rightarrow 2y = 25 \rightarrow y = 12.5$. Check to see if those values work for what Dave pays: if $x = 5$ and $y = 12.5$, then 2 halibut steaks cost $10 ($2 \times 5 = 10$) and 4 salmon steaks cost $50 ($4 \times 12.5 = 50$), so he spends a total of $60, which is true. So is (A) the answer? Be careful! What if you had tried (C) first? If $x = 10$, then $y = 10$ because $10 + 2y = 30 \rightarrow 2y = 20 \rightarrow y = 10$. These numbers for x and y also work in the second equation: 2 halibut steaks are $20 ($2 \times 10 = 20$) and 4 salmon steaks are $40 ($4 \times 10 = 40$), so Dave spends a total of $60 ($20 + 40 = 60$), which is true. There can't be multiple correct answers, so since there is not enough information provided about the price of the fish steaks, the correct answer is (D). Note: normally you don't need to check all the answers when you use PITA. This one is a tricky question!

36. **B** Pay attention to the information above the problem. Choice (D) is a trap answer. $(1 + 5) = (6)$. Since the value inside the parentheses is even, use the definition for x is even: $(x) = \frac{1}{2}(x)$. Plug in 6 for x and simplify: $\frac{1}{2}(6) = 3$. Since $(6) = 3$, the correct answer is (B).

37. **D** Since there are variables in the question and answers, plugging in for x, calculating a target value, and finding the answer choice that matches would be an option. However, another way to solve the problem would be to distribute the 2: $2(4z + 1) = (2 \times 4z) + (2 \times 1) = 8z + 2$. This matches (D), which is the correct answer.

38. **B** On this stem-and-leaf plot, the values in the "stem" column are hundreds and tens digits and the values in the "leaf" column are the ones digits. For example, a stem of 10 and a leaf of 8 represent 108. To find the median of this data set, locate the number in the middle. There are 27 numbers in this set, so the middle number will be the 14th number, which is the 2 in the leaf column in stem row 13, which equals 132. The correct answer is (B). Note: if you have trouble trying to determine the middle number, just use the leaf numbers and cross off one number from the beginning and one number from the end of the list until you reach the middle term. Don't forget to add the stem part to the beginning of the number.

39. **C** To find the average, use $T = AN$. The *Total* will be the sum of the monkeys at the 3 zoos: $3 + 8 + 16 = 27$. There are 3 zoos, so the *Number of items* is 3. Divide to find the *Average*: $\frac{27}{3} = 9$. Thus, the average is 9, and the correct answer is (C).

40. **A** Since there are variables in the question and answers, plug in a value for the cost of one of the items to determine the cost of the other items. If a steak costs $10 and it is $4 more than a hamburger, then a hamburger costs $6. If a hamburger costs $6 and it is $4 more than a grilled cheese sandwich, then a grilled cheese sandwich is $2. Six grilled cheese sandwiches cost $12 since $2 \times 6 = 12$.

If 6 grilled cheese sandwiches cost $2x$, then $x = 6$ because $2x = 12$ and $\frac{12}{2} = 6$. The question asks how much 4 steaks and 2 hamburgers cost. Steaks are \$10 each and hamburgers are \$6 each, so the total cost will be \$52 since $(4 \times 10) + (2 \times 6) = 40 + 12 = 52$. The correct answer will be the one that equals 52. Plug 6 in for x and check each answer choice. Choice (A) equals $2(6) + 40 = 12 + 40 = 52$. Choice (B) equals $2(6) + 48 = 12 + 48 = 60$. Choice (C) equals $6(6) + 34 = 36 + 34 = 70$. Choice (D) equals $12(6) + 40 = 72 + 40 = 112$. Since it is the only one that matches the target value of 52, (A) is the correct answer.

41. **C** A solution set is the set of all numbers that make the inequality true. One method of solving this question is to plug in values from the answer choices (PITA). For example, if $x = 0$, then $|3 - 2(0)| > 9$. Multiply to get $|3 - 0| > 9$, and then subtract to get $|3| > 9$. The absolute value of 3 is 3, so $3 > 9$, which is not true. Eliminate any answer choices that include 0 as a possible value for x, so cross off (A) and (B). Try another number. If $x = 4$, then $|3 - 2(4)| > 9$. Multiply to get $|3 - 8| > 9$, and then subtract to get $|-5| > 9$. The absolute value of -5 is 5, so $5 > 9$, which is also not true. Therefore, eliminate (D), which would include $x = 4$ as a possible solution. The correct answer is (C), which includes the complete solution set for this inequality. Note: another way to do this problem is to solve the inequality for x. If you chose to solve this way, don't forget to flip the sign if you multiply or divide by a negative number.

42. **D** Since there are variables in the question, plug in values for x and y. If $x = 2$ and $y = 3$, then $100xy = 100(2)(3) = 600$ and $xy = (2)(3) = 6$. Now the question reads 600 is what percent of 6. Translate the English words into their math equivalents: $600 = \frac{x}{100} \times 6$ and solve for x: $600 = \frac{x}{100} \times 6 \rightarrow 600 = \frac{6x}{100}$. Multiply both sides of the equation by 100 to get $60{,}000 = 6x$. Divide both sides by 6 to get $x = 10{,}000$. The correct answer is (D). Note: setting up a proportion $\left(\frac{600}{6} = \frac{x}{100}\right)$, cross-multiplying, and solving for x works too.

43. **D** If Ismail's and Lakshmi's home are in the same direction from the school, then their homes would be 4 miles apart since $8 - 4 = 4$. However, if Matt lives 4 miles west of the school and Laura lives 8 miles east of the school, then their homes are 12 miles apart since $8 + 4 = 12$. There are other possibilities as well, so without knowing which direction they both live, there is not enough information to determine the distance between their homes. The correct answer is (D).

44. **B** Use a ratio box. The numbers for the ratio row are provided in the answer choices, so use the answers (PITA). Remember to add the 2 numbers in the ratio row to get the total. Since the ratio total has to be a number that is divisible by the real value total (\$2,000), eliminate (A) and (D) since

6 + 1 = 7 (A) and 2 + 1 = 3 (D) yield totals that are not divisible by 2,000. Start with one of the remaining choices and fill in the values into a ratio box. For (B),

	Larger	Smaller	Total
Ratio	5	3	8
Multiplier			
Real Value			2,000

What number does 8 need to be multiplied by to get 2,000? 250. Therefore, 250 goes in all the cells for the multiplier row.

	Larger	Smaller	Total
Ratio	5	3	8
Multiplier	250	250	250
Real Value	1,250	750	2,000

The question states that the difference between the two amounts is half of their average. Remember to find average, use $T = AN$. The *Total* ($2,000) and the *Number of things* (2 partners) are given. Therefore, divide the *Total* by the *Number of things* to get the *Average*: $\frac{2,000}{2} = 1,000$. If $1,000 is the average, then half the average is $500 $\left(\frac{1,000}{2} = 500\right)$. The difference between the larger and smaller amounts should be $500, which is true for this answer choice since 1,250 − 750 = 500. Thus, the correct answer is (B). Note that (C) will not work because the difference between the larger and smaller amounts will be $1,200, which does not fit the restrictions of the problem.

45. **A** Since there are variables in the question and answers, plug in a value for *j*. If *j* = 2, then *j* + 5 = 2 + 5 = 7. Next, calculate the values. Two coins each worth 10 cents is a total value of 20 cents since 2 × 10 = 20. Seven coins each worth 25 cents is a total value of 175 cents since 7 × 25 = 175. Thus, all 9 coins have a value of 195 cents (20 + 175 = 195). The question asks for the total value, so the correct answer will be the one that equals 195. Plug 2 in for *j* and check each answer choice. Choice (A) equals 35(2) + 125 = 195. Choice (B) equals 35(2) + 5 = 75. Choice (C) equals 10(2) + 130 = 150. Choice (D) equals 2(2) + 5 = 9. Since it is the only one that matches the target value, (A) is the correct answer.

46. **D** To find the probability of an event, find the total of what is wanted out of the total possible outcomes:

Probability = $\frac{\text{the number of what you want}}{\text{the total number}}$. If the first randomly selected coin is a penny, the

probability would be $\frac{\text{penny}}{\text{total}} = \frac{6}{18}$. Making a second selection means that there is one fewer item overall to choose from, so the total decreases by 1. The probability of choosing a quarter as the second coin would be $\dfrac{\text{quarter}}{\text{total}} = \dfrac{5}{17}$. To find the probability of BOTH events, multiply the fractions together: $\dfrac{6}{18} \times \dfrac{5}{17}$. There is no need to actually multiply the fractions—pay attention to how the answer choices are written. The correct answer is (D).

47. **A** Use the formula provided and plug in the given values to solve for the radius. $V = \dfrac{1}{3}\pi r^2 h \rightarrow$ $12\pi = \dfrac{1}{3}\pi r^2(4)$. Divide both sides by π to get $12 = \dfrac{1}{3}r^2(4)$. Multiply both sides by $\dfrac{3}{1}$ to cancel the fraction on the right side to get $36 = r^2(4)$. Divide both sides by 4 to get $9 = r^2$. Finally, take the square root of both sides to find $r = 3$. The correct answer is (A). Note: Another way to approach this problem is to use the answer choices rather than solve for r. Remember that the answer choices represent possible values of the radius. Use PITA to see which value of r will make the equation equal to 12π. Only (A) will work.

Chapter 12
Middle Level
ISEE Practice Test

This test is also available in an online format when you register this book at PrincetonReview.com. See the *Get More (Free) Content* page after the Table of Contents for instructions.

Middle Level ISEE Practice Test

Be sure each mark *completely* fills the answer space.

SECTION 1 - Verbal Reasoning

1 Ⓐ Ⓑ Ⓒ Ⓓ	9 Ⓐ Ⓑ Ⓒ Ⓓ	17 Ⓐ Ⓑ Ⓒ Ⓓ	25 Ⓐ Ⓑ Ⓒ Ⓓ	33 Ⓐ Ⓑ Ⓒ Ⓓ
2 Ⓐ Ⓑ Ⓒ Ⓓ	10 Ⓐ Ⓑ Ⓒ Ⓓ	18 Ⓐ Ⓑ Ⓒ Ⓓ	26 Ⓐ Ⓑ Ⓒ Ⓓ	34 Ⓐ Ⓑ Ⓒ Ⓓ
3 Ⓐ Ⓑ Ⓒ Ⓓ	11 Ⓐ Ⓑ Ⓒ Ⓓ	19 Ⓐ Ⓑ Ⓒ Ⓓ	27 Ⓐ Ⓑ Ⓒ Ⓓ	35 Ⓐ Ⓑ Ⓒ Ⓓ
4 Ⓐ Ⓑ Ⓒ Ⓓ	12 Ⓐ Ⓑ Ⓒ Ⓓ	20 Ⓐ Ⓑ Ⓒ Ⓓ	28 Ⓐ Ⓑ Ⓒ Ⓓ	36 Ⓐ Ⓑ Ⓒ Ⓓ
5 Ⓐ Ⓑ Ⓒ Ⓓ	13 Ⓐ Ⓑ Ⓒ Ⓓ	21 Ⓐ Ⓑ Ⓒ Ⓓ	29 Ⓐ Ⓑ Ⓒ Ⓓ	37 Ⓐ Ⓑ Ⓒ Ⓓ
6 Ⓐ Ⓑ Ⓒ Ⓓ	14 Ⓐ Ⓑ Ⓒ Ⓓ	22 Ⓐ Ⓑ Ⓒ Ⓓ	30 Ⓐ Ⓑ Ⓒ Ⓓ	38 Ⓐ Ⓑ Ⓒ Ⓓ
7 Ⓐ Ⓑ Ⓒ Ⓓ	15 Ⓐ Ⓑ Ⓒ Ⓓ	23 Ⓐ Ⓑ Ⓒ Ⓓ	31 Ⓐ Ⓑ Ⓒ Ⓓ	39 Ⓐ Ⓑ Ⓒ Ⓓ
8 Ⓐ Ⓑ Ⓒ Ⓓ	16 Ⓐ Ⓑ Ⓒ Ⓓ	24 Ⓐ Ⓑ Ⓒ Ⓓ	32 Ⓐ Ⓑ Ⓒ Ⓓ	40 Ⓐ Ⓑ Ⓒ Ⓓ

SECTION 2 - Quantitative Reasoning

1 Ⓐ Ⓑ Ⓒ Ⓓ	9 Ⓐ Ⓑ Ⓒ Ⓓ	17 Ⓐ Ⓑ Ⓒ Ⓓ	25 Ⓐ Ⓑ Ⓒ Ⓓ	33 Ⓐ Ⓑ Ⓒ Ⓓ
2 Ⓐ Ⓑ Ⓒ Ⓓ	10 Ⓐ Ⓑ Ⓒ Ⓓ	18 Ⓐ Ⓑ Ⓒ Ⓓ	26 Ⓐ Ⓑ Ⓒ Ⓓ	34 Ⓐ Ⓑ Ⓒ Ⓓ
3 Ⓐ Ⓑ Ⓒ Ⓓ	11 Ⓐ Ⓑ Ⓒ Ⓓ	19 Ⓐ Ⓑ Ⓒ Ⓓ	27 Ⓐ Ⓑ Ⓒ Ⓓ	35 Ⓐ Ⓑ Ⓒ Ⓓ
4 Ⓐ Ⓑ Ⓒ Ⓓ	12 Ⓐ Ⓑ Ⓒ Ⓓ	20 Ⓐ Ⓑ Ⓒ Ⓓ	28 Ⓐ Ⓑ Ⓒ Ⓓ	36 Ⓐ Ⓑ Ⓒ Ⓓ
5 Ⓐ Ⓑ Ⓒ Ⓓ	13 Ⓐ Ⓑ Ⓒ Ⓓ	21 Ⓐ Ⓑ Ⓒ Ⓓ	29 Ⓐ Ⓑ Ⓒ Ⓓ	37 Ⓐ Ⓑ Ⓒ Ⓓ
6 Ⓐ Ⓑ Ⓒ Ⓓ	14 Ⓐ Ⓑ Ⓒ Ⓓ	22 Ⓐ Ⓑ Ⓒ Ⓓ	30 Ⓐ Ⓑ Ⓒ Ⓓ	
7 Ⓐ Ⓑ Ⓒ Ⓓ	15 Ⓐ Ⓑ Ⓒ Ⓓ	23 Ⓐ Ⓑ Ⓒ Ⓓ	31 Ⓐ Ⓑ Ⓒ Ⓓ	
8 Ⓐ Ⓑ Ⓒ Ⓓ	16 Ⓐ Ⓑ Ⓒ Ⓓ	24 Ⓐ Ⓑ Ⓒ Ⓓ	32 Ⓐ Ⓑ Ⓒ Ⓓ	

SECTION 3 - Reading Comprehension

1 Ⓐ Ⓑ Ⓒ Ⓓ	9 Ⓐ Ⓑ Ⓒ Ⓓ	17 Ⓐ Ⓑ Ⓒ Ⓓ	25 Ⓐ Ⓑ Ⓒ Ⓓ	33 Ⓐ Ⓑ Ⓒ Ⓓ
2 Ⓐ Ⓑ Ⓒ Ⓓ	10 Ⓐ Ⓑ Ⓒ Ⓓ	18 Ⓐ Ⓑ Ⓒ Ⓓ	26 Ⓐ Ⓑ Ⓒ Ⓓ	34 Ⓐ Ⓑ Ⓒ Ⓓ
3 Ⓐ Ⓑ Ⓒ Ⓓ	11 Ⓐ Ⓑ Ⓒ Ⓓ	19 Ⓐ Ⓑ Ⓒ Ⓓ	27 Ⓐ Ⓑ Ⓒ Ⓓ	35 Ⓐ Ⓑ Ⓒ Ⓓ
4 Ⓐ Ⓑ Ⓒ Ⓓ	12 Ⓐ Ⓑ Ⓒ Ⓓ	20 Ⓐ Ⓑ Ⓒ Ⓓ	28 Ⓐ Ⓑ Ⓒ Ⓓ	36 Ⓐ Ⓑ Ⓒ Ⓓ
5 Ⓐ Ⓑ Ⓒ Ⓓ	13 Ⓐ Ⓑ Ⓒ Ⓓ	21 Ⓐ Ⓑ Ⓒ Ⓓ	29 Ⓐ Ⓑ Ⓒ Ⓓ	
6 Ⓐ Ⓑ Ⓒ Ⓓ	14 Ⓐ Ⓑ Ⓒ Ⓓ	22 Ⓐ Ⓑ Ⓒ Ⓓ	30 Ⓐ Ⓑ Ⓒ Ⓓ	
7 Ⓐ Ⓑ Ⓒ Ⓓ	15 Ⓐ Ⓑ Ⓒ Ⓓ	23 Ⓐ Ⓑ Ⓒ Ⓓ	31 Ⓐ Ⓑ Ⓒ Ⓓ	
8 Ⓐ Ⓑ Ⓒ Ⓓ	16 Ⓐ Ⓑ Ⓒ Ⓓ	24 Ⓐ Ⓑ Ⓒ Ⓓ	32 Ⓐ Ⓑ Ⓒ Ⓓ	

SECTION 4 - Mathematics Achievement

1 Ⓐ Ⓑ Ⓒ Ⓓ	11 Ⓐ Ⓑ Ⓒ Ⓓ	21 Ⓐ Ⓑ Ⓒ Ⓓ	31 Ⓐ Ⓑ Ⓒ Ⓓ	41 Ⓐ Ⓑ Ⓒ Ⓓ
2 Ⓐ Ⓑ Ⓒ Ⓓ	12 Ⓐ Ⓑ Ⓒ Ⓓ	22 Ⓐ Ⓑ Ⓒ Ⓓ	32 Ⓐ Ⓑ Ⓒ Ⓓ	42 Ⓐ Ⓑ Ⓒ Ⓓ
3 Ⓐ Ⓑ Ⓒ Ⓓ	13 Ⓐ Ⓑ Ⓒ Ⓓ	23 Ⓐ Ⓑ Ⓒ Ⓓ	33 Ⓐ Ⓑ Ⓒ Ⓓ	43 Ⓐ Ⓑ Ⓒ Ⓓ
4 Ⓐ Ⓑ Ⓒ Ⓓ	14 Ⓐ Ⓑ Ⓒ Ⓓ	24 Ⓐ Ⓑ Ⓒ Ⓓ	34 Ⓐ Ⓑ Ⓒ Ⓓ	44 Ⓐ Ⓑ Ⓒ Ⓓ
5 Ⓐ Ⓑ Ⓒ Ⓓ	15 Ⓐ Ⓑ Ⓒ Ⓓ	25 Ⓐ Ⓑ Ⓒ Ⓓ	35 Ⓐ Ⓑ Ⓒ Ⓓ	45 Ⓐ Ⓑ Ⓒ Ⓓ
6 Ⓐ Ⓑ Ⓒ Ⓓ	16 Ⓐ Ⓑ Ⓒ Ⓓ	26 Ⓐ Ⓑ Ⓒ Ⓓ	36 Ⓐ Ⓑ Ⓒ Ⓓ	46 Ⓐ Ⓑ Ⓒ Ⓓ
7 Ⓐ Ⓑ Ⓒ Ⓓ	17 Ⓐ Ⓑ Ⓒ Ⓓ	27 Ⓐ Ⓑ Ⓒ Ⓓ	37 Ⓐ Ⓑ Ⓒ Ⓓ	47 Ⓐ Ⓑ Ⓒ Ⓓ
8 Ⓐ Ⓑ Ⓒ Ⓓ	18 Ⓐ Ⓑ Ⓒ Ⓓ	28 Ⓐ Ⓑ Ⓒ Ⓓ	38 Ⓐ Ⓑ Ⓒ Ⓓ	
9 Ⓐ Ⓑ Ⓒ Ⓓ	19 Ⓐ Ⓑ Ⓒ Ⓓ	29 Ⓐ Ⓑ Ⓒ Ⓓ	39 Ⓐ Ⓑ Ⓒ Ⓓ	
10 Ⓐ Ⓑ Ⓒ Ⓓ	20 Ⓐ Ⓑ Ⓒ Ⓓ	30 Ⓐ Ⓑ Ⓒ Ⓓ	40 Ⓐ Ⓑ Ⓒ Ⓓ	

Section 1
Verbal Reasoning

40 Questions	Time: 20 Minutes

This section is divided into two parts that contain two different types of questions. As soon as you have completed Part One, answer the questions in Part Two. You may write in your test booklet. For each answer you select, fill in the corresponding circle on your answer document.

Part One – Synonyms

Each question in Part One consists of a word in capital letters followed by four answer choices. Select the one word that is most nearly the same in meaning as the word in capital letters.

SAMPLE QUESTION: <u>Sample Answer</u>

     TRUTH: Ⓐ Ⓑ ● Ⓓ

     (A)   dread
     (B)   marriage
     (C)   reality
     (D)   relevance

Go on to the next page. →

VR

Part Two – Sentence Completion

Each question in Part Two is made up of a sentence with one blank. Each blank indicates that a word is missing. The sentence is followed by four answer choices. Select the word that best completes the meaning of the sentence as a whole.

SAMPLE QUESTION:

The question was so ------- that the best student in class got it wrong.

(A) coarse
(B) difficult
(C) funny
(D) long

Sample Answer

Ⓐ ● Ⓒ Ⓓ

Go on to the next page. ➔

Part One – Synonyms

Directions: Select the word that is most nearly the same in meaning as the word in capital letters.

1. UNUSUAL:

   (A) friendly
   (B) happy
   (C) new
   (D) peculiar

2. ASSISTANCE:

   (A) call
   (B) disability
   (C) service
   (D) teaching

3. REALITY:

   (A) dream
   (B) fact
   (C) rarity
   (D) security

4. DIMINUTION:

   (A) assessment
   (B) leniency
   (C) reduction
   (D) restitution

5. CONTENTED:

   (A) diplomatic
   (B) disgusted
   (C) mammoth
   (D) satisfied

6. BOUND:

   (A) badgered
   (B) confused
   (C) obliged
   (D) relieved

7. FALTER:

   (A) drop
   (B) hesitate
   (C) question
   (D) replenish

8. CONTAINED:

   (A) eliminated
   (B) held
   (C) raging
   (D) wooden

9. REVERE:

   (A) disdain
   (B) esteem
   (C) faith
   (D) reliance

10. DILIGENT:

   (A) defensive
   (B) hardworking
   (C) lazy
   (D) obsessive

Go on to the next page. ➜

11. DETRIMENTAL:

   (A) harmful
   (B) knowledgeable
   (C) tentative
   (D) worrisome

12. VOW:

   (A) argue
   (B) claim
   (C) please
   (D) pledge

13. ASPIRATION:

   (A) focus
   (B) hope
   (C) injury
   (D) trend

14. BASHFUL:

   (A) argumentative
   (B) serious
   (C) shy
   (D) tolerant

15. SINISTER:

   (A) elderly
   (B) erratic
   (C) uncomfortable
   (D) wicked

16. DISCLOSE:

   (A) hide
   (B) remove
   (C) reveal
   (D) undress

17. CONGEAL:

   (A) coagulate
   (B) help
   (C) recede
   (D) weaken

18. INUNDATE:

   (A) enter
   (B) flood
   (C) migrate
   (D) strive

19. STEADFAST:

   (A) constant
   (B) optional
   (C) quick
   (D) restful

20. RUTHLESS:

   (A) counterfeit
   (B) unofficial
   (C) unsparing
   (D) victorious

Go on to the next page. ➜

Part Two – Sentence Completion

Directions: Select the word that best completes the sentence.

21. Myron was able to remain completely -------; he never took sides in any of the disagreements around the house.

    (A) biased
    (B) interested
    (C) neutral
    (D) thoughtful

22. Since the great drought left the soil completely useless, the people of that country were forced to ------- food from other countries.

    (A) export
    (B) import
    (C) report
    (D) sell

23. Because he was annoyed by even the smallest grammatical error, Mr. Jones reviewed all the students' papers ------- before grading them.

    (A) crudely
    (B) helplessly
    (C) inefficiently
    (D) meticulously

24. Eric doesn't merely dislike racism; he ------- it.

    (A) abhors
    (B) moderates
    (C) questions
    (D) studies

25. Sharon's anger was too great: David simply could not ------- her with his charm.

    (A) irritate
    (B) manipulate
    (C) pacify
    (D) terrify

26. Even though the accident led to serious damage to our property, our ------- lawyer didn't present a convincing argument and we received no compensation.

    (A) discerning
    (B) fatalistic
    (C) incompetent
    (D) professional

27. After months of petty disputes, the two countries finally decided to sit down at a table and have a ------- discussion.

    (A) friendly
    (B) hostile
    (C) lengthy
    (D) pressing

28. Although the thief claimed that he accidentally picked up the stolen watch, the jury judged his action -------.

    (A) deliberate
    (B) frantic
    (C) impractical
    (D) misguided

Go on to the next page. ➞

29. In order to be a good doctor, you don't need to be ------- yourself, just as a good architect does not have to live in a fancy house.

    (A) educated
    (B) handsome
    (C) healthy
    (D) thoughtful

30. Pete's coach was ------- when Pete followed up his winning season with an even better performance this year.

    (A) disappointed
    (B) gratified
    (C) relieved
    (D) upset

31. While many species, such as wolves, travel in groups, the cheetah is a ------- animal.

    (A) dangerous
    (B) pack
    (C) solitary
    (D) territorial

32. During his years in the Senate, Jones felt ------- about speaking up at all, while most of the other senators were aggressive and argumentative.

    (A) blithe
    (B) contented
    (C) favorable
    (D) timid

33. The politician's speech was so ------- that nearly everyone in the room decided not to vote for him.

    (A) feeble
    (B) monotonous
    (C) persuasive
    (D) unique

34. The corporation did not have a ------- system for promotions; each department was free to use its own discretion in advancing employees.

    (A) dignified
    (B) favorable
    (C) forgiving
    (D) uniform

35. Only from years of training can a gymnast hope to become ------- enough to master Olympic-level techniques.

    (A) agile
    (B) mature
    (C) passive
    (D) strict

36. Though Mr. Fenster was known to be ------- toward his neighbors, he always welcomed their children as trick-or-treaters at Halloween.

    (A) belligerent
    (B) cheerful
    (C) courteous
    (D) direct

Go on to the next page. →

37. The ------- young man talked back to his parents and teachers alike.

    (A) dreary
    (B) insolent
    (C) nervous
    (D) respectful

38. While the painting's brushstrokes seem -------, they are actually carefully planned out.

    (A) flagrant
    (B) haphazard
    (C) intricate
    (D) paltry

39. The Declaration of Independence is premised upon ------- principles, such as protecting life, liberty, and the pursuit of happiness.

    (A) united
    (B) lofty
    (C) predictable
    (D) variable

40. Our teacher advised us not to get too caught up in the ------- of information in the textbook, or we could lose the "big picture" of its theory.

    (A) minutiae
    (B) principles
    (C) scope
    (D) thought

STOP. If there is time, you may check your work in this section only.

STOP

QR

Section 2
Quantitative Reasoning

---

37 Questions	Time: 35 Minutes

This section is divided into two parts that contain two different types of questions. As soon as you have completed Part One, answer the questions in Part Two. You may write in your test booklet. For each answer you select, remember to fill in the corresponding circle on your answer document.

Any figures that accompany the questions in this section may be assumed to be drawn as accurately as possible EXCEPT when it is stated that a particular figure is not drawn to scale. Letters such as *x, y,* and *n* stand for real numbers.

Part One – Word Problems

Each question in Part One consists of a word problem followed by four answer choices. You may write in your test booklet; however, you may be able to solve many of these problems in your head. Next, look at the four answer choices given and select the best answer.

EXAMPLE 1:

Sample Answer

● Ⓑ Ⓒ Ⓓ

What is the value of the expression

$1 + 3 \times (4 \div 2) - 5$?

(A) 2
(B) 3
(C) 4
(D) 8

The correct answer is 2, so circle A is darkened.

Go on to the next page. ⟶

Part Two – Quantitative Comparisons

All questions in Part Two are quantitative comparisons between the quantities shown in Column A and Column B. Using the information given in each question, compare the quantity in Column A to the quantity in Column B, and choose one of these four answer choices:

(A)   The quantity in Column A is greater.
(B)   The quantity in Column B is greater.
(C)   The two quantities are equal.
(D)   The relationship cannot be determined from the information given.

	Column A	Column B	Sample Answer
EXAMPLE 2:	$\frac{2}{3}$ of 9	$\frac{1}{3}$ of 18	Ⓐ Ⓑ ● Ⓓ

The quantity in <u>Column A</u> (6) is the same as the quantity in <u>Column B</u> (6), so circle C is darkened.

EXAMPLE 3:

Sample Answer

Ⓐ Ⓑ Ⓒ ●

When integer x is multiplied by 2, the result is greater than 10 but less than 16.

<u>Column A</u>   <u>Column B</u>
x 7

Since $10 < 2x < 16$, $5 < x < 8$. Thus, as x can equal 6 or 7, there is not enough information given to determine the relationship. Circle D is darkened.

Go on to the next page. ⟶

NO TEST MATERIAL ON THIS PAGE

Part One – Word Problems

Directions: Choose the best answer from the four choices given.

1. $54 \times 3 =$

    (A) 123
    (B) 150
    (C) 162
    (D) 172

2. What is the area of a square with a side of length 2 ?

    (A) 2
    (B) 4
    (C) 6
    (D) 8

3. $3 \times 2 \times 1 - (4 \times 3 \times 2) =$

    (A) 18
    (B) 6
    (C) −6
    (D) −18

4. Vicky scored 80, 90, and 94 on her three tests. What was her average score?

    (A) 81
    (B) 88
    (C) 90
    (D) 93

Questions 5–6 refer to the following graph.

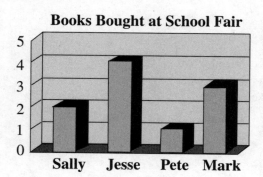

Books Bought at School Fair

5. Who bought the most books at the school fair?

    (A) Sally
    (B) Jesse
    (C) Pete
    (D) Mark

6. Sally and Mark together bought how many more books than Jesse?

    (A) 1
    (B) 2
    (C) 3
    (D) 5

Go on to the next page. →

QR

7. $\dfrac{1}{2} + \dfrac{3}{4} =$

   (A) $\dfrac{3}{8}$

   (B) $\dfrac{5}{4}$

   (C) $\dfrac{3}{2}$

   (D) $\dfrac{5}{2}$

8. What is the value of the digit 7 in the number 4,678.02 ?

   (A) 7
   (B) 70
   (C) 700
   (D) 7,000

9. Jason has several books in his room, 20% of which are fiction. The other books are nonfiction. If he has 5 fiction books, how many nonfiction books does he have?

   (A) 5
   (B) 10
   (C) 20
   (D) 25

10. $\dfrac{7}{0.35} =$

   (A) 0.2
   (B) 2
   (C) 20
   (D) 200

11. Which of the following is closest in value to 5 ?

   (A) 4.5
   (B) 5.009
   (C) 5.01
   (D) 5.101

12. Janice went to the butcher and bought six pounds of hamburger. If the bill was $18.50, which of the following is closest to the cost per pound of the hamburger?

   (A) $2.00
   (B) $3.00
   (C) $5.00
   (D) $6.00

13. Which of the following numbers is closest to the square root of 175 ?

   (A) 9
   (B) 13
   (C) 22
   (D) 30

14. Laurie was reading a book that had an illustration on every odd-numbered page. If there are 32 numbered pages in the book, how many illustrations are there?

   (A) 15
   (B) 16
   (C) 17
   (D) 31

Go on to the next page. ➔

15. If $6y + 8 = 20$, what is the value of $3y + 4$?

   (A)   2
   (B)   8
   (C)   10
   (D)   12

16. A lecture hall's maximum capacity of 56 has increased by 75%. What is the new seating capacity after the increase?

   (A)   42
   (B)   70
   (C)   98
   (D)   112

17. When a number is divided by 8, the quotient is 11 and the remainder is 2. What is the number?

   (A)   11
   (B)   22
   (C)   72
   (D)   90

The following graph shows the amount of rainfall in Miller County for the years 1942–1946.

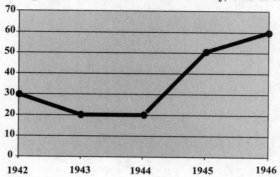

Average Inches of Rainfall in Miller County, 1942–1946

18. When did the greatest increase in rainfall occur in Miller County?

   (A)   Between 1942 and 1943
   (B)   Between 1943 and 1944
   (C)   Between 1944 and 1945
   (D)   Between 1945 and 1946

19. The temperature at 6 A.M. was 32°. If the temperature increased at a constant rate of 3° per hour all day, what was the temperature at 1 P.M.?

   (A)   35°
   (B)   43°
   (C)   47°
   (D)   53°

20. What is the volume of a box with length 4 cm, width 3 cm, and height 2 cm?

   (A)   6 cubic centimeters
   (B)   9 cubic centimeters
   (C)   12 cubic centimeters
   (D)   24 cubic centimeters

Go on to the next page. →

QR

②

Part Two – Quantitative Comparisons

Directions: Using all information given in each question, compare the quantity in Column A to the quantity in Column B. All questions in Part Two have these answer choices:

(A) The quantity in Column A is greater.
(B) The quantity in Column B is greater.
(C) The two quantities are equal.
(D) The relationship cannot be determined from the information given.

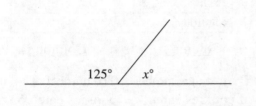

	Column A	Column B
21.	x	55

A rectangle with sides x and y has an area of 12.

	Column A	Column B
22.	The length of x	The length of y

	Column A	Column B
23.	$\sqrt{9} + \sqrt{25}$	$\sqrt{9 + 25}$

The quadrilateral *ABCD* has an area of 12.

24.	Column A	Column B
	The perimeter of *ABCD*	15

Go on to the next page. ⟶

Answer choices for all questions on this page.

(A) The quantity in Column A is greater.
(B) The quantity in Column B is greater.
(C) The two quantities are equal.
(D) The relationship cannot be determined from the information given.

Martha had $20. She gave half of her money to her sister, Linda. Linda now has $30.

Column A	Column B

25. The amount of money Martha now has / The amount of money Linda had originally

$$4x + 7 = 63$$
$$\frac{y}{3} + 6 = 15$$

Column A	Column B

26. x / y

Column A	Column B

27. The area of a rectangle with length 3 and width 4 / The area of a square with a side of 3

Number of Cookies Eaten Each Day

Wednesday	3
Thursday	2
Friday	1
Saturday	3

Column A	Column B

28. The average number of cookies eaten each day / The number of cookies eaten on Thursday

Column A	Column B

29. $\sqrt{0.64}$ / $\sqrt{6.4}$

Go on to the next page. →

Answer choices for all questions on this page.

(A) The quantity in Column A is greater.
(B) The quantity in Column B is greater.
(C) The two quantities are equal.
(D) The relationship cannot be determined from the information given.

Avi bought 5 oranges and 6 peaches. The total price of the fruit was $1.10.

Column A	Column B
30. The cost of one orange	The cost of one peach

Column A	Column B
31. $-(5)^6$	$(-5)^6$

a represents an odd integer greater than 9 and less than 15.

b represents an even integer greater than 9 and less than 15.

Column A	Column B
32. $a \times 3$	$b \times 4$

A 12-sided die with faces numbered 1 through 12 is rolled.

Column A	Column B
33. The probability that the result is even	The probability that the result is prime

Go on to the next page. ⟶

Answer choices for all questions on this page.

(A) The quantity in Column A is greater.
(B) The quantity in Column B is greater.
(C) The two quantities are equal.
(D) The relationship cannot be determined from the information given.

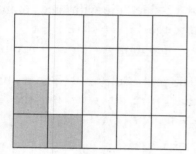

The original price of a shirt now on sale was $50.

	Column A	Column B
	Column A	Column B

36. | The price of the shirt after two 20% discounts | The price of the shirt after a single 40% discount |

Column A	Column B

34. The fractional part of the figure that is shaded

$\dfrac{3}{20}$

37. The slope of the line with points (3, 8) and (5, 2) | The slope of the line $6x - 2y = -8$

Melvin brought home a large pizza with 12 slices.

Column A	Column B

35. The number of slices left if Melvin eats 50% of the pizza | The number of slices left if Melvin eats one-third of the pizza

STOP. If there is time, you may check your work in this section only. STOP

RC

Section 3
Reading Comprehension

36 Questions

Time: 35 Minutes

This section contains six short reading passages. Each passage is followed by six questions based on its content. Answer the questions following each passage on the basis of what is <u>stated</u> or <u>implied</u> in that passage. You may write in the test booklet.

STOP. Do not go on
until told to do so.

Questions 1–6

Line

1   When most people think of the history
2 of transportation, they think of the invention
3 of the wheel as the starting point. The
4 wheel was invented around 3500 B.C.E.,
5 more than 5,000 years ago. Before then,
6 transportation was a difficult process,
7 especially for those who had anything to
8 carry. During prehistoric times, the only
9 way to get around was to walk. Children
10 and possessions were strapped to someone's
11 back if they needed to be carried. If the
12 load was too heavy for one person, it could
13 be strapped to a pole and carried by two.
14 The sledge was developed as a way to
15 drag a heavy load. Sledges were originally

16 just logs or pieces of animal skin upon
17 which a load was strapped and dragged.
18 In time, runners were put on the sledge,
19 and it evolved to what is now called a sled.
20 Around 5000 B.C.E., the first animals were
21 domesticated, or tamed. Then, donkeys and
22 oxen were used to carry heavy loads and
23 pull sledges. It wasn't until almost 1,500
24 years later that wheeled vehicles appeared.
25 It is believed that the wheel was invented
26 in Mesopotamia, in the Middle East. About
27 300 years later, the Egyptians invented the
28 sailboat. These two inventions changed
29 transportation forever.

Go on to the next page. ➡

RC

1. The primary purpose of the passage is to

   (A) describe some of the things people used for transportation long ago
   (B) describe the reasons that led to transportation discoveries
   (C) explain the evolution of the sled
   (D) give a detailed history of transportation

2. The passage suggests that prehistoric man used all of the following for carrying things EXCEPT

   (A) animals
   (B) children
   (C) poles
   (D) primitive sleds

3. The passage implies that early man

   (A) was incapable of inventing the wheel any earlier than 3500 B.C.E.
   (B) was interested in farming
   (C) was interested in finding ways to help carry things
   (D) was outgoing and friendly

4. It can be inferred from the passage that the reason animals were domesticated was

   (A) to help carry large loads
   (B) to move people and possessions around quickly
   (C) to provide family pets
   (D) to ward off danger

5. Which of the following describes the author's attitude toward the invention of the wheel?

   (A) Admiration
   (B) Disdain
   (C) Indifference
   (D) Regret

6. The passage suggests that the sledge was

   (A) a precursor to the sled
   (B) invented in conjunction with the wheel
   (C) made exclusively of animal skin
   (D) the only tool used for transportation at the time

Go on to the next page. ➞

Questions 7–12

Line

1   Bison and buffalo are not the same
2 animal. For years, American bison were
3 mistakenly referred to as buffalo. Due to
4 this confusion, there are many references
5 to buffalo in the United States. There is the
6 city of Buffalo in northwestern New York
7 state. In addition, the buffalo appeared
8 on the U.S. nickel for many years at the
9 beginning of the twentieth century. This is
10 often referred to as the "Buffalo Nickel" to
11 distinguish it from the current nickel with
12 Thomas Jefferson on the front. Buffalo are
13 actually found in Asia, Africa, and South
14 America. Bison roamed the North American
15 western plains by the millions just a couple
16 of centuries ago. Because the bison were so
17 widely hunted, however, their numbers fell
18 greatly. In fact, as of a century ago, there
19 were only about 500 left. They were deemed
20 near extinction, but due to conservation
21 efforts, their numbers have increased. There
22 are approximately 50,000 bison living today
23 in protected parks. Though they may never
24 be as abundant as they once were, they are
25 not in danger of extinction as long as they
26 remain protected.

Go on to the next page. ➡

7. The primary purpose of the passage is to

   (A) applaud conservation efforts
   (B) explain the genetic difference between the bison and the buffalo
   (C) explain why people confuse the buffalo and the bison
   (D) give some background on the American bison

8. The passage implies that the primary difference between the buffalo and the bison is

   (A) their geographic location
   (B) their number
   (C) their size
   (D) when they existed

9. As used in line 19, the word "deemed" most closely means

   (A) found
   (B) hunted
   (C) ruled
   (D) eaten

10. According to the passage, what can be hoped for as long as the American bison is protected?

    (A) They will be as plentiful as they once were.
    (B) They will disturb the delicate ecological balance in the plains.
    (C) They will face even greater dangers.
    (D) They will probably not die out.

11. According to the passage, the primary reason that the American bison is no longer near extinction is

    (A) conservation efforts
    (B) lack of interest in hunting them
    (C) loss of value of their fur
    (D) the migration of the animals

12. In line 6, the author mentions the city of Buffalo in order to

    (A) criticize a hunting practice
    (B) establish the reason for a particular currency
    (C) illustrate a common misunderstanding
    (D) pinpoint the first sighting of buffalo in New York

Go on to the next page. ⟶

Questions 13–18

Line

1   The Greek philosopher Aristotle
2 had many students, but perhaps none so
3 famous as Alexander the Great. As a child,
4 Alexander was known for his intelligence
5 and bravery. The lessons he learned from
6 Aristotle left him with a lifelong love of
7 books and learning. But it was not his love
8 of books that made him famous. Alexander,
9 in 336 B.C.E., became the king of a small
10 Greek kingdom called Macedonia. He was
11 only twenty at the time. He went on to
12 invade country after country: Persia (now
13 known as Iran), Egypt, and all the way
14 to parts of India and Pakistan. Alexander
15 conquered most of what was then the
16 "civilized world." He brought with him the
17 Greek way of thinking and doing things. He
18 is considered one of the great generals and
19 kings of history and is responsible for the
20 spread of Greek culture throughout much of
21 the world.

Go on to the next page. ➞

3

13. Which of the following would be the best title for the passage?

   (A) "Alexander the Great: King and Conqueror"
   (B) "Aristotle: Teacher of the Kings"
   (C) "Greek Culture"
   (D) "The History of Macedonia"

14. As used in line 16, the word "civilized" most closely means

   (A) barbaric
   (B) educated
   (C) friendly
   (D) well-mannered

15. The tone of the passage is most like that found in

   (A) a diary entry from an historian
   (B) a letter from an archaeologist
   (C) a philosophy journal
   (D) a reference book

16. According to the passage, one of the things that was so impressive about Alexander was

   (A) his ability to teach
   (B) his great integrity
   (C) his handsome features
   (D) his intelligence and culture

17. The passage suggests that Aristotle

   (A) encouraged Alexander to spread culture
   (B) helped foster Alexander's love of books
   (C) supported Alexander's military career
   (D) taught Alexander military strategy

18. According to the passage, when Alexander invaded a country, he

   (A) enslaved citizens
   (B) freed oppressed people
   (C) spread Greek ideas
   (D) toppled monuments

Go on to the next page. ➞

Questions 19–24

Line

1   Everyone has had attacks of the
2 hiccups, or hiccoughs, at one point in his or
3 her life. Few people, however, think about
4 what is happening to them and how hiccups
5 begin and end.
6   The diaphragm is a large muscle,
7 shaped like a dome, that sits at the base
8 of the chest cavity. As one breathes, the
9 diaphragm gently contracts and relaxes
10 to help the process. Occasionally, an
11 irritation near the diaphragm or a disease
12 may cause the muscle to spasm, or contract
13 suddenly. The spasm will suck air into the
14 lungs past the vocal cords. A small flap
15 called the epiglottis tops the vocal cords so
16 that food will not accidentally enter into
17 the windpipe. The sudden spasm of the
18 diaphragm causes the epiglottis to close
19 quickly. Imagine the pull of air into the
20 vocal cords from the spastic diaphragm
21 hitting the closed epiglottis. This moves
22 the vocal cords, causing the "hic" sound
23 of the hiccup. Although most people don't
24 really worry about the hiccups, attacks may
25 last for days. The exhaustion of hiccupping
26 for days on end has been fatal in certain
27 rare cases. Home remedies abound—from
28 breathing into paper bags to squeezing on
29 pressure points that supposedly relax the
30 diaphragm.

Go on to the next page. ⟶

| For more free content, visit PrincetonReview.com

19. The primary purpose of the passage is to

    (A)   describe a common occurrence
    (B)   prescribe a treatment
    (C)   settle a dispute
    (D)   warn about a danger

20. According to the passage, one possible cause of hiccups is

    (A)   a sudden rush of air
    (B)   an irritant near the diaphragm
    (C)   breathing in and out of a paper bag
    (D)   the closing of the epiglottis

21. As used in line 24, "attacks" most closely means

    (A)   advances
    (B)   assaults
    (C)   bouts
    (D)   threats

22. The passage suggests that which of the following makes the "hic" sound of the hiccup?

    (A)   the diaphragm
    (B)   the lungs
    (C)   the stomach
    (D)   the vocal cords

23. According to the passage, the hiccups can be fatal due to

    (A)   fatigue from days of hiccupping
    (B)   home remedies that are toxic
    (C)   the humiliation of hiccupping for days on end
    (D)   the irritant to the diaphragm

24. The author mentions "hiccoughs" in line 2 in order to

    (A)   correct an improper usage
    (B)   define a technical term
    (C)   indicate an alternate spelling
    (D)   weaken a misguided argument

Go on to the next page. ⟶

Questions 25–30

Line

1 During the winter months in many
2 regions, food can be extremely scarce. For
3 the wildlife of these areas, this can be a
4 great problem unless animals have some
5 mechanism that allows them to adapt. Some
6 animals migrate to warmer climates. Others
7 hibernate to conserve energy and decrease
8 the need for food. Prior to hibernation, an
9 animal will generally eat a lot to build up a
10 store of fat. The animal's system will "feed"
11 off the fat stores throughout the long cold
12 winter months. When the animal hibernates,
13 its body temperature decreases and its body
14 functions slow down considerably. The
15 dormouse's heartbeat, for example, slows
16 down to just a beat every few minutes. Its

17 breathing also becomes slow and its body
18 temperature drops to just a few degrees
19 above the temperature of the ground around
20 it. All these changes decrease the need for
21 fuel and allow the animal to survive long
22 periods without any food. It is a mistake
23 to think that all hibernating animals sleep
24 for the whole winter. In fact, many animals
25 hibernate for short spurts during the winter.
26 They may wake for an interval of mild
27 weather. Scientists have now discovered
28 the chemical that triggers hibernation. If
29 this chemical is injected in an animal in the
30 summer months, it can cause the animal to
31 go into summer hibernation.

Go on to the next page. ➞

25. The primary purpose of the passage is to

   (A) compare the hibernating dormouse with other hibernating animals
   (B) debunk some common myths about hibernation
   (C) discuss the discovery of the chemical that causes hibernation
   (D) explore some basic information about hibernation

26. As used in line 7, the word "conserve" most closely means

   (A) expend
   (B) help
   (C) reserve
   (D) waste

27. According to the author, each of the following happens to a hibernating animal EXCEPT

   (A) it goes into a dream state
   (B) its body temperature drops
   (C) its breathing slows
   (D) its heartbeat slows

28. Which of the following can be inferred as a reason a hibernating animal may interrupt its hibernation?

   (A) A day or two of stormy weather
   (B) An overabundance of food
   (C) A week in which there was no snow
   (D) A week in which the temperature was well above freezing

29. According to the author, if the chemical that triggers hibernation is injected into an animal when it would not normally hibernate, the chemical may

   (A) allow the animal to shed extra fat stores
   (B) cause an out-of-season hibernation
   (C) cause body functions to slow to a halt
   (D) decrease an animal's need for food

30. The tone of the passage is best described as

   (A) amazed
   (B) concerned
   (C) indifferent
   (D) informative

Go on to the next page. ➞

<u>Questions 31–36</u>

Line

1   The theater is one of the richest art
2 forms. The excitement of opening night
3 can be felt by the people waiting to watch
4 a performance and by the performers and
5 workers backstage waiting for the curtain
6 to go up. Live theater is thrilling because
7 no one really knows how well the play
8 will go until it is performed. Many people
9 collaborate to bring a play to life. There
10 are playwrights, directors, set designers,
11 costumers, lighting technicians, and,
12 of course, actors. If the performance is
13 a musical, the skills of a songwriter, a
14 choreographer (the person who composes
15 the dances), and musicians are also
16 required. The word *theater* comes from the
17 Greek *theatron*, which means "a place for
18 seeing." One concept from Greek theater
19 that is still seen in some plays today is the
20 "Greek Chorus." This consists of several
21 actors/characters watching the action of the
22 play (almost like the audience) and then
23 commenting on what they just saw with
24 either reactions or dialogue. Although most
25 people think of the theater in terms of a play
26 performed on the stage, theater has taken
27 on a much broader meaning in the modern
28 world. You may find yourself walking into
29 a theater with no seats in the rows. Instead,
30 you are seated among the set pieces, which
31 makes you part of the setting. Sometimes
32 theater may come to life on a street corner,
33 or in a classroom. The excitement of theater
34 is in its very nature—it is an art form that
35 changes as it is interpreted in different
36 ways by different people. That is probably
37 why the works of the greatest playwright
38 of all time, William Shakespeare, are still
39 performed and enjoyed today, both in
40 classic and new interpretations.

Go on to the next page. ➡

31. The best title for the passage might be

    (A) "A Brief History of Theatrical Productions"
    (B) "Modern Theater: Adventures in Acting"
    (C) "Shakespeare: Our Greatest Playwright"
    (D) "The Excitement of Theater"

32. According to the passage, the primary reason that theater is so exciting is that

    (A) it derives from a Greek custom
    (B) it is performed live
    (C) plays are often well written
    (D) there are so many people working on it

33. The passage suggests which of the following about modern theater?

    (A) It always draws great attention from the audience.
    (B) It has been interpreted in a more varied fashion.
    (C) It is less exciting than classic theater.
    (D) There are mostly Shakespearean plays performed.

34. The author's attitude toward theater can best be described as

    (A) admiring
    (B) ambivalent
    (C) apathetic
    (D) neutral

35. In line 1, the word "richest" is best understood to mean most

    (A) diverse
    (B) entertaining
    (C) terrifying
    (D) wealthy

36. The passage suggests that the plays of Shakespeare

    (A) are more often given new interpretations today than at any other time
    (B) are more popular today than during Shakespeare's time
    (C) have been performed in a variety of ways
    (D) will always be considered the world's greatest

STOP. If there is time, you may check your work in this section only. STOP

Section 4
Mathematics Achievement

| 47 Questions | Time: 40 Minutes |

Each question is followed by four suggested answers. Read each question and then decide which one of the four suggested answers is best.

Find the row of spaces on your answer document that has the same number as the question. In this row, mark the space having the same letter as the answer you have chosen. You may write in your test booklet.

SAMPLE QUESTION:

Sample Answer

(A) ● (C) (D)

What is the perimeter of an equilateral triangle with a side length of 4 in.?

(A)   8 in.
(B)   12 in.
(C)   16 in.
(D)   24 in.

The correct answer is 12 in., so circle B is darkened.

STOP. Do not go on until told to do so.

STOP

NO TEST MATERIAL ON THIS PAGE

1. In the decimal 0.0987, the digit 9 is equivalent to which of the following?

    (A) $\dfrac{9}{10}$

    (B) $\dfrac{9}{100}$

    (C) $\dfrac{9}{1,000}$

    (D) $\dfrac{9}{10,000}$

2. What is the least common multiple of 6, 9, and 12 ?

    (A)   3
    (B)   36
    (C)   72
    (D)   324

3. Which of the following equals 5 ?

    (A) $30 - 12 \div 2 \times (3 + 7)$
    (B) $30 - 12 \div (2 \times 3 + 7)$
    (C) $(30 - 12) \div 2 \times 3 + 7$
    (D) $30 - 12 \div 2 \times 3 - 7$

4. $\dfrac{5}{7} + \dfrac{2}{11} =$

    (A) $\dfrac{10}{17}$

    (B) $\dfrac{10}{77}$

    (C) $\dfrac{7}{18}$

    (D) $\dfrac{69}{77}$

5. $7\dfrac{1}{2}$ hours is how many minutes more than $6\dfrac{1}{4}$ hours?

    (A)   45
    (B)   60
    (C)   75
    (D)   90

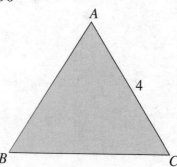

6. What is the perimeter of equilateral triangle *ABC* shown above?

    (A)   12
    (B)   15
    (C)   18
    (D)   It cannot be determined from the information given.

Go on to the next page. ➡

7. Which of the following is 20% of 200 ?

(A) 20
(B) 30
(C) 40
(D) 100

Questions 8–10 refer to the following chart.

Day	Temperature (in degrees Celsius)	Snowfall (in centimeters)
Monday	2	3
Tuesday	6	3
Wednesday	3	4
Thursday	13	1

8. What was the total amount of snowfall for the four-day period shown?

(A) 44 cm
(B) 40 cm
(C) 11 cm
(D) 10 cm

9. On which day was the snowfall the greatest?

(A) Thursday
(B) Wednesday
(C) Tuesday
(D) Monday

10. What was the average temperature for the four-day period?

(A) 24°C
(B) 20°C
(C) 11°C
(D) 6°C

11. $\dfrac{100}{0.25} =$

(A) 4
(B) 40
(C) 400
(D) 4,000

12. If $5 \times 31 = 100 + \_$, what number goes in the _?

(A) 55
(B) 51
(C) 50
(D) 36

13. Gwen planted six tomato plants. Half of them died. She then planted one more. How many tomato plants does Gwen have now?

(A) 3
(B) 4
(C) 5
(D) 6

Go on to the next page. ⟶

14. The public library charges one dollar to rent a video game overnight, with a fifty-cent charge for each day the video game is late. If Tracey returns a video game three days late, how much does she owe all together?

    (A) $1.50
    (B) $2.00
    (C) $2.50
    (D) $3.50

15. $0.45 \times 100 =$

    (A)   4,500
    (B)   450
    (C)   45
    (D)   4.5

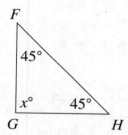

16. In triangle *FGH* shown above, the value of angle *x*, in degrees, is

    (A)   30
    (B)   45
    (C)   50
    (D)   90

17. If a dozen eggs cost $1.20, then 3 eggs cost

    (A)   30¢
    (B)   36¢
    (C)   40¢
    (D) $3.60

18. Boris and his friend Bruce collect baseball cards. If Bruce has 12 baseball cards and Boris has three times as many baseball cards as Bruce, what is the average number of cards in the boys' collections?

    (A)   7.5
    (B)   18
    (C)   24
    (D)   48

19. What is the perimeter of a rectangle with length 3 and width 2 ?

    (A)   6
    (B)   8
    (C)   10
    (D)   12

20. $\dfrac{3}{5} \times \dfrac{2}{7} =$

    (A) $\dfrac{3}{8}$

    (B) $\dfrac{6}{35}$

    (C) $\dfrac{31}{35}$

    (D) $\dfrac{21}{35}$

Go on to the next page. ➜

4

21. If Kenny can run three miles in 45 minutes, how long will it take him to run five miles?

 (A) 1 hour
 (B) 1 hour 15 minutes
 (C) 1 hour 30 minutes
 (D) 2 hours

22. Which fraction is greater than $\frac{5}{11}$?

 (A) $\frac{3}{8}$

 (B) $\frac{2}{7}$

 (C) $\frac{4}{9}$

 (D) $\frac{4}{7}$

23. If the perimeter of a square is 36, what is its area?

 (A) 16
 (B) 36
 (C) 64
 (D) 81

24. Maureen studied for two hours before school. After school, she studied for twice as long as she had before school. What was the total number of hours she studied in the day?

 (A) 4
 (B) 6
 (C) 8
 (D) 12

25. $\dfrac{40(37 + 63)}{8} =$

 (A) 450
 (B) 500
 (C) 1,250
 (D) 4,000

26. 0.347 =

 (A) $\dfrac{7}{10} + \dfrac{4}{100} + \dfrac{3}{1,000}$

 (B) $\dfrac{3}{100} + \dfrac{4}{10} + \dfrac{7}{100}$

 (C) $\dfrac{4}{100} + \dfrac{3}{10} + \dfrac{7}{1,000}$

 (D) $\dfrac{3}{10} + \dfrac{4}{1,000} + \dfrac{7}{100}$

27. Which is the prime factorization of 36 ?

 (A) $3 \times 3 \times 3 \times 2$
 (B) $3 \times 3 \times 2 \times 2$
 (C) $3 \times 2 \times 2 \times 2$
 (D) $6 \times 3 \times 2$

Go on to the next page. ➞

Questions 28–30 refer to the following chart.

Train Fares from Monroeville to Perkins' Corner

Fares	Weekday Peak	Weekday Off-Peak	Weekend & Holiday
One Way	$6.00	$5.00	$4.50
Round-Trip	$12.00	$10.00	$9.00
10-Trip Ticket	$54.00	$45.00	$40.00
Children Under 11	$1.00	$0.50	Free with Paying Adult

28. How much would it cost two adults and one child under the age of 11 to travel one way from Monroeville to Perkins' Corner on a weekend?

(A) $25.00
(B) $20.50
(C) $18.00
(D) $9.00

29. The price of a weekday peak fare ten-trip ticket is what percent less than the cost of purchasing ten one-way weekday peak fare tickets?

(A) 10%
(B) 20%
(C) 50%
(D) 100%

30. How much more does it cost for one adult to travel one way during the weekday peak fare period than for one adult to make the trip on the weekend?

(A) $0.50
(B) $0.75
(C) $1.00
(D) $1.50

31. Mr. Schroder swims laps at the community pool. It takes him 5 minutes to swim one lap. If he swims for 60 minutes without stopping, how many laps will he swim?

(A) 8
(B) 10
(C) 12
(D) 14

32. $10^3 =$

(A) 10×3

(B) $10 + 10 + 10$

(C) $10 \times 10 \times 10$

(D) $\dfrac{10}{3}$

Go on to the next page. ➞

33. A video game system initially cost $100. During a sale, the store reduced the price by 10%. Two days later, the store reduced the new price by 20%. What was the final price?

   (A) $68
   (B) $70
   (C) $72
   (D) $80

34. Mr. Hoffman has a rectangular box that is 10 centimeters wide, 30 centimeters long, and 4 centimeters high. What is the volume of the box?

   (A)   44 cm^3
   (B)   120 cm^3
   (C)   300 cm^3
   (D) 1,200 cm^3

35. Dr. Li sees an average of nine patients an hour for eight hours on Monday and for six hours on Tuesday. What is the average number of patients she sees on each day?

   (A)   54
   (B)   63
   (C)   72
   (D) 126

36. If $q + 9 = 7 - p$, what is the value of $q + p$?

   (A) −16
   (B)   −2
   (C)   2
   (D)   16

37. Which of the following is the product of two consecutive even integers?

   (A)   0
   (B) 15
   (C) 22
   (D) 30

38. Two triangles, *ABC* and *XYZ*, are similar. Triangle *ABC* has lengths of 3, 4, and 5. Which of the following could be the corresponding lengths of triangle *XYZ* ?

   (A) 3, 3, and 3
   (B) 4, 5, and 6
   (C) 6, 8, and 10
   (D) 13, 14, and 15

39. The perimeter of a square whose area is 169 centimeters is

   (A) 52
   (B) 48
   (C) 44
   (D) 42

40. If three-fourths of the 240 employees at Tigger's Toys are at a party, how many of the employees are NOT at the party?

   (A)   60
   (B)   80
   (C) 120
   (D) 180

Go on to the next page. ⟶

41. Jose and Greg are going on a 20-mile walk for charity. If they walk $\frac{1}{4}$ of the distance in the first two hours, and $\frac{1}{5}$ of the entire distance in the next hour and a half, how many miles do they have left to walk?

    (A)   9
    (B)   10
    (C)   11
    (D)   12

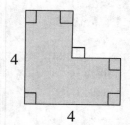

4

4

42. What is the perimeter of the shaded area in the figure above?

    (A)   15
    (B)   16
    (C)   24
    (D)   It cannot be determined from the information given.

43. A field hockey player scored an average of 3 goals per game for 12 games. How many points did she score in all 12 games?

    (A)   4
    (B)   20
    (C)   24
    (D)   36

44. What is the volume of a box with length 8, width 4, and height $\frac{1}{4}$?

    (A)   8
    (B) $12\frac{1}{4}$
    (C)   32
    (D)   128

45. The price of a $30 hat is decreased by 20%. What is the new price of the hat?

    (A) $10.00
    (B) $12.00
    (C) $20.00
    (D) $24.00

Go on to the next page. ➞

MA

46. There are 5 oatmeal cookies, 6 brownies, and 8 granola bars in a jar. If an item is selected at random, what is the probability of selecting a brownie?

(A) $\dfrac{1}{6}$

(B) $\dfrac{6}{19}$

(C) $\dfrac{8}{19}$

(D) $\dfrac{6}{13}$

47. Which of the following is equivalent to $\dfrac{2}{3}x = 6 - y$?

(A) $2x = 6 - 3y$

(B) $3y - x = 6$

(C) $2x + 3y = 18$

(D) $2(x + 3y) = 18$

STOP. If there is time, you may check your work in this section only.

STOP

Essay

You will have 30 minutes to plan and write an essay on the topic printed on the other side of this page. **Do not write on another topic. An essay on another topic is not acceptable.**

The essay is designed to give you an opportunity to show how well you can write. You should try to express your thoughts clearly. How well you write is much more important than how much you write, but you need to say enough for a reader to understand what you mean.

You will probably want to write more than a short paragraph. You should also be aware that a copy of your essay will be sent to each school that will be receiving your test results. You are to write only in the appropriate section of the answer sheet. Please write or print so that your writing may be read by someone who is not familiar with your handwriting.

You may make notes and plan your essay on the reverse side of the page. Allow enough time to copy the final form onto your answer sheet. You must copy the essay topic onto your answer sheet, on page 3, in the box provided.

Please remember to write only the final draft of the essay on pages 3 and 4 of your answer sheet and to write it in blue or black pen. Again, you may use cursive writing or you may print. Only pages 3 and 4 will be sent to the schools.

Directions continue on next page.

REMINDER: Please write this essay topic on the first few lines of page 3 of your answer sheet.

Essay Topic

If you could change one thing about your school, what would you change and why?

- Only write on this essay question
- Only pages 3 and 4 will be sent to the schools
- Only write in blue or black pen

NOTES

_____

_____

_____

_____

_____

_____

_____

_____

_____

_____

_____

_____

STUDENT NAME_____**GRADE APPLYING FOR**_____

You must write your essay topic in this space.

_____

_____

_____

Use specific details and examples in your response.

_____

_____

_____

_____

_____

_____

_____

_____

_____

_____

_____

_____

_____

_____

_____

_____

_____

Page 3

Page 4

Chapter 13:
Middle Level ISEE
Practice Test:
Answers and
Explanations

ANSWER KEY

ISEE ML Verbal Reasoning 1

1. D	5. D	9. B	13. B	17. A	21. C	25. C	29. C	33. A	37. B
2. C	6. C	10. B	14. C	18. B	22. B	26. C	30. B	34. D	38. B
3. B	7. B	11. A	15. D	19. A	23. D	27. A	31. C	35. A	39. B
4. C	8. B	12. D	16. C	20. C	24. A	28. A	32. D	36. A	40. A

ISEE ML Quantitative Reasoning 2

1. C	5. B	9. C	13. B	17. D	21. C	25. B	29. B	33. A	37. B
2. B	6. A	10. C	14. B	18. C	22. D	26. B	30. D	34. C	
3. D	7. B	11. B	15. C	19. D	23. A	27. A	31. B	35. B	
4. B	8. B	12. B	16. C	20. D	24. B	28. A	32. B	36. A	

ISEE ML Reading Comprehension 3

1. A	5. A	9. C	13. A	17. B	21. C	25. D	29. B	33. B
2. B	6. A	10. D	14. B	18. C	22. D	26. C	30. D	34. A
3. C	7. D	11. A	15. D	19. A	23. A	27. A	31. D	35. B
4. A	8. A	12. C	16. D	20. B	24. C	28. D	32. B	36. C

ISEE ML Mathematics Achievement 4

1. B	6. A	11. C	16. D	21. B	26. C	31. C	36. B	41. C	46. B
2. B	7. C	12. A	17. A	22. D	27. B	32. C	37. A	42. B	47. C
3. D	8. C	13. B	18. C	23. D	28. D	33. C	38. C	43. D	
4. D	9. B	14. C	19. C	24. B	29. A	34. D	39. A	44. A	
5. C	10. D	15. C	20. B	25. B	30. D	35. B	40. A	45. D	

EXPLANATIONS

Section 1 Verbal Reasoning

1. **D** Unusual is the opposite of usual, which is defined as regular or normal. The answer should match the opposite of usual or normal. Only (D), peculiar, matches this meaning.

2. **C** If you are unsure of the meaning of this word, try to use it in a sentence. An example would be "the pedestrian could not stand up after his fall without assistance." Assistance is defined as help or aide. The only choice that matches this definition is (C), service.

3. **B** Reality comes from the word "real"—it has to do with facts and what is happening in real life. The only choice that matches this meaning is (B), fact.

4. **C** Try to think of other words that sound like diminution: diminish. To diminish something means to tear it down or lessen it in some way. The best match to this meaning is (C), reduction.

5. **D** Contented is a form of content, which is defined as a state of happiness. The best match to happiness in these choices is (D), satisfied.

6. **C** Bound can be used in several different ways, so try it in a few different sentences. For example: The oath of office bound the President to stay within the law; in my dream I was bound to a skateboard and couldn't get off! In both of these examples, the meaning of bound means to be obligated or tied down to something. This best matches (C).

7. **B** To falter is defined as to hesitate or to waver. The best match for this definition is (B), hesitate.

8. **B** What does it mean to contain something? It means to keep it closed off or boxed in. This best matches (B), held.

9. **B** Try to think of other words that are related to or sound like revere: reverential, reverence, reverend. A reverend, for example, is a religious official whose job is to offer reverence to a deity. Reverence means to honor or worship; to revere someone or something means to honor or think highly of that person or thing. The best match for this meaning is (B), esteem.

10. **B** What does it mean to work diligently? To work tirelessly or very hard. The best match for the meaning of diligent is hardworking, (B).

11. **A** Detrimental is defined as harmful or destructive. The best match for this definition is (A), harmful.

12. **D** What are phrases that you heard the word "vow" used in? Marriage vows, a vow of silence, I vow revenge. A vow is a type of promise or pact. This meaning best matches (D), pledge.

13. **B** To have aspirations is to aspire to something. To aspire means to reach for or to dream of. The best match for this meaning is (B), hope.

14. **C** Where have you heard the word bashful before? One of Snow White's Seven Dwarves was named Bashful, the shy one. Bashful is defined as shy or retiring. This best matches (C), shy.

15. **D**   Sinister is defined as having evil intent. This best matches (D), wicked.

16. **C**   To disclose information means to share or provide information. This best matches (C), reveal.

17. **A**   Congeal might be a word you have heard in science class or when you have had a cut; congeal means to become thicker, as in when the blood from a cut congeals and the cut stops bleeding. This best matches the meaning of (A), coagulate, another word for congeal.

18. **B**   To inundate means to overwhelm or overcome. The best match for this meaning is (B), flood.

19. **A**   Steadfast is related to steady, which means to stay the course or remain firm. This best matches the meaning of constant, (A).

20. **C**   Ruthless is defined as without sympathy or concern. This best matches the definition of unsparing, (C).

21. **C**   Pay attention to the clues in the sentence. The second half of the sentence indicates that Myron never took sides in any disagreements. The missing word most likely means unbiased or undecided. This best matches (C), neutral. Choices (A) and (B) are the opposite of this meaning, and (D) does not relate to being undecided. Choice (C) is the correct answer.

22. **B**   Pay attention to the clues in the sentence. The first half of the sentence indicates that the drought left the soil completely useless. The second half of the sentence discusses food. Since food can't come from useless soil, the missing word must mean requested or brought in. This best matches (B), import. Choice (A) means to send out, so it cannot be correct. Choices (C) and (D) do not mean to bring in, so they can also be eliminated. Choice (B) is the correct answer.

23. **D**   Pay attention to the clues in the sentence. The first part of the sentence indicates that Mr. Jones does not like even small grammatical errors, which means that he likely checked the students' papers closely. The missing word must mean closely. The only choice that matches this meaning is (D), meticulously. Choices (A) and (C) are the opposite of this meaning, and (B) does not relate to the sentence. Choice (D) is the correct answer.

24. **A**   Pay attention to the clues in the sentence. The first part of the sentence indicates that Eric is strongly against racism, so the missing word must mean something like "strongly against" or "hates." The only answer that matches this meaning is (A), abhors. Although it may be true that Eric questions racism, as in (C), abhors more strongly matches "dislikes." Choice (A) is the correct answer.

25. **C**   Pay attention to the clues in the sentence. The first part of the sentence states that Sharon's anger was "too great." David couldn't do something because of it in the second part of the sentence. This indicates David couldn't overcome her anger, so the missing word must mean "overcome her anger." The best match for this meaning is (C), pacify.

26. **C**   Pay attention to the clues and direction words in the sentence. The first part of the sentence indicates that serious damage to property occurred. But that part of the sentence starts with "even though," indicating an opposite meaning later in the sentence. So even though there was damage, the lawyers did not do a convincing job. So the lawyers did not to a good job. The missing word must match the meaning "did not do a good job," which best matches incompetent, (C).

27. **A** Pay attention to the clues in the sentence. It states that after months of disputes the countries finally decided to sit down and do something. The time shift indicates they made some kind of change, so they are no longer in a dispute when they sit down. The missing word must mean the opposite of dispute, which best matches (A), friendly.

28. **A** Pay attention to the clues and direction words in the sentence. The first part of the sentence indicates that the thief claimed his crime was an accident. But that part of the sentence starts with "Although," indicating an opposite result later in the sentence. The missing word must mean "on purpose," the opposite of accident. This best matches (A), deliberate.

29. **C** This sentence is making an analogy. The second part of the sentence says that to be a good architect you don't need to live in a fancy house, which is something architects build as part of their jobs. The first part of the sentence is about doctors. What do doctors do for part of their jobs? They try to make or keep people healthy. The missing word must be healthy, (C).

30. **B** Based on the clues in this sentence, Pete is doing a better and better job as time goes on. This indicates that he is most likely impressing his coach with his performance. The missing word must mean impressed, which best matches (B), gratified.

31. **C** Pay attention to the clues and direction words in the sentence. The first part of the sentence states that wolves travel in packs, but starts that idea with the word "while" and goes on to discuss what cheetahs do. The use of the word "while" indicates a difference between wolves and cheetahs, so it is likely that cheetahs do not travel in packs. The missing word must mean "lone" or "individual." This meaning best matches (C), solitary.

32. **D** Pay attention to the clues and direction words in the sentence. The second part of the sentence states that the senators were argumentative, but starts that idea with the word "while." The use of the word "while" indicates a difference between these senators and Jones, who is mentioned earlier in the sentence. So it is most likely that Jones is not argumentative. The missing word must mean "not argumentative," which best matches (D), timid.

33. **A** Pay attention to the clues in the sentence. The sentence says that no one ended up voting for the politician, so it sounds as though his speech was not very good. The missing word must mean "not very good." This best matches (A), feeble. Choices (C) and (D) are both positive words, so they cannot be the answer. Although monotonous, (B), is a negative word, it is more related to the physical sound of the speech as opposed to how good it was. Choice (A) is the correct answer.

34. **D** Pay attention to the clues in the sentence. The second part of the sentence states that each department was free to advance employees as it saw fit. The missing word must mean that there was no standard system for promotions. The best match to this meaning is (D), uniform.

35. **A** Pay attention to the clues in the sentence. The sentence says it takes years of training for a gymnast to become something. What would likely happen after a gymnast trains for years? They would be very good. The missing word must mean very good at gymnastics. The best match for this meaning is (A), agile, as agility is a very good quality for gymnasts to have.

36. **A**   Pay attention to the clues and direction words in the sentence. The second part of the sentence states that Mr. Fenster was welcoming to children on Halloween, but starts that idea with the word "though." The use of the word "though" indicates a difference between how Mr. Fenster treats the children versus how he treats his neighbors in general. It seems that he treats his neighbors differently than he treats the children, so the missing word must mean "mean" or "angry." This best matches (A), belligerent.

37. **B**   Pay attention to the clues in the sentence. The sentence says the young man talked back to his parents and teachers, so the missing word must mean "rude" or "disrespectful." The best match for this meaning is (B), insolent.

38. **B**   Pay attention to the clues and direction words in the sentence. The second part of the sentence states that the brushstrokes are actually carefully planned. The first part of the sentence starts with "while," which indicates a shift within the sentence. This must mean that while they seem the opposite of planned, they are in fact planned. So the missing word must mean the opposite of planned. The only word that matches this meaning is (B), haphazard.

39. **B**   Pay attention to the clues in the sentence. The sentence says the Declaration of Independence is based on principles, which it then lists. The principles listed are very important ones to our society, so the missing word must mean important. The only choice that matches this meaning is (B), lofty.

40. **A**   Pay attention to the clues in the sentence. The teacher does not want the students to lose the "big picture." Therefore the students shouldn't get too lost in the details or nuances of the information. The missing word must mean "details" or "nuances." The only word that means details or nuances is (A), minutiae.

Section 2 Quantitative Reasoning

1. **C** $54 \times 3 = 162$, so the correct answer is (C). Stack the numbers to multiple, or you can break the problem into two steps: $50 \times 3 = 150$ and $4 \times 3 = 12$. When you add 150 and 12 together, you get 162.

2. **B**   To find the area of a square multiply two sides together. Since each side of the square is equal, use the formula $A = s^2$. The side length of this particular square is 2, so the area of the square would be 4: $A = s^2 = 2^2 = 4$. The correct answer is (B).

3. **D**   Remember to use order of operations (PEMDAS). First, simplify inside the parentheses multiplying from left to right: $(4 \times 3 \times 2) \Rightarrow (12 \times 2) \Rightarrow (24)$. Next, multiply from left to right: $3 \times 2 \times 1 - 24 \Rightarrow 6 \times 1 - 24 \Rightarrow 6 - 24$. Finally, subtract from left to right: $6 - 24 = -18$. The correct answer is (D).

4. **B** Use $T = AN$. Find the *Total* by adding all of Vicky's test scores together: $80 + 90 + 94 = 264$. She took 3 tests, so 3 is the *Number of items*. Divide to find her *Average*: $\frac{264}{3} = 88$. The correct answer is (B).

5. **B** Use the graph provided to find out which student bought the most books at the school fair. The tallest bar indicates which student bought the most books. Sally bought 2 books, Jesse bought 4 books, Pete bought 1 book, and Mark bought 3 books. Since Jesse bought the most books at the school fair, (B) is the correct answer.

6. **A** Use the graph provided to find the number of books the students bought. Sally bought 2 books and Mark bought 3 books, so together they bought 5 books. Jess bought 4 books. Therefore, Sally and Mark together bought 1 more book than Jesse did ($5 - 4 = 1$). The correct answer is (A).

7. **B** When adding fractions with unlike denominators, find a common denominator first. For this question, multiply the first fraction by 2 so that $\frac{1}{2}$ becomes $\frac{2}{4}$. Next, add the numerators together to get the final sum: $\frac{2}{4} + \frac{3}{4} = \frac{5}{4}$. The correct answer is (B).

8. **B** For the number given, 7 is two spots to the left of the decimal which is the tens place. Seven 10s (or 7 groups of 10) is equal to 70, so the correct answer is (B).

9. **C** If 20% of Jason's books are fiction and he has 5 fiction books, then 20% of something is equal to 5: $\frac{20}{100}(x) = 5$ or $0.20x = 5$

   Divide 0.20 from both sides to get $x = 25$. Therefore, Jason has a total of 25 books. To find out the number of nonfiction books he has, subtract 5 from 25. The result is 20, making the correct answer (C). Another way to solve the problem is to determine that if 20% are fiction, then 80% are nonfiction. If 5 books are equal to 20%, then four times that would equal 80%: $4 \times 5 = 20$. Note that answer (D) represents the total number of books Jason has.

10. **C** Long division is one way to approach division with decimals. $\frac{7}{0.35}$ can be written as $0.35\overline{)7}$. Move the decimal to the right two times to get rid of the decimal in the divisor and also move the decimal to the right two times in the dividend: $35\overline{)700}$. The result is $35\overline{)700}^{\,20}$, so the correct answer is (C). Another option is use the answer choices (PITA). Multiply the answer choices by 0.35 to see which one equals 7. Choice (C) is the only option that works.

11. **B** To find the answer closest in value to 5, find the answer that has the smallest distance between itself and 5. Choice (A) is 0.5 from 5. Choice (B) is 0.009 from 5. Choice (C) is 0.01 from 5. Choice (D) is 0.101 from 5. Therefore, the one closest to 5 is (B) since $\frac{9}{1,000}$ is a shorter distance than $\frac{5}{10}, \frac{1}{100}$, and $\frac{101}{1,000}$.

12. **B** Use the answers (PITA) to determine the closest cost per pound. Janice bought 6 pounds of hamburger. If each pound cost $2.00 (A), then she paid $12.00. If each pound cost $3.00, then she paid $18.00 (B). If each pound cost $5.00, then she paid $30.00 (C). If each pound cost $6.00, then she paid $36.00 (D). The closest option to $18.50 is (B), which is the correct answer.

13. **B** Use the answers (PITA) to determine the number that is closest to $\sqrt{175}$ since 175 is not a perfect square. In (A), 9 would be $\sqrt{81}$. In (B), 13 would be $\sqrt{169}$. In (C), 22 would be $\sqrt{484}$. Stop after (C) because (D) will be even greater. The closest to the $\sqrt{175}$ is (B), which is the correct answer.

14. **B** If there are 32 numbered pages in Laurie's book, then there are 16 odd-numbered pages (odd numbers from 1–31) and 16 even-numbered pages (even numbers from 2–32). Since illustrations appear on every odd-numbered page, there are 16 total illustrations. The correct answer is (B).

15. **C** One way to solve this problem is to solve for y in the first equation: $6y + 8 = 20$. Subtract 8 from both sides to get $6y = 12$. Divide both sides by 6 to get $y = 2$. Next, plug 2 in for y in the second equation: $3y + 4 = 3(2) + 4 = 6 + 4 = 10$. The correct answer is (C). If you noticed that $3y + 4$ is half of $6y + 8$, then $3y + 4$ will equal half of what $6y + 8$ equals. $\frac{20}{2} = 10$, which is the correct answer.

16. **C** If the lecture hall's current capacity is 56 seats, then the increased capacity will be greater than 56. Eliminate (A). The capacity increased by only 75%, so eliminate (D), which represents a 100% increase. $\frac{3}{4}(56) = 42$, so the lecture hall's capacity increased by 42 seats. $56 + 42 = 98$. Therefore, the correct answer is (C).

17. **D** Use long division to check each answer. In (A), 8 goes into 11 once with a remainder of 3. In (B), 8 goes into 22 twice with a remainder of 6. In (C), 8 goes into 72 exactly nine times, so the remainder is 0. In (D), 8 goes into 90 eleven times with a remainder of 2. Therefore, (D) is the correct answer.

18. **C** Use the graph provided and the answer choices to determine when the greatest increase in rainfall occurred. There was no increase between 1942 and 1944, so eliminate (A) and (B). From 1944 to 1945, there was an average increase of 30 inches. Keep (C). From 1945 to 1946, there was an average increase of 10 inches. Since the increase in (C) is greater, it is the correct answer.

19. **D** There are 7 hours between 6 A.M. and 1 P.M. Therefore, if the temperature increases at a constant rate of 3 degrees per hour, then the temperature at 1 P.M. will be 21 degrees higher than it was at 6 A.M. ($3 \times 7 = 21$). If it was 32 degrees at 6 A.M., then the temperature at 1 P.M. is 53 degrees ($32 + 21 = 53$). The correct answer is (D).

20. **D** To find the volume of a box, use the formula $V = l \times w \times h$. Plug the given dimensions into the formula: $V = 4$ in $\times 3$ in $\times 2$ in $= 24$ in^3. Therefore, (D) is the correct answer.

21. **C** There are 180° in a straight line. Subtract 125 from 180 to find the degree measure of x: $180 - 125 = 55$, so $x = 55°$. Since both columns are equal, the correct answer is (C).

22. **D** To find the area of a rectangle, use the formula $A = l \times w$. Since the side lengths are x and y, plug in values that will equal 12 when multiplied together. For example, if Column A equals 1, then Column B would equal 12, and Column B would be greater, so you can eliminate (A) and (C). However, if Column A equals 12, then Column B would equal 1, making Column A greater. Therefore (B) can be eliminated, and the correct answer is (D).

23. **A** The value of Column A is 8 since $\sqrt{9} = 3$ and $\sqrt{25} = 5$ and $3 + 5 = 8$. Column B can be rewritten as $\sqrt{34}$; however, 34 is not a perfect square so the value of $\sqrt{34}$ will have to be approximated. Since $\sqrt{25} = 5$ and $\sqrt{36} = 6$, then the value of $\sqrt{34}$ is between 5 and 6. Since that range is less than 8, Column A is greater. The correct answer is (A).

24. **B** The area formula of the quadrilateral is $A = l \times w$. The area of the figure (12) and one side (3) are given. Therefore, the missing side length is 4 since $12 = 3 \times w$ and $\frac{12}{3} = 4 = w$. To find the perimeter of a shape, add up all the sides. In a rectangle, opposite sides are equal, so since $AD = 3$, then $BC = 3$, and since $AB = 4$, then $DC = 4$. $3 + 4 + 3 + 4 = 14$, so Column A equals 14. Since 14 is less than 15, Column B is greater. The correct answer is (B).

25. **B** If Martha has $20, then half of her money is $10: $\frac{1}{2}(20) = 10$. If Martha gives away $10, then she has $10 left, which is the value of Column A. If, after receiving $10 from her sister, Linda now has $30, then Linda originally had $20: $30 - 10 = 20$. Thus, Column B equals $20. Since Column B is greater, the correct answer is (B).

26. **B** To determine the value of Column A, solve for x in the equation: $4x + 7 = 63$. Subtract 7 from both sides to get $4x = 56$. Then divide both sides by 4 to get $x = 14$. Column A equals 14. To determine the value of Column B, solve for y in the equation: $\frac{y}{3} + 6 = 15$. Subtract 6 from both sides to get $\frac{y}{3} = 9$. Then multiply both sides by 3 to get $y = 27$. Column B equals 27. Since Column B is greater, the correct answer is (B).

27. **A** To find the area of a rectangle, use the formula $A = l \times w$. Since $l = 3$ and $w = 4$, then $A = 3 \times 4 = 12$. Thus, Column A equals 12. To find the area of a square, multiply two sides together. Since each side of the square is equal, use the formula $A = s^2$. The side length of this square is 3, so $A = 3^2 = 9$. Thus, Column B equals 9. Since Column A is greater, the correct answer is (A).

28. **A** Use the table provided to find the values of the two columns. To find the average number of cookies eaten each day, use $T = AN$. The *Total* is the sum of all the cookies eaten: $3 + 2 + 1 + 3 = 9$. The *Number of items* is 4 since there are 4 days. Divide the *Total* by the *Number of items* to get the *Average*: $\frac{9}{4} = 2.25$. Therefore, Column A equals 2.25. According to the table, the number of cookies eaten on Thursday is 2. Since Column A is greater, the correct answer is (A).

29. **B** Estimation will work well for this problem. For Column A, 0.64 is less than 1, so $\sqrt{0.64} < \sqrt{1}$. Since $\sqrt{1} = 1$, then $\sqrt{0.64} < 1$. Therefore, Column A is less than 1. For Column B, 6.4 is between perfect squares 4 and 9. Since $\sqrt{4} = 2$ and $\sqrt{9} = 3$, then $2 < \sqrt{6.4} < 3$. Therefore, Column B is between 2 and 3. Since that range is greater than any number less than 1, Column B is greater. The correct answer is (B).

30. **D** Since the prices of an orange and a peach are not given, plug in values. If 1 orange costs 4 cents, then 5 oranges cost 20 cents: $5 \times 0.04 = 0.20$. Since 6 peaches would cost 90 cents ($1.10 - 0.20 = 0.90$), then 1 peach would cost 15 cents: $0.90 \times 6 = 0.15$. Column A equals 4, and Column B equals 15. Currently, Column B is greater. However, since the prices of the fruit are not given, remember to plug in more than once! If 1 orange costs 10 cents, then 5 oranges cost 50 cents: $5 \times 0.10 = 0.50$. Since 6 peaches would cost 60 cents ($1.10 - 0.50 = 0.60$), then 1 peach would cost 10 cents: $0.60 \div 6 = 0.10$. In this instance, Columns A and B both equal 10. Since Column B is not always greater, nor are the two columns always equal, the correct answer is (D).

31. **B** Pay attention to the parentheses and remember order of operations (PEMDAS). For Column A, 5 will be raised to the 6th power first and then multiplied by –1, so Column A will be a negative number. For Column B, –5 will be raised to the 6th power, so the result is a positive number. Since Column A is negative and Column B is positive, the correct answer is (B). Note that it is not necessary to calculate $5 \times 5 \times 5 \times 5 \times 5 \times 5$. Simply knowing that one column is negative and one column is positive will allow you to answer the question correctly!

32. **B** If a represents an odd integer greater than 9 and less than 15, a could be 11 or 13. If b represents an even integer greater than 9 and less than 15, b could be 10, 12, or 14. Therefore, Column A could equal 33 (11×3) or 39 (13×3). Column B could equal 40 (10×4), 48 (12×4), or 46 (14×4). In every instance, Column B is greater than Column A, so the correct answer is (B).

33. **A** To find the probability of an event, find the total of what is wanted out of the total possible outcomes: Probability = $\dfrac{\text{the number of what you want}}{\text{the total number}}$. If the die has 12 sides numbered 1 through 12, then there are 6 even-numbered sides (2, 4, 6, 8, 10, and 12). Thus, Column A equals $\dfrac{6}{12}$. From 1 to 12, there are 4 prime numbers (2, 3, 5, and 7), so Column B equals $\dfrac{4}{12}$. Since Column A is greater, the correct answer is (A).

34. **C** For column A, there are 20 total squares and 3 that are shaded, so the fractional part that is shaded is $\frac{3}{20}$. Since the two columns are equal, the correct answer is (C).

35. **B** If Melvin eats 50% of 12 slices, then he will eat 6 out of 12 slices or $\frac{1}{2}$ of the pizza, so there will be 6 slices left (12 − 6 = 6). Column A equals 6. If Melvin eats $\frac{1}{3}$ of the pizza, then he will eat 4 out of 12 slices, so there will be 8 slices left (12 − 4 = 8). Column B equals 8. Since Column B is greater, the correct answer is (B).

36. **A** If the shirt was originally $50, the first 20% discount would be $10 off: 0.2(50) = 10. The new price of the shirt is $40 (50 − 10 = 40). After a second 20% discount, which is a discount of $8 since 0.2(40) = 8, the shirt will be $32 (40 − 8 = 32). Column A equals 32. If the shirt had only been discounted once by 40%, the discount would be $20: 40% of 50 is 0.4(50) =20. The new price of the shirt would be $30 since 50 − 20 = 30. Column B equals 30. Since Column A is greater, the correct answer is (A).

37. **B** To find the slope of a line with two given points, use the slope formula: $\frac{y_2 - y_1}{x_2 - x_1}$. For Column A, the slope equals $\frac{2-8}{5-3} = \frac{-6}{2} = -3$. Therefore, Column A equals −3. To find the slope of a line with a given equation, rewrite the equation in slope-intercept form: $y = mx + b$, where m represents the slope. For Column B, isolate y in the equation $6x − 2y = −8$. Subtract $6x$ from both sides to get $−2y = −6x − 8$. Next, divide both sides by −2 to get $y = 3x + 4$. Therefore, the slope is 3, and Column B equals 3. Since Column B is greater, the correct answer is (B).

Section 3 Reading Comprehension

1. **A** On primary purpose questions, ask yourself "Why did the author write this story? What is the main takeaway for this story?" The story is focused on the history of early modes of travel. Choice (C) is focused only on one form of transportation, so it is too specific. Choice (D) is too general; this story is about the history of early transportation, not transportation in general. And (B) is incorrect as the focus is not on the motivation for travel but rather on modes of travel. Choice (A) is the correct answer.

2. **B** On Except/Not/Least questions, cross check each answer choice and write a "T" for true and an "F" for false for each answer choice, based on the passage. The false answer will be the correct choice. Lines 21–23 mention donkeys and oxen being used to pull sledges, so (A) is true. Although children are mentioned in line 9, they are not being used to carry things, so (B) is false. Poles are mentioned as being used to carry goods in line 13, so (C) is true. And primitive sleds are discussed in lines 15–19 as a form of transport for goods, so (D) is true. Choice (B) is the only false answer, and so is therefore correct.

3. **C** This is a very open-ended question, so check each answer with the information in the passage. Answer (A) is too extreme; the passage never indicates that early man was incapable of anything. Farming is not mentioned in the passage, which eliminates (B). There is also no mention of early man being outgoing or friendly, so (D) is wrong as well. Only (C) is supported by the passage, since the entire focus is on man's history of different ways of transporting goods.

4. **A** This is a specific question, so make sure to go back to the passage and find the answer. Animals are mentioned in lines 20–23. The only information provided is that they were first tamed around 5000 B.C.E., and they were used for transporting heavy loads and pulling sledges. This best supports (A). Although (B), (C), and (D) may seem like likely answer choices, they are never explicitly stated in the passage. Choice (A) is the correct answer.

5. **A** This question asks about the author's attitude toward the invention of the wheel, so pay attention to what the author says about that particular invention. Then eliminate choices that don't match the story. The author begins and ends the passage discussing the wheel. Quite clearly they find this to be an important invention, which eliminates (C). The author says positive things about the wheel, so neither (B) nor (D) makes sense. The only possible answer is (A), admiration.

6. **A** This is a relatively open-ended question about a specific subject in the passage, so make sure to check each answer choice with the passage. Lines 18–19 state that the sledge evolved into the sled, which supports (A). The sledge was invented before the wheel, so (B) is incorrect. Choice (C) is too extreme; the passage says early sledges were made from logs as well as animal skins. Eliminate (C). Choice (D) is also too extreme due to the word "only" and so is not supported by the passage. The correct answer is (A).

7. **D** On primary purpose questions, ask yourself "Why did the author write this story? What is the main takeaway for this story?" The story is focused on providing factual information about the American bison. This best matches (D). Choice (A) is much too specific; (B) and (C) are not mentioned in the passage. Choice (D) is the correct answer.

8. **A** This is a specific question, so make sure to find the answer in the story. The actual buffalo is mentioned only twice in the story, lines 1–3 and lines 12–14. The passage states that buffalo and bison are different animals, and that they are found on different continents. This best matches (A), they differ by geographical location. The author does not mention the size or number of buffalo, which eliminates (B) and (C). Both buffalo and bison are found today, so (D) is not a difference. Choice (A) is the correct answer.

9. **C** When asked a vocabulary in context question, focus on what the word means in the sentence. In line 19, deemed most nearly means "categorized" or "listed," which best matches answer (C). No other choice matches the context of the sentence.

10. **D** This is a specific question, so make sure to find the answer in the story. Protection of the bison is discussed in the last lines of the passage, where it states that the bison is not in danger of extinction as long as it is protected, although they may never be as plentiful as they were. This refutes (A), so it can be eliminated. Choice (C) is the opposite of what is stated in these lines, so it can be

eliminated. The ecological balance of the plains is not mentioned, so (B) can be eliminated. Only (D) matches the passage.

11. **A** This is a specific question, so make sure to find the answer in the story. Lines 19–21 state that due to conservation efforts the bison has been saved from near extinction. This best supports (A). Choice (B) is the opposite of this; they were near extinction due to being hunted. Choices (C) and (D) are not mentioned in the passage, so (A) is the correct answer.

12. **C** When a question asks why an author includes a line in the passage, ask yourself "What purpose does this line serve?" The author mentions the city of Buffalo as part of a list of the things in America that are named after buffalo. The other items on this list show the different ways in which we used the buffalo when we were really referring to bison. This best supports (C). Choice (B) is deceptive as it refers to the next example of the nickel, not the city of Buffalo. Choice (A) comes from a different area of the passage and does not answer this question. And (D) is never mentioned in the passage. Choice (C) is the correct answer.

13. **A** This question is a "main idea" question in disguise. Ask yourself the "so what?" of the story. This story is about the life and influences of Alexander the Great. The only answer choice that focuses on Alexander the Great is (A), making it the best and only correct answer choice.

14. **B** When asked a vocabulary in context question, focus on what the word means in the sentence. In line 16, civilized most nearly means "advanced or forward thinking," based on the following sentences that stress "ways of thinking." This best matches (B), educated.

15. **D** On tone questions, eliminate answer choices that are too extreme or don't make sense based on the passage. This passage is very informative and fact based. It's not from a personal perspective, which eliminates (A) and (B). The story is focused on historical facts rather than philosophical aspects, which best supports (D) over (C). Choice (D) is the correct answer.

16. **D** This is an open-ended question, as there are many impressive things discussed about Alexander. Check each answer choice with the information in the passage. The passage says that Aristotle is the teacher, not Alexander, so eliminate (A). Integrity is never mentioned in the passage, so eliminate (B). Alexander is never described as being handsome, eliminating (C) as well. The passage does discuss Alexander's intelligence in lines 4–5 and his culture in lines 16–17 (his ways of thinking and doing things), making (D) the best answer.

17. **B** This question asks about Aristotle, who is discussed in the first few lines of the passage. Lines 5–7 state that Aristotle's teachings left Alexander with a lifelong love of books, which best supports (B). There is no indication that Aristotle influenced Alexander's military approach or strategy, so eliminate (C) and (D). There is also no indication that Aristotle encouraged Alexander to do anything, let alone something as specific as spreading culture, eliminating (A). Choice (B) is the correct answer.

18. **C** This is a specific question, so make sure to find the answer in the story. Alexander's conquering is discussed in lines 11–21, where it states he conquered most of the "civilized world" and brought the "Greek way of thinking and doing things" to those places. This best supports (C). None of the things listed in (A), (B), and (D) are mentioned in the passage.

19. **A** On primary purpose questions, ask yourself "Why did the author write this story? What is the main takeaway for this story?" The story is focused on what hiccups are and how they occur in the human body. This best supports (A), describe a common occurrence. Although the subject of remedies is mentioned at the end of the passage, the passage does not prescribe a treatment so eliminate (B). There is no dispute mentioned, eliminating (C) as well. Although the potential danger of hiccups is mentioned, that is not the primary purpose of the passage, which eliminates (D). Choice (A) is the correct answer.

20. **B** This is a specific question, so make sure to go back and find the answer in the passage. As the passage begins to describe how hiccups occur in line 8, it says it is an irritant that begins the process of developing hiccups. This best matches (B). A paper bag is mentioned as a remedy to the hiccups, not the cause, eliminating (C). Choices (A) and (D) include information mentioned in the passage, but they come after an irritant has already prompted a spasm. Choice (B) is the best answer.

21. **C** When asked a vocabulary in context question, focus on what the word means in the sentence. In line 24, "attacks" is referring to the hiccups mentioned early in the sentence. The best meaning of the word attacks then is most likely "fits." This best matches (C), bouts. Choices (A), (B), and (D) are all synonyms of attacks, but do not work in the context of the sentence.

22. **D** This is a specific question, so make sure to go back and find the answer in the passage. The "hic" noise is mentioned specifically in line 22, and states that it is the movement of the vocal cords that prompts this sound. This supports (D) as the correct answer.

23. **A** This is a specific question, so make sure to go back and find the answer in the passage. The passage discusses the fatal possibility of hiccups in lines 25–27, due to exhaustion. This best matches (A), fatigue from hiccups. None of the other answers are supported by the passage.

24. **C** When asked why the author includes a word or phrase in the passage, ask yourself "Why is this word or phrase there? What point does this make?" The inclusion of the word "hiccoughs" is a very brief aside that merely demonstrates another word used to refer to the same phenomenon. This best supports (C). It is not a correction, definition, or an attack on an argument, so (A), (B), and (D) can all be eliminated. Choice (C) is the correct answer.

25. **D** On primary purpose questions, ask yourself "Why did the author write this story? What is the main takeaway for this story?" The story is focused on the phenomenon of hibernation. Although all four answer choices contain information that is provided in the passage, all except (D) are too specific. The passage is focused on the general information regarding hibernation, making (D) the correct answer.

26. **C** When asked a vocabulary in context question, focus on what the word means in the sentence. In line 7, conserve most nearly means to "store" or "save up." This best matches (C), reserve. Choices (A) and (D) are the opposite meaning, and (B) does not match the context of the sentence as well as (C).

27. **A** On Except/Not/Least questions, cross check each answer choice and write a "T" for true and an "F" for false for each answer choice, based on the passage. The false answer will be the correct choice. There is no reference to a "dream state" in the passage, so (A) is false. Lines 12–14 discuss the possible drop in body temperature for some animals, which makes (B) true. The following lines also discuss the possibility of slower heartbeats and breathing in some animals, so (C) and (D) are also true. Choice (A) is the only false answer, and is therefore correct.

28. **D** This is a specific question, so make sure to go back and find the answer in the passage. In lines 26–27, it states that an animal may wake from hibernation when there is mild weather. This best supports (D). Food is not mentioned as a motivation to break hibernation in the passage, only weather, which eliminates (B). Choice (A) is the opposite of mild weather, so it can be eliminated. Although (C) may seem like a good choice, just because there isn't snow doesn't mean the weather is favorable. Choice (D) is the best answer.

29. **B** This is a specific question, so make sure to go back and find the answer in the passage. The chemical that causes hibernation is discussed in lines 27–31, where it states that if the chemical were injected into an animal in the summer months it might cause the animal to go into summer hibernation. This best supports (B). None of the other answer choices are supported from these lines.

30. **D** On tone questions, eliminate answer choices that are too extreme or don't make sense based on the passage. This passage is a very fact-based review, which best supports (D), informative. The author does not come off as overly impressed with hibernation, which eliminates (A), nor do they seem concerned, which eliminates (B). It is unlikely that the author would write a passage about something that doesn't interest them, which eliminates (C). Choice (D) is the correct answer.

31. **D** This question is a "main idea" question in disguise. Ask yourself the "so what?" of the story. The passage focuses on the experience of theater. Although Shakespeare is mentioned in the passage, (C) is much too specific an answer for a main idea question; eliminate it. Choices (A) and (B) are also much too specific; the passage is not focused on any specific productions, modern or otherwise. The only choice that matches the overall main idea of the passage is (D).

32. **B** This is a specific question, so make sure to go back and find the answer in the passage. The author discusses why the theater is "thrilling" in lines 6–8. According to the author, it is the live nature of the theater that makes it so thrilling. This best matches (B). The author goes on to discuss the Greek origin of the word theater, but that does not answer this question so (A) is incorrect. There is no mention of plays being thrilling because they are well written or have several people working on them, which also eliminates (C) and (D). Choice (B) is correct.

33. **B** This is an open-ended question, so make sure to check all four answer choices and remember your process of elimination guidelines. Choice (A) has extreme language; there is no indication that modern theater always does anything. Eliminate that choice. The passage does not state that one form of theater is better than another, which eliminates (C). Although Shakespeare is mentioned in the passage, it does not say modern theater is mostly comprised of those plays. Eliminate (D). The only possible answer is (B), which is supported by the information in lines 24–33, in which the variety of modern forms of theater is discussed.

34. **A** On tone questions, eliminate answer choices that are too extreme or don't make sense based on the passage. The author is very positive about the theater in this passage, which eliminates (B), (C), and (D) since those are all neutral words. Only (A), admiring, works based on the passage.

35. **B** When asked a vocabulary in context question, focus on what the word means in the sentence. In the first line, "richest" is being used in a positive manner by the author. They go on to say that live theater is very exciting and thrilling. "Exciting" and "thrilling" best match (B), entertaining. Choice (D), wealthy, is too literal a meaning for "richest." Choice (C) is very negative, which doesn't match the tone of the passage. And (A) doesn't fit with the topic discussed in the first lines of the passage. Choice (B) is the correct answer.

36. **C** This is a specific question, so make sure to go back and find the answer in the passage. Shakespeare's plays are mentioned in the last lines of the passage. These lines state that the works of Shakespeare are still performed today in a variety of interpretations. This best matches (C). Choices (A) and (D) contain extreme language; eliminate them. The passage never states that Shakespeare is more popular today than during his time, eliminating (B) as well. Choice (C) is the correct answer.

Section 4 Mathematics Achievement

1. **B** Since the digit 9 is two places to the right of the decimal, it is in the hundredths place and would be equivalent to nine one-hundredths or $\frac{9}{100}$. The correct answer is (B). Choice (A) is nine-tenths and would be one place to the right of the decimal. Choice (C) is nine one-thousandths and would be three places to the right of the decimal. Finally, (D) is nine ten-thousandths and would be four places to the right of the decimal.

2. **B** The least common multiple of a set of numbers is the smallest number that is divisible by all members of the set. Use the answer choices (PITA). Choice (A) can be eliminated because 3 is a factor, not a multiple, of 6, 9, and 12. In (B), 36 can be divided by 6, 9, and 12 evenly (6 times, 4 times, and 3 times). Since there is no smaller number that works, (B) is the correct answer.

3. **D** Remember to use order of operations (PEMDAS) and check each answer choice. Choice (A) equals $30 - 12 \div 2 \times (3 + 7) = 30 - 12 \div 2 \times (10) = 30 - 6 \times 10 = 30 - 60 = -30$. Choice (B) equals $30 - 12 \div (2 \times 3 + 7) = 30 - 12 \div (6 + 7) = 30 - 12 \div (13) = 30 - \frac{12}{13}$, which is not an integer and therefore not equal to 5. Choice (C) equals $(30 - 12) \div 2 \times 3 + 7 = (18) \div 2 \times 3 + 7 = 9 \times 3 + 7 = 27 + 7 = 34$. Finally, (D) equals $30 - 12 \div 2 \times 3 - 7 = 30 - 6 \times 3 - 7 = 30 - 18 - 7 = 12 - 7 = 5$. Therefore, the correct answer is (D).

4. **D** When adding fractions with unlike denominators, find a common denominator first. For this question, multiply $\frac{5}{7}$ by 11 and multiply $\frac{2}{11}$ by 7. Add the numerators of the fraction to get the final sum: $\frac{55}{77} + \frac{14}{77} = \frac{69}{77}$. The correct answer is (D).

5. **C** Remember that when subtracting mixed numbers, make sure the fractions have a common denominator. For this question, multiply $\frac{1}{2}$ by 2 to get $\frac{2}{4}$. Subtract the numerators of the fractions: $\frac{2}{4} - \frac{1}{4} = \frac{1}{4}$. Next, subtract the whole numbers: $7 - 6 = 1$. Be careful! The question is looking for minutes, not hours, so convert $1\frac{1}{4}$ hours to minutes. There are 60 minutes in 1 hour and 15 minutes in $\frac{1}{4}$ hours, so there is a total of 75 more minutes: $60 + 15 = 75$. The correct answer is (C).

6. **A** To find the perimeter of a shape, add up all the sides. In an equilateral triangle, all sides are equal, so if one side is 4, all three sides are equal to 4. Thus, the correct answer is (A), since $4 + 4 + 4 = 12$.

7. **C** To find 20% of 200, multiply 0.2 and 200 to get the result: $0.20 \times 200 = 40$. Therefore, the correct answer is (C). Choice (A) would be 10% of 200, (B) would be 15% of 200, and (D) would be 50% or half of 200.

8. **C** Use the chart provided to find the total snowfall for the four-day period. Add the amount of snowfall for each day: $3 + 3 + 4 + 1 = 11$. The correct answer is (C).

9. **B** Use the chart provided to determine which day had the greatest amount of snowfall. Both Monday and Tuesday each had 3 inches of snowfall. On Wednesday, there was 4 inches of snow. On Thursday, there was 1 inch of snow. Therefore, the greatest amount of snow was on Wednesday. The correct answer is (B).

10. **D** To find the average temperature, use $T = AN$. The *Total* is the sum of all temperatures: $2 + 6 + 3 + 13 = 24$. The *Number of items* is 4 since there are 4 days. Divide the *Total* by the *Number of items* to get the *Average*: $\frac{24}{4} = 6$. The correct answer is (D). Note that (A) is incorrect because 24 is the total degrees for the four-day period.

11. **C** Long division is one way to approach division with decimals. You can write $\frac{100}{0.25}$ as $0.25\overline{)100}$. Move the decimal to the right two times to get rid of the decimal in the divisor and also move the decimal to the right two times in the dividend: $25\overline{)10000}$. The result is $25\overline{)10000}$ with 400 on top, so the correct answer is (C). Another option is use the answer choices (PITA). Multiply the answer choices by 0.25 to see which one equals 100. Choice (C) is the only option that works.

12. **A** To find the missing part of this equation, simplify the left side of the equation first: $5 \times 31 = 155$. The equation now looks like $155 = 100 +$ ___ . To determine what goes in the blank, subtract 100 from 155 or use the answer choices (PITA). Try (A): $155 = 100 + 55$. Since this is the only answer choice that makes the right side of the equation equal to 155, the correct answer is (A).

13. **B** If half of the 6 tomato plants that Gwen planted died, then she lost 3 tomato plants: $\left(\dfrac{1}{2} \times 6 = 3\right)$. If Gwen then planted another tomato plant, she would have 4 total tomato plants: 3 + 1 = 4. Therefore, the correct answer is (B).

14. **C** To rent the video game, Tracey had to spend $1. Since she returned the video game 3 days late, she had to pay $0.50 for each late day, so she owed another $1.50 since 0.5 × 3 = 1.5. The total amount she paid for the video game rental is $2.50 because 1 + 1.5 = 2.5. Thus, the correct answer is (C).

15. **C** When multiplying a decimal by 100, simply move the decimal two places to the right so that 0.45 becomes 45, making the correct answer (C). Multiplying by stacking will also work. 45 times 100 equals 4,500. Don't forget to move the decimal two places to the left to get 45.

16. **D** There are 180° in a triangle. The given angles are each 45°, so they represent a total of 90°. Subtract 90 from 180 to get 90°, so the correct answer is (D) because 90° + 45° + 45° = 180°.

17. **A** There are 12 in a dozen, so 12 eggs cost $1.20. Therefore, the cost of 1 egg is 10 cents: $\dfrac{1.2}{12} = 0.1$. If 1 egg costs 10 cents, then 3 eggs cost 30 cents: 0.1 × 3 = 0.3. The correct answer is (A).

18. **C** If Boris has three times as many baseball cards as Bruce and Bruce has 12, then Boris has 36 cards: 12 × 3 = 36. To find the average number of cards between the two boys, use $T = AN$. The *Total* will be the sum of the boys' baseball cards: 36 + 12 = 48. The *Number of items* is 2 since there are 2 boys. Divide the *Total* by the *Number of items* to get the *Average*: $\dfrac{48}{2} = 24$. The correct answer is (C). Note that (D) is incorrect because 48 is the total number of baseball cards between the 2 boys.

19. **C** To find the perimeter of a shape, add up all the sides. In a rectangle, opposite sides are equal, so if the length is 3, then the side opposite of it will also be 3. If the width is 2, then the side opposite of it will also be 2. Add all the sides: 3 + 2 + 3 + 2 = 10. Thus, (C) is the correct answer. Note that (A) is incorrect because 6 would be the area of this rectangle: $l \times w = 3 \times 2 = 6$.

20. **B** To multiply fractions, multiply the numerators together and multiply the denominators together: $\dfrac{3}{5} \times \dfrac{2}{7} = \dfrac{6}{35}$. The correct answer is (B).

21. **B** If Kenny can run 3 miles in 45 minutes, then he can run 1 mile in 15 minutes since $\dfrac{45}{3} = 15$. If he runs 5 miles, then it will take him 75 minutes (15 × 5 = 75) or 1 hour and 15 minutes since there are 60 minutes in 1 hour. Therefore, the correct answer is (B). Note that estimation can help eliminate some of the answer choices. Since Kenny runs 3 miles in 45 minutes, 6 miles would take him twice that amount of time. The question asks for the time it would take him to run 5 miles,

so eliminate (C) because 1 hour and 30 minutes is twice as long as 45 minutes (the time to run 6 miles), and eliminate (D) because in 2 hours he would run farther than 6 miles.

22. **D** There are several ways to solve this problem (e.g., using the Bowtie method or finding a common denominator for the fractions). Another option would be to convert the fractions to decimal form: $\frac{5}{11} = 0.45\overline{45}$. Choice (A) equals 0.375, (B) is about 0.286, (C) equals $0.4\overline{4}$, and (D) is about 0.571. The only answer that is greater than $\frac{5}{11}$ or $0.45\overline{45}$ is 0.571, or (D).

23. **D** The perimeter of a shape is the sum of all the sides. In a square, all four sides are equal, so if the perimeter is equal to 36, then each side equals 9 because $\frac{36}{4} = 9$. To find the area of the square multiply two sides together. Since each side of the square is equal, use the formula $A = s^2$. Therefore, the area is 81 because $9^2 = 81$. The correct answer is (D).

24. **B** If Maureen studied twice as long after school than she did before school, she studied for 4 hours after school: $2 \times 2 = 4$. For that day, she studied a total of 6 hours because $2 + 4 = 6$. The correct answer is (B). Note that (A) is incorrect since it only represents the number of hours she studied after school.

25. **B** Remember to use order of operations (PEMDAS). Start with parentheses first! $\frac{40(37 + 63)}{8} = \frac{40(100)}{8} = \frac{4,000}{8} = 500$. The correct answer is (B).

26. **C** Use process of elimination. 0.3 is equivalent to $\frac{3}{10}$, so eliminate (A) and (B). 0.04 is equivalent to $\frac{4}{100}$, so eliminate (D). Therefore, the correct answer is (C).

27. **B** Draw a factor tree of 36.

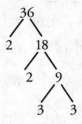

The prime factorization of 36 is $2 \times 2 \times 3 \times 3$ or $2^2 \times 3^2$. Therefore, (B) is the correct answer. Note that (D) contains a number that is not prime (6).

28. **D** Use the chart to determine each price. If one adult buys a one-way weekend train ticket, it will cost $4.50. Therefore, two one-way adult tickets cost $9.00. Children do not pay to ride the train on the weekend, so the total cost is $9.00 $(4.5 + 4.5 + 0 = 9)$. The correct answer is (D).

29.   **A**   Use the chart to determine each price. The cost of 1 weekday peak fare ten-trip ticket is $54.00. The cost of purchasing 1 one-way weekday peak fare ticket is $6.00, so the cost of 10 such tickets is $60.00 (6 × 10 = 60). To find percent change, use the formula: % change = $\dfrac{difference}{original} \times 100$. The difference of the two prices is $6.00, and the original price is $60.00. Note that when the question says *percent less*, the *original* will be the larger number.

$$\frac{difference}{original} \times 100 = \frac{60-54}{60} \times 100 = \frac{6}{60} \times 100 = \frac{600}{60} = 10$$

Therefore, the correct answer is (A).

30.   **D**   Use the chart to determine each price. The price for 1 adult to travel one way during the weekday peak fare period is $6.00. The price for 1 adult to travel one way on the weekend is $4.50. The question asks how much more it costs this adult to travel during a weekday peak time versus to travel on the weekend. It costs $1.50 less since 6 − 4.5 = 1.5. Thus, the correct answer is (D).

31.   **C**   If Mr. Schroder can swim 1 lap in 5 minutes, then set up a proportion to find how many laps he can swim in 60 minutes: $\dfrac{1 \text{ lap}}{5 \text{ min}} = \dfrac{x}{60 \text{ min}}$. Cross-multiply to get $5x = 60$. Then divide both sides by 5 to get $x = 12$. Therefore, he can swim 12 laps in 60 minutes. The correct answer is (C).

32.   **C**   When in doubt with exponents, expand them out. $10^3 = 10 \times 10 \times 10$. Therefore, the correct answer is (C).

33.   **C**   If the video game system originally cost $100, a 10% discount would be $10 off: 0.1 × 100 = 10. The new price of the video game system is $90 (100 − 10 = 90). When the new price of the video game system is reduced by 20%, which is a discount of $18 since 0.2 × 90 = 18, the final price will be $72 (90 − 18 = 72). Therefore, the correct answer is (C).

34.   **D**   To find the volume of a box, use the formula $V = l \times w \times h$. Plug the given dimensions into the formula: $V = 30 \text{ cm} \times 10 \text{ cm} \times 4 \text{ cm} = 1{,}200 \text{ cm}^3$. Therefore, (D) is the correct answer.

35.   **B**   Use $T = AN$. For this problem, you'll use $T = AN$ three times. The first $T = AN$ will represent Monday. The *Average* (9) and the *Number of items* (8 hours) are given. Multiply to find the *Total* number of patients seen that day: 9 × 8 = 72. The second $T = AN$ will represent Tuesday. The *Average* (9) and the *Number of items* (6 hours) are given. Multiply to find the *Total* number of patients seen that day: 9 × 6 = 54. Finally, the third $T = AN$ will represent the *Average* number of patients she sees each day. To find the *Total*, add the total patients seen on Monday and the total patients seen on Tuesday to get 72 + 54 = 126. To find the *Number of items*, pay attention to the question. It asks for the average number of patients she sees on each *day*. There were 2 days, so the *Number of items*

is 2. Divide the *Total* by the *Number of items* to find the *Average*: $\frac{126}{2} = 63$. Therefore, the correct answer is (B). Note that (A) is incorrect because 54 is the total patients seen on Tuesday, (C) is incorrect because 72 is the total patients seen on Monday, and (D) is incorrect because 126 is the total number of patients seen on the two days.

36. **B** Since there are variables in the question and answers, plug in a value for q or p. If $q = 2$, then $2 + 9 = 7 - p$. Simplify the left side of the equation to get $11 = 7 - p$. Isolate p to get $p = -4$. The value of $q + p = -2$ because $2 + (-4) = -2$. Therefore, the correct answer is (B).

37. **A** Use the answer choices (PITA) to determine which one is the product of two consecutive even integers. Choice (A) could be the product of 0 and 2, so it is the correct answer. Note that (B) is incorrect because 15 is the product of 3 and 5, which are consecutive *odd* integers. Choice (D) is incorrect because 30 is the product of 5 and 6, which are consecutive but not both even integers. Choice (C) is not the product of consecutive integers.

38. **C** Similar triangles are triangles that have the same angle measures and corresponding sides have the same ratio. Thus, if triangle *ABC* has side measures of 3, 4, and 5, then the sides of triangle *XYZ* should have the same ratio. Only (C) will work. If the sides of triangle *ABC* are each multiplied by 2, the result is 6, 8, and 10, which are possible side lengths for triangle *XYZ*. Therefore, the correct answer is (C). Note that (A) is incorrect because triangle *ABC* is not equilateral, so triangle *XYZ* will not be either.

39. **A** If the area of the square is 169 cm, then use the area formula to find the length of one side of the square: $A = s^2$. If $169 = s^2$, then $\sqrt{169} = s$. Thus, $s = 13$. Since all four sides of a square are equal, each side equals 13. To find the perimeter of a shape, add up of all the sides: $13 + 13 + 13 + 13 = 52$. The correct answer is (A).

40. **A** If $\frac{3}{4}$ of the employees are at the party, then only $\frac{1}{4}$ of the employees are NOT at the party. Eliminate (C) and (D) since the answer should be less than half of 240. Note that (C) equals $\frac{1}{2}$ of 240 and (D) equals $\frac{3}{4}$ of 240. If $\frac{1}{4}$ of the employees are NOT at the party, then 60 employees did not attend because $\frac{1}{4} \times 240 = 60$. The correct answer is (A).

41. **C** Break word problems into bite-sized pieces. If Jose and Greg walk $\frac{1}{4}$ of the distance in the first 2 hours, they will walk 5 miles since $\frac{1}{4} \times 20 = 5$. If they walk $\frac{1}{5}$ of the entire distance (20 miles) in the next 1.5 hours, then they will walk 4 miles: $\frac{1}{5} \times 20 = 4$. The number of miles remaining is 11 since $20 - 5 - 4 = 11$. Therefore, (C) is the correct answer.

42. **B** To find the perimeter of a shape, add up all the sides. Even though the shape is odd looking and not all sides are labeled, the sides opposite of a labeled side can still be determined because opposite sides will still be equal.

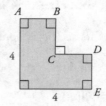

Thus, $AB + CD = 4$ since they are opposite the base, which is equal to 4. Furthermore, $BC + DE = 4$ since they are opposite the left side of the shape, which is equal to 4. Therefore, the perimeter is 16 since $4 + 4 + 4 + 4 = 16$. The correct answer is (B).

43. **D** Use $T = AN$. The *Average* (3) and the *Number of items* (12 games) are given. Multiply to find the *Total* number of points scored: $12 \times 3 = 36$. Therefore, the correct answer is (D).

44. **A** To find the volume of a box, use the formula $V = l \times w \times h$. Plug the given dimensions into the formula: $V = 8 \times 4 \times \dfrac{1}{4} = 8$. Therefore, (A) is the correct answer.

45. **D** If the hat costs $30, then a 20% decrease would be $6 since $0.2 \times 30 = 6$. The new price of the hat would be $24 because $30 - 6 = 24$. The correct answer is (D).

46. **B** To find the probability of an event, find the total of what is wanted out of the total possible outcomes: Probability $= \dfrac{\text{the number of what you want}}{\text{the total number}}$. The item wanted is a brownie, so any 6 could be chosen. The total number of items in the jar is 19 since $5 + 6 + 8 = 19$. Therefore, the probability of selecting a brownie is $\dfrac{6}{19}$. The correct answer is (B). Note that (C) is incorrect since $\dfrac{8}{19}$ is the probability of choosing a granola bar.

47. **C** Since there are variables in the question and answers, plug in a value for x or y. If $x = 3$, then $\dfrac{2}{3}(3) = 6 - y$. Simplify the left side of the equation to get $2 = 6 - y$. Isolate y to get $y = 4$. Using these values for x and y, check each answer choice to see which one works. In (A), $2(3) \neq 6 - 3(4)$ since $6 \neq -6$. In (B), $3(4) - 3 \neq 6$ since $9 \neq 6$. In (C), $2(3) + 3(4) = 18$ since $18 = 18$. Finally, in (D), $2(3 + 3(4)) \neq 18$ since $30 \neq 18$. Therefore, the correct answer is (C). Another option is to multiply both sides of the equation by 3 to get rid of the fraction: $\left(\dfrac{2}{3}\right)x = 6 - y$ becomes $2x = 3(6 - y)$. Distribute the 3 to get $2x = 18 - 3y$. Finally, add $3y$ to both sides to get $2x + 3y = 18$, which is (C).